The Psychology of Feeli

The concepts of betrayal, vengeance and forgiveness have long been a major part of religious doctrine throughout the world. However, only in recent times has the impact of these emotions become of interest to those involved in psychological study. In *The Psychology of Feeling Sorry*, Peter Randall links contemporary psychological research with religious teachings and doctrine that have provided spiritual guidance for hundreds of years.

Illustrated with explanatory narratives, Randall fuses religious precepts with psychological theory concerning one of the least understood but most common of human emotions: feeling bad about one's 'sins'.

Using an eclectic approach, Randall explores how much of what is believed within the domain of faith is now supported by modern psychological research. This book will be of interest not only to those with religious beliefs, but also to psychologists, psychotherapists, students, and anyone with an interest in the intersection of psychology, psychotherapy and theology.

Peter Randall is a retired Chartered Psychologist and Fellow of the British Psychological Society.

To Andi

from Pete

The Psychology of Feeling Sorry

The weight of the soul

Peter Randall

Routledge
Taylor & Francis Group

LONDON AND NEW YORK

First published 2013
by Routledge
27 Church Road, Hove, East Sussex BN3 2FA

Simultaneously published in the USA and Canada
by Routledge
711 Third Avenue, New York, NY 10017

Routledge is an imprint of the Taylor & Francis Group, an informa business

British Library Cataloguing in Publication Data
A catalogue record for this book is available from the British Library

Library of Congress Cataloging in Publication Data
  Randall, Peter (Peter Edward)
  The psychology of feeling sorry: the weight of the soul/Peter Randall.
  p. cm.
  1. Guilt. 2. Remorse. 3. Grief. 4. Repentance. I. Title.
  BF575.G8R36 2012
  152.4'4—dc23
  2012020065

ISBN: 978-0-415-60046-0 (hbk)
ISBN: 978-0-415-60047-7 (pbk)
ISBN: 978-0-203-08089-4 (ebk)

Typeset in Garamond
by Florence Production, Stoodleigh, Devon

MIX
Paper from
responsible sources

FSC
www.fsc.org **FSC® C004839**

Printed and bound by CPI Group (UK) Ltd, Croydon, CR0 4YY

For my wife, Marilyn, with love

Contents

Acknowledgements   viii
Preface: the weight of the soul   ix

1   The stirrings of conscience   1

2   Interpersonal relationships and betrayal   28

3   Interpersonal relationships, religion and vengeance   48

4   Shame, guilt and remorse   78

5   Remorse and criminal offending   105

6   Religion, spirituality and remorse   126

7   Forgiveness   159

8   Remorse, empathy, forgiveness and therapy   188

9   The weight of the soul   211

    Notes   236
    References   242
    Index   267

Acknowledgements

The material for this book has been some 40 years in collection and many people have assisted throughout this time in a variety of ways. I have received a great deal of their help and support throughout my career as a psychologist and my thanks go out to all of them. They know who they are – I took up enough of their time. I would like to make particular mention of my friend Mike Donohue, now sadly deceased, who taught me a lot about counselling – not just about his practice but also the vital empathetic backdrop that helped many distressed people regain their belief that they were worth something after all. I also want to warmly mention Dr Don Kendrick whose under-graduate module on human aggression so inspired me many years ago that I continue my own study in that to this day.

I would like to thank Derek Brooks and his colleagues at Leven public library, East Yorkshire. They are brilliant at acting successfully on my weird requests for esoteric literature without so much as a raised eyebrow.

Disclaimers

Although the contents of this book refer to various personal and mental health issues, it does not contain any material that provides therapeutic suggestions or guidance to people in distress. While I have sympathy with anyone in spiritual or psychological distress, I can only suggest that they seek assistance from appropriately qualified professionals.

I regret any errors in translation and interpretation of scriptural material that derive from quotations. I note that there are variations evident in translation of some material between sources.

Preface
The weight of the soul

Background

This book is an attempt to link contemporary psychological theory and research concerning the sorrowful feelings following interpersonal wrongdoing with religious teachings and doctrine that have offered guidance over hundreds of years. It is not an erudite tome that offers far-reaching additional knowledge to further either psychology or religion; it does not review the work of the great moral philosophers or espouse particular theological and psychological ideologies. Hopefully, it is also not a sententious rehash of some of the more florid material that has appeared in the areas of forgiveness and religious belief. Instead, it takes an eclectic approach to material relevant to one of the most common problems that afflict people, that of the feelings of profound sorrow arising from betrayal within interpersonal relationships. The study of this invariably painful experience falls not only within the domain of psychology, the scientific study of human behaviour and mental processes, but also of religious doctrine that provides a moral benchmark for many people, against which they critically judge the rightness of their behaviour.

I start with a brief description of the background to my studies that have led to the writing of this book. These studies began with a strong research interest from my undergraduate days in the area of human aggression. At its earliest, this interest encompassed all forms and manifestations of human aggression, including the vastly complex behaviours that we subsume under the hideously simple label of 'war'. Gradually, however, the inevitable buffeting of time and exposure to the panorama of emotion in day-to-day human relationships led me to narrow my focus. In particular, I became appalled at the enormous daily struggle of a largely unrecognised mass of school children against the predations of powerful bullies. At that time the study of bullying in childhood was emerging quite rapidly and becoming the massive research and practice topic that it is today.

Many strategies for alleviating this scourge have been established and offered up to parents, teachers and agencies dealing with children and young people. Among these were bullying 'hotlines'. My friend, Mike Donohue, now sadly deceased, was both a counsellor and teacher. Together we established a local hotline and, almost immediately, were nearly overwhelmed by a tidal surge of distress calls. Staggeringly, adults made nearly half of the calls. These callers were bullied at work, in their local community and often in both. Others were being abused at home within their intimate relationships. Many simply required support, guidance or assistance over employment rights. Others needed counselling or psychiatric sessions and medication to help them. We arranged those services as best we could.

I am neither a counsellor nor a clinician in the sense of offering therapy. Nevertheless, I did interview many victims and perpetrators for the purposes of information gathering to inform potential intervention.[1] Often issues of forgiveness and remorse emerged, particularly when some victims had also been perpetrators of bullying or some other behaviour that had been regarded as a betrayal by the recipients. Victims sometimes felt able to forgive significant cruelties when their bullies expressed remorse and many of the latter expressed sincere regret for their actions. Sometimes there was forgiveness but no regret; at other times there was sincere remorse but no forgiveness. Occasionally, devoutly religious people forgave the perpetrators of their hurt but on other occasions equally devout people turned their faces away from expressions of heartbreaking remorse and abject apology.

In addition, my experience of other forms of aggressive abuse, particularly the non-accidental injury of children, provided many examples of remorse as the consciences of perpetrators were sparked by the consequences of their actions. Child abusers spoke of their suicidal thoughts as they acknowledged the betrayal of their children; workplace bullies expressed shame over the way they had threatened co-workers; managers acknowledged their abuses of power in casting blame unfairly, and husbands, wives and partners cringed at the way their supposed loved ones had been reduced to nervous wrecks by manipulation and threat. Prisoners found religion and poured out their regrets in prayer and confession. Expressions of remorse and forgiveness were inextricably interwoven in the clinical narratives of the people involved. Inevitably, my interest in the expressions of human aggression began to incorporate these issues also.

The study of forgiveness is another that has burgeoned recently, particularly in the United States. It is noteworthy that this study has examined this uniquely human behaviour from both academic and practice orientations. In particular, the role of forgiveness within the realm of interpersonal relations has received much study. Many university-based researchers have tapped a rich vein of students responding to matters of troubled romantic relations and betrayal, using psychometric surveys. Shame, guilt and apology are included among the topics under investigation, alongside forgiveness and reconciliation.

In general terms, however, the behaviour of remorse has been significantly less thoroughly investigated than that of forgiveness despite evidence that forgiveness is often withheld until victims become convinced that expressions of remorse have been genuine. The role of conscience as a motivator of significant change in relationship behaviour is also much less studied and it seems to me that there has been little attempt to link the psychological basis of expressions of regret and remorse to other disciplines, such as theology, where they have been given great importance and much attention over hundreds of years. These lacunae are surprising and suggest the need of some redress.

Wrongdoing and betrayal

This book cannot be concerned with the whole multitude of betrayals that are perpetrated throughout the functioning of humankind. Thus, atrocities of war, torture and genocide are excluded, as are all types of wrongdoings perpetrated by offenders against victims not known to them. Instead, this book is concerned with harm and betrayal that takes place between people who are well known to each other, often intimately. In essence, these take the form of betrayals of the trust between people who are important to each other for any of a number of reasons. These reasons could include support, nurturance, affection, personal development, stimulation, succour, the meeting of dependency needs (e.g. as in parenting), a recognised duty of care and any other type of relationship between two or more people who depend on a state of loyalty between each other. Examples of such people are parents, romantic partners, close friends, dependents, elderly relatives, carers and members of the caring professions. Betrayal of relationships by these people of those who trust them is often devastating and associated with long-term harm. In many cases, not only the victims suffer but also many offenders who eventually come to feel such sorrow over their actions that their days are forever tainted by remorse and their lives become marinated in shame and guilt.

I emphasise that the betrayals referred to here are interpersonal. This is intended to limit the scope of consideration to a manageable level. It is also recognition that these are the betrayals that are of particular concern to most people as they go through their daily lives. There are few adults who have not experienced the pain of being let down or the sorrowful guilty feelings of letting others down. The impact of these betrayals is very often the cause of deep emotional harm, even mental health difficulties that require professional assistance from counsellors, psychologists or doctors. Infidelity in romantic relationships is a particularly strong example where feelings of betrayal are frequently coincident with the experience of depression.[2]

Obviously, there are other forms of betrayal that are very important. For example, the dictionary definition tends towards the betrayal of one's country through the divulgence of secret information. Although this behaviour may have impact on many thousands of individuals, the betrayal of trust is indirect and largely impersonal. In addition, the traitors may argue that they feel no remorse as they are ideologically driven and acting out of principle.

In addition, there are forms of betrayal of interpersonal relations that are so intense and horrifically damaging that they are beyond the scope of this book. The sexual abuse of children, for example, is excluded because the motivations for this horrendous behaviour are so extensive in range and the motivations of perpetrators acknowledging their abuse so tied to societal and legal responses that it is almost impossible to provide examples of genuine remorse confidently. Even abuse through the passive collusion of a partner or other party[3] is so multifaceted that, in my experience of child-protection investigations, expressions of remorse are often part of an attempt to avoid the removal of children into the care system. I am convinced that this topic could not be dealt with responsibly within a publication that is not specific to child abuse.

Physical abuse and the neglect of children are also excluded. These betrayals of children fall within the general domain of child abuse and are mentioned only in relation to the remorse shown by adults who caused such harm that they have come to the attention of child protection agencies. I acknowledge that some of the most genuine, heartfelt remorse that I have encountered is that of highly stressed parents who have harmed their infants in a moment of absolute desperation. The presence of remorse in these situations is regarded as a vital ingredient of future risk assessment. It can be part of the determination of whether the aggression that brought the parent to the attention of the child protection agencies was impulsive or instrumental. Aggression is considered instrumental if the parent believes it is a justified means of managing a child's behaviour. Such parents are likely to blame their children and feel little or no genuine remorse; clearly, they are likely to respond in much the same way if similar circumstances arise again. Conversely, aggression is thought of as impulsive if the parent knew it was unjustified, did not believe the child was to blame and expressed genuine remorse.[4] Such parents are less likely to respond in the same way under similar circumstances, particularly if they are given effective support and therapy. Obviously, great care has to be taken to ensure that the expressions of remorse are genuine and that the abuser is not 'cheating' in order to make a good impression on the agency's staff. I believe that this area of interpersonal wrongdoing is too substantial and important for me to cover adequately in this book.

The last comments, however, mention one example of cheating by individuals in order to avoid some aversive event. I have sometimes been asked, during discussions on remorse arising from the betrayal of intimate relations, why I make little reference to the behaviour of cheating. Certainly, it has been extensively researched, particularly so in relation to the variety of strategies used by men and women in respect of infidelity and their different motives for extra-relationship sexual behaviour. I have not made use of 'cheating' in this book because it is not a concept that is often employed in the common ground between religious and psychological debate. It is a relatively 'new' concept in this very old field of enquiry and is often used as a media colloquialism for promiscuity. Cheating, in common parlance, crosses a wide spectrum of human activity from the sexual betrayal of intimate relationships through to the manipulation of outcomes in sporting events. Increasingly, in the context of infidelity, it is viewed as having significant evolutionary significance[5] as a means of increasing the benefits derived from intimate dyadic relations, such as acquiring an improved partnership for child rearing.[6] This comment is not meant to disparage a study of cheating as behaviour worthy of investigation elsewhere, but I have to impose limits on the range of human behaviours that are under consideration here. In addition, whereas 'betrayal' is viewed almost universally as unacceptable, 'cheating' lies in a somewhat more acceptable grey area, having complex age, gender and family circumstance influences that render cross-disciplinary investigation open to significant obfuscation.

Conscience and remorse

The acknowledgement of the role of conscience in the recognition of wrong-doing and the expression of remorse has long exercised theologians and moral philosophers who propounded increasingly sophisticated arguments from medieval times onwards. By then, the study of conscience had advanced significantly. Two important concepts had been formulated, *conscientia* and *synderesis*. The former was seen as 'knowledge within oneself', the particular attitudes of individuals to specific instances of right and wrong behaviour, whereas the latter was viewed as the 'spark of conscience', the assumed ability of the individual's mind to understand the principles of moral reasoning and the drive to do good. Two distinct opinions concerning the linkage between conscience and synderesis had evolved by the late Middle Ages. Franciscan theologians, as represented particularly by Bonaventure, held that both are innate facets of practical reasoning and cross-stimulate each other such that there may be improvement of moral judgement with age and experience. The second, led particularly by Aquinas, was based on intellectual judgement. Synderesis was conceptualised as an intellectually based set of constructs that provide general guidance to conscience for application in specific situations. Thus, individuals can choose to 'listen' to this guidance in order to avoid potential wrongdoing in a given situation or ignore it in favour, for example, of pleasurable self-gratification. This viewpoint resonates well with contemporary psychological explanations of the function of conscience.

In very general terms, religious conceptualisation of conscience associates it with the divine, a universal drive to goodness and the morality that is unique to human beings. Such a stance does not always fit comfortably with secular and scientific considerations where cognitive, experiential and emotional qualities are emphasised. These lead towards a position where the development and manifestations of conscience owe more to a combination of genetic potential and learned behaviour intrinsic to the culture the individual develops within. The seeming lack of congruence between these views may, however, be more apparent than real. Both the religious and secular camps appear to share an understanding that, whatever its source, conscience is an intellectual judgement that differentiates right from wrong based on principles, rules, values and societal norms that, collectively, shape the morality espoused by individuals. Although the vocabulary defining the outcome of these judgements varies across religions and between religion and science, it seems generally accepted that a self-examination of one's behaviour that results in finding nothing blameworthy is associated with a feeling of relief and strengthened integrity. Conversely, an adverse judgement may lead to feelings of shame, guilt, remorse and regret.

The vocabulary associated with feeling sorry about one's wrongdoings is extensive and frequently used interchangeably. Here are some of the terms used in this context with an attempted summary at their widely accepted meanings:

Conscience: often referred to as an inner direction providing guidance about the rightness or wrongness of one's behaviour.

Remorse: feeling very regretful; and/or guilty because of an acknowledged wrongdoing; being sorry for one's personal responsibility concerning that wrongdoing.

Regret: sadness or (in religion) repentance about acknowledged wrongdoing.

Shame: painful feelings of humiliation and/or distress caused by the acknowledgement of wrongdoing.

Guilt: the unpleasant and aversive feeling arising from having done wrong.

Contrition: the state of feeling remorseful and penitent aroused by guilt.

Apology: typically, a regretful acknowledgment of an offence or failure made directly by the perpetrator usually to the victim(s).

Repentant: the feeling or expression of sincere regret or remorse about one's wrongdoing or, in religion, sin. Often, the repudiation of the aspects of one's character that generated the wrongdoing and a resolve to do one's best to extirpate those aspects. Sometimes, there is a resolve to atone by making amends for the harm that one has done.

Penitent: feeling or showing sorrow and regret for having done wrong and seeking forgiveness from God.

Atonement: reparation for a wrongdoing and, in religion, the expiation of sin. This is extended in Christian faith to include the concept of 'vicarious atonement'; the belief that Jesus took upon himself the weight and consequences of human transgression vicariously.

Vengeance: the punishment inflicted or retribution exacted for an injury or wrong.

As may be seen, these terms suffer from repetition of meaning, redundancy and ambiguity. Indeed, why should they not? The concepts that underpin them are diffused in clarity by the factors of significant interpersonal differences of understanding as well as by variations between religions, cultures and subcultures. I find, however, that people generally do seem to understand each other when these terms appear in everyday usage, despite the apparent lack of clarity.

That is not, however, an adequate basis for scientific enquiry. If there is a significant degree of variation, then attempts should be made to delineate some meaning that can guide investigation. This book is about feeling sorry, that sensation associated with remorseful ideations of one's personal agency in wrongdoing. An important question that arises from this asks how 'tight' is the understanding of remorse when used in the context of perpetrators feeling sorry for their actions or failures to act? For example, can perpetrators who feign remorse be said to show remorse or are they merely actors on a stage portraying a character type that is not real? Is their subsequent make-believe penitence valid if it fools the victims into feeling that there is a recognition of the harm done to them and a genuine sorrow that it was inflicted?

What about displays of being sorry that appear to be 'over the top'? For example, do people who display extreme regret over a trivial wrong, such as a forgotten shopping date, seem as credible as a motorist who shows extreme regret over running down and killing a pedestrian? Can a serial killer who claims to have found God before repudiating his crimes, appear to be genuinely remorseful to a parole board?

Jefferie Murphy[7] provides a useful differentiation between two types of remorse that may lead to repentance. He states that repentance is the remorseful acceptance of one's wrongdoing, the refusal to accept the traits of character that were associated with the wrongdoing, coupled with a resolve to banish those traits and atone for the damage done. This embracing conceptualisation is, he believes, generally correct and useful but does not fully reflect the complexity of remorse. He suggests that not all expressions of guilt among morally guided people are necessarily associated with remorse. For example, the breaking of a promise that was of great importance to the person to whom it was made should stimulate feelings of guilt, but if there were no long-term painful or damaging consequences, it is likely that the term 'remorse' might be considered too extreme. Murphy suggests that the experience of remorse is more closely associated with extreme and powerful guilt feelings that are proportional to the grave seriousness of acknowledged wrongdoing.

In addition, Murphy considers that not only the degree of severity of the wrongdoing is important, but also that a sensation of hopelessness is essential and associated with an inconsolable 'bite' of a guilty conscience. He refers to the French medieval belief in the 'agenbite of inwit' as one type of remorse.

Dan Michel, a monk of Canterbury, brought this concept to England in a translation of 1340 and referred to the prick (agenbite) of conscience (the Old English word 'inwit', meaning an inner sense of right and wrong). Murphy suggests remorse of this type appears to engage more than guilt only and believes that the wrongdoing is so serious that the harm done can never be made right again such that the victim is irrevocably and permanently harmed. Clearly, a comparatively trivial wrong, such as a broken promise to go shopping, cannot generally constitute such a profound assault on the injured party. Murphy speaks of rape, murder and torture by way of comparison and comments that even if wrongdoers could impose an 'eye for an eye' form of atonement on themselves, there would still be no cessation of the inconsolable feeling of remorse because the self-imposed punishment is voluntary and so not comparable with the vicious deeds forced on the victims, robbing them of their autonomy.

I accept the force of the argument that remorse is a complex phenomenon and that Murphy's, and no doubt other, distinctions are viable. Nevertheless, I return to my comment above, that when used within the communications of most people, there is a reasonably effective shared understanding of descriptions such as 'remorse' and 'feeling sorry'. As a consequence, this book does not make such distinctions and uses the description in the form of an amalgam of the different types of remorse.

The weight of sin

It is hardly surprising that those who have found their conscience troubled by wrongdoing and the harm they have done to others, should express a feeling of being weighed down with guilt and often a need to 'unload' that weight through remorse and acts of contrition. Many people from different faiths have told me that confessing their sins has given them a profound feeling of forgiveness and cleansing. They explain that they feel unburdened, lighter of spirit and closer to their families and friends.

The 'weight' of one's sins is an age-old concept. According to Christian mythology, St Michael, the patron saint of warriors, is the guardian of the souls of the deceased. It was his duty to weigh both their good deeds and unreconciled bad deeds in perfectly balanced scales in order to determine whether they should go to heaven or hell. As with many other Christian beliefs, this was a plagiarised version of much older non-Christian mythology. For example, during the Judgement of Osiris from Ancient Egyptian myth, the soul's 'heart' was given to Osiris who, in the Hall of Truth, used a great golden scale to balance it against the white feather of Ma'at, the symbol of truth and harmony. If the soul's heart weighed less than the feather, it was allowed to enter into heaven, the blissful Field of Reeds. If, however, the heart was heavier than the feather, it was thrown to the floor and there consumed by Amenti, a horrific god with the face of a crocodile, the front of a leopard and the rear of a rhinoceros. The luckless person then ceased to exist.

What, then, of the influence of religion[8] on remorse and repentance? These concepts have been an essential ingredient of humanity's spiritual life long before psychology existed in any formal sense. In my experience, the understandings of these guides to moral behaviour are still very strongly associated with religious belief and doctrine, even among those who have no strong faith. Thus, remorse is often associated with moral guidance acquired from doctrinal and other religious teaching and this, perhaps, begs the question as to whether non-believers can feel truly remorseful about wrongdoing. It is certainly the case that many criminals allege that they have experienced[9] a religious conversion that has caused them to become remorseful and penitent, but is religious belief really the *sine qua non* of genuine remorse? I am of the view that such an opinion is based on simplistic consideration and argument. For example, extremist beliefs sometimes lead religious fundamentalists to perpetrate appalling attacks on innocent people. Although many of these perpetrators express regret for the harm suffered, it is rare indeed that there is any repentance or even acknowledgement that the assaults committed were wrong and against moral codes. Instead, it is typically the case that these extremists use their religious beliefs to support their horrendous behaviour and claim that their God will reward them for violence against victims unknown to them. It is perverse that religion has been used for centuries as the excuse for behaviour that resists even the most lenient judgement of wrongdoing. Thus, these perpetrators can transform themselves from the murderers they are in the eyes of most of humanity into devout soldiers who are engaged in a righteous struggle and superior to the point of being deserving of the rewards of martyrdom. Whereas many violent criminals can accept they have overstepped the boundaries of law and decency, these violent extremists sometimes delude themselves that they deserve lesser punishments or none at all. No logical argument, therefore, can be made convincingly that religious belief is a necessary or sufficient condition for remorse and repentance although, perversely, such beliefs may well be causally associated with criminal behaviour of the worst kind. In addition, many atheist and agnostic individuals have extremely well-developed empathetic responses to the people they have harmed and express sincere remorse and repentance.

It is not my intention to attempt a sceptical argument against those who profess religious conversion. As a person without formal religion, it would not be appropriate for me to repudiate such experiences out of disbelief only. Nevertheless, there are significant difficulties in accepting the arguments of some who claim conversion and then argue they have been born again as different and better people such that they are no longer the same individuals whose perpetration of harmful wrongdoing would have led to adverse judgement of them.

People who acknowledge wrongdoing are unlikely now to fear the consumption of their souls by hungry crocodile gods, but many do fear divine retribution and a sentence to hell. Others fear more earthly retributions or simply feel weighed down by the punishments of their own consciences, their guilt and shame. The subtitle of this Preface reflects a belief that one's soul may be weighed down by an accretion of one's wrongdoing over the life course. One purpose of the book, therefore, is to explore the psychological processes that create this 'weight' and, if possible, to reconcile them with much older religious doctrine. I endeavour to present the developmental, learning, personality and social factors that contribute to this process within the domains of contemporary spiritual, religious and cultural discourse. It is believed that feeling genuinely sorry for wrongdoing is an important therapeutic experience, relieving this weight and restoring a sense of self-worth. Modern psychological study helps to bring substance to this subject and is illustrated by vignettes about people[10] who have come to acknowledge their responsibility for harm done to others.

Content

This section provides a brief description of the material in this book on a chapter-by-chapter basis. It may appear that some topics are rather incongruent with the book's title but each has a significant association with profound remorse after wrongdoing and this justifies inclusion. Each chapter has a summary and, for those chapters where it is appropriate, a section dealing with implications for practice. Illustrative vignettes are provided to support main issues where appropriate. Religious material is drawn mostly from the major world religions (defined by numbers of adherents) and is presented in no order of personal preference.

I The stirrings of conscience

Research studies have indicated that wrongdoing leading to the harming of others that is not followed by feelings of remorse can be indicative of deficits in the development of conscience. This chapter examines the development of conscience from childhood and the links it has to feeling sorry for harm done to others.

2 Interpersonal relationships and betrayal

This chapter provides a discussion of the nature and impact of betrayal with particular reference to transgression within interpersonal relationships. Current theoretical considerations of the complexities of betrayal are presented and the impact upon 'victims' is discussed. Some examples are provided to illustrate important points and the door is opened to a discussion of potential responses from victims.

3 Interpersonal relationships, religion and vengeance

The religion-orientated concept of vengeance, or revenge as it is more usually referred to, is considered in its context as a response to real or perceived grievance. This chapter leads on from the second because the instinct of revenge is very strong among the victims of betrayal. As the philosopher Nussbaum opined, the act of vengeance often differs from the original wrongdoing only in the sequence of events and because it is a response rather than the original act. This rather Old Testament view is no longer congruent with a modern-day morality that often subscribes more to the fallacy of 'Two wrongs make a right'.[11] This kind of decision-making may lead to vengeful behaviour that has as many irrational and destructive consequences for the victim seeking vengeance as for the perpetrator. There may be damage done to the victim's integrity, social standing and personal safety simply for the sake of getting one's own back. What makes people seek out such a pyrrhic victory? This chapter considers the predictors of vengeance (e.g. age, gender, religious background, narcissism, global self-esteem, acknowledging remorse) and the factors that may make victims step back from thoughts of revenge to consider other options such as forgiveness. One of these factors might be that some victims do not want a weight on their own souls arising from a refusal to forgive.

4 Shame, guilt and remorse

Perpetrators of harm to others may acknowledge their responsibility to a greater or lesser extent. Some may feel guilty about their actions. This does not necessarily mean that their feelings will go beyond this. They may be able to rationalise why they acted as they did and some even blame the victims (e.g. as in many cases of domestic violence and sexual assault). In terms of contemporary theory, guilt may be experienced but not necessarily as a motivation for further action that benefits the victim. Perpetrators might, however, develop patterns of negative affect as a consequence of acknowledging guilt that may, in turn, lead to remorse. This trend is evident in case studies of perpetrators who have gone on from acknowledgement of guilt to the expression of remorse. Parallels are to be found in religious belief.

5 Remorse and criminal offending

This chapter examines the expressions of remorse from criminal offenders before, during and after their trials. This is now such an important area of multidisciplinary concern that it is worthy of separate investigation. The judiciaries of several countries attend to expressions of remorse that affect sentencing in particular. In addition, many guilty prisoners (and some on remand) claim to have found God and wish to demonstrate a newly acquired moral code that will turn them away from further wrongdoing. Both psychological and legal studies reveal opposed views on whether expressions of remorse and acquired spirituality are worth considering during the legal process. Is finding religion in prison a sufficient reason for the mitigation of a sentence or not? If it is, what tests should be applied in order to detect deception? There are many studies and published opinions. This chapter presents a cross-section and gives examples to support the main pros and cons. For example, some authorities provide forceful opinion against taking account of remorse, whereas others argue equally strongly in favour of the spiritual components of restorative justice that include remorse.

6 Religion, spirituality and remorse

Given the importance that most cultures attach to religion (and spirituality in general) is it important to consider the religious/spiritual connotations of remorse, particularly as they relate to relevant psychological processes. That some perpetrators 'feel sorry' for the harm they caused is of central importance to the interwoven consideration of their forgiveness. Likewise, the healing powers of acknowledging guilt (perpetrator) and turning from a lifetime of vengeful grudge-bearing (victim) are thought to benefit mental health. The acolytes of all major religions have sought to encourage these benefits for millennia; now modern counsellors and psychotherapists pursue the same goals. It is very important, therefore, to the consideration of the interaction of victims and perpetrators to provide comment on the potential influences of religion and spirituality.

7 Forgiveness

This chapter deals mainly with forgiveness in relation to transgressions within interpersonal relationships. This is an important area for study because it provides a potentially strong link between the responses of victims to perpetrators. Behaviour of perpetrators that is indicative of remorse, of regret for their wrongdoing, is one of the more powerful influences on victims that may increase the probability of forgiveness and reconciliation. A review of the contemporary psychological understanding is provided and the religious connotations are considered.

8 Remorse, empathy, forgiveness and therapy

Therapies for the trauma of betrayal of close relationships are redolent with processes that link religion/spirituality with contemporary psychology. This chapter does not seek to describe specific therapies in detail; such an endeavour is beyond the scope of this book and has been well served by other publications. Instead, this chapter seeks to observe the dimensions of remorse and forgiveness that are bound up in the processes through which sincere acceptance of blame by the offender become enmeshed with the gradual erosion of the victim's negative emotions to a point where it becomes possible to consider forgiveness, if not reconciliation. Central to this movement are the workings of empathy: from the offender in relation to the pain suffered by the victim and from the victim in relation to the pain associated with the sincere portrayal of remorse. The role of therapeutic endeavour in this movement is considered.

9 The weight of the soul

The final chapter examines a difficult time near the end of life when the experience of feeling sorry may rise to a particularly critical point. At this time people realise the opportunity for acting on remorse may have passed and they may also experience anxiety about what happens to them in the afterlife. How sorry they feel for wrongdoing, particularly the betrayal of relationships, may be intensified by their conceptualisation of events after death (including judgement and punishment), particularly if these have been shaped by religious doctrines that may have been important to them throughout much of their life course. Thus, this content completes an examination of the factors underpinning feeling sorry for wrongdoing that began with the development, during childhood, of conscience (Chapter 1). I will also attempt to provide an amalgam of the disparate opinions and multidisciplinary sources that contribute to this book. In short, the evidence is that, for most people the burden of guilt or vengeful grudge bearing is a heavy weight to bear. This burden leaves little space for any 'feel-good' factor and unresolved transgression within intimate relations always seems to leave its weight on the soul.

Chapter 1

The stirrings of conscience

Lord Byron's line from *The Giaour* 'No ear can hear nor tongue can tell the tortures of the inward hell' (1813), reminds us that conscience is as much a source of pain and discomfort as it may be a reassurance of good moral fibre. The pains evoked by stirring conscience have stimulated a mass of compelling attempts to describe its impact on those troubled by their wrongdoings. The simile of conscience as a quiet oppressive voice is exemplified by Mahatma Gandhi's comment, 'The only tyrant I accept in this world is the still voice within'. The power of troubled conscience to unman us is also frequently referred to; for example, William Shakespeare's famous line points out, 'Thus conscience does make cowards of us all . . .'. He understood that the workings of our conscience might lead us to painful feelings of remorse when we act against our moral values. This is congruent with the writings of Paul (e.g. Romans, 2:15) who sees conscience as an internal witness of our behaviour, accusing us according to its wrongness. On the positive side, however, we may experience a sense of integrity or righteousness when our behaviour meets our moral standard.

What is this quiet tyrant of our private minds? How can it guide our conduct and punish our shortcomings? How is it shared with our fellows such that the essence of our personal morality is also part of a communal benchmark enabling cooperative social behaviour? Are we born with it or does it steal up on us with age and experience? It can evoke strong emotions, yet is it emotional or merely cognitive? Does one's religion cause conscience to develop or merely influence it? Questions on the nature of conscience has been the subject of philosophical debate for centuries and its development in terms of moral thinking has exercised psychologists in countless research studies.

For the purposes of this chapter, conscience is considered to comprise both the cognitive and emotional processes that constitute people's internalised moral regulator of their behaviour.

Relatively recently, psychologists have examined the role of moral emotions, such as empathy and guilt, in moral behaviour. There has been a significant change of opinion on the validity of studying such individually based experiences of emotionality in relation to moral behaviour with an increasing awareness that such experiences may inhibit immoral behaviour and motivate prosocial moral behaviour. Previously it had been argued that the non-deliberate nature of emotional experience militates against the rational and considered judgement that is assumed to underpin moral behaviour. In addition, emotions are not considered to be impartial in that they are usually focused on specific instances or events and reflect personal and self-interested perspectives. It is a purpose of emotionality to energise action that is focused on personal perceptions of problems rather than on a broader perspective that requires intellectual deliberation. Not surprisingly, therefore, a common excuse for grossly undesirable behaviour is that an excess of emotional lability robbed wrongdoers of their reason and overcame their customary restraints. It was argued, therefore, that emotionality is counterproductive to the manifestation of moral behaviour.

Yet this cannot be wholly or always true, as examples abound of moral emotions that have led to highly organised and considered actions. On occasion, these events have led people to take up arms in order to save others from oppression, their revulsion at ethnic cleansing or other monstrous behaviour having animated them to violent remedies. At these times their moral compass and strength is defined not by cold intellectualism but by loathing, sadness and an overwhelming urge to protect the vulnerable from unendurable wrongdoing. Whereas the purely intellectual response might have been to stand by and remain detached, the moral emotional imperative has been to take sides and do whatever is needful. Indeed, it may be harder for those who are deficient in emotionality to evince moral responses generally as they lack the spurs of compassion and humanity.

Ben-Ze'ev (1997), for example, argues that we do have a responsibility over our emotions that emanates from indirect control over the circumstances eliciting them. He contends that the partial or biased nature of human emotions can impart a moral perspective of particular circumstances in addition to that provided by intellectual processing. Consequently, they enable the establishment of core values and commitments that form the fundamental guidelines of moral behaviour. This analysis of the influence of emotion on moral behaviour fits well within the general psychological conceptualisation of emotion as changing patterns of physiological arousal, feelings, cognitions and behaviours that are made in response to personally significant circumstances. Both basic and higher-order emotions are thought to be involved with moral behaviour. For example, Kochanska's (1997) report on multiple pathways to conscience described the importance of fearfulness (a basic emotion) as a possible enhancer of the developmental rate of conscience. In addition, Walker and Pitts (1998) studied moral maturity and reported on moral excellence in terms of higher-order factors. The results of their research led them to describe the highly moral individual as one who holds strongly to a range of values and principles that reflect externalised moral guidelines and the internal workings of conscience. Integrity is prized and revealed as an awareness of personal agency such that this individual is committed to acting according to the ideals of compassion for others, helpfulness and the maintenance of relationships through reliability and fidelity.

In essence, therefore, the role of emotionality in the development and functioning of conscience is now accepted despite some caveats about labelling. Both basic and higher-order 'moral' emotions may be assumed to play a part in the workings of conscience and the following section provides a summarised consideration of this.

The moral emotions

Moral emotions are a vital but seldom regarded facet of functional prosocial decision-making and consequent behaviour. They are, therefore, integral to the composition of conscience. One description of them, provided by Haidt (2003), is that they are coupled to the welfare of people other than oneself and also to the interests of society in general. These emotions supply the motivating force to avoid causing harm to others and to behave in a manner that is considered 'good' within one's society. Typically, the moral emotions are subdivided into categories relating to their impact on the individual (e.g. Eisenberg, 2000). For example, among the self-conscious emotions there are those that are negatively experienced, such as guilt, shame and embarrassment, and those that are positively experienced, such as pride, gratitude and the underlying feelings of empathic processes.[1]

The self-conscious moral emotions

Self-conscious emotions are those elicited by the sometimes painful processes of self-examination. Although self-examination may start unbidden and unnoticed, it cannot remain so as awareness must bloom for self-consciousness to be engaged and for the resulting emotion to energise some response. At the point where self-consciousness occurs, the self becomes aware that it is evaluating its functioning or potential functioning within the circumstances that have stimulated the process. Thus, it is not always necessary for there to have been an overt behavioural response to have occurred in order that the self begins to subject itself to scrutiny; it is enough that individuals can become aware of how they might behave under the prevailing circumstances that is sufficient to stimulate an emotional response. Consequently, it is not unusual to hear people state that they are 'ashamed' of their own thoughts, or of 'looking over their shoulders' as though they had been observed merely thinking about potential wrongdoing. It is probable that this emotional response to 'wrong' thinking is engendered by a prior history of acting poorly in similar circumstances, in which case the negative self-conscious emotion is a punisher for past behaviour. This anticipatory response provides a firm guide about what not to do, whereupon the individual has an opportunity to respond in a morally acceptable way instead.

Apparently, therefore, moral self-conscious emotions impart prompt sanctions upon behaviour by punishing that which is or could potentially be unacceptable or reinforcing behaviour that is deemed morally correct. The emotions of guilt, shame, embarrassment, self-approval and pride provide a moral compass for a route to take or one that has already been taken.

It is axiomatic, however, that none of this is possible for those individuals who are insensitive to such emotions. The feeling of shame is only available to those who are disposed to the experience of shame. Thus, Tangney (1990), in her paper on the assessment of proneness to shame and guilt, states that *emotion disposition* is the propensity to experience an emotion across a range of circumstances. If, for example, the specific emotion was guilt, then those who are highly disposed to its occurrence would be more likely to experience it if they catch themselves anticipating acting badly and also are more likely to experience it as a consequence of actually acting badly.

Embarrassment

Examination of the broad spectrum of relevant literature indicates that shame and guilt are the negative moral emotions that have been studied most during research enquiry into the nature and development of conscience. These are given particular attention in the next section, but some mention of the emotion of embarrassment is appropriate here, given that it is sometimes considered within the same grouping as guilt and shame.

Eisenberg (2000) reviewed contemporary understanding of the negative self-conscious emotion of embarrassment. She reflected opinion that embarrassment can be differentiated from guilt and shame in that it has antecedents, experience and displays that are not evident in respect of other emotions. For example, in comparison with shame, Miller and Tangney's (1994) findings suggest that embarrassment was less intense, less enduring, resulted from less grave behavioural transgressions and associated with less serious outcomes. The negative feelings were not as likely to be associated with self-directed anger and disgust. The research findings of Robbins and Parlavecchio (2006) on embarrassment and shame indicate that embarrassment includes feelings of surprise at one's unintended behaviour and a concern that observers have observed failings in the self that is presented to them rather than the preferred 'core' self. They suggest that these elements are less likely to be evident in experiences of shame. Indeed, the nature of the embarrassing incidents may even be a source of amusement to the person involved, whereas that is unlikely to be the case for shame. In short, there is agreement that embarrassment is distinguishable from other negative self-conscious moral emotions and has only a minor role, if any, in moral functioning.

Shame and guilt

The following are definitions of shame and guilt provided by Ferguson and Stegge (1998) and cited by Eisenberg (2000) that are used within this section. It is acknowledged that they are open to argument but provide a basis for the ensuing discussion.

> *Shame:* a dejection-based, passive, or helpless emotion aroused by self-related aversive events. The ashamed person focuses more on devaluing or condemning the entire self, experiences the self as fundamentally flawed, feels self-conscious about the visibility of one's actions, fears scorn, and thus avoids or hides from others.
>
> (Ferguson and Stegge, 1998, p. 20)

> *Guilt:* an agitation-based emotion or painful feeling of regret that is aroused when the actor actually causes, anticipates causing, or is associated with an aversive event
>
> (Ferguson and Stegge, 1998, p. 20)

It is broadly accepted that shame and guilt are moral emotions. As Thomaes *et al.* (2010) point out, both are elicited by moral transgressions that reflect badly on one's moral credibility and may evoke empathetic concerns about the harm done to victims of those transgressions. In addition, it is axiomatic that the experience of shame and guilt is possible only if the individuals involved are possessed of a morality that delineates right from wrong (e.g. Eisenberg, 2000). Finally, it is acknowledged that from the internalised lessons of childhood socialisation, shame and guilt are potential self-punishers of moral transgression that provide an opportunity to back away from wrongdoing or to do better in future. As such, they act as motivators for moral behaviour (e.g. Olthof *et al.*, 2000).

As stated above, shame and guilt have been the subjects of much, if not the majority of research studies on moral emotions. Indeed, Thomaes *et al.* (2010) among others regard them as the quintessence of moral emotions. Their significance was captured by Gaylin (1979) in his comment that they are noble emotions, essential to the maintenance of civilised society, and vital to the development of the refined and elegant qualities of human potential, namely generosity, service, self-sacrifice, unselfishness and duty. Given this level of importance it is, perhaps, surprising to find that many people – clinicians, researchers and laypeople alike – have tended to use the terms 'shame' and 'guilt' as synonyms. In particular, shame has received less attention, probably because guilt has been perceived to be a higher order indicator of conscience at work, with shame being a component of it.

Tangney *et al.* (2007) report that there have been three kinds of effort to distinguish between them. The first examines a distinction based on the nature of eliciting events, while the second is founded on the public versus private nature of the wrongdoing. The third is an intrapersonal judgement based on the degree to which the wrongdoer considers the emotion-eliciting transgression to be a failure of their whole self rather than a particular instance of their behaviour ('It's not like me to behave like that'). Of these, the first appears to have received the greatest attention. Generally, however, it is found that research into reports of the personal experiences of children and adults of shame and guilt following wrongdoing events do little to differentiate between the two emotions. Tracey and Robins (2006) report that there appears to be little distinction between those transgressions that evoke either one or the other. Whereas many common examples of transgressions were described, including cheating, stealing, lying, disobedience and failing to help others, there were no consistent trends as to whether the subjects reported experiencing shame or guilt associated with them. Some subjects reported shame, whereas others reported guilt for the same wrongdoing. It would appear, therefore, that the nature of the event when wrongdoing has occurred does not have much to do with the distinction between shame and guilt.

Despite these complexities, current psychological theory does differentiate between these two moral emotions. There is some evidence that shame is elicited by a wider range of circumstances that include both moral and non-moral failures and wrongdoings, whereas guilt is more specifically linked to moral transgressions (e.g. Smith *et al.*, 2002). As a consequence, the degree of doubt about guilt's provenance within the range of moral emotions is slight. That of shame is less secure. To further the argument that shame is a true moral emotion, Tangney and her colleagues call upon the 'Big Three' ethics of morality (Tangney *et al.*, 2007) proposed by Shweder and colleagues (e.g. Shweder *et al.*, 1997). This proposal originated with the commonplace observation that different cultures value different moral rules. Thus, Shweder and colleagues reported that the conventional moral judgement of people from the Indian culture is bound by strict social rules that are universally applied. These are founded on community duties and sometimes on religious doctrine. The morality of people from the United States, however, was less constrained by such rules and they espoused instead, a morality founded on individual rights. Subsequent analysis by Shweder and colleagues led them to conclude that it is possible to reduce a base-set of universal moral concepts to a 'Big Three' group of ethics – namely, the ethics of autonomy, the ethics of community and the ethics of divinity (Shweder *et al.*, 1997). It is postulated that these three can coexist within cultures but with varying degrees of emphasis according to the individual differences of each culture.

The *Ethic of Autonomy* defines the individual as the source of moral authority. This moral system is founded in people's rights to pursue their needs and desires but also on fairness and justice.

The *Ethics of Community* are founded upon respect for others and authority, loyalty, honour, effective self-control, and behaviour appropriate to social roles and duties to other individuals, family, community, nation, and other interpersonal groups that define a person's identity. In essence, the ethic of community locates individuals as members of groups to which they have commitments and obligations. It is these responsibilities that provide the basis of the individual's moral beliefs and values (Arnett *et al.*, 2001).

The *Ethics of Divinity* evolved from the study of two distinct religious traditions: American monotheistic Christianity, and Indian polytheistic Hinduism, with core concepts shared by both types of tradition. In essence, the concepts underpinning these ethics locate individuals as spiritual entities subject to a higher order. The self is connected to a higher force, and the body is considered sacred thereby making vital the keeping of its purity (e.g. Haidt *et al.*, 1993). Although the ethics of divinity do not require faith in any particular religion, they adhere to belief or faith in divine or natural law. These beliefs may well be rooted in religious authorities and texts (e.g., the Bible, the Koran, the Vedas scriptures), as well as duties and sanctions associated with supernatural forces (e.g. Arnett *et al.*, 2001).

Shweder's publication of the Big Three codes of ethics prompted many research studies across cultures and nationalities and, in general, the results have supported the usefulness of the conceptualisation. Guerra and Giner-Sorolla (2010) reviewed much of this research as part of their validation of a quantitative measure of the Big Three moral codes: namely, the Community, Autonomy and Divinity Scale (CADS).

Returning to Tangney's arguments favouring shame as a moral emotion, she and her colleagues take the view that it is less associated with the ethics of autonomy but more strongly with those of community and divinity. When an instance of an individual's behaviour is essentially oriented towards self-gratification but obviates the requirements of social obligation or produces breaches of religious doctrine, then there will be an experience of the negative emotion of shame. Consequently, therefore, shame may be said to function as a sanction against selfish acts and as a motivator of future improved behaviour.

Moral pride

This section leaves consideration of those self-conscious moral emotions that are experienced negatively and considers an example that is experienced positively. Pride is a positively experienced emotion, at least until it comes just before the proverbial fall from grace. It is described as being elicited by socially approved acts or by being a socially respected person (Tangney *et al.*, 2007). Its force is thought to reinforce other approved behaviour and so increase the probability of repetition. Although it is a powerful motivating force, it has not been closely studied; indeed, Tangney and her colleagues describe it as the neglected sibling of the self-conscious emotions. In addition, Eisenberg (2000) points out that although pride is a self-evaluative emotion and that it can be elicited by moral behaviour, it has been researched mostly in relation to achievement. As a consequence, its role in the functioning of conscience is imperfectly understood.

Tracy and Robins (2004a) acknowledge that much of the research on pride has emphasised the experience of that emotion in association with achievement, usually in respect of occupational, educational or sporting attainments. Nevertheless, they argue that most people strive to be good, decent and to treat others well (Tracy and Robins, 2004b) such that success in these leads to feeling authentic pride. This may act as a positive motivation reinforcer for behaving in morally acceptable ways according to the Big Three ethics. Tracy and Robins (2007) distinguish between authentic pride that is associated with self-esteem and hubristic pride that provides only a 'short cut' to a status that is probably unwarranted and short-lived. The latter is not a viable self-conscious moral emotion and Tangney *et al.* (2007) refer to hubris as the 'evil twin' of pride.

Other-focused moral emotions

The consideration of moral emotions above has examined the self-conscious emotions (embarrassment, shame, guilt and pride) that arise when individuals scrutinise and pass judgement on their core selves or instances of their behaviour given the benchmark of their own moral standards. Psychologists, notably Haidt (e.g. 2000, 2003), have extended the range for consideration by the addition of other-focused emotions that are elicited by judging the behaviour of others in the light of the same moral standards. The other-focused emotions include the negative ones of 'righteous' anger, contempt and disgust, and the positive ones of gratitude and elevation.

Rozin and colleagues have provided several studies on the negative emotions of anger, contempt and disgust (Rozin *et al.*, 1999). They cite Izard's reference to them as the *hostility triad* and locate each within Shweder's Big Three triad of moral emotions.

Righteous anger

The emotion of anger is not usually thought to fall within the moral domain. The range of eliciting circumstances is very broad and need not be associated with moral infringement; indeed, animals are capable of displaying anger and are not known for their moral codes. In human terms, for example, a valid parking ticket may well elicit anger but there is usually no sense that the traffic warden had breached a moral code in issuing it. In addition, anger may be directed against events associated with inanimate objects such as the car that fails to start or the television that expires in the middle of a favourite programme. In general, anger is elicited when events occur that thwart, frustrate or injure and a person or object is held (correctly or incorrectly) to be directly responsible.

Righteous anger, however, appears to be associated with a particular type of anger-evoking stimuli that is characterised by infractions of the observers' moral standards arising from the behaviour of others. On occasion, the experience of righteous anger may result in remediating action taken by observers. In terms of the Big Three, evidence suggests that righteous anger is experienced particularly when observers believe that what they witness is a violation of the ethic of autonomy (Rozin et al., 1999).

Contempt and disgust

Whereas the emotions of contempt and disgust are also the results of observing the behaviour of others that offends against the moral codes of the observers, they are less likely than righteous anger to result in action taken against the perpetrators.

Contempt is the feeling that a person or a thing is beneath consideration, worthless or deserving scorn, and is thought of as a 'cold' emotion that asserts the moral superiority of individuals or groups over other individuals or groups. Racism is associated with contempt as is social classism. Rozin and colleagues found from American and Japanese subjects that violations of social hierarchy elicited contempt for the violators and proposed that this emotion was aroused by unacceptable events censored by the ethics of community (Rozin et al., 1999).

Disgust is thought of as having its roots in the distaste of violations of civilised maintenance behaviours that separate humans from animal species. These are mainly to do with hygiene, waste elimination, eating and other bodily functions, including sexual behaviour. Appropriate behaviours associated with the civilised management of these functions are obviously pragmatic, but also have cultural and religious connotations. For example, virtually the whole Book of Leviticus is a manual for the maintenance of hygiene as a demonstration of religious conformity. It provides instructions on a wide variety of issues from skin diseases, through bodily discharges to homosexuality and bestiality. These reflect religious concerns with pollution of self and taboo behaviour, and the impact of these on spirituality. Rozin and colleagues believe this association with the sacred provides sufficient reason to link disgust to the ethics of divinity (Rozin et al., 1999). It does not, however, suggest why the disgust individuals experience over the animalistic behaviour of others should extend to their social behaviour also. Haidt (2000) suggests that this is the result of the aspirations humans have towards godliness. He states that as human cultures usually organise their spiritual aspirations along a vertical dimension with their god or gods at the pinnacle of moral perfection, then any base immoral or amoral behaviour tends to debase the perpetrator towards the lowest end inhabited by devils and the morally bankrupt. This draws on many tenets of ancient religion and Haidt cites the medieval Christian belief in the *scala naturae* (natural ladder), decreed by God, and more often referred to as The Great Chain of Being, a medieval concept describing a strict, hierarchical linkage of all life and matter. Thus, disgust is experienced by observers of those individuals whose behaviour tends to move them down the chain. Haidt (2000) describes this as people experiencing revulsion when witnessing moral depravity.

Gratitude

It is perhaps useful to introduce this emotion with the comment that 'gratitude' is derived from the Latin *gravia*, meaning 'grace' as well as 'gratefulness'. Emmons and McCullough (2003) refer to it as a moral virtue stemming from the pleasant feeling of being the recipient of another's kindness, freely given. Their research led them to conclude that the experience of gratitude benefited people in terms of psychological resilience, physical health and the quality of daily life. Gratitude is good for us.

From previous study, McCullough and colleagues concluded that gratitude could be described as a moral emotion because of its impact on prosocial behaviour (McCullough *et al.*, 2001a). They ascribe a threefold function to gratitude that allows it to be considered as such an emotion. First, it draws attention to the moral prosocial behaviour of benefactors; second, it motivates grateful recipients to act in a kindly prosocial way towards not only their benefactors but also to others; and third, the expression of gratitude encourages benefactors to display future moral behaviour. This may be found in the sometimes harshest of human interpersonal environments, that of commerce. For example, DeSteno *et al.* (2010) reported research demonstrating that gratitude functions to stimulate cooperative economic exchange even when that entails the reduction of individual financial gain. DeSteno and his colleagues found that increased gratitude is a direct antecedent of increased communal profit at the expense of individual gains. In addition, the increased benefaction was evident whether or not the beneficiary was known to the benefactor, thereby demonstrating that expectation of reciprocity, or simple mutual 'back scratching', was not a significant factor.

Elevation

The principal researcher of elevation as a moral emotion has been Haidt (e.g. Haidt, 2003). He believes that it is elicited by acts of virtue that motivate people to behave more virtuously themselves and his research suggests that it is experienced more often by individuals from Asian cultures than those from the West. Subjects in Haidt's study reported feeling motivated to help others and to become better people themselves. This suggests that it functions at a very high order of moral emotion.

The moral emotional process of empathy

Unlike the moral emotions described above, empathy is not a separate emotion; it is usually conceptualised as an integrated emotional and cognitive process and, as such, is a vital ingredient of conscience. It can be other-directed or self-directed. Eisenberg (2000) provided a definition of other-directed empathy as an emotional response that arises from the apprehension or comprehension of another person's emotional situation and is similar to that which this person is experiencing or would be expected to experience. This definition makes clear that the experience of empathy requires the integration of emotion and cognition, a combination that has been understood for over thirty years. Feshbach (1975), for example, proposed that there are three facets involved. The first is the cognitive ability to understand that the other people have their own perspective. This is referred to as Theory of Mind and it is the ability to understand that other people have thoughts and beliefs that are different from one's own. The second requires the cognitive ability to identify and assess the emotional state of others, and the last is the affective capacity to personally experience a range of emotions sufficient to match the range of other people's.

It appears that empathy is most likely to be elicited when empathic people observe similarities between themselves and those they may empathise with. Researchers note that the probability and accuracy of empathy is higher when there are similarities of culture, status, living circumstances and frequency of interaction. Conversely, there is evidence that distortion of empathy can occur according to the nature of the emotional background of the empathiser that may colour the judgement of those witnessing people in certain contexts. Distinctions are made between empathy and sympathy, the latter being a feeling of concern for another but is not necessarily a sharing of that person's emotion. Empathy, however, is other-directed and frequently linked to altruistic helping behaviour (e.g. Levenson and Ruef, 1997).

The development of conscience

A question about conscience posed in the opening section above was 'Are we born with it or does it steal up on us with age and experience?' Not surprisingly, the answer is rather open. As will be described, some facets of conscience are inbuilt in terms of child temperament and others arise from the experiences of socialisation at the hands of the principal caregivers, usually the child's parents. Thus, in part conscience does steal up on us with age and experience, and this process begins in infancy and early childhood. There is no potential end to the process as far as our present state of understanding is concerned and we can keep on learning the lessons of conscience for as long as we are able.[2] This section examines the early processes that provide us with the foundations of our conscience that life builds on from the materials of experience.

There are several theoretical perspectives concerning the development of conscience or moral judgement. Among the most influential there are four that have attracted particular attention: psychoanalytic theory, social learning theory, personality theory and cognitive developmental theories. The first of these begins with the psychoanalytic perspective dating back to the work of Freud. In essence, psychoanalytic theory posits that morality develops through humans' conflict between their instinctual drives and the demands of society. Guilt is the driving force that fashions the inhibition of these drives and allows the emergence of moral function. Support for this perspective is likely to come from those who believe that humans have innate basic drives that need to be controlled by the guidance of a maturely developed conscience. Social learning theory, in contrast, takes its behaviourist perspective from experiences of moral behaviour occurring within the individuals' external environments. Thus, children and young people develop their morality as a consequence of learning the rules of acceptable behaviour from others whom they imitate and are subsequently positively reinforced (rewarded) for displaying the same or similar behaviour.

Personality theories take a broader stance and propose an holistic approach that acknowledges the 'force' of all the factors that combine to fashion individual human development. This is attractive to those who conceive of humans as having a huge store of potentialities from which to develop many adaptive prosocial skills. Cognitive developmental theories are concerned with the development of reasoning such that the understanding of conscience is that it is one important product of that process. This viewpoint is important to theorists, theologians and others who consider that the most significant defining characteristics of the human species are its unique reasoning abilities and capacity for moral judgement.

Kohlberg's stage model

One of the most influential cognitive models of the development of conscience was proposed by the American psychologist, Lawrence Kohlberg, who published his reformulation (Kolberg, 1973) of Piaget's cognitive-developmental theory on the moral judgement of children (Piaget, 1932). Piaget's well-known theory of cognitive development demonstrated that children's reasoning grows through different stages, moving from the concrete to the formal or abstract. Kohlberg applied a similar progression through a sequence of developmental stages to the mature emergence of conscience.

Kohlberg's theory states that people go through six stages equally divided between three levels of moral development: pre-conventional morality, conventional morality and post-conventional morality. Conventional morality was considered to be the level reached by the majority; individuals had to move through the stages in order and acquired their developmental impetus from socialisation with other people.

Level One pre-conventional morality concerns the development of children from about four to ten years of age. It comprises two stages, the first of which is about obedience and punishment for wrongdoing. Thus, children do the right thing (i.e. that required by their caregivers) because they wish to avoid punishment. Kohlberg referred to Stage Two as the instrumental-relativist stage wherein moral judgement is not motivated by an awareness of morality to guide their behaviour but rather by the desire for self-gratification. Thus, children who behave well (i.e. according to the requirements of their caregivers) get what they want as rewards.

Kohlberg's Level Two, conventional morality, develops during late childhood to adulthood and consists of the third and fourth stages. The third stage is characterised by the growth of interpersonal concordance and is referred to as the 'Good boy/nice girl' stage. Here, the moral judgement that underpins conscience is induced by the need to maintain the acceptance and approval of others, particularly of the peer group. The major fear that attends this stage is that of rejection and disapproval and parents observe the force of peer pressure at work on their adolescent children. With further maturation, individuals move to the fourth stage of moral judgement that includes an understanding of the need for observance of law and community regulations and adhering to the obligations of duty to others.

Level Three is the post-conventional level of higher focused morality. It also has two stages, the fifth and sixth, and is not attained by everyone. Stage Five is that of social-contract legalistic orientation. The individual's moral judgement is based on respect for the community and social order, and is a genuine awareness of the need to act appropriately for the general good. The sixth and final stage is that of universal ethical-principle orientation. This considers not only the moral viewpoint of society but also allows reflection on the possibility that some extenuating circumstances can modify and extend moral choices. These may be understood as matters of conscience that transcend Level Two moral judgement. Thus, the fundamentals of morality such as human rights, justice, fairness and the preservation of human dignity provide an initial benchmark for the working of conscience, but ultimately these may be tempered by deeper review and reasoning if individuals are to make the best moral judgements they can in particular extenuating circumstances.

Kohlberg's developmental theory has been widely accepted and is still regarded as inspirational work. He is not without his critics, however, and some of the most trenchant must be acknowledged here, albeit in brief summary. Some important criticisms arise from the feminist perspective and the Kohlberg–Gilligan controversy of the eighties is particularly well known. In essence, Gilligan (1982) challenged Kohlberg's belief in the universality of moral development according to the stages of growth on the grounds that it was founded on male-dominated early research using boys, and that the moral development of girls is quite different (e.g. Clifford, 2002). As women's experience and socialisation throughout the world differs across almost every culture, it should be apparent that their moral development might differ significantly from that of men. Gilligan's position moved against the grain of early thinking in moral philosophy that women developed less mature moral systems than men and that their morality revolved more around an ethic of care, whereas that of men centred more on an ethic of justice. In Kohlberg's terms, this would mean that women were less likely than men to move to the pinnacle of his levels of moral development. Clearly, this is wrong, as even the most meager examination of the published works of female moral philosophers will reveal.

Other criticisms of Kohlberg's theory included concerns that his studies improperly restricted experimental results to an essentially Western, urban culture with primarily intellectual and upper-class conceptions of morality. Other sources of moral guidance were therefore undervalued, such as that pertaining to rural and working-class people, those with tribal heritage or those having Eastern moral backgrounds. Kohlberg came to realise that when going further than the broad cognitive developmental approach of age-related moral growth, the specific stage model and concept of universal development across cultures needed some revision. In general terms, however, a wealth of research over the years has supported in broad measure the developmental trends Kohlberg described. Indeed, a thorough recent review of the research literature led to the conclusion that his belief in the universality of basic moral development was largely correct in principle (Gibbs *et al.*, 2007).

The interplay of temperament and socialisation

A strong movement within the study of conscience development arises from research on the ways in which children's temperaments interact with their experiences of socialisation. Grazyna Kochanska at the University of Iowa and her colleagues have pursued the study of this interaction in commendable detail. This section presents a brief summary of this profitable contribution to our understanding of how conscience emerges from human infancy onwards.

Their study has been based on a series of investigations of how young children shift from the external regulation of their behaviour as provided by their adult caregivers to the self-regulation provided by internalised mechanisms. While it is the case that external regulation is seldom absent from daily living, taking the form of laws and other sanction-based prescriptions for behaviour, the majority of social interaction and interpersonal behaviour is mediated by internal regulation. We do what we should do because we have our own internalised standards to guide us.

Kochanska and colleagues have examined particularly the first six years of life, as this is the period when the transition to internal regulation is first apparent. They consider in particular two major components of conscience, moral emotions and moral conduct (e.g. Kochanska and Aksan, 2006). They use the construct of conscience (or morality) to discuss the growth of the autonomous internalised guidance that becomes independent of external authority, starting in early childhood. They note that psychoanalytic theorists had originally studied conscience in respect of development from infancy but the influence of cognitive-developmentalists such as Piaget and Kohlberg had brought about a shift of focus to adolescence. Subsequently, however, the growing influence of the study of younger children in the context of social-domain theory has reawakened interest in conscience development and the very young. Social-domain theory suggests that from as young as three years, children seek to take ownership of different domains of social knowledge, including that of morality. They defend their declaration of right to act within these domains (be it about hair style, friendships, behaviour, etc.) on the grounds of personal choice, freedom and autonomy. Their routes to growing autonomy appear to be relatively similar across cultures (e.g. Helwig, 2006).

In addition, there is a growing awareness that young children, previously thought to be unable to internalise rules and standards of conduct, do, in fact, have a complex moral life based on internalised guidance. For example, Laible and Thompson (2000) reported findings shared with other studies that young children (four years) from mother–child dyads characterised by high mutual responsivity, gained significantly high scores on maternal reports of conscience development, concern over shared good feelings, cooperation without reminders with parental requests and greater internalisation of rules.

The shifting viewpoint on conscience development is propelled further by another source of information, the inclusion of research on psychopathology. For example, Frick and Ellis (1999) studied children with conduct disorder in relation to age of onset and the manifestation of callous and unemotional traits. They commented that temperaments characterised by low behavioural inhibition could prejudice the maturation of the conscience-relevant developments of guilt and empathy, and suggest this may lead to the growth of the callous-unemotional traits. Subsequently, Frick and colleagues have strengthened their view that developmental difficulties with the growth of conscience arising from problematic temperamental factors are associated with the callous-unemotional traits of conduct disorder (e.g. Frick and White, 2008). In addition, there have been robust linkages of the emergence of psychopathy with temperamental and socialisation factors associated with differential outcomes in the development of conscience (e.g. Blair, 2006). It is noteworthy also that interest in the psychopathology of autism has led to the examination of the general deficit evident in the development of empathetic capacity of young children with the disorder. This appears to be related to their difficulties in establishing both physical and representational sense of self (Roth-Hanania *et al.*, 2000).

The outcomes of these movements have reinforced investigation of early development in respect of the growth of conscience and of the factors within it of individual differences and personality. The extensive programme of thorough research in these areas conducted by Kochanska and her colleagues has led to some definitive outcomes (see Kochanska and Aksan, 2006, for review). Their model of conscience development follows that of Feshbach (see p. 11) in that three interconnected facets develop with age —namely, moral emotions, moral conduct and moral cognitions. Their findings suggest that the first of these is principally the discomfort of feeling guilty associated with either a transgression or the anticipation of that emotion.

It is the case that there is no royal road along the developmental journey that a child makes in respect of these facets of conscience. Research studies reveal significant variation between individuals throughout this journey. Kochanska and her colleagues have found it beneficial to focus on two major sources of the individual differences. These are (1) the biologically based characteristics of children's temperaments, and (2) the nature of their experiences of socialisation, mainly involving those experiences derived from the early relationships they have with their caregivers (usually their parents).

Kochanska and Aksan (2006) review their findings from three large longitudinal studies of community samples of a hundred families. The first study was of mothers and children from toddler status; the second study extended from infancy to early primary school; and the final study was of both parents and their infants up to age three years. The main data was collected from behavioural observations of the children and the families. Some reports were taken from teachers. The findings support the opinion that moral emotions and moral conduct develop at much the same rates. As the children grew to experience discomfort (guilt) during wrongdoing, so their capacity to engage in rule-mediated behaviour increased. Thus, the more sorry that children feel about their transgressions, the more likely they are to inhibit future wrongdoing. Kochanska and Aksan (2006) report that three principal insights into the development of conscience were revealed by their results. The first is that both moral emotions and moral conduct are consistently evident across situations. Thus, although children's early conscience does function within situation specific contexts, its application can be more general. Second, the concurrent correlations between moral emotions and moral conduct are significant. This suggests moderate coherence between the two and that the products will also be stable rather than functioning disparately. The third finding was a moderate degree of longitudinal stability over consecutive assessments. This provides additional evidence of the stability of conscience at work as self-regulation achieves greater potency and reliability.

The variation between children in relation to their acquisition of mature conscience has been well recorded. A number of researchers have noted that there is variation between children and within children over their willingness to respond to parental requirements for acceptable behaviour (e.g. Maccoby, 1999). Some adopt an eager receptivity on most occasions but only sulkily bow to parental pressures on others. Other children may be uniformly resistant. The degree of willingness is seen as a critical issue for the vital development of autonomous self-regulation. Thus, how quickly and smoothly the transition to internalised guidance for social conduct proceeds depends in large measure on the motivation children have to comply with the standards of behaviour instructed and required by their parents and other caregivers.

This area of investigation by Kochanska and colleagues has been fruitful. Their results indicated that children who demonstrated the greatest commitment to compliance with caregivers' wishes were those who could demonstrate well-regulated behaviour in the absence of surveillance. They were also able to display 'moral' solutions to hypothetical problems where potential self-gratification competed adversely with the welfare needs of others. Those children who revealed the most mature conscience development at age four years were those most eager to use their mothers as models of behaviour.

Thus far, the evidence indicates that conscience develops from an early age and that the two major components of moral emotions and moral conduct grow consistently at a similar rate. Individual differences exist such that the route to mature conscience is not identical for all children. Further research suggests that this is due in large measure to the variations of child temperament and how the experiences of interaction affect the development of guilt particularly. With regard to temperament, research has shown that several inhibiting systems are influential as part of a complex interaction, with social experiences leading to individual variation and the 'developmental plasticity' referred to by Posner and Rothbart (2000). In relation to the issues concerning the development of conscience, two core components are investigated: *fearfulness*, which is associated with passive, reactive inhibition, and *effortful control*, which is the child's voluntary, active and vigilant control of behavioural impulses.

Children who have elevated fearful responses are inhibited in unfamiliar situations that may appear to them to be somewhat threatening. They are likely to be shy, slow to approach or explore novel stimuli, find separation from parents to be difficult and often seem anxious and distressed. This fearful inhibition has been linked to conscience development; it is assumed that children experience anxiety as a result of wrongdoing and this negative feeling effectively punishes the wrongdoing and reduces the probability of it being repeated.

The inhibition arising out of fearfulness is contrasted with that consciously exerted by children who practise effortful control. This is the skill that some children show from about age two years when they suppress a prohibited but strongly positive response in favour of a less pleasant but required and approved response. It is also a core requirement of moral behaviour whereby self-gratification has often to be foregone in favour of less personally desirable but approved behaviour. Kochanska and colleagues have hypothesised that effortful control is a probable support for emergent behaviour that is compatible with societal values. The socialisation afforded by family life is a further spur to the development of conscience and would also be a source of variation between children.

There has been particularly relevant interest in the parental disciplinary response to children's undesirable behaviour (e.g. Kerr *et al.*, 2004). In addition, related research studies have led to a substantial volume of information about the quality and style of early relationships. These have examined in detail the key ingredients of parent–child attachment, including parental sensitivity and availability, nurturance and stress management. Sroufe and his colleagues carried out a longitudinal study of thirty years' duration. He reports the key points from the mass of data accumulated and drew conclusions about the importance of early relationships (Sroufe, 2005). While variation in these relationships (specifically infant–caregiver attachment) do not relate well to all outcomes, it is clear that they are important to the instigation of complex developmental processes. Although no causal property can be claimed, the impact of the quality of early relationships is very considerable on pathways of development and connection to many vital developmental functions, including those relevant to the self-regulations of emotions and behaviour. Aksan and colleagues discuss their construct of mutually responsive orientation (MRO) that is the relationship between parent and child characterised by being positive, cooperative and mutually binding (Aksan *et al.*, 2006). They state that the extent to which MRO develops in any given parent–child relationship has an important bearing on the socialisation process. Their construction of an observation coding system for important components of MRO provided evidence that these are stable across early mother–child and father–child relationships.

When the two constructs of child temperament and socialisation are examined jointly it is suggested that for fearful children, gentle parental discipline is the most effective response because it modifies behaviour appropriately and also facilitates internalisation. It is predicted also that increasingly power-assertive discipline for fearless children may modify their behaviour in the desired direction but, in the longer term, is unlikely to promote internalisation because of increasing anxious arousal, including resentment and anger. For such children, the MRO style of parenting is more likely to promote internalisation. In essence, Kochanska and Aksan (2006) report that these predictions are supported by their research. They showed that gentle maternal discipline that reduces power assertive interaction was a significant predictor of the internalisation of appropriate conduct in respect of fearful children's conduct. This was true for concurrent parent–child

responding as well as that across time. In respect of fearless children, interactions characterised by attachment security and maternal responsiveness (major
traits within MRO) predicted the development of internalisation, again both
concurrently and longitudinally.

In summary, therefore, it is clear that conscience is the product of a complex
developmental process where factors of child temperament and parental
socialisation come together from early life to provide a basis for future
autonomous self-regulation.

Conscience and the influence of religion

Does being religious influence the development of a believer's conscience?
Or does being a member of a religious community, congregation or other group
of believers cause conscience to become more developed than that of individuals
who have no such faith-based membership? Do religious parents have a better
probability of developing their children's conscience than those parents who
have no faith? The answers appear to be in the affirmative but, typically, there
are significant caveats. This section provides a brief discussion of these.

It is often assumed by theists that religion maintains the moral order of
society. This is hardly surprising given that only about two per cent of the
population professes to atheism and only a further 12 per cent claim to have
no formal religious beliefs. Consequently, theists, as the overwhelming
majority, may feel that they are right to assume that religion is the bastion
of morality. The Christian philosopher J.P. Moreland adopts a tone of moral
authority in stating that morality is 'more at home' and less *ad hoc* when placed
in a theistic universe. He argues that as God has the property of goodness
and that as humans are made in God's image, then it follows that to be human
is not merely a matter of biology but also morality, an essence of God's
goodness (Moreland, 1987). An illogical but frequently taken step from this
argument is that there is no morality without religion, which places atheists,
agnostics and those with no firm religious belief in a strange no-man's land.

Not surprisingly, there is robust contrary argument and Stark (2001) states
unequivocally that there is no evidence to show that observance of religious
faith has significant independent influence upon morality. Sadly, research as
well as common experience indicates that not all religious people can aspire
to a warm and empathetic regard for other people. It is axiomatic that whereas
one can easily lay claim to high moral principles, that does not necessarily
guarantee competence in the harder task of applying them. Research results
suggest that being religious does not necessarily bestow or improve the moral
reasoning ability that is vital to conscience. It is the manner in which religious
constructs are processed that is important (e.g. Duriez and Soenens, 2006).
Those who follow a literal interpretation of their chosen religious sources
strictly and without question are at risk of a restrictive, prejudicial
fundamentalism that is manifest as a deficiency in empathy but strong in

intolerance and authoritarianism. These traits are in marked contrast to those people who affirm their faith after weighing their beliefs against disciplined argument from other sources and authorities. They tend towards tolerance and benevolence; show willingness to listen to the differing viewpoints of others and do not reject them out of hand as do those adherents to faith who brook no alternative interpretations of their religious lore. Under these conditions religious faith can bring about a restriction of moral judgement and cuts off the routes to the full development of conscience. It is probable also, that such devotees do not provide the models of moral behaviour and styles of parenting that their children require in order to develop their conscience fully (e.g. Berkowitz and Grych, 1998.

Authoritarianism is not associated positively with child rearing. Authoritarian parents generally do not encourage independent thinking and seek to promulgate behavioural standards through insistence on obedience to a set standard of conduct, often underpinned by their religious beliefs. Obedience is regarded as a virtue and is maintained by punitive, forceful strategies (e.g. Baumrind, 1966). If, therefore, a parent's strong religious beliefs lead to authoritarianism, it is probable that their parenting style will be negatively influenced and restrictive of their children's opportunities for the development of conscience.

In general, research on religion and the cognitive elements of conscience indicates that among Islamic, Christian, Jewish and Buddhist samples, engagement in religious practice and community support is associated with empathetic understanding, willingness to help others and benevolent attitudes. These traits were not found to be artefacts of gender, social desirability bias, attachment security, empathy or honesty (e.g. Saroglou et al., 2005). This does not mean that there is, however, always a universal benevolence in that what is considered an appropriate social response and to whom it should be made depends on religious affiliation (e.g. Hunsberger and Jackson, 2005). Indeed, strictly orthodox and fundamentalist observance is, for some adherents, associated with discrimination, prejudice and egoism. This is associated also with a greater tendency to hold unforgiving attitudes (e.g. Cohen et al., 2006). It appears that while most religious people espouse values that exemplify the presence of mature conscience, there are limiting factors for some that restrict the behaviour associated with such values to particular recipients who together constitute a singularly religious 'in-group'. Outsiders are met with significantly reduced benevolence. Day (2010) provides a thorough review of relevant research and concludes that there are distinct religious attitudes that affect the workings of conscience. He finds that variables of ethnicity, cultural interpretation, gender and social attitudes are linked to religious mediating factors; these include tradition, stances of faith pertaining to particular religious communities, and the dissimilar conceptualisations of correct moral functioning held by different faiths. The conclusion is inevitable, therefore; religion does have an impact on the development of conscience but, although this impact is usually positive, it is not always so.

Nevertheless, however, the world's major religions purvey a similar message to parents about their responsibilities for the moral development of their children and have been doing so for hundreds of years before the advent of psychology as a discipline. Although the term 'conscience' is infrequently found in scriptural material, the components of conscience are expressed in appropriate ways. Trust, empathy, honesty, regard for others, generosity, protection of the vulnerable and the avoidance of wrongdoing feature largely in the traits to be taught and encouraged by parents. Using Islam as an example, while it is true that the Qur'an has more to say about the duties children have to their parents than parents have to their children, the direction of good parenting is clear, particularly for fathers,[3] and covers both physical and spiritual development. Islamic teaching gives parents the duty to love, respect and bring up the children they are blessed with, in the Islamic faith and in a manner that benefits them in this life and in the hereafter. Parents should encourage their children to do good and refrain from evil deeds.

Nurturing the growth of conscience

Parents and committed teachers observe the chaos in the world around them and understand that much of it is the product of failed, misguided or absent moral guidance. They see children and young people 'going wrong', and harming themselves and others as a consequence. Although worried adults may not share the vocabulary of psychologists, they understand intuitively that these young people lack an internalised code of conduct and so fall prey to the corrosion caused by unrestrained self-gratification. Throughout recorded history, every generation of parents and caregivers has looked worriedly at young children and wondered how best they may nurture the stirrings of conscience. This is not a modern phenomenon; it is the lot of all who genuinely strive to nurture the young and employ their best endeavours to create the most favourable circumstances for the vital lessons about what is right and wrong. Publications for parents on child rearing have swirled like confetti around bookshops and supermarket shelves over decades. Many have provided basic common-sense advice, but others have spawned more fears and doubts than they have alleviated. Diehard authoritarians spout the virtues of aggressive discipline that results in alienation, fear of punishment and devious schemes to avoid detection. Permissive gurus have corroded the will of parents to set boundaries and failed to encourage respect for the standards of behaviour required to live at peace in the community. It is inevitable that, after decades of studying the growth of conscience and the well-springs of moral judgement, the question is asked of theoreticians: 'What works?'.

Unsurprisingly, perhaps, the answer is not simple but, as all parents know, nothing about child rearing is. Typically, what works does not achieve perfect results but gets by well enough to mould most young people into generally empathetic individuals who respond to others with sympathy and understand the meaning of cooperation and the need for self-restraint. At the heart of this modest but vital outcome is an intuitive parental awareness that there is no single, definitive route to follow, but an evolving child-centred approach that brings together knowledge of the child's temperament with moral teaching that involves discussion, modelling correct behaviour, reinforcement, encouragement and preservation of the child's self-esteem.

Guidance to parents and other caretakers is, of course, available. The findings presented above that conscience is the product of a complex developmental process involving child temperament and parental socialisation, provide a significant entry point into approaches that can be modified to suit the individual. Kochanska and her colleagues' work provides an explanation of why conscience develops given the right nurturance, and other psychologists offer procedural advice. Of these, Berkowitz and Grych (1998) offer a clear sequential strategy that is summarised here.

They identify four attributes of children's moral development that it is desirable to promote. These are:

Social orientation: moral behaviour that is motivated by an interest in and concern for other people.

This is fostered by the quality of attachment between mother and child from early infancy. Securely attached infants have mothers who respond swiftly and consistently to their behavioural signals of need and distress. They continue to do this as their children become toddlers and their relationship becomes characterised by that described above as the mutually responsive orientation (MRO). This ensures that the relationship between parent and child is positive, cooperative and mutually binding.

Self-control: the capacity of individuals to control their own behaviour and to refrain from engaging in behaviour that violates acceptability when not under supervision.

In terms of parenting, Maccoby and Jacklin (1980) have described five ways that parents can help their children develop self-regulation from the early impulsivity of infancy. The first is the duty to provide protection from harm arising from potentially dangerous impulsivity by utilising successful and consistent management as circumstances arise. The second is the need for parents and caregivers to help infants deal with emotions at a time when they have no capacity to do that for themselves. This includes the gentle management of emotional outbursts, particularly when the child's wants are thwarted by necessity. Maccoby and Jacklin's third point concerns the teaching of coping skills, including how to refocus attention away from a desire for self-gratification that cannot be fulfilled immediately. Their next suggestion concerns gradually encouraging children to predict the consequences of their own impulsive actions and the fifth is a reminder to parents that their own behaviour in front of their children should provide clear models of self-control.

Compliance with external behavioural standards: learning to internalise the external standards of acceptable and required behaviour.

The parenting style associated with the development of compliance with external behavioural requirements is that which has been described above, instructive rather than power-assertive, modeling of pro-social conduct, reinforcing of correct behaviour and consistent. The MRO style appears to be effective.

Self-esteem: developing a positive evaluation of one's own worth and, in the context of this section, coming to understand that one is valued by important others such as parents and other caregivers.

Parents can encourage this development through warm acceptance of their children, setting and maintaining clear boundaries for their children's behaviour, while allowing (within acceptable limits) self-expression and demonstrating respect for their children's individual personalities and opinions.

In addition, Berkowitz and Grych also identify four core facets of moral functioning that are vital to the acquisition of conscience and are open to positive parental influence. These are:

Empathy: the ability to understand and share the feelings of others, including their pain and distress.

Suggestions about parenting include support for parental induction, which is the patient explanation of their behaviour to children and demonstrating how that behaviour affects them. Counter-productive strategies are power-assertive discipline and the withdrawal of love from their children. In essence, parents who explain why their parenting behaviour is as it is, particularly emphasising consequences to others, are more likely to develop their children's empathy.

Conscience: in this context, the internalisation of the standards of 'right' behaviour, the self-examination of concordance with those standards and apology and reparation for harm done to others, as well as the monitoring of others' wrongdoing.

In respect of parenting, much of the relevant background has been described above. The role of developing feelings of guilt is of great significance and the use of non-power assertive discipline by parents leads to better outcomes. The work of Kochanska and colleagues may be returned to here as they have demonstrated the positive impact on child empathetic development of mother–child reciprocity. This involves demonstration of maternal empathy as well as low power assertive discipline with good mutual affectivity.

Moral reasoning: Berkowitz and Grych make use of Kohlberg's model of staged development of moral reasoning (see p. 13) for their suggestions on this area of development. They review evidence that highlights parental discipline style and family communication strategies as being of particular importance.

Altruism: the potential to give to others at a cost to oneself. This moral attribute is not just about selflessness. It is part of a set of character strengths that include being sociable, insightful, competent, assertive and advanced in skills such as social judgement. It is linked also to strengths in moral reasoning and to the formation of mature relationships.

Style of parenting is at the core of the growth of altruism. In my experience, parents of children who successfully develop altruism tend to be highly supportive and put themselves and their own needs behind those of their children and others generally. They are nurturing, explain the consequences to other people of desirable and undesirable behaviour, set consistent behavioural boundaries, expect their children's behaviour to be as mature as it can be, given age and stage of development, and encourage their children to accept some responsibility for the welfare of others, pets and tasks that benefit the family.

The eight psychological attributes above are therefore the key 'ingredients' of conscience that Berkowitz and Grych believe should be promoted as an integral part of child development. They go further to discuss the 'tools' that parents can utilise to enable this development to occur successfully and identify five core processes. These are:

Induction: One of the earliest descriptions of this parenting style was provided by Hoffman (1970). He defined it as the parents' explanations with respect to their own actions, values and disciplinary behaviours. Hoffman believed their use of induction encouraged children to learn about the reasons behind their parents' actions, rather than simply mimic the behaviour. The parents' discussion of their disciplinary behaviour should include explanations of the consequences of their children's behaviour on other people[4] such as other children, parents, teachers and other caregivers. It is noteworthy that, among parents with religious beliefs, the use of induction was associated with sanctification of parenting and higher scores for their children on measures of moral conduct (Volling *et al.*, 2009).

Nurturance: Nurturing parenting is not only responsive, encouraging, warm and supportive, it is also the basis for the demonstration of respect for their children and a celebration of their worth. The parents have discussions with their children about the moral implications of their behaviour, but do so in an emotionally supportive and respectful manner that does not threaten the child's self-esteem.

Demandingness: This is not a polite term for parents who act like martinets and demand unattainably high standards of behaviour from children on the grounds of 'because I said so'. Instead, the parents establish expectations of their children's behaviour that are realistic and attainable; they supply the appropriate guidance and support to ensure that their children are able to succeed in reaching those expectations and they monitor their children's behaviour to ensure that their expectations are met, stepping in with support and guidance if problems are occurring. Finally, parents positively reinforce success with their praise and occasional use of other rewards.

Modelling: this refers to the provision of clear models of moral behaviour that children can imitate or internalise. It is teaching by example, and, in this context, it requires that parents not only deal respectfully with each other and their children but everyone they encounter, particularly when their children are present to observe them. It is axiomatic that children learn from poor models as well as good. Thus, parents who denigrate, coerce and act aggressively with each other provide that behaviour as a model of adult interpersonal interaction. Whatever desirable behaviour they may promote in discussions will be overwhelmed by the strength of the rancorous lessons they model.

As children acquire the representational skills that come with language development, they become more able to internalise some standards of behaviour that are described to them rather than observed by them. Parents, therefore, may 'model' appropriate moral conduct by talking to their children of relevant events from their day, using words to represent behaviour that has been a moral response to particular situations. In addition, talking about events seen on television by the family members that concern charity, altruism and generally putting other people first are all opportunities to help children understand the widespread nature of moral conduct and so broaden the range of adult models. This will not work effectively if the parents' own behaviour is manifestly different.

Democratic family decision-making and living: as suggested above, the observable process of respecting children and their opinions has a beneficial impact on the development of conscience. Democratic parents are more likely to be rewarded by children having higher self-esteem, greater altruism and compliance based on internalisation of behavioural standards. This does not mean that parental wishes should always evolve from interminable family discussion, but that there is sufficient give and take generally to constitute an appreciation of having a voice that is listened to. Such parents respect children's opinions, made from within their developmental compass, as meaningful contributions to decision taking and the resolution of conflicts.

Berkowitz and Grych (1998) provide a chart summarising these processes in relation to the psychological attributes they promote. The following may be of some assistance also:

Attributes required	Influential processes
Social orientation	Nurturance
Self-control	Demandingness, modelling
Compliance	Nurturance, democratic family living
Self-esteem	Nurturance, demandingness, democratic family living
Empathy	Induction
Conscience	Induction, nurturance, democratic family living
Moral reasoning	Induction, nurturance, democratic family living
Altruism	All five processes

Many parents can utilise these processes without having heard of them in these terms. Generations of parents have engaged their children successfully in these developmental processes with no other guidance than that from their own experienced parents, siblings and circle of friends. Not all parents are so fortunate, however, and I have had considerable professional experience of working with, for example, parents who were the luckless victims of poor alternative care systems or homes where alcoholism and criminality swamped all external attempts to convey information and provide support. Other parents experience severe doubts about either their motivation or their potential for parenting. It is for these parents that education and structured programmes are vital. We can only hope that our societal conscience will always urge finding the time and resources to help them.

Summary

Conscience is a facet of our judgement that enables us to distinguish right from wrong. Positive feelings associated with it, such as that of pride, reinforce behaviour that meets our own moral standards and those of the society we live in. Negative feelings, such as those of shame and guilt, punish transgressions of those standards. Being sorry about our past and present transgressions is an integral guiding force for improved future self-regulation. Conscience has three major components: moral emotions, moral reasoning and moral conduct. In general, these develop at similar rates and have their roots from infancy in early manifestations of temperament and the quality of socialisation lessons arising from interactions with parents and other caregivers. As these come together, conscience emerges in stages of maturation that roughly follow similar trends between individuals. Authoritative and nurturing styles of parenting are associated with good outcomes for the development of conscience, whereas authoritarian and punitive styles are associated with less successful outcomes. Although benevolent religious faith is generally associated with empathy, nurturance and support for others, this is less likely to be true for those believers who espouse an overly authoritarian application of religious belief. There is no evidence that any one of the major religious faiths studied has a better influence on the development of conscience than the others or that those people without religion are incapable of the moral judgement that is the overt manifestation of conscience. Some psychopathologies are, however, associated with diminished or absent development of conscience. In general terms, therefore, the remorseful sting of conscience is available to mostly everyone and few individuals can truthfully claim to have escaped the discomfort of being sorry for wrongdoing.

Chapter 2

Interpersonal relationships and betrayal

Introduction

The American playwright Steven Dietz knows how severe the pain of betrayal can be, and much of his work concerns the effects of personal betrayal and deception. The potency of these effects is well reflected in his comment, 'One should rather die than be betrayed. There is no deceit in death. It delivers precisely what it has promised. Betrayal, though . . . betrayal is the willful slaughter of hope.' Most people regard betrayal of a partner, family or friends to be one of the most serious interpersonal transgressions that an individual can commit. The discovery that a loved one has been treacherous, has violated the joint 'rules' through which trust is reciprocated within a close relationship, can be devastating to those betrayed. Feelings of outrage swirl furiously with those of despair and bewilderment. Often all hope is lost, not only for the future of the relationship but also for regaining the victims' sense of worth and place in their familiar world. Such is the intensity of feeling, it is small wonder that perpetrators are shunned or treated with extreme suspicion for as long as it takes for the impact of their offence to heal from the immediacy of a raw wound to become the scar of unpleasant memory. And that can be a very long time; indeed, as the American playwright Arthur Miller believed, 'Betrayal is the only truth that sticks'.

Betrayal cuts across all types of interpersonal relationships, ranging through those of children who suffer the parental treachery of abuse to those of people who learn of the perfidy of their friends. It is, however, the complex arena of intimate relationships that attracts the greatest public attention to betrayal. From the sensationalist gleeful scrabbling of the tabloids to the sober investigations of serious journalism, no stone is left unturned where infidelity may hide. This should not cause surprise given the time, effort and prodigious resources that humans devote to seeking out potential partners, and establishing and maintaining romantic relationships. When they are not working on their own relationships, they like to know about those of others.

It is axiomatic that romantic relationships are vitally important to most people and typically attract great effort and emotional investment from them.

They are prepared to accept this even though their relationships may become dysfunctional and present more problems than rewards. Perhaps the struggle for union with others reflects the understanding that two or more stand a better chance of surviving contentedly than one alone. The task of raising children and nurturing them to maturity is an added incentive for many. Economic inducements exist also in that often two can live as cheaply as one – but with more fun. It is the case, however, that among all the incentives that exist to encourage the formation of intimate relationships, the basic 'need to belong' is as powerful as any. Betrayal may be the ultimate dissolution of belonging and threatens all the 'comforts' and reassurance that relationships bring.

Although romantic relationships are those that spring most readily to mind, close friendships may be just as important for many people. In general, people are happier when they are part of a friendship group (e.g. Sharma, 2010), although it does not appear that the degree of happiness is directly associated with the number of friends a person may have. Thus, people who have five friends or less seemed to rate their happiness as highly as those with five friends or more (National Opinion Research Center General Social Survey, reported by Myers, 2000). People with extravert tendencies particularly enjoy and feel happy with social contacts (e.g. Pavot et al., 1990) but paradoxically they do not necessarily have more friends than anxious introverts who generally feel fairly miserable (e.g. Hotard et al., 1989).

People gamble that their relationships will endure. They understand that they are more comfortable with others or one other rather than remain alone. Indeed, in comparison with people who have few or no reciprocal associations with others, those who have close supportive relationships with family, romantic partner, friends, work colleagues, fellow team or church members and even Internet groups may enjoy significant benefits in addition to that of companionship. For example, research demonstrates that there are health and longevity benefits (e.g. Cohen, 1988). Thus, people with serious illnesses such as heart disease who enjoy good social support are more likely to have better survival prospects than those who do not (e.g. Case et al., 1992). Conversely, the failure of important social relationships is associated with negative outcomes for health; for example, the possible weakening of immune systems associated temporally with fragmenting relationships may lead to an increase of rates of disease (e.g. Kaprio et al., 1987).

It is probable that the most intensely studied interpersonal romantic relationship is that of marriage. Although the religious significance of this appears to be in decline across the world, it is nevertheless of great importance to a substantial proportion of the adult population. Married couples that share religious beliefs experience benefits that they ascribe to their joint faith. Dollahite and Lambert (2007) investigated the marital satisfaction of 57 middle-aged married couples. They reported:

> We found that religious involvement helped to sanctify marriage by helping couples set aside sacred time to spend together, share a holy vision and purpose, enhance interpersonal virtues, find spiritual help in conflict resolution, and receive divine relational assistance.
>
> (p. 305)

Betrayal of marriage through adultery is proscribed by all major religions and the scriptures provide fierce punishments. For example, the Law of Moses stated that the penalty for adultery was death by stoning (Deuteronomy 22:21). Even being attracted to a woman was deemed to be a sin; Matthew records the words of Jesus on this subject as, 'That whosoever looketh on a woman to lust after her hath committed adultery with her already in his heart' (Matthew 5:28).

Research findings generally reveal that in contrast with individuals who have not married or are separated or divorced, married people's survey responses indicate that they are happier and generally more satisfied with their lives. Using data from national surveys of over 20,000 people in 19 countries, Mastekaasa (1995) confirmed the strong positive relationship between marriage and happiness. He reported that people who were previously married experience less social well-being than spouses and those who had never married. Divorced and separated individuals experienced less happiness than widowed people. This finding appears to be stronger for men but married people generally show a smaller risk of depression. A really strong vote in favour of the value married partners attach to their status is the finding that the majority believe that their spouse is their best friend and would marry the same person again (e.g. Greeley, 1991). Although there is a variety of influences that link marriage to happiness and well-being, including personal–social competencies, a prevailing conclusion of much research is that married people experience happiness because of the benefits (support, companionship, commitment, acceptance) that marriage brings them (e.g. Mastekaasa, 1995).

It is clear, therefore, that the potential destruction of these benefits by acts of betrayal is likely to be a powerful antecedent for feelings of outrage and despair. The question may be asked as to whether the same or similar factors influence unmarried partners in romantic relationships generally. Although the research evidence is not as extensive, it does appear that similar factors are influential such that the effects of betrayal are also alike, although not perhaps as strongly felt. Thus, Feldman *et al.* (2000) found that the young adults sampled were strong in their disapproval of betrayal in relationships generally because of the damage done to the betrayed. There were, however, some mediating dynamics. For example, male respondents were considerably more likely to accept sexual betrayal perpetrated by male transgressors, and this trait skewed the findings concerning sexual betrayal. In addition, there are significant findings that reveal attachment style to be an important determinant of what may happen to couples after one has betrayed their intimate relationship. Jang *et al.* (2002) studied the responses of 213 participants who reported betrayal of a romantic relationship. The results showed that respondents with a secure attachment style tended to talk about the betrayal with the transgressor; conversely those with anxious/ambivalent attachment styles were more likely to try to avoid the issue. Both groups, however, often maintained their relationships, unlike those respondents with an avoidant attachment style who were more likely to terminate their relationship with the transgressors on discovery of the betrayal. Evidently, therefore, betrayal has a powerful negative impact on romantic relationships that is largely independent of marital status. The experience is illuminated starkly by the following.

Michael and Alice married when both were aged 23 years. They met at their church activities and both were devout Christians who had made a lot of money for various charities by marathon running. Alice had moved into their community but Michael had always lived in the area where he was well-liked and respected. He described their time together as 'exuberant' and was thrilled to have met a young woman with as deep a love of Christianity as he had.

They married less than two years after meeting whereupon their relationship was finally consummated. Michael had thought of Alice as '. . . a chaste girl' who had fended off his clumsy attempts at sex prior to marriage. He felt surprised that she had '. . . really come alive sexually' after their wedding. Michael had thought that they were both '. . . utterly committed to each other' and 'joined together for life in God's love'.

Michael's enthusiasm for his marriage was scarcely diminished by a steadily increasing '. . . waspishness from Alice'. She became somewhat intolerant of him and occasionally belittled his intelligence. This attitude hurt him but was not a surprise as he had always thought that he was her intellectual inferior because she was a graduate and he had barely scraped a few low-grade GCSEs. Rather more hurtful, he found that at church meetings and other social gatherings she seemed to distance him in favour of more able and witty conversationalists. He noted that her telephone calls to her mother and brother became more frequent, longer and secretive, yet their news relayed to him grew shorter and more vague. Her time spent at work also got longer and Alice's interest in make-up, usually quite low, increased significantly.

Michael became embarrassed after the event of their separation because he had not guessed that Alice was having an affair. He thought that he had been hopelessly naïve and '. . . far too trusting', an opinion shared by his friends who eventually told him that he was the last person to know what Alice had been doing. Nevertheless, Michael was shrewd enough to understand that there are always '. . . friends who are wise after the event'.

In fact, Alice had conducted two extra-marital sexual relationships simultaneously, both with married men who were clients of her boss. She was sufficiently audacious to warn Michael against speaking to her employer in case she lost her job before a transfer to another area could take place.

Michael discovered later that Alice's behaviour had occurred before she moved into his community; indeed, she had had to move because of the fall-out from previous affairs with married men. He was saddened to discover that her church and charitable activities were largely a front, a type of presentational package to help project an image of spirituality and goodness.

Michael was devastated by the collapse of his marriage. His despair and anger never turned to violence but he sincerely believed that this was only because his priest and genuine friends '. . . sat on me'. His thoughts were of revenge and he ranted that Alice had not just betrayed him but also had betrayed God, before whom she had made her marriage vows. Michael made telephone calls to Alice's friends and family that were filled with tirades of abuse, blaming them for continuing to talk to her and questioning their own sexual morality on the grounds that they were colluding with an adulteress.

Michael's own employer was also a genuinely good friend. He was greatly saddened by these events and turned a blind eye to the lower standard of Michael's work. He and his wife supported Michael with meals, trips to social events and over-night stays when the young man seemed too upset to be by himself. They spent hours listening to Michael's vitriolic outpourings of betrayal and loss. These continued for some months after the separation but gradually died down, only to peak again around the time that divorce proceedings were initiated. A new theme emerged whereby Michael reminisced about early happy events Alice and he had shared but reinterpreted them to find evidence of her deceit even then. Virtually every pleasure they had had together became infused with his vitriol as he recounted them to anyone who would listen.

In retrospect, it is clear that Michael's mental health had reached such low ebb that psychological intervention would have been desirable. As it happened, however, his kind Christian friends gently reminded him of a core theme of his faith based on love for others, selflessness and forgiveness. His priest helped him understand how his vengeful behaviour and talk was at odds with the Christian love that he had built his life upon.[1] Michael later came to understand that his religion had brought him '. . . a release from corrosive revenge', but he also accepted that this was not the only protective factor that had saved him from further psychological damage. He had received a letter of remorse from Alice who thanked him for the love he had shown her and asked forgiveness for all the harm she had caused him and his family. This letter came at a time when he was beginning to return to his faith and enabled him to turn away from thoughts of revenge and bitterness. They exchanged letters and eventually met. To his surprise, Michael found that his anger was muted although he could no longer find a basis for trust. Her remorse seemed genuine and her expressions of shame and guilt encompassed not only the hurt she had caused him but also that caused to their parents, close relatives and friends. She spoke of her disgrace and the damage she had done to her sense of self-worth. Of great importance to Michael was the fact that she wanted his forgiveness but understood that he could not be expected to give it. He gave her this but also told her that he did not want to see her again once their affairs were settled and their marriage was '. . . laid to rest'.

This example of betrayal, remorse and forgiveness provides a number of insights into the complexities of transgression within romantic relationships. It reveals how the intimacy and mutual joy of the relationship provides great benefits to the partners and how betrayal of the underpinning principles of loyalty and trust gives rise to outrage and vengefulness. Also revealed, however, is how a shift away from anger can be made to a state of forgiveness fuelled by forces such as religious belief or some other source of guidance on how to behave towards transgressors. Lastly, this case demonstrates that the remorse of the transgressor can act as a powerful catalyst for this shift from revenge to forgiveness. It is perhaps the single most important factor in the repair of betrayal; it does not always lead to the re-establishment of a damaged relationship, but it invariably assists both the victim and the transgressor in the improvement of their own perceptions of themselves. However, before it is possible to examine the processes stretching from an act of betrayal to remorse, it is first necessary to consider the multifaceted nature of this act and why it is perceived to be betrayal.

The anatomy of betrayal

What is betrayal?

The *Oxford English Dictionary* states that to betray is to act treacherously towards a country, to reveal information that might aid an enemy. It states also that it is be disloyal to others, to prove false. These terms do little to encompass the feelings of those betrayed whose opinions on the subject are apt to be rather more emotive. The intensity of feeling appears often to be in some way directly proportional to the importance of the norm(s) broken within the relationship by the betrayer. All relationships are governed by 'rules' or norms that the partners subscribe to, although there is unlikely to be any formal statement of them. The norms may differ between romantic partnerships and estimates of importance may also diverge. Thus, a particular act of betrayal within one relationship may be viewed very differently by the partners of another.

This important facet of relationships is reflected in the definition of betrayal provided by Finkel and Rusbult (2002). They state:

> In the context of close relationships, we define betrayal as the perceived violation by a partner of an implicit or explicit relationship-relevant norm. Betrayal may be said to have occurred when the victim believes that the perpetrator has knowingly departed from the norms that are assumed to govern their relationship, thereby causing harm to the victim.
>
> (p. 957)

Norms within relationships are essentially rule-based and, according to interdependence theory, are the consequences of processes by which partners within a given relationship sculpt the behaviour of each other. It is believed that strong interdependence of partners creates significant opportunities for mutual influence and adaptation such that self-oriented behaviours designed to meet the immediate needs of the individual are supplanted by behaviours that sustain the needs of both. The 'rules' that govern the new behaviour constitute the essential norms for the behaviour that maintains the integrity of the relationship. Thus, 'Each person's self is sculpted by the partner; each person's dispositions, values, and behavioral tendencies come to reflect the particular conditions of interdependence experienced with the partner' (Rusbult *et al.*, 2005, p. 377). The norms that guide expectations of relationships and the behaviour required within an individual's own relationship is sometimes called a 'script'. This is made up of beliefs and expectations about the ways in which the relationship typically unfolds in predictable situations (e.g. Knee, 1998).

It is the case, however, that not all broken rules in relationships constitute a betrayal. Most couples would accept that if one of them forgets the rule that he or she always does the Friday shopping, then the resulting difficulties do not seriously harm the relationship or cause the other to feel betrayed. Such rules may simply be established because they reflect matters of expedience and become a norm within the relationship. Most people would agree that the broken rules that lead to a partner feeling betrayed are those that have the force of moral obligation. Whereas Friday shopping does not usually have such a force, a norm concerning sexual fidelity does have for the majority of people in mutually interdependent relationships. Infidelity is an obvious rule breach but some rules, of enormous significance to particular couples, are not so obvious. Three of these are shown below; in each case the breach of these rules, regarded by the 'victims' as vows defining their lives together, led to relationship collapse.

'He knew that I would never leave my Dad and always helped me look after him, even before we married. We both accepted that we couldn't leave Dad. Then he went and got a promotion 90 miles away. How did he expect me to cope with Dad then? Dad's lived here all his life and wouldn't move with us.'

'When we decided to get married Keith was keen to convert to Catholicism. For nearly 20 years he came with me to Mass every Sunday — our Church was very important to us. Now he's stopped going — he says he doesn't believe any longer and I hate going to church alone. I really feel that he's betrayed me as well as God.'

'We meet up with lots of caravanning friends every year at the club's annual outing. We've been doing that since before we got married. We agreed that we'd carry on doing that for as long as we could. I love going. Now she says she's fed up and wants to go abroad instead. We don't get long holidays and can't do both things. She can't change the rules just like that, can she? What else is she going to get fed up with?'

These norms were idiosyncratic and would not be expected to cause the end of most relationships despite people being able to understand why they were regarded as very important to the partners involved. In each case, the norms of the relationships had sculpted each partner's behaviour and expectations. All was stable as long as each individual's behaviour remained in temporal synchronicity with that of his or her partner (Vallacher *et al.*, 2005); betrayal was experienced when this coordination failed. In short, the basis for trust was broken.

The behaviour and significance of betrayal

The adaptive behaviour within relationships includes routines of relationship maintenance. Within these, some behaviours are accommodative; that is, they are constructive and arise to repair or inhibit the potential harm caused by inconsiderate behaviour from the other partner (e.g., Rusbult *et al.*, 1991). Other behaviours that assist the maintenance of the relationship are the deprecation of possible alternative relationship partners (e.g. Johnson and Rusbult, 1989) and the act of self-sacrifice whereby a partner gives up the opportunity of a desirable event in order to protect the relationship (e.g. Van Lange *et al.*, 1997). These behaviours are largely defensive and arise when there is a threat to the relationship; that is, when some other behaviour would constitute a violation of the relationship norms such that betrayal might be perceived. In general terms, as Fitnes (2001) points out, any kind of behaviour that violates the norms for a relationship may be perceived by a hurt partner as betrayal, depending on how he or she views the severity of the harm done.

Common acts of betrayal that are reported by wronged partners are infidelity (sexual and emotional), lying and other forms of deception, and increasingly the use of online pornography, erotic chat lines and cyber-dating (e.g. Witty, 2005). Of these, research has concentrated largely on sexual and emotional infidelity[2] and it may be presumed that, at least until the ready availability of the Internet, these remained the most serious and frequent acts of betrayal. Although these evoke intense emotions in both sexes, there are some gender differences. For example, Becker *et al.* (2004) used hypothetical scenarios involving both sexual and emotional infidelity. Subjects of both sexes were asked to rate how jealous, angry, hurt and disgusted they would be. The results revealed no gender differences for anger, hurt or disgust, but sexual infidelity produced greater anger and disgust, despite significantly less hurt, than emotional infidelity. The results indicated, however, that the jealous response to an emotional infidelity did discriminate between the sexes in that women reported significantly greater intensity in their emotional reactions than men. People of both sexes who were in a committed relationship also showed high levels of reporting intensity of jealousy than those who were not.

A belief in gender differences concerning infidelity has been fairly strong and based on considerable research. For example, in 1985 Glass and Wright reported that men's extramarital relationships were generally more sexual, whereas women's were more emotional. For both men and women, sexual and emotional extramarital involvement occurred for those partners with the greatest marital dissatisfaction. In general, it has been thought that men are more distressed by a partner's sexual infidelity, whereas women are more upset by a partner's emotional infidelity because the sexes are exposed to different potential adaptive problems when their relationships are betrayed. With no thought for political correctness, it has been hypothesised that women fear the loss of their partner's resources, whereas men are fearful of becoming cuckolds. Harris (2002) investigated jealousy in respect of 196 adult men and women of homosexual and heterosexual orientations. Significantly, the heterosexual adults showed a gender difference in responses to a forced-choice question about hypothetical infidelity. No gender differences, however, were found when participants were asked to recall personal experiences of a partner's actual infidelity. Both sexes, regardless of sexual orientation, reported being less distressed by a partner's sexual infidelity than by a partner's emotional infidelity.

The latter finding suggests that it is the hurt of rejection in favour of another more preferred person that is particularly damaging and/or that sexual infidelity is attributable to the baser motive of lust. This resonates with findings concerning the relationship that rejection, or its prospect, has with self-esteem. It is axiomatic that rejection in favour of someone who is loved more will harm a partner's self-esteem, but there is strong evidence that self-esteem is a factor that may be antecedent to the perception of rejection. For example, Murray et al. (2002) wrote, 'People with low self-esteem have difficulty finding evidence of a partner's acceptance in the most accommodating behavioral realities' (p. 556). Indeed, Murray et al. (2000) found that, in respect of both dating and marital relationships, partners with low self-esteem underestimate how positive their partner values them on specific traits. Further research (Murray et al., 2002) amplified understanding of the impact of rejection or perceived rejection in relation to self-esteem.

Three experiments investigated how needs for acceptance within relationships influence the capacities of partners with low or high self-esteem to shield their relationships from harm. Subjects were encouraged to believe that their partners perceived problems in their relationships. Perceptions of three partnership variables were measured: partner's acceptance, partner enhancement and closeness. Subjects with low self-esteem put too much emphasis on to problems, believing them to be, '. . . a sign that their partner's affections and commitment might be waning' (p. 556). Their response was to disparage their partners and diminish their closeness to them. Conversely, partners with higher self-esteem were less sensitive to rejection. They asserted their relationships against the threats and supported their partners. Murray and her colleagues were led by their findings to opine that, 'Ironically, chronic needs for acceptance may result in low self-esteem people seeing signs of rejection where none exist, needlessly weakening attachments' (Murray *et al.*, 2002, p. 556). This appeared to be the case for a man who, with considerable insight, was able to link his general low self-esteem to a strong trait of perceiving rejection by his long-suffering wife.

'For as long as I can remember I have always been behind everyone else. At school I believed I was the poorest in lessons and the clumsiest at football. When I did well in exams – that was just good luck. When I got promoted it was because someone had made a mistake, not because I was the best candidate. When I won a prize for poetry – that was because the other entrants were even worse than me, not because I was good. I drive my wife mad by getting her to do things like pay bills or book the holidays because otherwise I'll just mess things up. Every man who sees us together must wonder what a lovely lady like her is doing with a loser like me. If I've accused her once of being attracted to another man, I've done it a thousand times. Sometimes I distance myself from her as if that might deaden the pain when she finally leaves me for someone better.'

Another common cause of feeling betrayal in a relationship is lying or other deception practised by one partner against the other. These behaviours are included among a group of relationship 'trials' that are sometimes referred to as aversive interpersonal behaviours (e.g. Kowalski, 1997). Teasing, complaining, arrogance and dependency are also exemplars of these behaviours. Most people in a close relationship prize and expect truthfulness. They do not anticipate being deceived by their partner into accepting false information. When lied to, they make an apparently obvious assumption that the lying is a form of self-preservation, a strategy that puts the liars first and their partners and relationships a poor second.

Kowalski *et al.* (2003) used male and female students to write victim and perpetrator narratives in order to explore the structural elements of specified aversive interpersonal behaviours (betrayal, lying, improprieties, teasing, complaining, arrogance and dependency) and test for individual differences in the perceptions of these behaviours. The results demonstrated that whereas significant victim/perpetrator differences were found, there was variation relating to the specific aversive behaviour being examined. Thus, victims perceived betrayal, lying, teasing, and arrogance more negatively in contrast to perpetrators. There was no difference in respect of complaining and dependency. Moreover, victims considered betrayal, lying and arrogance to be more aversive than the other behaviours. In contrast, perpetrators felt more guilt about betrayal than when complaining or engaging in high dependency.

The result that victims and perpetrators appear to have differing opinions about the severity of lying and deception is congruent with the outcomes of other studies that examined these aversive behaviours in a different way. For example, Barbee *et al.* (1996) reported 70 per cent of participants admitted they had lied to their current partner at least once. It is noteworthy, however, that 79 per cent of these 'perpetrators' reported that their lies were told in order to protect their partners; a dubious altruistic motive that implies they regarded the behaviour as a minor or justifiable betrayal. This opinion is unlikely to be shared by deceived female partners because as Levine *et al.* (1992) report, in contrast with men, women feel that lies are serious relational transgressions. In addition, once lying was uncovered women were more likely than men to find other negative aversive events; as Kowalski *et al.* (2003) opined, 'The loss of honesty in the relationship may lead to a cascade of other losses' (p. 471). This opinion appears to underpin the following comments of wives who discovered that their husbands had lied to them 'for their own good'.

'Raafe lied to me about his gambling on horses races. If my neighbour hadn't seen him coming from the betting shop and told me I might never have known. He had just told me he was having to spend more on petrol for work because his sales area had got bigger. He apologised a lot when I confronted him and he did stop gambling; he even offered to let me doll out his money each day. He said he lied because he knew that his gambling would hurt me when we didn't have much spare money. But I started to think of other things that I hadn't liked; the way he cut my Dad off when he was talking and refusing to come with me when I visited him. He had started going off on Saturday with his mates, knowing that we used to go shopping together that day and have coffee. He seemed to be getting more distant.'

'Frank said he'd got me a birthday present but it got nicked at work. He wasn't even at work on the day that was supposed to have happened. It was another lie. When he did admit he hadn't remembered, he said he'd been too busy to get to the shops and he didn't want to upset me by saying he'd forgotten me. Now I can't stop thinking that everything he says is a lie and how else he might be deceiving me? I'm not worth being remembered – I feel humiliated as well as lied to.'

The last comment introduces the feeling of being humiliated, another common aversive behaviour complained of by victims of their own partners. Transgressional behaviour in close relationships inevitably brings with it the humiliation of being devalued, cast aside, shamed and judged to be worthless. Whatever the specific form of betrayal the transgression has taken, these feelings serve to make the trauma more intense. Hartling *et al.* (2000) wrote of the disempowering context of humiliation and of the profound, enduring influences that this has on future life. They quote Miller and Stiver's (1995) comment that

> we become so fearful of engaging others because of past neglects, humiliations, and violations . . . we begin to keep important parts of our experience out of connection. We do not feel safe enough to more fully represent ourselves in relational encounters.

(p.1)

This wound of humiliation endures like a stiff scar, preventing many betrayed people from fully trusting in the formation of healthy interpersonal relations again. This outcome is encapsulated in the following sad disclosure.

'When Halfa went back to her family with our daughter I thought it was because she wanted to have time for her parents to get to know their grandchild. Later I found out that she really wanted to be near her second cousin, a man she had loved from teenage. Apparently, I was about the only one of our friends and her relatives who didn't know the real reason. When I found out and confronted her over the phone she just giggled and said, "Sorry, I thought you knew. Perhaps you should open your eyes more often". I can't trust even myself now – when I think someone is worth getting to know better I can't bring myself to think that she won't think of me being as big a fool as Halfa did.'

Research has shown that humiliation makes conflict within close relationships much worse and lowers the probability of reconciliation. This is to be expected given that refraining from humiliating one's partner is an important 'rule' within most relationships, particularly within those norms that define the interpersonal behaviour that is expected in public (e.g. Jones and Gallois, 1989).

It is important also to be aware of the link that humiliation has to other potentially more dangerous transgressional behaviours within close relationships. Watts and Zimmerman discuss 'intimate partner violence', which is more often referred to as domestic violence, and ranges from kicks, slaps and punches through assaults with a weapon to murder. They state that these behaviours are '. . . frequently accompanied by emotionally abusive behaviours such as . . . ongoing belittlement or humiliation . . .' (Watts and Zimmerman, 2002, p. 1233). It is my professional experience that such behaviour, used on a regular basis, may be a precursor to domestic violence. This was certainly the experience of Cathy, a young mother who, along with her youngest child was brutally assaulted by her then partner, Adam.

'Adam came over all kind and sweet to me and the kids when we first met. I really welcomed a relationship with him after the kid's father left us to concentrate on his boozing. Only a few months after he moved in Adam turned nasty. He used to make fun of me to his friends and people we met in the shops. He told my Mum that I was useless and was lucky not to have the kids in care. She told him to stop humiliating me; he just laughed and said "sorry". But he didn't stop. Next he stopped me going to see her, started dolling out my benefit money and hiding my mobile. The beating started soon after that.'

Whatever its nature, there is little doubt that the impact of betrayal may last for many years even if the transgression is forgiven. This is true for damage done to other close but non-intimate relationships that provide support networks of individuals. For example, Hansson *et al.* (1990) investigated the responses of older adults to transgression within relationships and reported that, 'In many cases, the event had occurred much earlier in their life, but had retained its symbolic impact across a lifetime' (p. 451).

Clues of infidelity and evidence of betrayal

Marriage is a common practice in virtually every known culture. Although the ceremony is becoming less popular, the establishment of long-term intimate relationships is still a prevalent human behaviour. Likewise, the practice of infidelity within those relationships is also found in most cultures and the rate of such behaviour varies extensively. Shackelford and Buss (1997) reviewed a number of studies and found a variation of rates of extramarital affairs ranging from 26 to 76 per cent for women and from 33 to 75 per cent for men.

Allen *et al.* (2005) reported on more recent studies using large representative samples. They state that approximately 22–25 per cent of men and 11–15 per cent of women report involvement in extramarital affairs. These rates are likely to be underestimates because some subjects refused to disclose this information. It is also true that these samples included younger people who might not then have engaged in extramarital affairs and may or may not do so eventually. Wiederman (1997) used older subjects and reported that up to 34 per cent of men and 19 per cent of women reported involvement in extramarital sex at some time in their lives. Situational factors are known to influence rates. For example, Lawoyin and Larsen (2002) found that infidelity rates rose for Nigerian men during the postpartum abstinence period of their wives; in addition, the rates were significantly higher for rural than for urban-dwelling men.

This flood of infidelity is not limited to particular regions or countries, it knows no bounds of ethnicity or religion and it crosses all the sociopolitical divides that humans can create. Betzig (1989) reported that she studied 160 cultures across the world, finding evidence that infidelity was the most common cause of marriage failure. It is clear, therefore, that infidelity stands a high chance of being discovered, even if the transgressors hide the behaviour rather than admit to it voluntarily. This arises often because the transgressors have given prior cause for suspicion such that their partners are engaged in a search for disloyalty. Should they be uncertain of what to look for there are countless websites that are full of advice. Although mostly sensationalist, it appears that many of the clues described on the Web are congruent with research evidence. The less extreme provide a range of indicators that are based on the observations of reasonable people. The range includes:

• Changes of attitude towards family life, reflecting less enthusiasm for it, and a developing lackadaisical trend tainted with boredom and increasing emotional distancing.

- A decrease in emotional and physical intimacy.
- Sporadic exaggeration of affection for the partner.
- An increased willingness to find fault with the partner.
- A growing unwillingness to really engage with a partner's concerns, interests and opinions.
- A shutting out of conversations or news presentations concerning infidelity, divorce and related topics. Opinions about unfaithful partners change relatively suddenly, veering towards greater permissiveness.
- Changes in work patterns such that less time is spent at home or with the partner generally and more time is spent at work than was usually the case.
- Renewed interest in personal appearance coincides with an atypical spending on clothes or grooming products.

This list is not exhaustive but is representative of indications that are unlikely to escape the attentions of most long-term partners in close relationships. In most cases they represent 'interruptions' of normal patterns of joint daily life. In some respects these interruptions mirror the changes in daily life that first occurred when the existing partnership evolved initially. The major difference is that deception is an added factor. Berscheid was one of the first social psychologists to initiate the scientific study of romantic love. In 1983 she proposed an application of Interruption Theory to relationship formation and maintenance (Berscheid and Peplau, 1983). In essence this sets out a scenario whereby the day-to-day behaviours of individuals become pleasantly 'interrupted' by the inclusion of another person who becomes intensely important. The opportunities afforded by the growing attraction create conviviality in carrying out routinised behaviours together. Once the relationship has coalesced into a mutual sharing of lives these routinised behaviours become the new norm. When one of the partners begins to behave outside of the norms of the relationship by abandoning parts of the routines then interruptions occur that are strange, uncomfortable and unwelcome to the other partner. It is these that may sow the seeds of suspicion. They become potential signs of deception.

In line with this, Shackelford and Buss (1997) investigated laypeople's beliefs about possible clues, hinting that a partner was engaging in sexual or emotional infidelity. They made use of over 1,200 people in their first study and over 2,200 in their second. The first required the subjects to nominate behaviour that elicited suspicions of sexual or emotional infidelity. The second study required that the subjects consider how revealing each suspicious behaviour was of either sexual or emotional infidelity. The data was subject to factor analysis that yielded 14 factors of clues. These included Angry and Argumentative, Exaggerated Affection, Sexual Boredom and Relationship Dissatisfaction. Twelve factors differentiated sexual from emotional infidelity; for example, Relationship Dissatisfaction was thought more indicative of emotional infidelity whereas Sexual Boredom was thought more indicative of sexual infidelity. Interestingly, women gave higher ratings for differentiation than men did. This suggests that they attached greater significance to the behaviours regarded as suspicious. These results appear to be in line with the lay observations listed above and support an opinion that many partners will be accurate in suspecting serious transgressions of infidelity, no matter how cleverly their partners may try to hide their behaviour. It is probable, therefore, that almost all inexplicable overt 'interruptions' of normal daily functioning within a relationship will be noted with concern by a suspicious partner. Once alerted, more rigorous evidence of betrayal is sought and subsequently many transgressing partners are exposed and brought to book.

What happens next?

No discussion of betrayal would be complete without consideration of what happens after the transgressions are discovered. As has been stated above, the discovery or disclosure of betrayal in a close relationship is likely to be devastating for the injured partner unless the relationship was not truly close. The discovery may also be injurious to the transgressor for a variety of reasons, some simple and others that are almost labyrinthine in their complexity. Case (2005) states: 'The disclosure is most healing when it is honest, free of blame or excuse-making, and with sincere remorse. It also needs to include any specifics that clarify significant hurtful acts within the overall betrayal' (p. 50). Sadly, in my experience, many disclosures and/or discoveries of betrayal fail to fulfil these criteria. The extent of the betrayal is often hidden and further deception is used to prevent a full revelation of details.

A common reason for this is the desire of many transgressors to reduce the degree of harm they will suffer if the full extent of their behaviour is revealed to their partners, friends, family, church congregation or employers. They fear loss of esteem and the shame of condemnation.

'I wanted to tell him all the truth about my affair but I didn't want to harm my reputation either. The details would get out and people would be hard on me – I'd lose my standing in the village. We'd have to move. I just don't have that much humility.'

'It's one thing getting found out and quite another telling the full truth. If my wife knew everything she'd tell her parents and that would be the end of my business. They cast a lot of clout in the business community and they'd finish me. I'll not have that, I've worked too hard.'

Shame and the preservation of self-image are therefore powerful inhibiting factors acting against full disclosure. As long ago as 1937 Gordon Allport suggested that in the interests of self-esteem, there might be concealment of weaknesses that may result in self-deception and also shield against unwelcome harm (Allport, 1937). Thus, the avoidance of shame is likely to create a further act of deception. Nagel (2002) believes that although people may be aware of the shameful nature of some aspects of their behaviour, they are also aware that there is a considerable difference between self-acknowledgement of it and admitting it openly. Thus, as Nagel (2002) suggests, 'Concealment includes not only secrecy and deception but also reticence and non-acknowledgment' (p. 4). This heady brew of ingredients for deception is targeted mainly at preserving the perceived esteem of perpetrators, both in their own minds and those they seek to impress. Branden (2001) believes that in the effort to create or maintain the illusion of intact self-esteem, people shackle themselves '. . . to chronic psychological fraud – moved by the desperate sense that to face the universe without self-esteem is to stand naked, disarmed, delivered to destruction' (p. 110).

Some perpetrators, however, become aware that being overtly ashamed of their behaviour can have adaptive value in that their partner sees that they are remorseful and may look more favourably upon them. This does not necessarily mean that these perpetrators admit to the full truth of their betrayal; they may feel that they do not have to if their partners are already showing signs of being at least partially appeased. The appeasement value of overt shame has been recognised from the time of Charles Darwin who described the non-verbal displays associated with it (Darwin, 1872). Subsequently, there have been descriptions of the facial expressions that signify it; these include gaze aversion and lowering of the eyelids as well as the 'hang-dog' expression consistent with diminished tone of the facial muscles (e.g. Tomkins, 1963). Gilbert and McGuire (1998) describe these as submissive displays enabling individuals '. . . de-escalate and/or escape from conflicts' (p. 102). There is some evidence also that these displays may even elicit sympathy in others. For example, Tsoudis and Smith-Lovin (1998) made use of vignettes of perpetrators and victims to demonstrate how emotional displays can influence the judgements of mock juries. This effect was not lost on one unfaithful perpetrator who commented on his discovery of this appeasement value.

'I genuinely felt sorry and rotten to the core. I had betrayed my wife who didn't deserve treatment like that. I felt so bad that I was ill and looked it. She's always hated seeing me like that and started to lose a lot of her rage at me. I'm afraid that I then made my mind up to keep back the extent of my affairs so as not to cause her – and me – further harm. So more lies. Anyway, she forgave me and is still none the wiser all this time later.'

This last vignette provides an example that even when offenders are truly sorry for their transgressions, they may still dissemble when showing remorse. It seems also quite common that transgressors claim that they deceived their partners and others close to them for reasons that were acceptable. They may claim that they were protecting others from hurt, that their betrayals were unintended, or even due to situational factors beyond their control (e.g. Leary *et al.*, 1998). There is a tendency also for some perpetrators to try and ascribe blame to the people that have been hurt: Leary *et al.* (1998) stated, ". . . compared with victims, perpetrators tended to indicate that the event was an accident or that the victim had precipitated the event and, thus, deserved to be hurt" (p. 1235). It appears also that perpetrators, perhaps when it suits them, may fail to acknowledge the negativity their betrayal evoked in victims and the degree of harm they had caused. Leary *et al.* (1998) stated,

> Perpetrators did not seem to realize how much victims distrusted and disliked them, and they underestimated the victims' hostility toward them as well. Most of the victims thought the perpetrator knew they were hurt, and, of course, all of the perpetrators knew they had hurt the victim's feelings (or else they would not have recounted the event). . . . Thus, perpetrators' misperceptions were confined primarily to how the victim felt about them. In part, perpetrators may have inaccurately gauged victims' reactions because victims concealed the strength of their negative feelings.
>
> (p. 1236).

It is also possible that the underestimate of victims' reactions is associated with the manner in which perpetrators account for their betrayal. If the perpetrator is motivated by a desire to repair the harm done to the relationship, then it may be expected that the account would be enveloped within a context of remorse and apology. If, however, the perpetrator is motivated by a desire to terminate the relationship, the account is more likely to be delivered in a heartless and rejecting manner. In short, the account of the transgression is often carefully crafted to facilitate the perpetrator's relationship goals.

There is, of course, a possible third goal. A perpetrator may hope for forgiveness but also want to end the relationship. The issue of forgiveness will be examined in a subsequent chapter but, for the purposes of this discussion, it is important to understand what it means to some perpetrators. Typically, to forgive means to stop feeling angry with someone who has caused harm; the meaning is similar to that of absolution, whereby the guilty party's wrongdoing is set aside and he or she becomes free of blame for that act. An alternative meaning is perhaps more attractive to some perpetrators who want to end the relationship but on an equal basis. This meaning is to cancel a debt. If that goal is achieved, then the perpetrator may feel free to walk away from the relationship with dignity, owing nothing to the ex-partner.

The nature of the account given by the perpetrator has significant bearing on the final outcome of the act of betrayal. The most honest, remorseful and least excuse-making style is liable to be preferred by victims and offers the highest probability of a positive reception. Any movement away from that ideal account meets greater negativity. Gonzales *et al.* (1994) examined this in relation to the effects of offender blameworthiness and offender accounts on victims' responses. They asked subjects to imagine that they were the victims of an offence against them and then to write rejoinders to accounts given by the offenders. The subjects were also asked to rate the interpersonal consequences of the offence. The results indicated that offenders' blameworthiness and the accounts they gave influenced both the content of victims' responses and how they chose to phrase them. The rejoinders became more negative for both content and communicative style in response to the degree of culpability and diminishing credibility of accounts. The ratings provided by the victims of the interpersonal consequences were affected by both offenders' blameworthiness and the nature of their accounts. The probability of mitigation decreased with intentional rather than neglectful offences and lack of credibility of accounts. These findings are augmented by subsequent research that has studied the 'goodness of fit' between the content and style of the perpetrators' accounts and the expectations and perceptions of their victims. Thus, if both parties are focused on the repair of harm done by transgression, then there is a good fit. Conversely, if the foci differ between the parties, then the fit is poor and repair is less probable. For example, Santelli *et al.* (2009), having made use of three robust methodologies, reported that

> In demonstrating that the effect of repentance on forgiveness differs as a function of one's regulatory focus, this study has shown that regulatory fit or mismatch between victims and repentant transgressors can indeed influence forgiveness. These findings also offer one potential explanation for those instances in which forgiveness, despite repentance, is not as forthcoming as would normally be expected.
>
> (p. 391)

In short, it is probable that mismatch does not encourage victims to believe that the accounts given by perpetrators 'feel right'. This is considered again in Chapter 7.

In general, transgressors who wish to repair their situation will offer apology and show (convincing) genuine remorse. This is true over a wide range of contexts from interpersonal relationships (e.g. Younger *et al.*, 2004) to defendants on trial in criminal proceedings (e.g. Bibas, 2006). If the perpetrator does not appear to be genuinely remorseful, judgement is likely to be harsher. Perpetrators must appear to be submissive, unconditionally in the wrong and morally inferior to their victims or those standing in judgement. Their experience of guilt must be overt, such that their victims can see empathy for the hurt they have caused and their desire to lessen it. Indeed, there is an opinion that victims experience satisfaction if they see that they have made those who have offended them suffer from the feeling of guilt (e.g. Baumeister *et al.*, 1995).

Even such abasement cannot, however, guarantee forgiveness or a softer sentence. Whether or not there is absolution and reconciliation depends only to a limited extent on what the perpetrator does; victims will not necessarily forgive and forget, no matter how abject the apology. The urge towards punishment of the perpetrator may be too strong. Finkel and Rusbult (2002) comment that

> the degree to which a victim is inclined toward vengeance rather than forgiveness varies across interactions and may be moderated by the severity of betrayal, the importance of the domain in which betrayal occurs, and the specific emotions and cognitions that accompany a given act. . . . given that betrayals cause harm, violate moral obligations, and create an interpersonal debt, we suggest that betrayal typically engenders impulses such as vengeance and demands for retribution.
>
> (p. 958)

Thus, the victims' initial inclinations are antithetical to forgiveness and relationship repair. In order to move beyond that state there has to be some shift on the victim's part that enables the perpetrator's remorse to influence subsequent decision-making. The research carried out by Finkel and Rusbult (2002) indicates that a pro-relationship transformation of motivation is required and they identify strength of commitment to the relationship as a viable catalyst. They claim that strong commitment to the relationship throughout its history promotes pro-relationship cognitive events, pro-relationship motivations and a trend towards forgiveness. It is probable that this helps pave the way for growing positive attitudes to perpetrators' remorse.

It is hard to view the impact of this force in real-life betrayal situations as victims find it hard to consider their commitment at a time when they perceive that their partner has demonstrated the opposite. The following comments demonstrate the converse, however – a lack of victim commitment associated with a consistent refusal to consider the perpetrator's remorse and apology.

'Sam was not the man I really wanted to be with – he was good to me and I admit that he indulged me and my whims. In fact, our relationship was about me – not us. I don't doubt that he loved me but I took that for granted. I'm not the sort of person to believe that getting my own back is a good idea but when I discovered that he had been having an affair I was enraged. How dare he? Was I no longer special, no longer worth making a huge effort for? He kept on saying that he was really sorry for hurting me, that he had let us down and done wrong. I believed him but just didn't care enough for it to make a difference. I just wanted to stay angry, leave him and pay him out by having affairs of my own. That's exactly what I did.'

Remorse is not always enough to pay off the debt of betrayal but without it there is little prospect of relationship repair. Likewise in contexts other than close relationships, restoration of a transgressing individual's equal place in society depends extensively on how credible their expressions of remorse are. The factors that underpin the development of remorse and the credibility of its expression are the subject of further discussion.

Summary

Betrayal of intimate relationships is potentially devastating and frowned on by all age groups, both genders, and by both religious and non-religious people. Infidelity within intimate relationships has a severe impact on victims irrespective of marital status. Not only are the 'rules' of the relationship broken, but also the rejection associated with infidelity causes harm to victims' self-esteem and confidence.

Although offenders may not judge their transgressions to be as severe as do their victims, most do accept that betrayal has occurred. Many feel profoundly sorry and seek to express their remorse. Displays of their feelings of sorrow may influence the victim's response to the betrayal. Apparently, genuine remorse and revelations of the pain associated with shame and guilt may mollify victims' vengeful feelings. Offenders may, however, be less than candid in exposing the full extent of their betrayals if circumstances are such that they may succeed in mollifying their injured partners without further disclosure. Thus, being truly sorry for the harm done to a romantic partner is no guarantee that all will be revealed or that self-interest is no longer a powerful incentive for deception. Further consideration of this area is given in Chapter 7.

Chapter 3

Interpersonal relationships, religion and vengeance

Introduction

At the end of the last chapter, there was a clear message that remorse and apology were not enough to divert a betrayed woman from acting on her vengeful feelings. She gained great satisfaction from doing so. Perversely, however, the same woman generally did not agree with an 'eye for an eye' code of behaviour. In common with most of us, she did not subscribe to the morality of vengeance. Yet, when the injury was hers, she was able readily to put aside such scruples and take her revenge. This is one aspect of the behaviour of vengeance or revenge that makes for paradox. Arindam Chakrabarti, a moral philosopher, took this as a clear indication that vengeance is 'a bad idea. A very popular, widespread and even much-admired idea, but nonetheless an extraordinarily bad idea' (Chakrabarti, 2005, p. 33). The basis of his judgement is that it is contradictory to believe that to behave vengefully is wrong and then do just that. He points out that the desire of victims to teach a painful lesson by acting as the perpetrators had behaved when causing the harm is to model their own behaviour on that of the perpetrators and so, in actuality, to learn from them. In addition, vengeance may result in several foolish and self-destructive consequences for the vengeance seeker. Their vengeful behaviour can lead to losses of social support and standing within the community, weakened friendships, diminished self-respect and compromised personal safety. Despite this, vengeance remains as fashionable now as it was when Thomas Kyd introduced the highly popular revenge tragedies to the Elizabethan stage in 1592. Some people seem willing to go to any lengths to secure vengeful justice, even if theirs is a pyrrhic victory.

The apparent folly of this pursuit is possibly at the heart of Juvenal's comment, 'In vengeance is found the abject pleasure of an abject mind'. His satirical representations of the deeply flawed hierarchy of pagan Rome might well have led him to view such behaviour as abject and the product of dismal minds. He may even have agreed with Henry Bohn, the seventeenth-century British publisher, who believed that 'Forgiveness is the noblest vengeance'. This chapter considers the predictors of vengeance, including age, gender, religious belief and background, and personality factors such as narcissism. Also included are some comments about influences that may make victims step back to consider other options such as forgiveness. One of these influences may well be that some victims do not want a vengeance-driven refusal to forgive, adding its weight to their own souls.

Mixed messages of religious teaching about vengeance

Although most contemporary societies claim to frown on the pursuit of vengeance, this has not always been the case. Indeed, religion has played a large part in its promulgation with mixed messages about its acceptability. For example, Jewish and Old Testament scriptures portray a fierce and vengeful God who is to be feared; one who may be called on to punish the perpetrators of crimes against the innocent. Thus, 'The apocalyptists firmly believed that God would respond to the innocent suffering of the righteous . . .' (Carlson, 1982, p. 90). The New Testament, however, refutes such constructs and presents a different view of God, one who espouses forgiveness rather than retribution, a principle enshrined in the oft-quoted passage, 'If someone strikes you on the right cheek, turn to him the other also' (Matthew 5:39), said when Jesus repudiated the ancient tenet of 'life for life, eye for eye, tooth for tooth, hand for hand, foot for foot, burn for burn, wound for wound, bruise for bruise' (Exodus, 21:23–25). Although this ancient oath probably referred to the Israelite law of equivalency, which has modern-day representation in the law of torts (compensatory damages), it has been taken literally as an advocation of bloodthirsty vengeance. As such, it more probably had its origins in the Code of Hammurabi (the sixth Babylonian king, *c*. 1790 BC) and translated as 'If a man puts out the eye of an equal, his eye shall be put out'. I have heard several perpetrators of violent acts of revenge quote the phrase 'an eye for an eye' as a vindication of their assaults on others. Some have added further justification by commenting, 'It says so in the Bible'. Despite this commonly held and rudimentary misunderstanding of a small and over-used segment of scripture, Judaism has a clear opinion on the ill-advised behaviour of vengeance: 'Who takes vengeance or bears a grudge acts like one who, having cut one hand while handling a knife, avenges himself by stabbing the other hand' (Jerusalem Talmud, Nedarim 9.4).

There is some evidence that predilection to particular aspects of Old and New Testament scripture has a significant influence on how Christian individuals consider the opposing roles of vengeance and forgiveness. For example, from his study of religious belief in the southern states of the US, Ellison determined that those most likely to accept the validity of vengeance were also more likely to view God as a stern judge and master, giving divine punishments to perpetrators. He stated:

> Southern religion is distinguished by its strong preoccupation with the attainment of individual salvation from punishment at the hands of a wrathful God. Popular southern theology stresses the themes of moral punishment and divine punishment prominent in the Old Testament. These images may legitimize interpersonal violence in defense of the less powerful or in retaliation for deliberate affronts.
>
> (Ellison, 1991, p. 1233)

Ellison concluded that biblical literalists were likely to hold more positive attitudes towards vengeance in contrast with others who are less accepting of the belief that the Bible is the literal word of God. For such vengeance-oriented literalists, biblical themes centred on revenge for interpersonal transgressions are of particular relevance and, according to Ellison (1991), they are quite willing to make use of them as justifications.

Islam appears to send an unequivocal message about choosing forgiveness rather than vengeance. For example, 'if any show patience and forgive, that would truly be an affair of great resolution' (Qur'an, 42:43). There is also strict guidance about the degree of recompense that may be sought for a harm done. This should not be greater than the original harm and should not trespass beyond that which is lawful: 'The recompense for an injury is an injury equal thereto' (Qur'an, 42:40). Even so, it is obvious that such guidance is open to abuse and may be used to condone excessively vengeful acts that are essentially self-seeking. Consequently, the same verse continues, 'but if a person (the victim) forgives and makes reconciliation his reward is due from Allah for Allah loveth not those who do wrong' (Qur'an, 42:40). Indeed, forgiveness is one of the most important moral traits counselled by the Qur'an: 'Hold to forgiveness, command what is right, but turn away from the ignorant' (Qur'an, 7:199). For these reasons, adherents to Islam are portrayed as peaceful, forgiving, tolerant and compassionate and, in the words of the Qur'an, 'restrain anger and pardon (all) men; for Allah loves those who do good' (Qur'an, 3:134).

A legend advancing the Islamic view of vengeance concerns the devout Hadrat Ali whose bravery in battle led to him being popularly referred to as 'Asadullah' (The Lion of Allah). The legend tells how Hadrat Ali overpowered an enemy in a crusade. Just as he was about to behead the opponent, the man spat in his face. Hadrat Ali immediately stood back and told the man to go free. When asked why, Hadrat Ali replied that he would have taken the man's life for the Cause of Allah, but if he did so after the insult of spitting, his action would be tinged with personal vengeance for which he would have to account on the Day of Judgement.

This guidance makes clear that the Qur'an does allow an exact and equivalent degree of retribution for a harm done, similar to the Judaist law of equivalency, but that forgiveness is preferable and pleasing to Allah. Despite this apparent clarity, there are modern instances of 'an eye for an eye' concept of retribution being applied rigidly. For example, in 2004 an Iranian woman was blinded in both eyes by a fellow student who threw acid in her face after she had rejected his advances. She went to Spain for facial reconstruction surgery. An Iranian Court ruled that, under the Sharia principle of *qias* (equivalency), she could blind him by dripping acid into his eyes.[1] Furthermore, in 2010 a family requested of a judge that the spinal column of a young man be damaged in order to punish him for the damage he did to his victim in a fight two years previously. The victim had lost a foot and was paralysed. In apparent acceptance of the family's plea for justice under Islamic law, the judge sought a hospital that would be willing to carry out the punishment.

Given the apparently mixed messages that exist between sacred scriptures and clear examples of formalised vengeful behaviour, it is not surprising that individuals will bypass courts and other legal agencies of retribution and take the law into their own hands. Clearly, however, there is a distinction to be drawn between vengeance and justice. Sikhism, for example, has a place in its philosophy for justice and avenging wrongs, but eschews personal vengeance. The wearing of the Sikh sword is symbolic of independence, self-respect and temporal and spiritual power. It is to be used to protect the vulnerable and the oppressed. It must not be used for conquest or vengeance, but its use should not be refused when oppression, injustice and tyranny threaten the common good.

Vengeance or justice?

This chapter opened with a comment from Arindam Chakrabarti that vengeance was 'a very bad idea'. It would seem that he is in agreement with the major world religions on this, despite mixed messages from interpretations of the scriptures that condone equivalent acts of vengeance under particular circumstances and through formal channels, such as an authorised state legal system. Wreaking personal vengeance is not condoned, but it seems that some individuals or groups feel there is sufficient latitude of interpretation to allow them to act vengefully.

The criminal justice system is as lacking in clarity, particularly where the legal process has reached that point where juries must consider the evidence presented to them. Then, no matter how professional the conduct of judges, and defence and prosecution counsels, the matter rests with laypeople who bring with them their own personal views of what justice is. Most are likely to derive some satisfaction from seeing the guilty punished, of 'getting their just deserts' from retributive justice.

Two alternatives are part of a largely undecided debate on the role of punishment. The first, and apparently most commonly held, is that punishment of the offender is retribution and is an end in itself. A wrong has been done; the scales of justice have been tipped towards evil and are to be rebalanced by punishment of the offender. This is a sufficient justification.

Few, it appears, are likely to consider the second utilitarian alternative where the aim is not punishment per se but a form of teaching that will minimise the future likelihood of offending by the perpetrator.

There has been considerable research on the motivations that underpin the affective and cognitive components of the desire to see the guilty punished. For example, Carlsmith and colleagues carried out a series of studies using approximately one thousand people and concluded that, 'When faced with a prototypical wrongdoing action, a harm intentionally inflicted on another by a perpetrator, people assign punishment to give the perpetrator his or her just deserts (deservingness) rather than to achieve any future utility. Although participants expressed support for deterrence as a goal of punishment at an abstract level, they failed to assign punishment in a way that was consistent with this stated goal . . . Their punishment assignments were instead consistent with a theory of punishment based on the moral deservingness of the perpetrator' (Carlsmith *et al.*, 2002, p. 295). Does this harsh criterion come into being simply because individuals who come together as jurors are somehow transformed into vengeful disciplinarians who have a need to smite the ungodly? The evidence of research is that individuals act in accordance with their beliefs in what is just and, unless prompted otherwise, are liable to formulate their decision-making in accordance with retributive justice. In general terms, 'citizens' perception of the fairness of the criminal justice system is a major determinant of their adherence to its codes. When laypersons' intuitions fail to align with punishments assigned by judges, their perceptions of the justice system become less positive, and hence their likelihood of complying with the code decreases' (Darley *et al.*, 2000, p. 678). In addition, individuals who perceive themselves to be disadvantaged or part of a poorly regarded underclass are more likely to experience negative emotions such as anger and frustration that lower their threshold for potentially retributive responding (e.g. Stouten *et al.*, 2009).

This strongly punitive attitude is not, however, cast in tablets of stone. Although considerable evidence indicates strongly that individuals believe in and pursue vengeance-oriented justice, there is also evidence that its opposite may be prompted. Humans are not only vengeance seekers, but may also show altruism and find value in forgiveness. Some individuals may regard this as being 'soft on crime' or wrongdoing in general. This is not necessarily the case, however. Forgiveness is not about ignoring wrongdoing and neither is it an abrogation of the duty to reprove perpetrators nor a weakening of punishment. As Aquino and colleagues comment, 'Condoning an act is equivalent to denying the wrongness of an act . . . We can . . . forgive the sinner but not condone the sin' (Aquino *et al.*, p. 213). This may sound like a semantic hairsplitting that would lead only to the dilution of justice in order to offer merciful responses to perpetrators. Wenzel and Okimoto (2010) argue, however, that a sense of forgiveness may be fostered if a broader conceptualisation of justice is engendered that includes restorative[2] as well as retributive functions. In support of this, Karremans and Van Lange (2005) found that the concept of justice (primed by seeing the image of Justitia[3]) acted to enhance rather than inhibit forgiving traits when considering hypothetical offending. In similar vein, Wenzel and Okimoto (2010) found that the feeling of justice further mediated the effects of the forgiveness expression in terms of reducing hostile emotions, revenge motivation and retributive attitudes, as well as increasing the willingness to reconcile with the offender. Their findings indicate that forgiveness can facilitate a sense of justice for victims and so diminish thoughts of vengefulness in favour of benevolence towards the offender. They comment that these findings are

> quite different from the common view among forgiveness researchers that justice is no longer considered an issue once people have made the decision to forgive . . . Rather than abandoning justice, forgiveness can contribute to the subjective restoration of justice.
>
> (Wenzel and Okimoto, 2010, p. 414).

It is clear, however, that individuals with strongly vengeance-oriented attitudes to perpetrators are unlikely to accept an augmentation of their belief in retributive justice by the addition of a commitment to restorative processes. Forgiveness and vengeance are impossible bedfellows when the swirling emotions stimulated by serious crimes blinker perspectives of anything other than punishment. A characteristic of most well-established criminal justice systems is that offenders are punished at a level of severity proportional to meet the severity of their crimes. Thus, punishment is a proportional and core requirement of justice being done; perpetrators should get what they deserve on a rational basis devoid of strong emotion. Sadly, this ambition may not always be realised as Freedman (1997) describes in respect of the death penalty. It is probable that jurors are motivated to exact vengeance on murderers on the grounds that they deserve to experience the torments and dread of their victims. The US Federal Judge Richard Nygaard commented about the death penalty,

> Revenge. The ultimate payback. As a retributory tool, death works wonderfully. The desire for revenge is the dark secret in all of us. It has, I suppose, been so since the beginning of time. It is human nature to resent a hurt, and each of us has a desire to hurt back.
>
> (1994, p. 7)

Age and gender as predictors of vengeance

Leaving aside religious and cultural determinants, there are other significant factors, acting separately and in combination, that influence an individual's propensity to vengeful behaviour. For example, research has shown consistently that men, across age, are likely to be more vengeful than women (e.g. Brown, 2004). Cota-McKinley *et al.* (2001) found that while men are more likely than women to experience vengeful attitudes, this gender effect did not extend to the readiness to seek revenge in particular situations. Stuckless and Goranson (1992) found that men hold more positive attitudes towards vengeance and also that there were significant positive correlations between trait anger[4] and vengeance. These findings are congruent with research evidence that males obtain higher scores than females on measures of general aggression. For example, Maccoby and Jacklin (1980) carried out a meta-analysis on studies concerning male aggression from humans as young as six years and of primates. Their findings led them to conclude that there was a biological predisposition toward aggressive behaviour for males, particularly in the presence of other males. Although this biological theory was challenged (e.g. Tieger, 1980), the finding that males are more generally aggressive than females remains. In addition, Kendrick and Sheets (1993) found that males are more likely also to recall and report more and lengthier violent and murderous phantasies than females where co-workers and strangers are cast in the role of victims. The fantasies of females were more likely to represent family members than did those of males, but this was merely a function of the fact that males had more fantasies across categories including family members, not because males had fewer phantasies concerning family members than females.

Age is also a significant variable. A number of studies across a wide range of situational contexts have demonstrated that the propensity for vengeance diminishes as individuals get older. Thus Sommers *et al.* (2002), when researching their Organisational Revenge Scale, found that scores were moderately correlated with age. Likewise Baron *et al.* (1999) examined aggression in the workplace and determined that age, gender and the physical location of individual's workplaces were all variables associated with the occurrence of aggression. Randall (1997, 2002) has also reported on combinations of personal–social and environmental influences on aggression taking the form of workplace bullying. Cota-McKinley and her colleagues' research using the Vengeance Scale (Stuckless and Goranson, 1992) made use of a sample of rather young students. They stated that age was a significant predictor of scores on the scale in that 'the wisdom of age' was associated with a decrease in vengefulness (Cota-McKinley *et al.*, 2001, p. 348). Fascinating data on age and vengefulness arises from the study of wrath aroused by road and traffic incidents. For example, Hennessy and Wiesenthal (2002, 2004) researched driver aggression and driver violence, and found that violence was associated with a combination of mild aggression and vengeance. Thus, aggressive drivers tended to be more violent but only for those having heightened levels of dispositional vengefulness. Drivers with more than five years' driving experience showed a decrease in mild aggression as they got older, but those with moderate levels of dispositional vengefulness hardly altered with age in respect of their level of aggressiveness. Paradoxically, however, mild driver aggression increased as highly vengeful drivers got older. The authors suggested that as motor vehicles often provide a protective environment (e.g. anonymity, ease of escape) in respect of conflicted circumstances, it is safe for highly vengeful drivers to express aggressive behaviour. Presumably, the increasing years of experience of such circumstances provide reinforcement for such traits among drivers who are predisposed to vengefulness. In general terms, however, feelings of vengefulness in respect of conflicted interpersonal relationships are found to diminish with age.

Personality factors as predictors of vengeance

Thus far, religion, age and gender variables have been considered as predictors of dispositional and active vengefulness. Personality factors also provide effective insights into these individuals who are likely to harbour vengeful thoughts and even engage in vengeful behaviour. More particularly, both the Big Five factor model (these factors are openness, conscientiousness, extraversion, agreeableness and neuroticism, often summarised as OCEAN, Costa and McCrae, 1992) and the Three Factor model (these factors are psychoticism, extraversion and neuroticism, or PEN, Eysenck, 1985) have yielded predicted and significant results. With regard to the Big Five taxonomy of personality (e.g. John, 1990), it was predicted that dispositional vengefulness would be associated with the factor of neuroticism. Individuals who score highly on this factor are predisposed to being easily angered into taking offence, although neuroticism does not account for all variance concerning the experience of angry feelings (e.g. Martin and Watson, 1997).

In addition, it has been predicted that the factor of agreeableness is associated with lowered dispositional vengefulness. It is associated with traits that would be in conflict with vengeful feelings, such as kindness, trust and altruism. Individuals who score well on this factor tend to have empathetic and altruistic traits for family and non-family when associated with high emotional stability (e.g. Ashton et al., 1998) and so are unlikely to show high levels of dispositional vengefulness.

It is acknowledged, however, that these two factors from the Big Five do not provide the full picture of the underpinnings of dispositional vengefulness. Thus, although McCullough et al. (2001b) found that vengefulness was negatively correlated with agreeableness and positively with neuroticism, measures from the Big Five model accounted for only 30 per cent of the vengefulness variance. They state:

> Vengefulness also is positively related to negative affectivity/Neuroticism and negatively related to Agreeableness and satisfaction with life. Thus, vengeful people tend to experience greater levels of negative affect, lower levels of life satisfaction, and perhaps, difficulty maintaining harmonious interpersonal relationships. Although personality taxonomies such as the

Big Five taxonomy help to characterize the nature and structure of vengefulness, vengefulness does not appear to be reducible to a linear combination of the Big Five.

(McCullough *et al.*, 2001b, p. 609)

Psychoticism and vengeance

The Three Factor model of personality offers a further predictive variable. This model is comprised of the psychoticism, extraversion and neuroticism (PEN) main factors. Of these, psychoticism is particularly interesting because it is not only associated with dispositional vengeance but also with spirituality and religiosity, unlike any of the Big Five factors (MacDonald, 2000).

Eysenck (1967a) described psychoticism as a primary dimension with tough-mindedness at one extremity and tender-mindedness at the other. Individuals who score highly on this factor tend to be aggressive, deficient in empathy, antisocial and generally dislike conformity to social expectations. Several studies have demonstrated that psychoticism is consistently and inversely related to religiosity. For example, Dunne *et al.* (1997), who used the Eysenck Personality Questionnaire (EPQ), found that high scores were inversely related to the incidence of personal prayer and church attendance. They also found that

> EPQ measures of P and N were associated with frequency of church attendance for both men and women. In addition, women who rarely or never attended church were more introverted than those who did so at least occasionally, although it is interesting that women who attended church very frequently also scored relatively low on the E scale. With this large and diverse adult sample, we were able to examine whether associations between personality and religious practice are equivalent across a wide age span. Given that there were no statistically significant interactions with age, we can conclude that the associations between personality and frequency of church attendance are similar in young and older adults.
>
> (Dunne *et al.*, 1997, p. 530)

The meta-analysis carried out by Saroglou (2002) also determined that psychoticism scores predict low religiosity; conversely, agreeableness and conscientiousness from the Big Five are positively and more strongly associated.

It is noteworthy that the majority of studies that have examined the relationship between psychoticism and religiosity have predicted a negative linear relationship. This is to be expected given that the psychoticism factor tends to emphasise at its upper end traits of impulsivity, poor socialisation and empathy deficits. Religiosity, however, tends to be found in people who are well socialised, empathetic and exercise personal restraint. It is not surprising, therefore, that the expected negative correlation is found consistently. In addition, as has been described, some strongly religious individuals tend to be hostile, show empathy deficits and have little tolerance for others whose beliefs do not coincide with theirs. These traits share similarities with those of individuals who score highly on the psychoticism factor. It is predicted, therefore, that there should be a discernible positive association between psychoticism and specific aspects of religiosity, independent of the generally negative one.

An interesting study by Jorm and Christensen (2004) provides support for this by demonstrating not only an inverse trend between psychoticism and religiosity but also a quadratic trend. They made use of the Index of Religiousness (Zuckerman et al., 1984). This scale has three items: 'How often did you attend regular religious services during the past year?' (six-point scale ranging from 'never' to 'more than once a week'); 'Aside from how often you attended religious services, do you consider yourself to be deeply religious, fairly religious, only slightly religious, not at all religious, or against religion?'; and 'How much is religion a source of strength and comfort to you?' (four-point scale ranging from 'none' to 'a great deal') (Jorm and Christensen, 2004, p. 1435). The subjects also completed the Eysenck Personality Questionnaire (EPQ-R, Eysenck and Eysenck, 1991) that provided the psychoticism scores.

In essence, the results showed that the most and least religious quartiles of their sample of 7,000 adults tended to be higher in psychoticism. This is evidence of a curvilinear relationship between the two variables. One interpretation of this finding is provided by Jorm and Christensen who believe it is possible that 'extremist religiosity attracts some people who are rejecting of conventional values. Certainly, the association of religious extremism with authoritarian power, violence and persecution of differing beliefs would support this view' (Jorm and Christensen, 2004, p. 1440). One is reminded by this comment of the traits of biblical literalists who have been discussed previously.[5]

Other studies have linked psychoticism to vengefulness. For example, Bellah et al. (2003) made use of both the three- and Big-Five-factor models in their study of vengefulness. Psychoticism, from the Three Factor model was revealed as the best predictor of vengefulness. Agreeableness, from the Big Five, was revealed as the best inverse predictor. Johnson and Butzen (2008) extended the study of psychoticism and vengefulness further by including the variable of Christian religious commitment. Theirs was a small sample of 67 Christian graduate students who completed the Mauger Forgiveness Scale. This is a self-administered test with a Likert Scale ranging from 'strongly agree' to 'strongly disagree'. The items include questions about forgiveness of self and forgiveness of others. Composite scores representing both of these constructs are derived. Low forgivingness for each trait is represented by high scores (Mauger et al., 1992). The subjects also completed the Eysenck Personality Questionnaire (EPQ-R, Eysenck and Eysenck, 1991). As described previously, this provides scores for psychoticism, extraversion and neuroticism.

In addition, the subjects completed the Religious Commitment Inventory (RCI–10). This is a modification of a previous version described by McCullough *et al.* (1997). That version had seventeen items arranged on a Likert scale dealing with various behaviours associated with religious commitment (e.g. making charitable contributions, reading publications about faith, praying, living according to religious precepts, defending their faith against criticism). The version used in the Johnson and Butzen (2008) study was found to be statistically more robust but utilised only ten items (Worthington *et al.*, 2003).

Johnson and Butzen found that

> Psychoticism, Extraversion and Neuroticism were all significantly related to vengefulness, with Psychoticism and Extraversion emerging as most predictive. Higher levels of Psychoticism and Neuroticism are associated with greater levels of vengeance, while higher levels of Extraversion are associated with lower levels of vengeance.
>
> (2008, p. 334)

Clearly, these findings generally support those obtained in previous studies and it is noteworthy that the authors suggest that higher levels of neuroticism may be associated with vengefulness because of a raised probability that those individuals experience the angry ruminations that characterise thoughts of vengeance (e.g. McCullough *et al.*, 2001b).

The findings concerning psychoticism revealed that it was the only statistically significant variable to predict religious commitment, albeit inversely. Thus, individuals whose scores are high on the Psychoticism scale are less likely to show higher levels of religious commitment as measured by the RCI–10. Extraversion was associated with religious commitment but was not significantly predictive. Johnson and Buzen speculate that their small sample size might have been influential. The sample size might also have been insufficient to replicate the curvilinear association of psychoticism and religiosity reported by Jorm and Christensen (2004). Another possibility is that the ten items of the RCI–10 are dissimilar in terms of their specificity to that of the three-item scale employed by Jorm and Christensen (see above). This may have resulted in different aspects of religiosity being assessed, with consequent impact on the direction of the resulting trends.

Narcissism as a predictor of vengefulness

It seems axiomatic that those individuals who show traits of dispositional forgiveness are unlikely also to show significant traits of dispositional vengeance.

Brown (2004) hypothesised that although people who are highly likely to forgive perpetrators are unlikely to be vengeful about them, the reverse proposition need not be true. Thus, people who are unlikely to be forgiving do not also have to be vengeful. He asked what distinguishes people who are low in forgiveness and also low in vengefulness from those who are low in forgiveness but high in vengefulness. He hypothesised that narcissism might be a differentiator.

His review of research on narcissism was supportive of this hypothesis. Leaving aside those individuals whose narcissistic traits are so elevated that their presentation justifies a diagnosis of Narcissistic Personality Disorder (see APA, DSM-IV-TR, 2000, p. 714), there are those non-psychopathological individuals who are excessively self-centred, believe that they are more deserving than others, bathe in the opinion that they are socially powerful and influential, are less open to error and feel generally superior to 'ordinary' people. Egocentricity dominates their social interactions and their personal–social relations are predicated by an insistence that they are beyond criticism. They are intolerant of negative feedback and resistant to change. Under laboratory conditions where narcissists were subjected to experimentally engendered social rejection, their responses were more aggressive than those of non-narcissists. They were, however, no angrier or more aggressive than non-narcissists after a period of social acceptance. It was considered that 'narcissism was not correlated with aggression or anger after an experience of social acceptance. Thus, the highest levels of aggression seem to require both high narcissism and an experience of social rejection' (Twenge and Campbell, 2003, p. 269). In addition, it has long been understood that narcissism and empathy are negatively related (e.g. Watson et al., 1984). The combination of significantly elevated egocentricity, aggressive response to social rejection (as in failed interpersonal relations) and empathy deficits are highly predictive of vengeful traits.

Brown (2004) tested the hypothesis that narcissism would differentiate between people with low forgiveness but either high or low vengefulness. He made use of 248 undergraduate subjects who took a personality inventory tapping narcissism, a scale recording dispositional forgiveness and the Vengeance Scale of Stuckless and Goranson (1992). In addition, a self-esteem inventory was administered also to assess global, normal non-narcissistic self-worth.[6] The results demonstrated that subjects who were low in dispositional forgiveness were more vengeful than those with high forgiveness. In addition, this trend was particularly evident among those who were also high in narcissism. The most dispositionally vengeful subjects were those high in narcissism and low in dispositional forgiveness. A later study by DeYoung (2009) with a sample size of 471 students revealed that subjects whose psychometric profile accorded with the criteria of narcissistic personality disorder were likely to be higher in dispositional vengefulness when contrasted with subjects showing an avoidant personality or those from a normal control group. It seems clear, therefore, that the presence of significantly elevated narcissism is a predictor of vengefulness.

Earlier in this chapter, the role of religion in respect of vengeance has been described in that some particularly zealous scripture literalists are known to be vengeful. It is noteworthy, therefore, that narcissism is associated with religious beliefs. Zondag and van Uden (2010) studied the relationship between two trait dimensions of narcissism (charted by Aktar, 1989), namely, overt and covert narcissism, with styles of religious coping.

Covert narcissism is a mask for an otherwise low level of self-esteem whereby the individual becomes hypersensitive to criticism. He or she is attracted to other narcissists and together they may espouse aggression and violence as a means of dealing with perceived criticisms or other threats. In addition, the covert traits of narcissism include power seeking coupled with a disregard for authority, delinquent tendencies and pathological lying. There is an 'on–off' relationship with moral and ethical behaviour that is coupled with a façade of false humility. The latter is often linked, in my professional experience, with assertions of strong religious belief and the manifestations of vengefulness. Overt narcissism is the 'public face' of the narcissistic individual and is associated with grandiosity, attention seeking, striving for adulation, good social 'charm' skills and a caricature of modesty. Relationships tend to be superficial and promiscuity often mars romantic and marital relations. Empathy is claimed but proves shallow and seldom is manifest in anything other than words rather than deeds.

The religious coping styles utilised by Zondag and van Uden (2010) are referred to as self-directive, collaborative, deferring and receptive, and are taken from the initial work of Kenneth Pargament. He believed that individuals might use their religious beliefs as coping styles to assist them during times of stress. Self-directed coping is used when individuals seek control of their circumstances independently rather than seek help from God. The deferring style is that used when the individual places the stressful situation entirely in God's hands for resolution, whereas the collaborative style involves a 'joint' approach in collaboration with God (see Pargament *et al.*, 1988). Subsequently, these coping styles were augmented by the addition of the receptive style (van Uden *et al.*, 2004) who hypothesised that the existing styles did not represent the belief of some individuals in a more impersonal God than was reflected in the original work. In addition, it was argued that not all people under stress necessarily focused on problem situations because, perhaps, they believe that not all problems can be solved, with or without God. A receptive coping style might allow them to accept what they cannot control. (Banziger *et al.*, 2008). These coping style are recorded by coping style scales.

Zondag and van Uden (2010) obtained results from self-completion questionnaires from 116 students. The results revealed a positive correlation between covert narcissism and the collaborative, deferring and receptive coping styles. Thus, the narcissistic dimension reflecting an anti-social, hostile and weak grip on empathetic and moral behaviour was unlikely to seek self-directing solutions for altering problematic stressful circumstances. Instead, the individual was more likely to await God's resolutions and/or accept that the problem was beyond his or her control. Thus, vengeful feelings about anyone associated with the onset of the stressful circumstances would become more likely. The overt narcissistic dimension was only correlated positively with the receptive coping style. Zondag and van Utan (2010) stated:

> No correlation was found with the other three styles. The only correlation is therefore with the style in which both the person and God remain passive. There is no correlation with styles in which either God or the person is active (or both). With overt narcissism, just as with covert narcissism, there is no similarity between the relational pattern of the dimension of narcissism and the coping style . . . This may mean that there is a basic trust that everything will work out well by itself.
>
> (p. 81)

It is probable, therefore, that narcissists are generally prone to vengefulness and may seek support in religious belief for their grandiosity and self-adulation. The Web pages of Joanna Ashmun (2008)[7] contain an interesting comment that is congruent with my experience of vengeful narcissistic individuals:

> Narcissists I've known also have odd religious ideas, in particular believing that they are God's special favorites somehow; God loves them, so they are exempted from ordinary rules and obligations: God loves them and wants them to be the way they are, so they can do anything they feel like – though, note, the narcissist's God has much harsher rules for everyone else, including you.

Narcissism appears to contaminate much religious belief. Devoted Christians, and doubtless sincere followers of other religions, may find much to lament in the styles of contemporary individual and communal worship. This is not just a matter of some religious leaders excusing terrorist atrocities on the grounds that God is served well by their perpetration; neither is it a distressing contemplation of the grandiose richness of clerical trappings while children from underdeveloped countries starve. Instead, it may be an opinion that liturgical worship has become a cipher for self-adulation. This depressing feeling is expressed by Monte Wilson[8] (2003) in the articles of the John March Ministries:

> Modern American Christianity is filled with the spirit of narcissism. We are in love with ourselves and evaluate churches, ministers and truth-claims based upon how they make us feel about ourselves. If the church

makes me feel wanted, it is a good church. If the minister makes me feel good about myself, he is a terrific guy. If the proffered truth supports my self-esteem, it is, thereby, verified.

Narcissism and psychoticism

Psychoticism, as measured by the Eysenckian scale, appears to have some communality of traits with narcissism. As has been described above, individuals who score highly on the Psychoticism scale lack empathy, are uncaring about others and show hostility. It seems likely that these traits are, at least in part, congruent with the narcissist's elevated sense of self-importance, superiority in relation to others, and preoccupation with entitlement. Raskin and Hall (1981) found that narcissistic scores on the Narcissistic Personality Inventory showed a significant positive correlation with both Psychoticism and Extraversion from the Eysenck Personality Inventory. In addition, a repetition of the test eight weeks later produced similar results.

It is reasonable to conclude, therefore, that a constellation of personality factors is influential in the determination of who is likely to display dispositional vengefulness. Narcissism, psychoticism and self-serving religious belief are particularly likely to mediate the traits of this disposition.

Vengeance, personality and Reinforcement Sensitivity Theory

Eysenck's three-factor model of personality stands out from some other models, including the Big Five. The difference arises from his hypothesis about the biological substrates of psychoticism, extraversion and neuroticism. Eysenck linked psychoticism to testosterone levels and the autonomic fight–flight system (e.g. Eysenck, 1967b). There has been considerable interest in this proposition and several modifications and alternatives have arisen. Popular among these is the linkage of psychoticism to sensitivity to aversive stimuli (fight–flight) associated with forebrain structures and dopamine, a neurotransmitter.

Reinforcement Sensitivity Theory (RST) is a biobehavioural model of personality that was founded on Eysenck's original hypothesis. It has undergone many modifications over the years and the reader is referred to Corr (2008) for a detailed exposition of the theory. In essence, however, RST is concerned with three interactive systems: the Behavioural Activation System, (BAS), the Behavioural Inhibition System (BIS) and the Fear–Flight–Freeze System (FFFS). These systems mediate the impact of goal conflict and reward on behaviour. The behavioural manifestations of these systems are distinguishable in respect of motivation and learning. The theory offers, therefore, a testable description of causality in respect of underlying structures of personality and the etiology of trait behaviours. This distinguishes it from other models, such as the Big Five, that are taxonomic only. MacLaren and colleagues provide a summary of neuropsychological systems converging with personality traits. They state: 'Human personality and psychopathology emerge out of individual variations in the sensitivity of the systems responsible for approach or avoidance behavior in situations that contain signals of reward and punishment' (McLaren *et al.*, 2010, pp. 142–3). According to the original RST (Gray, 1970), impulsivity results from an imbalance of the relative strengths of the systems that underlie responses to signals of reward versus punishment; anxiety results from elevated sensitivity to both punishment and reward signals. Thus, people who have high sensitivity to reward but who are relatively insensitive to punishment might tend towards impulsive behaviour. Harm-avoidant people who have high sensitivity to punishment but relative insensitivity to reward would often feel anxious and appear constrained in their behaviour. Those with high sensitivity to both punishment and reward might be best described as neurotic, vacillating between impulsive and fearful behaviour. Finally, people with very low sensitivity to both reward and punishment might not be particularly impulsive nor anxious, but poorly suited to changing environmental contingencies that require behavioral adaptation' (MacLaren *et al.*, 2010, p. 143).

At the heart of RST is the hypothesis that individual differences in sensitivity to rewards could be due, at least in part, to the three distinct neuropsychological systems that underpin consistent individual variation in the expression of emotional states. In essence, the Behavioural Activation System (BAS) is associated with conditioned signals of reward and is responsible for impulsive and extravert behaviour. The Behavioural Inhibition System (BIS) has been associated with conditioned signals of punishment and so is thought to be responsible for anxiety and neuroticism. Recently, the Fear–Flight System has been revised to take account of its control of flight, freezing and defensive fight. It is referred to as the FFFS.

The original FFS was considered to be responsible for fearlessness and the psychoticism factor from Eysenck's model. The revision of its role resulted in the FFFS being given a mediating role in respect of conditioned signals of punishment. Thus, the BIS has become more tightly associated with approach-avoidance behaviours in conflict situations. It is conceptualised as a system to inhibit behaviour by facilitating risk assessment, increasing autonomic arousal, heightening vigilance and anxiety. In its revised format, the RST claims, therefore, that goal conflicts are mediated by the BIS through the inhibition of potentially rash behaviours and engaging recall of their affectively negative consequences (MacLaren *et al.*, 2010). McNaughton and Corr (2004) suggest specific sites for the location of the three systems. They believe there is involvement of the amygdala, septo-hippocampal structures and the mesolimbic dopamine system.

In short, the RST provides a causal rather than taxonomic description of individual variation of stable traits of personality (i.e. psychoticism, extraversion and neuroticism) as well as crucial emotional responses (e.g. pleasure anticipation, fearfulness and anxiety). Clearly, therefore, RST measures should be predictive of vengefulness if they are descriptive of such stable personality traits and emotional states. Johnson *et al*. (2010) hypothesised that RST would predict vengefulness, and examined this in relation to BAS and BIS. They did not examine the FFF system because of the lack of an adequate measure. Their results indicated that both BIS and BAS predicted vengefulness. Specifically, individuals who are anxious but also express appetitively high levels of approach behaviour are likely to evince vengeful behaviour following on interpersonal affront. It would appear that their BAS activity achieves dominance over any inhibiting effect of anxiety. Raised BIS sensitivity predicted reduced forgiveness for self and others. The authors postulate that the capacity for forgiveness may be negated by BIS-mediated angry rumination over the transgressions. This would be congruent with the findings of McCullough *et al*. (2001b) that vengeful individuals are less forgiving and more prone to rumination.

As yet, I am unaware of any demonstration of FFFS predictability in respect of vengefulness, but it may be hypothesised that there will be a positive relationship. This arises from the fact that the FFFS is strongly linked to Eysenckian psychoticism, which is, as previously described, a robust predictor of vengefulness. At present, there appears to be a lack of a suitable test instrument to test this hypothesis and, indeed, Smillie *et al*. have commented that substantial work is needed on the definition of RST constructs and behaviours before there can be robust confidence in psychometric measures of them.

Vengeful rumination, grudge bearing and health

Vengeful rumination (e.g. Berry *et al*., 2005) and grudge bearing (e.g. Baumeister *et al*., 1998) are angry traits associated negatively with forgiveness in respect of damaged interpersonal relationships. In my professional experience, these two traits are either or both the antecedents and consequences of vengeful behaviour, which in any event is antithetical to forgiveness. Grudge bearing is certainly denounced within the scriptures of the major religions. For example, the Qu'ran provides: 'Those who spend in prosperity and in adversity, who repress anger and who pardon men; verily, Allah loves the good-doers' (Qu'ran, 3:134). The Bible contains a similar sentiment: 'Let all bitterness and wrath and anger and clamor and slander be put away from you, along with all malice. Be kind to one another, tenderhearted, forgiving one another, as God in Christ forgave you' (Romans 12:17–21). In Judaism, we are entreated: 'Do not take revenge and do not bear a grudge against a member of your people' (Parshas Kedoshim, 19:18). Contemporary psychological theory likewise provides plenty of reasons why grudge bearing should be minimised (e.g. Treynor *et al*., 2003).

Whereas vengeful rumination is a process of thinking deeply and angrily about taking some form of revenge against a perpetrator for a harm done, grudge bearing involves persistently being in the victim role and holding on to the negative emotions associated with the hurtful offence (e.g. Witvliet *et al.*, 2001). It can be argued that there are possible benefits arising from certain types of both traits. For example, in my professional experience constructive rumination can assist in the process of gradually releasing negative thoughts about perpetrators and moving towards forgiveness. In some cases, the longer the rumination has gone on, the more negative content has diminished and forgiveness becomes more likely.

Grudge bearing is also believed to have some benefits. For example, Baumeister *et al.* (1998) suggest that for some victims, grudge bearing is preferred when forgiveness is viewed negatively because then the victims would no longer have any claim against the perpetrators. The claim need not be a means of overtly sustaining some ascendency in terms of moral high ground. Obviously, forgiveness given only as a precedent to frequent reminders of why the perpetrator was forgiven is hollow indeed and lacks any claim to being genuine. The following vignette provides an example of this.

Jim managed to hide his excessive gambling from his wife, Ruth, for several years but his debts spiralled out of control and eventually she challenged him. Her initial anger appeared to cool when, in couple therapy, it was resolved that his gambling behaviour was probably associated with grief over the loss of their stillborn child. Ruth said that she had forgiven him and would support his efforts to return to the non-gambling individual he once was. Jim became aware, however, that any interaction with Ruth involving money was larded with references to 'his problem' and the need to be 'cautious' with his spending. This caution extended to locking away her purse even though Jim had never taken any money out of it. When attending what was supposed to be their final therapy session, Jim asked Ruth if she had really forgiven him or was subtly trying to punish him. She was able to acknowledge that she felt unable to forgive him although she wanted to. Ruth said their lost child was hers also and if she could bear the pain without harming their relationship then he should have been able to also.

Baumeister *et al.* (1998) suggest also that harbouring a grudge may be seen as some sort of defence against the reoccurrence of the transgression. One wonders how forgiveness is conceptualised by victims holding this opinion if they feel that withholding it is some guarantee of future good behaviour. It is clear, however, that grudge bearing is more likely if the perpetrator denies any wrongdoing or denies the seriousness of the harm done. Forgiveness is less easy under such circumstances and, indeed, it has also been recognised that apology with confession is much more likely to engender forgiveness (e.g. Weiner *et al.*, 1991).

Some grudge bearing is the consequence of the transgression being so awful that forgiveness would be impossible if not disloyal. For example, Baumeister *et al.* (1998) ask how the murder of a spouse or child could be forgiven. The following vignette concerns circumstances indicative of an unforgivable consequence.

John's wife Sandra was run over by a middle-aged business woman speeding in her powerful car while trying to send a text message. Sandra was pushing her disabled mother in her wheelchair when she was struck. She died two days later in hospital. The driver did not stop but was arrested because a bystander had provided the car's registration. The driver claimed not to have known that she had struck anyone despite obvious exterior damage to the front of her car. In addition, she did not express remorse and tried to mitigate her offence on the grounds that she was a substantial employer of local people whose earnings would suffer if she lost business through losing her license.

John suffered severe post-traumatic symptoms with depression. He ruminated constantly and angrily on the unfairness of his wife's death and the emptiness of life without her. John could not agree that he would benefit from trying to give up his vengeful thoughts, despite the gentle encouragement of his doctor, parish priest and friends. He grew angry at any mention of forgiveness and was convinced that if he weakened his hatred of the offender he would betray Sandra.

Some victims consider that forgiveness would be thought of as weakness by their friends and family. Publically harbouring the grudge offsets the possibility of being viewed as a weak person by others who believe forgiveness of transgression is symptomatic of cowardice.

Rafa's younger 14-year-old brother was stabbed in the back by a rival gang member. He was left with only one kidney, irreparable spinal damage and partial paralysis. In discussion with a school counsellor Rafa acknowledged that he and his brother had been provocative and constantly bullied the perpetrator. He stated adamantly, however, that he would not stop talking about revenge because his gang friends would think he was soft and cowardly. He believed that the more he spoke of revenge, the more support he got and the more he was able to believe that he and his brother had had no real responsibility for the incident.

A less obvious form of perceived grudge bearing may occur when a perpetrator seeks forgiveness and is refused by the victim. Jennings suggests that a request for forgiveness is perceived by the perpetrator as a 'costly, self sacrificial gift' (Jennings, 2003, p. 97). Some perpetrators are likely to feel harmed by their victim's refusal to forgive and then adopt victim status in their own right. This is congruent with the findings of Baumeister *et al.* (1990) that a lack of congruence between the perceptions of the original victim and original perpetrator lead to different interpretations of the offence, its severity and consequences. Original perpetrators may then believe that the failure of the original victim to forgive is an over-reaction that is harmful to them. Baumeister *et al.* (1990) describe how 'The perpetrator may even come to feel like a victim of unjust persecution' (p. 1002). In addition, perpetrators' opinions of their offending sometimes includes perceptions that their victims have contributed, in some way, to the reasons for the offence. Such perpetrators find self-forgiveness an easier task than those who shoulder the full blame (e.g. Zechmeister and Romero, 2002). In common with the findings of Baumeister *et al.* (1990) self-forgiving perpetrators view their transgressions as less serious than their victims. If this is the case, then such perpetrators are more likely than not to adopt victim status themselves in the face of a refusal to forgive by the original victim. A whole new cycle of grudge bearing may then ensue. The following vignette provides an example of such convoluted thinking.

Rhona had had a two-year affair with Wayne who was the husband of her sister, Jennifer. Wayne was filled with remorse over this affair and confessed his infidelity to Jennifer. The precipitating incident for this confession had been a very heated argument with Rhona when he tried to end their relationship. Jennifer and Wayne were reconciled eventually but Rhona's request for forgiveness was refused by her sister because she had tried to excuse her part in the affair by claiming that Wayne had been very seductive and begged her to love him. The more Rhona thought about the affair, the stronger she argued that it was mainly Wayne's fault and she wanted Jennifer to forgive her, particularly as she had been able to forgive herself. Jennifer was not convinced and refused immediately. This prompted a vitriolic response from Rhona who explained at length and repeatedly to their mutual friends that her sister was punishing her unfairly and deserved to be ignored by them until she apologised.

Whatever the causes of vengeful rumination and grudge bearing might be, it is clear that they are bad for one's health. Treynor *et al.* (2003) found that rumination was positively associated with depressive symptoms and that women were more susceptible than men to this outcome. In addition, Ysseldyk *et al.* (2007) found that dispositional forgiveness and vengefulness were moderately but negatively correlated. Both were associated with psychological health in the predicted direction. Thus, dispositional forgiveness was associated positively with psychological health and life satisfaction, while vengefulness was negatively associated. Ruminative processes were moderately associated with depressive affect (positive) and life satisfaction (negative). The results indicated, however, that ruminative processes associated with forgiving were different from those associated with vengefulness. It appears that an individual's disposition to be forgiving may reduce the degree of rumination. Thus a proactive side-effect of forgiving perpetrators may be a reduction in rumination associated with lower life satisfaction and depressive symptoms. Vengefulness was not correlated with depressive rumination but was negatively correlated with reflective rumination. This suggests to me that the disposition to vengefulness incorporates angry rumination for those individuals who engage in it and inhibits the cognitive processes that might enable a more relaxed or even forgiving approach to the perpetrator. This is a potentially self-defeating circumstance as failure to forgive (self or other) is associated with elevated depression scale scores for both men and women (Maltby *et al.*, 2001).

Research studies show that there are similarities between the impact on health of rumination and grudge bearing. In addition, physiological variables have also been included in some studies. For example, Witvliet *et al.* (2001) found that a grudge-bearing condition stimulated elevated negative affect, raised heart rate, increased blood pressure and skin conductance. These effects persisted considerably into recovery periods. In contrast, forgiving thoughts were associated with increase in perceived control and relatively lower physiological responses.

Witvliet and colleagues also found among military veterans with post-traumatic stress disorder (PTSD) that there was a link between difficulty in self-forgiving and negative religious coping,[9] depression, anxiety and PTSD severity. Difficulty in forgiving others was associated with depression and PTSD severity but not anxiety (Witvliet *et al.*, 2004). Messias et al. (2010) employed variables concerning other aspects of physical health in their investigation of grudge bearing. These included cardiovascular health, smoking and ulcers. They made use of data from over 6,000 Americans and found significant correlations between responses to a true–false item concerning grudge bearing ('Would you say this was true or false? I've held grudges against people for years', p. 184) and cardiovascular health (heart disease, heart attack, high blood pressure), chronic pain syndromes and peptic ulcers. It is probable, therefore, that serious health conditions are associated with grudge bearing, although it is not clear what, if any, causal relationship exists.

Turning away from vengeance

What encourages some victims to step back from their vengeful thoughts, grudge bearing and angry ruminations to adopt a neutral or generally less aggressive set of constructs about perpetrators and the harm they have caused? This is not necessarily the same as asking how victims can move from vengefulness to an act of forgiveness because it is not always the case that stepping back from vengeance seeking leads automatically to forgiveness. Indeed, there is a mistaken belief that forgiveness by victims includes pardoning the transgressions and reconciling themselves with the perpetrators. Although this might be true in some cases, genuine pardoning and reconciliation are not necessary conditions of forgiveness. Both of these may be granted without forgiveness although they would be indicative of a retreat from aspirations of vengeance. Worthington and Drinkard (2000) recognise that forgiveness may occur only in the minds of victims, whereas reconciliation involves both victims and perpetrators. They make the point in respect of the reconciliation goal of couple therapy:

Forgiveness for an interpersonal offense or injury does not necessarily imply that reconciliation will occur, nor does reconciliation between parties imply that forgiveness has occurred or will occur . . . Forgiveness is intrapersonal, whereas reconciliation is interpersonal. Forgiveness is granted, whereas reconciliation is achieved. Reconciliation might involve interpersonal interactions surrounding requesting, granting, and accepting forgiveness. Forgiveness, though, is intrapersonally experienced and should not be confused with interpersonal actions involving it . . .

(p. 94)

When victims genuinely move away from vengefulness it is clear that the valence of their feelings has altered at least from sharply negative to neutral. In some cases, the negative valence becomes positive, in that the vengeful feelings are replaced by benign and other positive feelings towards the perpetrators. The essential aspect of this movement, however, is that,

When people weaken negatively valenced responses, they no longer perceive themselves to be as strongly connected to the transgressor and/or transgression as they did previously. Weakening responses involves the attenuation of the intrusiveness or intensity of negative transgression-related thoughts or feelings.

(Thompson *et al.*, 2005, p. 320)

What processes bring about the attenuation of vengeful feelings? One possibility is simply that they erode with the passage of time. In my professional experience, people do report that the further they get away from the period of the offence or offending, the less important it seems. Their lives fill up with a variety of tasks, duties, responsibilities and pleasurable activities. All of these may be distractions that divert them from the pain of the wounds they suffered. Just as echoes of thunder die away, so the reverberations of interpersonal disloyalty, infidelity and abandonment may gradually become less intense.

The healing influence of time's passage is well known to most adults and many are apt to console those in pain with the message, 'You'll feel better soon, time is a great healer'. Indeed, many research studies suggest that this is correct. Despite the fact that many common tragedies, such as redundancy, abandonment, bereavement and divorce, usually impact dreadfully on individuals, research findings indicate that 'life events affect well-being for only short periods of time, and that people have an amazing ability to adapt to almost any life circumstance' (Lucas, 2005, p. 945). In support of this, Suh *et al.* (1996) found that significant changes in life events do cause disturbances but these lose their effects after three to six months.

There is a caveat, however. Although the effects of significant life changes do dissipate rapidly, this does not mean that there are no residual effects.

Lucas (2005) examined data from an 18-year panel study of more than 30,000 Germans in order to evaluate reaction and adaptation to divorce. Findings indicated that life satisfaction diminished as divorce approached but improved gradually over time. The improvement was not complete, however, in that satisfaction did not return to the level it was originally. People who married and did not divorce retained higher levels of life satisfaction. They also had higher levels of life satisfaction than the divorce group even before marriage. Clearly, therefore, the significant life change of divorce did have a long-term impact on life satisfaction but from a lower initial baseline. If this study were representative of the impact of life changes generally, it would appear that while time might heal it does not errode all scars.

It is my opinion that a significantly more deliberate reduction of vengeful-ness occurs when individuals make a decision that they have had enough of the bitterness of toxic thoughts and ruminations and want, in common parlance, to 'move on'. They may do so with or without formal therapeutic intervention and with or without the informal support of friends and family. In essence, through determined effort, these individuals alter their habitual styles of rumination from negative to positive valence. Negative rumination is, as described above, that most strongly associated with negative affect, including depressive symptoms and also adversely with forgiveness in respect of damaged interpersonal relationships. Constructive or positive ruminations are repetitive thoughts about 'positive self-qualities, positive affective experience, and one's favorable life circumstances that might amplify the positive affect' (Johnson et al., 2008, p. 705).

This shift represents an opportunity for victims of interpersonal transgres-sions to derive numerous benefits (e.g. Watkins, 2008). Positive thinking is associated with health benefits, particularly recovery from depressive symptoms. In addition, it facilitates recovery from traumatic and upsetting incidents and enables better preparedness against possible future stressful circumstances within interpersonal situations. These individuals achieve by themselves a major goal of therapists working with clients who experience negative affect because of harm done to them through betrayal of relationships. For example, Barber and colleagues state:

> Identifying and understanding the part that angry memories and thoughts of revenge play in relation to the failure to forgive is useful for the further development of forgiveness interventions. For practitioners dealing with forgiveness issues in therapeutic settings, encouraging the release of angry memories may be one way of reducing self-blame, or amelio-rating thoughts of revenge may be helpful in interventions to promote forgiveness in interpersonal conflict.
>
> (2005, pp. 259–60)

The roles of apology and repentance cannot be ignored in consideration of reasons why victims turn away from vengefulness. This topic will be examined further in another chapter, but some preliminary mention is appropriate here. Usually, the effects of apology have been studied in relation to acts of forgiveness within interpersonal relations and it is well founded in research that forgiving victims are considerably more likely to acknowledge apology than unforgiving victims (e.g. Zechmeister and Romero, 2002). In my opinion, however, forgiveness is at or close to the tipping point of a shift in victims' behaviour and there are preceding stages. Thus, whereas an apparently genuine apology might engender a reduction in vengeful thoughts and angry rumination, there is no guarantee that it will succeed in stimulating forgiveness any more than there can be a guarantee that forgiveness will result in reconciliation.

Vengeance and therapy

Not all victims can realign their vengeful feelings with more adaptive thoughts and healthy affect. They may need support and therapeutic intervention. These interventions have become increasingly targeted on the goal of forgiveness in recent years but initially had lacked a satisfactory operational definition of forgiveness to work towards. As Wade (2010) points out,

> Forgiveness has only recently entered the general consciousness of therapists and researchers. Before the 1990s a few therapists and clinicians were writing about or working on forgiveness with their clients, but the overall sentiment in research and practice appeared to be that forgiveness was not part of the psychological domain.
>
> (p. 1)

This is congruent with my experience of conversations with psychotherapists and counsellors as, even late on in the last decade, forgiveness was often thought of almost as a religious benefaction within the theological domain and not the business of general intervention strategies. That opinion may still be held as there is no definitive definition of forgiveness that cannot be challenged by faith-based argument. Nevertheless, within the domain of psychological intervention, forgiveness can be defined in operational terms that have the potential of being monitored objectively as treatment goals. Wade and Worthington (2005) argue that forgiveness is, 'a process that leads to the reduction of unforgiveness (bitterness, anger, etc.) and the promotion of positive regard (love, compassion, or simply, sympathy and pity) for the offender' (p. 160). While this makes clear that a shift away from vengefulness is necessary, it does not commit victims to reconciliations that they may not want and might leave them vulnerable to future harm. In addition, forgiveness is not necessarily about pardoning or condoning the transgression but, in the case of harm done within a valued relationship, it does include the enhancement of positive affect such as compassion, sympathy and sometimes even love. Perpetrators are still held accountable for the harm done, however, and are not necessarily as trusted as they were before. Given that forgiveness may become a reasonable and valid therapeutic goal, the next issue to be decided is that of the effectiveness of therapy. Does it work and, if so, what format might it take?

Wade *et al.* (2009) examined an explicit forgiveness intervention with an alternative treatment. The forgiveness intervention was based on a modification of Worthington's (2001) REACH intervention.[10] The alternative treatment had no explicit goal of promoting forgiveness but instead taught deep relaxation in a variety of simulated situations such as completing tests and going to job interviews. The measured treatment outcome was degree of forgiveness shown by the subjects according to the description given above. The subjects of this study were those used in a previous short-term study of intervention effects (Wade and Meyer, 2009). The group forgiveness-oriented treatment was that of REACH (see above and note 10). The process-oriented intervention was formatted according to Yalom's therapeutic factors for groups (see Montgomery, 2002, for description) but was not specifically targeted at forgiveness.

The results did not demonstrate that the focused intervention was superior to the alternative treatment. Both styles of intervention promoted forgiveness but none resulted in a significant increase in empathy. The degree of reduction in unforgiving dispositions was influenced significantly by the degree of contrition shown by offenders. Thus, the researchers concluded that the type of treatment might not be as important as other factors in the intervention.

Many studies of forgiveness-oriented interventions, like that of Wade and Meyer (2009) above, have only examined effectiveness over a limited period of weeks or a few months. It is reasonable to enquire if such interventions have a more enduring effect that would make them interventions of choice despite the finding that other more general formats achieved the same beneficial short-term effects. The study by Blocher and Wade (2010) reassessed subjects in a forgiveness-focused intervention two years after its cessation and found that subjects continued to experience reduced negative feelings towards perpetrators, less vengeful feelings concerning revenge and generally fewer psychological symptoms. Comparison of effects with a process-oriented intervention produced less clear results. Overall, the degree of forgiveness derived from both styles of intervention did not favour one over the other. Subjects' revenge ideation and psychological symptoms associated with the transgressions remained stable from the cessation of the intervention and there was no statistically significant difference between the interventions. Qualitative analysis, however, produced some evidence of differentiating trends. Blocher and Wade (2010) state:

> Despite the similarities in outcomes for the two treatment types, responses
> to . . . open-ended questions that addressed the helpfulness of the groups

seemed to favor the forgiveness group. The majority of the forgiveness group reported that treatment was helpful, that it had helped them with the specific hurt they intended to work on, that it had an impact on their personal relationships, and that they would want to participate in a similar experience in the future. Conversely, all the members in the process group indicated it had not helped their specific hurts; most of them reported it was not helpful and it did not have an impact on their personal relationships

(p. 69)

It is not clear, however, if this preference is likely to secure any long-lasting beneficial therapeutic effect or that it achieves primacy of intervention type in any other way.

Baucom and colleagues presented a rather different format for couple therapy in respect of harm caused by infidelity. They reviewed the traumatic effect of infidelity and describe why cognitive reframing of the infidelity and its causes assist the betrayed partners to regain a sense of control. They liken this process to themes that are common to forgiveness – based interventions (Baucom et al., 2005). A linkage of cognitive behavioural therapy (CBT) and forgiveness-oriented approaches seems constructive, therefore, in working not with the victim alone but with the couple. In recognition of the fact that victims may not be ready, however, to move on from thinking about the past transgression(s) to the 'now and the future' focus of CBT, the authors of the study introduce a third dimension, that of insight-oriented therapy (IOCT). The purpose of this is to help both parties understand their present relationship difficulties in the context of both their developmental histories with the goal of helping them discover how these histories have molded their relationship. This multi-modal and staged approach is referred to as the Infidelity-Specific Treatment Model.

Baucom et al. (2005) present the outcome of two small treatment studies and regard them as preliminary findings encouraging further research. Their description emphasises the importance of the victim's shift of negatively to positively valenced cognition and affect concerning the perpetrator. Dupree et al. (2007) provide a distillation of the practice-based evidence concerning the treatment of infidelity and it is clear that there is significant communality of goal setting and process within the broad range of treatments they examined. Given this communality it is quite probable that ostensibly different approaches will achieve similar outcomes in respect of the movement away from vengefulness that some betrayed partners can achieve.

Sandage and Worthington (2010) present a very different style of inter-vention to promote forgiveness. Their study of a psycho-educational interven-tion required ethnically diverse subjects to attend one of two seminars presented over six one-hour long sessions. A control group remained on a waiting list. All subjects were required to write a brief narrative describing an interpersonal offence they had experienced and to rate the intensity of the hurt they felt on a five-point Likert scale. The first group attended the Empathy Forgiveness Seminar that sought to promote forgiveness through affective and cognitive empathy, humility and gratitude. The second group attended the Self-Enhancement Seminar that focused on forgiving offenders in order to secure psychological and health benefits for themselves. There was no input or concentration upon empathy or benefits for the offenders. The waiting-list subjects received no inputs initially but were then assigned randomly to treatment seminar sessions around the mid-point.

Assessment data was collected before the seminars started, at post-test and again at a six-week follow-up. The results indicated that both the intervention groups were associated with a greater shift towards forgiveness than the waiting-list group at both the post-test and six-week assessments. Empathy was found to be associated with forgiveness irrespective of the seminar group attended. Shame-proneness was negatively associated with post-test forgiveness but guilt-proneness was positively associated with forgiveness scores at both post-test and six-week follow-up. This has some degree of congruence in that the negatively valenced traits of guilt and shame are differentiated from each other (see Chapter 1) and that the shame-prone individual is likely to evaluate both self and others negatively (e.g. Tangney, 1995). In my opinion, forgiveness becomes less probable under such circumstances. The results of this study, however, indicate strongly that the shift from vengefulness can be assisted by indirect intervention aimed at educating rather than treating individuals.

It has been recognised that spirituality and religion influence therapeutic effectiveness. For example, there has been considerable debate as to whether rational emotive behaviour therapy (REBT) can be used effectively with people who have a devout belief in God and religion. A partial reason for that argument arose as a consequence of the understanding that Albert Ellis, the main protagonist of REBT, was convinced that intense religious faith was antithetical to mental health and therefore to mental health therapy. Subsequent discussion among theoreticians and practitioners led to some significant consideration of this proposition. Eventually, Ellis concluded that 'REBT is compatible with some important religious views and can be used effectively with many clients who have absolutistic philosophies about God and religion' (Ellis, 2000, p. 29).

With specific reference to constructs of forgiveness, there are some significant theological divergences between religions. Christianity centres belief on atonement through the death of Jesus[11] whereas Islamic belief does not accept this ever happened or that Jesus is the Son of God, and asserts that forgiveness is a consequence of repentance and subsequent efforts to do good works.[12] In practice, however, there may be more similarities than differences between people of different religions during daily living. For example, Azar and Mullett (2001) found that there was a significant communality between

Moslems and Christians living in Beirut in that a general forgiveness construct seemed to exist outside of their theological differences. This study was based on responses of subjects of both religions and from different denominations within religions. It was found that 'the Druze, Shiite, and Sunni Muslims were willing to forgive to the same extent as the Catholic, Maronite, and Orthodox Christians'. In addition,

> neither the gender of the participant nor the age of the participant seemed to constitute an important factor . . . In contrast, education had a notable effect on willingness to forgive among both Muslims and Christians: The better educated people clearly indicated that they were more prepared to forgive than the less educated people.
>
> (Azar and Mullett, 2001, p. 179)

Of great significance was the finding that

> cancellation of consequences, intent to harm, and apologies, which had turned out to be important factors among Christians' willingness to forgive, were of similar importance for Muslims. By contrast, the religious and social similarity factors proved no more important among Muslims than among Christians. In general, the participants expressed an almost equivalent willingness to forgive whether the offender was a member of their own religious group or a member of another religious group.
>
> (p. 179)

These findings do not, however, offer therapists a carte blanche to offer any forgiveness directed therapy to any clients without due consideration of the influences of their religion, spirituality and culture.[13] There is a considerable volume of research literature in which these influences are addressed. Worthington and colleagues provide a summary review of this literature and demonstrate a forgiveness-oriented intervention based on REACH that was designed to take account of Christian belief and cultural issues in the Philippines. Their results indicated that 'an evidence-based program to promote forgiveness can be tailored to Christians and also to include elements from a disparate culture and still produce the same magnitude of effect sizes for forgiveness as found in the United States' (Worthington et al. 2010, p. 87).

It is tempting to suggest, therefore, that the shift from vengefulness to more positive feelings about perpetrators and transgressions in interpersonal relations should not be made independently of religious belief and culture, but that a common forgiveness-oriented format can be used when subject to such modifications as may assist clients feel that their religious and cultural identities have been accommodated.

In general terms, however, there does not appear to a be a therapeutic 'best-fit'; victims of interpersonal transgression do seem able to make use of different therapeutic strategies and benefit. A partial answer at least to the questions of what works and for whom, suggests interventions for most clients that stimulate empathy will have a positive effect of increasing the probability of forgiveness and thereby reducing feelings of vengefulness. This suggests that many people simply do not want to hang on to grudges, angry ruminations and the other weighty furniture of vengefulness. Perhaps they really do not want to be burdened by the millstone of vengeful thinking weighing heavily on their souls and await only the right stimulus to make the shift.

Summary

This chapter's focus is on vengeance as a common response to betrayal of interpersonal relations. Although vengeance is generally thought of as being the 'very bad idea' described by Chakrabarti and condemned by the scriptures of most major religions, it remains the almost instinctual response of many people to betrayal by trusted others. Even though most people generally understand that vengeance is not a desirable response, their prosocial arguments against it fall by the wayside when those they love and trust betray relationships they thought were secure. Moreover, the failure of legal systems to provide clear models of restorative rather than retributive justice does little to guide individuals who might otherwise turn away from vengeance.

It appears that personal instances of vengeful thoughts and behaviour may be given spurious credibility by the mixed messages available from religious doctrine and scripture. Vengeance comes easier when individuals accept religious doctrine without question. Those whose lives are defined by 'scripture literalism' find inconsistent guidance from their studies of the Bible, or the Qur'an or other scriptures to support their vengeful thoughts. Personality types also fuel the disposition to vengeance with the factor of psychoticism being particularly influential. In addition, narcissists who are greatly in love with themselves often experience vengeful feelings directed at others who are perceived to have harmed them or simply doubted the basis of their inflated sense of worth. It is not surprising that such people fall on fundamentalist rhetoric and religious doctrine as offering support to their views. This is reflected in their overt behaviour and their selection of religious coping strategies.

Although the strength of dispositional vengeance diminishes with age, the gender differentiation finds that males have a consistently greater predisposition to vengeance. Biological bases to this differentiation and associated personality traits may be explicable in terms of reinforcement sensitivity theory, although more work has to be done on the constructs underpinning the testing of this hypothesis.

Vengefulness poses a health hazard to those who engage in it. Angry rumination and prolonged grudge bearing are associated with significant and potentially serious physiological reactions. The negative emotions of vengefulness are best avoided or diminished, and many individuals turn away from vengeful thoughts in a conscious effort to improve their life quality. Positive, rather than angry, rumination assists with this shift but continued grudge bearing has little value other than to assert a form of continuous punishment of the transgressor and to maintain a presentation of strength rather than weakness.

Some victims wish to turn away from the torrid feelings associated with vengeful thoughts but are unable to do so alone or with the informal support of family and friends. Therapeutic intervention may assist them and perhaps even help them to forgive. Whereas research evidence does not find great support for particular therapeutic strategies, many clients find that specifically forgiveness-oriented strategies are preferable. Further consideration of therapeutic intervention is provided in Chapter 8.

It is clear, however, that the circumstance most particularly associated with a shift away from vengefulness to forgiveness is the genuine remorse of offenders who acknowledge their betrayal of relationships where trust was crucial. Expressions of personal agency and self-blaming associated with the act of betrayal, coupled with apology and repentance may demonstrate to victims that perpetrators feel profoundly sorry for the harm they have caused. Their remorse, if genuine, is the product of guilt and shame, two of the most potent motive forces of confession.

Chapter 4

Shame, guilt and remorse

Introduction

The moral philosopher Bernard Williams apprehended the vital link between shame and guilt when he commented that 'If we come to understand our shame, we may also better understand our guilt'. The understanding of the link develops with experience, but shame has long been thought to be experienced instinctually. Thus, Rodin's sculpture *Eve after the Fall* portrays the erstwhile innocent Eve lowering her head and turning her nakedness away. Her posture and pitiful attempt at concealment shout out self-loathing and shame. If Gershen Kaufman is correct, shame is an instinctual, physiological reaction of short duration (Kaufman, 1992) that 'becomes so acute as to create a binding, almost paralyzing effect upon the self' (p. 9). Thus, Eve was 'hard wired' to experience and express shame when she ate the forbidden fruit and was caught.

Did she also experience guilt? If Kaufman (1992) was again correct, then she would not have. In his opinion, guilt is a learned behaviour of self-directed blame with shame providing the affective component and contributing to the aversive experience of it. Adam and Eve, being innocent before the Fall, had no prior knowledge of wrongdoing and so would not have had opportunity to learn guilt. The self-destructive capacity for shame would not have 'taught' guilt until they experienced the aversive experience of discovery, punishment and expulsion from the Garden.

Albrecht Dürer's painting *The Fall of Man* depicts another aspect of shame, the desire of the shamed to offload the painful experience. In this painting Adam looks reproachfully at Eve who looks away and towards the serpent. Adam wants to blame Eve who, in turn, wants to blame the serpent. They may not have learned guilt at this stage in the Fall but they certainly seem aware of an urge to divest themselves of some of the responsibility. As Hess suggests,

> Such is the nature of shame in our relationships. Our inability to own and acknowledge our shame leads us to attack or accuse others, fending

off our own self-hatred, deflecting that which threatens to diminish us, poisoning our relationships.

(1997, p. 509)

The pain of being thought unworthy within one's social groups adds to the damage to self. Casey, writing as a theologian and survivor of abuse, states, 'Shame manifests itself in the fear of rejection and abandonment, in feeling unacceptable, and in the inability to trust' (Casey, 1998, p. 225). The experience of shame is the strongest signal that we may no longer be considered worthy, that within us lurks indecency and unseemliness, which, even if invisible to observers, is sufficient for us to shun ourselves, to hurry our mind's eye away from viewing our offending traits and seek instead some aspect that aspires to goodness. In the words of the Qur'an 'To those who do right is a goodly (reward) – Yea, more than in measure.[1] No darkness or abasement shall cover their faces'[2] (S.10.26).

The nature of shame

As stated in Chapter 1, shame is an aversive moral emotion elicited by social transgressions that reflect badly on one's integrity and may evoke empathetic concerns about the harm done to victims of those transgressions.

Shame stops us from being able to view ourselves as we would like to. It puts a block on self-admiration and casts a pall over bright thoughts of our successes. A sense of being undeserving can tinge every normal pleasure and a vigilant watch for shame's discovery taints every interaction. As one client put it, 'Shame makes me feel sorry on a daily basis. Sorry for the people I hurt and sorry for myself.'

The definition of shame provided by Chapter 1 was

a dejection-based, passive, or helpless emotion aroused by self-related aversive events. The ashamed person focuses more on devaluing or condemning the entire self, experiences the self as fundamentally flawed, feels self-conscious about the visibility of one's actions, fears scorn, and thus avoids or hides from others.

(Ferguson and Stegge, 1998, p. 20)

Added to this for some, in my professional experience, is a constant seeking of comparators with others, looking to find evidence that they have, perhaps, even more frailties and misdeeds to be ashamed of.

There is a rich vein of material on shame present in theological writing. Much of this provides a bridge to psychological opinion. Some of the material provides insights into both the institutions of orthodox religions and individual behaviour. For example, a number of theologians consider strict orthodoxy to contribute a sense of shame among the devout. With reference to Christianity, Pattison comments,

In failing to recognise and remember the difference between God and the church, the latter may fall into the temptation of idealising itself and seeing itself as perfect. This can have unfortunate consequences in relation to recognising and responding appropriately to shame and shamed people because idealisation may both actively foster shame and prevent its recognition and acknowledgment.

(Pattison, 2000, p. 284)

In a swingeing attack on fundamentalism, Boschen (2001) states,

Religious fundamentalists bear a burden of unhealthy guilt that we can call shame and the ways they conduct themselves in their religious world is directly related to their shame. That is, there is a direct link between the ethical behavior of religious fundamentalists and the shame they carry . . . When you hear sermons repeatedly calling you an evil sinner, when you hear often that you are dirty and unworthy, you can feel spiritually unclean.

(p. 21)

This is congruent with the views of Smedes (1993) who believes that shame in wrongdoers grows from being troubled by a voice saying that they have not fulfilled their duty of perfection and are therefore seriously flawed.[3]

Boschen (2001) argues that a number of 'rules' define the behaviour of fundamentalist churches and groups. Some of these rules also define the behaviour of shame-bound individuals in social contexts generally. Among them is the rule that states that others must be to blame for their failure to live up to impossible aspirations. Thus, for example, fundamentalists may blame their inability to be entirely free of sin on religious moderates whose interpretations of scripture and doctrine lack the rigidity of severe orthodoxy, thereby causing the pollution of moral lassitude. Likewise, shame-bound persons may blame others for tempting them into immorality or divergence from their struggle for perfect goodness.

Simon, a strict Salvationist, blamed a young woman in his congregation for getting him drunk and seducing him. Despite the fact that they soon married he continued for over 40 years until he died to blame her for tempting him into lasciviousness.

Sandra, a devout Catholic with equally devout parents and grandparents developed a close friendship with another young woman she met at a church charity event. Together they went shoplifting one day. Sandra was so afraid that her parents would find out from her priest, a close family friend, that she did not confess. Instead, she burned the clothes she had stolen and spent decades ruminating about how the other girl had led her into sin.

Alongside the rule of blame rests the rule of denial. Given that fundamentalism is often manifest in a drive for domination and power, it is axiomatic that the weakness of vulnerable feelings cannot be tolerated. Fear, loneliness, uncertainty, longing for companionship, stress and anxiety are all inimical to the desired presentation of steadfast strength and moral certainty that raises the self-image of the fundamentalist above the rest of weak and vacillating humanity. It is inevitable that such flaws must be denied and concealed behind a consuming and relentless drive to maintain the superior moral and doctrinal high ground. Similarly, in my experience, shame-bound individuals may strive to deny the feelings and events that bring them shame. They direct their energies into tasks that may appear to have little or no purpose and are not apparently worth the effort put into them. Some others turn to being exceptionally kind and self-sacrificing, often to the point of interfering with the independence of those they seek to help. The effort made to serve others with exceptional benevolence offers an image of self in which true but shameful feelings and thoughts are not reflected.

Boschen alludes to the withdrawal sometimes evinced by both shame-bound groups and individuals. When all else fails and the toxic feelings of shame begin to corrode the false imago of purity, withdrawing oneself from the source of conflict is a seemingly viable strategy. One is mindful of the isolation sought by religious groups splintered from their congregations by emerging doctrinal schisms during which accusations of not 'keeping the faith' add to the shame burden induced by severe orthodoxy. Just as these groups coalesce apart from the main congregation, so individuals may hide from shame by withdrawing from those others who remind them of their flaws and wrong doings.

Judaism and shame

The concept of shame is very important to Judaism where individuals' personal and religious potential are attained as members of family, tribe and nation. The Torah provides God's plan for individuals to live righteous lives within righteous communities in compliance with the principles laid down in the Torah. Transgression is a matter for the group, not just the individuals involved. Thus, the notion of individual salvation is much less significant in Judaism in contrast with Christianity. Physical and mental illness is closely associated with the burden of shame and traditional Jewish liturgy urges prayer for the sick to be cured of their illness and relieve them of this burden.

The Talmud, the assemblage of Jewish law, provides guidance on monetary compensation where shame is the result of reduced circumstances and others can be held responsible for causing shame to individuals by acting in such a way as to bring about a lowering of their status. A once frequently cited and traditional example of this is that of Levirate marriage. This requires that the brother of a deceased man must marry his brother's widow. Likewise, the widow is obliged to marry him.[4] She is shamed by the lowering of her social and economic status if the brother refuses to honour this obligation and the elders ensure that he shares the burden of her shame.

Compassion and community support are conceived of as vital to the reduction of shame and to the healing of wounds. To this end the daily recital of prayer includes several activities that 'know no limit'; that is, they cannot be overdone. The performance of them, and commitment to them, earns reward in this world and in the hereafter. The activities include visiting the sick, revering one's parents, being kind, regularly praying and studying, providing hospitality to strangers and making peace between fellow men. It is understood that few people are able to practise each activity on a daily basis but all believers should remind themselves each day of attempting to use their best endeavours. Although not explicit in doctrine, it is clear that such a prosocial goal is incompatible with the experience of overwhelming negative moral emotions, including shame and guilt.

Islam and shame

For Islamic societies, shame is inextricably linked to honour. In effect, the presence of public shame eradicates the honour of not just the individual but also the family. Dr Sania Hamady, an Arab scholar, wrote that shame, honour and revenge are the three fundamentals of Arab society that she believed might be described as shame-based (Hamady, 1960) such that individuals are deterred from transgression by the fear of public disgrace. In this context, Fluehr-Lobban (1994) referred to shame as the absence of honour and stated that the two were complementary but contradictory. This relationship between shame and honour is, according to sociologists, characteristic of Arab and Muslim cultures, but has also been attributed to the Mediterranean social complex in general. The Islamic shame-based culture operates successfully because honour is attached to groups rather than just to individuals. Whereas in Western cultures shame may be attached to individuals for their transgressions, the group shame-based culture attaches it to the apposite group, be that family, tribe and possibly even a nation state.[5] Thus, the actions or lack of conformity of one individual will damage the reputation, significance and influence of his or her own group. Not surprisingly, concealment of wrongs is considered to be a duty and far better than the shame of revelation; as an Arab proverb states, 'A concealed shame is two thirds forgiven'.[6] Lying, therefore, may be shameful or honourable, depending on the reason for it. Al Ghazali, the celebrated medieval Muslim philosopher and theologian, provided guidance about this. In essence, when either a lie or the truth would lead to the same good result, then the lie is wrong and the truth must be told. When, however, only a lie can produce a good result, then it is permissible to lie. There are similarities to the concept of the 'white lie' that leaves people in a state of ignorance when the truth might harm them. The words of the freelance writer Robert Brault are apposite: 'Today I bent the truth to be kind, and I have no regret, for I am far surer of what is kind than I am of what is true.' Clearly, it is easy to understand how lying may be considered an appropriate alternative to the shamefulness of a truthful revelation within an individual's group.

Shame may be eradicated and honour regained through revenge. Indeed, it is believed that the act of revenge is advocated in the Qur'an. The sentiment, 'Believers, retaliation is decreed for you in bloodshed' often appears in texts and Web pages (S 2:178). Translations differ, however. The official version of Saudi Arabia used by myself states instead, 'O ye who believe! The law of equality is prescribed to you in cases of murder'.[7] It is often thought by Westerners that some of the murders and other violent crimes committed by Islamic fundamentalists are angry acts of revenge. This is particularly true of wives being killed by enraged husbands who discover or allege infidelity. Increasingly, however, it is recognised in the Western world that these are honour killings as revenge for the shame inflicted on the husbands and their families. The act of murder is believed to be a means of regaining that honour.

A significant source of shame is a discovered failure to conform to expectations of the society in which the transgressor lives. As, however, the Qur'an does not provide an exhaustive list of prohibited 'sins', absolute conformity is sometimes thought to be relevant only to the individual's society. Thus, some Muslims are able to rationalise behaving outside their usual parameters of conformity when abroad in a society that is perceived as immoral and permissive by their community at home. For such individuals, morality and shame have territorial limits.

Christianity and shame

Nun Ioanna (1996) deplores the loss of shame from the heart of mankind. She sees modern morality in terms of the separation of virtue from its roots in Christianity such that an inevitable shamelessness of society makes true the words of the Prophet Jeremiah, 'Were they ashamed when they had committed abomination? Nay, they were not at all ashamed, neither could they blush' (Jer. 6:15). She refers to a growing shamelessness and blasphemous depravity that people no longer turn away from. In my lay opinion, this is hardly surprising given the remorseless movement towards egotistical self-gratification during this age of entitlement and overweening belief in undeserved self-worth.

It seems, however, that the scriptural basis in Christianity for considering shame is as conflicted as it is for other religions. In my opinion, the linkage to honour and conformity that is so strong in Islamic doctrine is not as forceful within Christianity but is still present to a degree that muddies rather than clarifies the construct of shame. Some content of the New Testament appears contradictory. For example, within the New Testament the book of Romans provides robust doctrinal guidance for individual social and interpersonal functioning as espoused by the early Christian church. Romans 13: 1–5 (NRSV) states:

> Let every person be subject to the governing authorities. For there is no authority except from God, and those that exist have been instituted by God. Therefore he who resists the authorities resists what God has appointed, and those who resist will incur judgment. For rulers are not a terror to good conduct, but to bad. Would you have no fear of him who is in authority? Then do what is good, and you will receive his approval, for he is God's servant for your good. But if you do wrong, be afraid, for he does not bear the sword in vain; he is the servant of God to execute his wrath on the wrongdoer. Therefore, one must be subject, not only to avoid God's wrath but also for the sake of conscience.

In short, conform to existing authority or be shamed and punished.

Paul appears to have made clear that formal interpretation of the scriptures is included as an authority to be obeyed. In his Second Epistle to Timothy he grants a great boon to biblical literalists by suggesting that scripture is the literal Word of God. He states, 'All scripture is given by inspiration of God, and is profitable for doctrine, for reproof, for correction, for instruction in righteousness' (2 Tim. 3:16).

This 'right-wing' dogmatism appears to be a significant contrast with the guidance of Jesus whose anti-authoritarian views are scattered throughout the New Testament scripture, often when he is portrayed in conflict over shame and honour with Pharisees or other authority figures. A good example is provided when Jesus is in public conflict with an official of a synagogue over an act of healing on the Sabbath. Luke (13:10–17) tells how the official is indignant that the 'work' of healing should take place on the Sabbath and demands that people wanting to be healed should come on other days. Jesus shames the official by saying, 'You hypocrites! Does not each of you on the Sabbath untie his ox or his donkey from the manger, and lead it away to give it water? And ought not this woman, a daughter of Abraham whom Satan bound for eighteen long years, be set free from this bondage on the Sabbath day?' In so doing, he was opposing the formal authority of a keeper of Jewish law, a supposed expert on the interpretation of the Torah. In this instance, therefore, formal authority is dispensed with as shameful and an alternative to orthodoxy is preferred. Despite this example and others like it, the rigidity of early Christianity appears to owe more to authoritarianism. Accordingly, therefore, it has the characteristics of a shame-bound religion.

South-Asian peoples and shame

Thus far, this chapter has considered the constructs of shame within monotheist religions. The construct has somewhat different roots within Hinduism, the largest polytheistic religion, which, in essence, reflects a culture of love, respect, honouring others and diminishing the importance of the presentation of self in order that the modest and untainted inner nature may be revealed. Over conversations with Hindu, Christian and Muslim Indians, I have, however, been struck by similarities of belief concerning spiritually appropriate interpersonal behaviour. Specific religious precepts seem to have less sway than those of culture for daily life, although depth of orthodoxy does mediate this somewhat as, indeed, it does elsewhere.

The cultures of the South Asian subcontinent do not typically find shame in failure to act according to law that proscribes the behaviour that is unacceptable; rather it is the failure to do what should be done. An example often given is that it would be quite ethical for an Indian to steal if that was the only way to help a friend or family member, whereas it would not be ethical for a Westerner. Benevolence is a highly priced virtue and is particularly attached to one's family and one's friendship groups. Individuals are not denoted solely by given names but by the family to which they belong. There are similarities to Chinese culture where individuals are seen literally as owing their lives to their parents.

Joan Miller, cultural psychologist, carried out several studies of the cultural differences between Indian and Western beliefs. She concluded that the primary function of the moral duty of Americans is to constrain their behaviour within societal norms. The moral duty for Hindus is to fulfil their social duties by acting benevolently and according to contextual sensitivity (e.g. Miller *et al.*, 1990; Baron and Miller, 2000). Failure to do so is shameful and reflects badly on the whole family, not just the individual. This also seems to be true, at least in part, for Indians of other religions, as I have noted above.

Psychology and shame

Tangney and her colleagues state that feelings of shame are often associated with a feeling of being small, worthless and powerless (Tangney *et al.*, 2007). Some clinicians have told me that many of their shamed clients spend a lot of time imagining how they would appear to others if their shameful actions had been observed, or if in some way their ruminations about their shame were transmitted to their friends, family and employers. Lewis (1971) suggests that there is a bifurcation in self-functioning in that the shamed person becomes both the cause of the shame and the object of condemnation. There has been considerable empirical support for this hypothesis. Tracy and Robins (2006), for example, found evidence of subjects' stable, irrepressible and internalised attributions for their failings that were positively related to shame. The following case study provides a good example of Lewis's suggestion.

Alice, a single-parent 34-year-old accountant, very cleverly embezzled a substantial sum of money from several of her clients. She did this in small amounts over a long period and was never detected. She spent the money on treats for her children and herself – nothing expensive enough to attract comment. She knew the risk of discovery was slight but was terrified that she would be exposed. Alice became anxious and low in mood; she experienced great shame but also condemned that part of herself that was perpetuating the theft and repeated often, 'This isn't me, I am not like this'. The embezzlement stopped when Alice remarried and moved to a new area. She claimed that she felt 'liberated' from her fears but her memories still carried the burden of shame around with her.

Shame is associated with avoidance behaviour as individuals attempt to hide from the situations that evoke shameful behaviour or memories of shameful behaviour. Dickerson and her colleagues have found associated physiologic factors and conclude 'that acute threats to the social self increase proinflammatory cytokine activity and cortisol and that these changes occur in concert with shame' (Dickerson *et al.*, p. 1191). They state also that these changes 'may support the withdrawal and disengagement behaviors that are observed in . . . humans experiencing shame in response to social self threats' (Dickerson et al., 2004, p. 1205). Lewis and Ramsey (2002) noted similar physiologic responses to shame and embarrassment in children as young as four years. If this is indeed the case, then, apart from external stimuli, there are internal changes that initiate or maintain the defensiveness, social distancing and painful feelings associated with shame. It is inevitable that the concealment of shame has a high priority in order to reduce both internal and external manifestations of shame. It appears, therefore, that contemporary psychological findings and theory are closely aligned with the practices of shame-bound religions in relation to the hiding of shame.

The nature of guilt

As stated in Chapter 1, guilt, like shame, is an aversive moral emotion elicited by social transgressions. It is experienced when an individual believes that they have done something wrong or failed to do something that is required by the moral code of the culture (and/or creed) they belong to. The definition chosen for Chapter 1 is, 'an agitation-based emotion or painful feeling of regret that is aroused when the actor actually causes, anticipates causing, or is associated with an aversive event' (Ferguson and Stegge, 1998, p. 20). This makes clear that the unpleasant experience of guilt is associated with the individuals' incorrect behaviour and not with low opinions of themselves.

The commonly held understanding of guilt is that it is a more adaptive emotion in respect of interpersonal functioning (e.g. Baumeister *et al.*, 1995) than shame. Whereas the latter is more closely associated with concealment and hiding from possible exposure, genuine guilt tends to promote action designed to alleviate its impact upon the individual. These actions are usually positive in that they are remorseful and aimed at some form of reparation.

Confession and apology are obvious examples; also common are assurances of lessons learned and promises of better behaviour in the future. Financial and other tangible forms of restoration may be offered. In general terms, the behaviour motivated by genuine guilt is designed to achieve an undoing of the harm done.

After being unfaithful to his wife for several years, Paul was relieved when the affair ended. He acknowledged that the one objective he had worked hardest at was concealment. It was exhausting to keep checking that he wasn't being followed or seen on a street with his lover; he spent hours working out which locations were likely to be safe and constantly monitoring his own behaviour for careless slip-ups. He finally realised that all this expenditure of energy was not only due to a huge fear of castigation by his peers but also an acknowledgement that he really loved his wife and did not want to hurt her. Once the affair was ended, Paul turned all the energy he had put into concealing his shame into responding to his guilt. He was very remorseful and wanted to try to make amends. Apology was out of the question because he could not confess to his wife without hurting her severely, but he could try to make amends secretly. Accordingly, he spent the money that would otherwise have been spent with his lover on treating his wife but, more particularly, he paid great attention to her widowed father and treated him whenever possible. It was his wife's great joy to look after her father and Paul's caring behaviour was greatly appreciated.

Are shame and guilt really different?

Many of the published works on shame and guilt from psychology, theology and moral philosophy are predicated by the proposition that they are different negative emotions. This is entirely reasonable as there is considerable support for this from theoretical, research and practice-driven perspectives. Despite the risks of repetition, it is worth summarising the common understanding. The conventional psychological perspective is aptly provided by Tangney and Dearing who state:

> In brief, shame is an extremely painful and ugly feeling that has a negative impact on interpersonal behavior. Shame-prone individuals appear relatively more likely to blame others (as well as themselves) for negative events, more prone to a seething, bitter, resentful kind of anger and hostility, and less able to empathise with others in general. In addition, individuals high in shame-proneness are more likely to blame others leading to a higher probability of verbal and physical aggression (e.g. Stuewig *et al.*, 2010). Guilt on the other hand, may not be that bad after all. Guilt-prone individuals appear better able to empathise with others and accept responsibility for negative interpersonal events. They are relatively less prone to anger than their shame-prone peers – but when angry, these individuals appear more likely to express their anger in a

fairly direct (and one might speculate, more constructive) manner. This is an intriguing pattern, and it is the aspect of shame and guilt that has the most direct implications – for parents, teachers, and clinicians alike.

(2002, p. 3)

The last sentence is noteworthy as it demonstrates the importance accorded to this differentiation between shame and guilt in respect of practical implications for parenting, personal–social education and therapeutic intervention.

Bernard Williams, moral philosopher, presents a similar delineation between shame and guilt, albeit with some additional elements concerned with the reactions of hypothetical observers. He states:

> What arouses guilt in an agent (person) is an act or omission of a sort that typically elicits from other people anger, resentment or indignation. What the agent may offer in order to turn this away is reparation; he may also fear punishment or may inflict it upon himself. What arouses shame on the other hand, is something that typically elicits from others contempt or derision or avoidance. This may equally be an act or omission, but it need not be: it may be some failing or defect. It will lower the agent's self-respect and diminish him in his own eyes. His reaction . . . is a wish to hide or disappear . . .
>
> (1993, p. 92)

Gabriele Taylor, a former St Anne's College philosopher, retains a conceptualisation that is based on the feelings of the individual. She states that shameful feelings are a degrading of a worthy self, whereas guilty feelings are concerned with 'the wrong done, not with the kind of person one thinks one is' (1985, p. 89).

Lewis Smedes, renowned ethicist and theologian, summarised the differentiation with commendably brevity: 'The difference between guilt and shame is very clear – in theory. We feel guilty for what we do. We feel shame for what we are' (Smedes, 1993, p. 9). This simple statement encapsulates the interdisciplinary agreements on the differences between these two negative emotions. Thus, people feel sorry not only for the harm they have caused others, but they also feel sorrow for being the kind of person who can cause such harm.

Much of the research work on shame and guilt is founded on the assumption of the accepted differentiation between them, but some results have not been supportive of it. As already considered in Chapter 1, it is evident that people label the same inappropriate behaviours as shameful and others as guilt-provoking. Similarly, Tangney and Dearing (2002) found that the intelligent, well-educated undergraduate students used as their subjects 'could not provide consistent, meaningful definitions of these common human emotions . . . (and)

... couldn't articulate any consistent clear differences between shame and guilt' (p. 11). It was only when Tangney and Dearing introduced counter-factual thinking to this study (i.e. they required the subjects to imagine how past events might have transpired if there had been some change to the situation or one's actions) that the distinction between shame and guilt emerged. They concluded that the differentiation was not intrinsic to the situation evoking the negative emotions but rather to the way 'in which people construe self-relevant negative events' (p. 24).

Tangney and Dearing provide examples of how two people may construe the same situation of wrongdoing differently, leading to a dissimilar experience of negative emotions. Casework often encounters the emotional impact of differential attributions in respect of similar events. The following examples show how two people attribute personal responsibility very differently in respect of a shared wrongdoing.

Mo and Patrick worked together in an open-plan office. They had little in common other than they liked to gossip. Their favourite location was the coffee machine where their over-heated imaginations came together to exaggerate the ordinary human failings of their fellow employees. Their scandal-mongering led to the rather trivial exposure of a young mother who sometimes sneaked out of the office early in order to collect her daughter from a child minder. She was warned by her manager and did make better arrangements but, unfortunately, Mo and Patrick did not stop talking about her and she had to leave her employment. Other employees rounded on Mo and Patrick who were surprised and rather alarmed at the vehemence of this response. They were told in no uncertain terms that they were pariahs and beneath contempt.

Mo felt guilty about her part in the events but resented being made to feel so; she excused herself by saying repeatedly that whistleblowers always suffered for telling the truth and 'anyway, my mouth just runs away with me'. She practised a lot of such self-talk and gradually came to believe her own propaganda. Patrick, however, felt ashamed and almost immediately found another job. He said that his whole personality had altered; from being chatty and outgoing to quiet, scared and withdrawing from company. He often went into long periods of rumination and self-criticism. He concluded that he was not the nice person he had wanted to be and was eventually diagnosed with depression.

It is noteworthy that Mo was able to mitigate the possibility of feeling shame using the cognitive strategy of self-talk: 'I was so busy, my mouth was on auto-pilot'. In other words, 'I'm not really a gossip but my mouth is when I'm distracted.'

In addition to the differentiated acceptance of shame and guilt between people, it is my experience that therapists have made inconsistent use of 'shame' and 'guilt' in their case notes, sometimes with serious consequences. The following provides an example.

Sandra was the pampered daughter of two wealthy parents who were very aware of their elevated station in life and liked to maintain appearances. Being caught out in socially unacceptable behaviour was a stain on their honour.

Sandra's boyfriend subjected her four-month old son to severe physical abuse on several occasions and eventually put the child in hospital with suspected brain injury from shaking. He objected to the child's cries because he couldn't concentrate on his studies. Sandra was not directly abusive but did not protect her son; she preferred each time to believe her boyfriend's assurances that he would not harm the child again. She put her feelings for the boyfriend ahead of her son's safety.

Sandra was assessed by members of a child-protection team who mistook her descriptions of shame for guilt about her passive abuse. They became convinced that she was genuinely remorseful about her son's experiences when in reality she was merely ashamed of her situation and her own parents' disgust. She had allowed the family name to become besmirched.

Her son was returned to her with inadequate supervision and suffered emotional abuse as eventually she blamed him for being the cause of losing her boyfriend and the respect of her parents. She did not blame herself for her son's continued injuries but only for losing the respect and approval of those who were most important to her.

I have found that for some people expressions of genuine guilt, even made just to themselves, are an amelioration or mitigation of shame. By acknowledging responsibility for transgressions, individuals may shift their focus away from considering a defective self and on to specific actions that have caused harm. It is easier to feel sorry about a particular wrongdoing than it is to punish one's whole self with the flagellum of shame. This displacement of shame towards a less painful end of the emotional spectrum may benefit not only wrongdoers but also their victims if the outcome of the shift leads to reparation. Pleading guilty may not only be cathartic for the wrongdoer who is relieved to 'get it off my conscience' but also for victims whose vengeful ruminations may be alleviated by a confession. In addition, I am aware that some offenders expect, and usually receive, a less demeaning response when they admit guilt than if their shame is exposed by others to contempt and derision.

The displacement of shame towards guilt is referred to as 'emotional substitution' by Lewis (1992) who believed that this arises because of shame that has not been acknowledged. He regards this as a normal process because individuals strive adaptively to dissipate corrosive feelings of shame when they arise. In a somewhat similar vein, Lindsay-Hartz *et al.* (1995) believe that guilt can involve an obscuring of a wrongdoer's motivations through the avoidance of the implications of undesirable actions for the sake of self-identity. For example, a person could feel ashamed of spreading specific malicious gossip in his place of employment but displace this to less corrosive guilt on the grounds that the gossip was true and the victim deserved it. This displacement probably helps the wrongdoer reduce the probability of shameful feelings about being a malicious gossip generally. Lindsay-Hartz and colleagues then suggest that if individuals come to acknowledge their true motivations honestly, they may then shift from guilt to shame. I acknowledge the shift between these negative emotions need not be unidirectional, but I have never encountered the shift from guilt to shame in practice.

The process of emotional substitution implies the existence of two distinct emotions between which wrongdoers may move. A counter-proposition, however, is that they are not so clearly differentiated and either shade into one another or are manifestations of the same emotion. This is possible and it is as reasonable to conceptualise shame-guilt as a spectrum emotion through which an individual may shift in response to a range of stimuli. This shift could become a specific therapeutic target for those individuals who obsess about their shameworthiness to a degree that is psychopathological or likely to become so. They may well be encouraged to shift their maladaptive cognitions about their derisory selves towards more adaptive thoughts about being guilty of specific acts and the potential for reparation.

Samuel made use of his roving commission as an insurance agent to make predatory sexual contact with young impressionable women in their own homes. He was sacked eventually after a tribunal hearing went against him. His wife left him, taking their two children with her, and he could only get low-paid work. Samuel experienced great shame and ruminated about how foolish he had been to lose everything he had achieved and the loss of his family's respect. It took him a long time to stop thinking solely about his folly, his loss and shame, and to begin to really consider the harm he had caused the vulnerable young women he had targeted. He made indirect reparation through charitable works set out for him by a counsellor attached to his local health centre.

As the above example suggests, the displacement from the chronic shame end of the spectrum involves weakening the primary insistence on 'self' or 'me' being overwhelmed by negative connotations in favour of a new focus on specific harm to 'them', the victims who would benefit from reparation. Even when reparation is not possible or is for some reason undesirable, the displacement to guilt enables wrongdoers to identify with those who have been harmed such that they can in some way make atonement by anticipating victims' reactions to their guilt and then inflict some form of penalty on themselves (e.g. Greenspan, 1993).

A somewhat amusing example is provided by a compulsive gambler whose lies about his losses caused his loyal wife great distress and depression, particularly when she found that her deceased mother's jewellery had funded his foolish bets on excessively slow horses. He fully acknowledged his guilt and shame, and begged his wife to tell him how he could make some form of reparation. She suggested that he should give up something, in addition to gambling, that was precious to him so that he could experience the pain of its loss. Aware of other uxorial sensitivities and growing impatience, he gave away all of his life-long space-consuming collection of football memorabilia.

The suggestion that shameful feelings may move towards guilt by the gradual weakening of the referents 'self' and 'I' finds some support from a consideration of conceptual semantics. Thus, Williams (1993) states that the fact that

> we have two words does not, in itself, imply there is any great psychological difference between shame and guilt. It might merely be that we set up an extra verbal marker within one and the same psychological field, in order to pick out some particular application of what would otherwise be shame
>
> (p. 89)

This elegant argument introduces another aspect to the question of differentiating shame and guilt. It is supposed that these negative emotions are universal, but it is the case that there is significant intercultural and religious variation in the way that emotions are labelled and understood. Herant Katchadourian, Stanford Emeritus Professor of Psychiatry and Human Biology, argues that cultural differences concerning emotionality are embedded in languages also (2010). He states that attempting to translate terms such as 'guilt' and 'shame' represents a source of possible confusion. Thus, he finds that there are no single-term synonyms for shame and guilt in Chinese. Instead, a number of terms appear to correspond to differentiated types of shame and that, in some contextual usage, guilt appears to be a subsidiary variation of shame. The fact that no word exists for an emotion does not mean that it does not exist and Katchadourian makes the point that we can find evidence of complex emotions through metalanguage[8] using the descriptions of the particular elements of these emotions. He suggests, for example, that the question 'How do you feel when you have lost someone dear to you?' is more likely to provide the essence of sadness than 'Do you feel sad?' (2010, p. 190).

One has to be aware, however, that this process of determining the understanding of a particular emotion by people with a different language and culture may be influenced by the framing of probe questions that are themselves culturally dependent. For example, if evaluating the concept of shame held by many Arabic peoples did not incorporate probes for dishonour, then the fact that dishonour, more so than wrongdoing, would be missed as a crucial antecedent of shame. Emotional universality cannot be assumed and differentiation cannot be demonstrated effectively.

Other considerations of the potential for differentiation may be found within the distinction between moral and non-moral evocations of shame and/or guilt. Smith *et al.* (2002) concluded from their research that

> public exposure of both moral (transgression) and nonmoral (incompetence) experiences was associated more with shame than guilt. Shame was

also more strongly linked with nonmoral experiences of inferiority, suggesting two core features of shame: its links with public exposure and with negative self-evaluation. The distinctive features of guilt included remorse, self-blame, and the private feelings associated with a troubled conscience.

(p. 138)

The linkage of shame to both moral and non-moral events in respect of exposure or the fear of exposure indicates differentiation rather than a single emotion with a broad range of expression.

Olthof and colleagues had examined the developmental context of the morality-identity distinction using children as subjects. Their test model encompassed situations that elicited primarily shame, or primarily guilt or both shame and guilt. The child subjects were aged 7–16 years and they were required to rate shame/guilt responses to these situations. Those subjects aged 12 years and older produced results that were consistent with morality-identity differentiation. Younger children found difficulty in attributing shame to moral transgressions in situations where there was no threat to identity. It would appear, therefore, that even comparatively young people (12 years and older) distinguish between shame and guilt in respect of the dimensions of morality and identity (Olthof et al., 2000).

Menesini and Camodeca (2008) carried out a further analysis of the shame-guilt awareness of children aged 9–11 years using intentional and unintentional situations eliciting guilt and shame in relation to their involvement in bullying, victimisation and prosocial behaviour (determined by peer nomination). Children in the prosocial group generally expressed more shame and guilt than bullies and children who were not involved. Victims of bullying expressed more shame than not-involved children. Situations of intentional harm generated more guilt than shame, whereas shame was expressed more strongly by children in neutral situations than by victims of harm. These results indicate that children who are generally prosocial experience more shame and guilt in the context of intended moral transgression than less well-socialised children. Shame but not guilt was expressed in relation to non-moral events and victims feel less shame when subject to harm inflicted intentionally. At the ages of these child subjects it seems clear that behavioural regulation is associated with the degree to which they express shame and guilt. In addition, they appear to be able to express shame but not guilt as an appropriate response to non-moral situations and distinguish these from non-shameful situations where they experience harm from others that is not of their making (i.e. becoming victimised).

These findings suggest that shame and guilt are distinct negative emotions and that their emergence is a part of normal child development. Additional evidence for differentiation arises from studies of the influence of affective states on decision-making. In essence, different emotions have different impacts on information processing and subsequent decision-making (e.g. Pham *et al.*, 2001). Distinct negative emotions convey distinct types of information causing decision-makers to address different goals in respect of mood repair (e.g. Raghunathan and Pham, 1999). The powerful negative emotions of guilt and shame should, if they are distinct, bring about dissimilar information states manifest as discrepant perspectives of the eliciting situation and so influence decision-making.

This was put to the test by Yang *et al.* (2010) who used 114 undergraduate subjects assigned randomly to one of three affect-inducing conditions: neutral, guilt and shame. Subjects in the neutral condition had read a series of commonplace events happening over the course of a day to a person named Sean. After the experimental groups (guilt and shame) had been subject to the affect-inducing manipulation (being asked to recall significant past emotional events of guilt or shame), all subjects were required to take part in the perspective-taking task of making judgements about the thinking of a person in a potentially difficult interpersonal situation. The results showed that, in comparison with the neutral group (no affect manipulation), the subjects in the guilt group showed better perspective taking than those in the shame group. Yang and colleagues concluded that, 'In general, the results suggest that an individual's inclination to take other persons' perspective into consideration has a differential effect on mood repair depending on whether behaviour is motivated by shame or guilt' (p. 605). Guilt was found to promote perspective taking, whereas shame tended to diminish it. Guilt, therefore, has better potential for decision-making aimed at repairing and improving social relationships. Conversely, the desire of shame-bound individuals to conceal their pain is more likely to promote withdrawal.

The foregoing indicates that there is support for both sides of the debate on the differentiation or unification of shame and guilt. At this time, Tangney is probably one of the leading researchers into these negative emotions and it is to her that I turn for last words on this subject. In concert with Peter Salovey, she provides the informed opinion that wide-ranging and exhaustive research studies 'underscore that shame and guilt are distinct emotional experiences, differing substantially along cognitive, affective, and motivational dimensions' (Tangney and Salovey, 2010, p. 249). This conclusion has significant implications for treatment, legal and educational activities, as well as the basis for future research and practice. Particular care needs to be taken in respect of multicultural and interfaith studies if the pitfalls of misunderstanding and misinterpretation are to be avoided.

However, no matter what stance one takes over the 'self' versus 'behaviour' distinction between shame and guilt, it is quite clear that we recognise their potency to make us very sorry, whether for ourselves, our victims or our actions. No matter how hard people try to deflect or weaken vilification coming from the victims of their wrongdoing by expressing false sentiments of guilt and accountability, it is clear that most of them, unless sociopathic, will not escape the self-inflicted derision of their shame. Others will seek to express remorse in the hope of making amends and at least partly clearing the slate.

Remorse and reparation

Gerald had reached the age of 76 when his feelings of guilt and shame finally matured into remorse. The halting process had lasted nearly 50 years, during which time Martin, his luckless victim, passed him on the street several times a week. They never spoke and Gerald came to believe that the 'silent treatment' was a punishment for his wrongdoing.

Both men were roughly the same age and had worked for the same small engineering firm. Martin had been made a shift supervisor and Gerald was a semi-skilled machine operator working under him. They had both been applicants for the promoted supervisory post and Gerald resented losing out. Martin had got the job on merit, being more experienced and better qualified. He was also well liked by the machine-shop employees and the managers. In contrast, Gerald was a quiet, rather morose man with a tendency to find fault in others too readily. A strict Presbyterian, he had little liking for contemporary culture and was apt to start quoting from the Bible whenever he thought his fellow employees talked of TV programmes he thought of as lascivious.

Gerald seethed with frustration and convinced himself that Martin had been given the job out of favouritism. When a series of thefts began at the works he began to spread rumours about Martin's police record for handling stolen goods. Martin had been 14 years old at that time and received a warning only. Gerald knew about this from a mutual friend at school. From then on Martin had led a blame-free life but this did not stop Gerald. Eventually, the spreading bad feeling against Martin led to him leaving the firm because he lost the confidence of the men on his shift. Within a few days he had lost his job, his reputation and his fiancé who did not want to marry an alleged thief.

Eventually, another employee was caught stealing but that was too late for Martin; his secret was out and there was no pleasing his detractors. He would have left the small town were it not for the needs of his ageing parents. Gerald was given Martin's old job but he lacked the ability to go further and stayed in it until retirement.

Although Gerald had persuaded himself that Martin deserved greater punishment for his teenage behaviour, he soon found no pleasure in his victory. He became ashamed of his actions, suffered depression and eventually his marriage failed as his wife could no longer stand his increasingly gloomy, isolated, shame-bound demeanour. She was unaware of what troubled him and thought it was her fault that he could not enjoy life. He expected that people at work would find out what he had done. This was unlikely, as staff turnover had removed most of the people who had been around during Martin's time. This did not stop Gerald believing that there were rumours passing around the factory about him. He held on to this belief even after his retirement.

Eventually, Gerald made the shift from egocentric shame only to a mix of guilt and shame. He became obsessed with the impact of his actions on Martin who subsequently had never managed to achieve satisfactory stable employment, remained unmarried, childless and badly off. Losing his job had had dire long-term consequences for Martin, and Gerald knew the responsibility for that had been his. He experienced deep regret and remorse, and wondered how he could make some form of reparation to Martin. It took him a long time to pluck up courage even to consider approaching Martin. During this time Martin became very ill and died in hospital. Gerald confessed to a mix of emotions at that time; on one hand he was relieved that he would not have to face Martin, but on the other he was distraught that he could not make reparation. With the help of a therapist, he undertook a series of regular charitable activities and devoted himself to helping the clients of these charities. Gerald felt that this helped him make atonement to God, but he knew that it was no substitute for the direct confession and apology that would have freed him of his self-loathing.

Remorse is the emotional expression of personal regret experienced by individuals after they have perpetrated some behaviour that they know to be shameful or have failed to do something that they should have done. Remorse inevitably follows genuine guilt, but some individuals may express false remorse without experiencing guilt in order to secure some personal benefit. Chiaramello *et al.* (2008) state that genuine remorse usually involves shame and guilt in varying proportions. In addition, they suggest that

> The intensity and duration of remorse would usually depend on the circumstances of the offense, the victim's attitude and, of course, the offender's personality. The ending of the remorse state could take many forms, which are probably directly related to the offender's and victim's personalities and the environment. Different forms of remorse naturally end with seeking forgiveness or other types of closure, such as complete denial or oblivion.
>
> (p. 384)

The vignette given above provides examples of several of these characteristics of remorse. Gerald, a religious man, certainly knew right from wrong and was ashamed that he had seized an opportunity to use old history to besmirch the reputation of a person he was intensely jealous of. He concealed the fact of his shame for many years but eventually guilt grew stronger. Martin's silence and his own biblical literalism created a punishing context for remorse that Gerald could not ignore. Martin's demise made direct atonement impossible so Gerald tried to make it indirectly through charitable works. He could not delude himself that this was a full substitute for confession and apology. Indeed, he would agree with Friedman (2006, p. 2) who states that 'Remorse without an apology may mean that both the victim and the offender suffer an entire life; there is no opportunity for healing'.

One of the most common expressions of remorse is apology, which is examined in Chapter 7. Some initial comments here are, however, appropriate for the further consideration of shame and guilt. Apology must seem credible for recipients to take it seriously. As Western criminal justice systems attach great significance to expressions of true remorse, it is not surprising that the 'ingredients' of genuine apology are of considerable interest. This has led to a commendable linkage of research in law and the behavioural sciences. Accordingly, Petrucci (2002) examined relevant literature and produced a summary of what elements contribute to credible apologies as expressions of genuine remorse. She states:

> Experts across several disciplines agree that the core elements of apology are as follows:
>
> (i)   an expression of remorse or regret, such as 'I'm sorry';
> (ii) an overt acceptance of responsibility for the harmful act;
> (iii) some type of offer of compensation, repair, or restitution; and
> (iv) a promise to avoid such behavior in the future.
>
> (p. 340)

Additional elements may make an apology even more effective. Where the transgression has been the betrayal of a relationship, a potentially effective apology could usefully include a desire that the relationship is improved from its post-betrayal state or even returned to its pre-betrayal state. In addition, the perpetrator should communicate distress in the form of guilt, anxiety and shame (e.g. Lazare, 1995). If the victim sees that the perpetrator is not experiencing these negative emotions, then the apology is likely to fail. Indeed, Lazare (1995) believes that many perpetrators fail to apologise because they do not want to seem weak by expressing guilt and shame; they fail to understand that genuine apology is evidence of a strong desire to help the victim regain strength and self-esteem. Genuine apology born of remorse is a powerful tonic for hurt and diminished victims. Engel (2001) summarises the benefits for the victim. She believes that

> By apologizing, we let the other person know that we regret having hurt him or her. Just as important, we let this person know we respect him, and we care about his feelings. It becomes one of the most effective tools for mending a relationship.
>
> (p.12)

The last sentence conveys the strong desire of many perpetrators for forgiveness and restoration of a positive relationship. The expression of sincere remorse is one of the few strategies that they have available to them, but it cannot be denied that there is pain involved.

Donna became estranged from her brother, Dick, after a trivial row that blew up into 11 years of recrimination followed by silence. Her oldest son, then 12 years old, had

*physically bullied Dick's 7-year-old daughter after she had teased his appearance.
The boy had apologised after the first occasion but there were two further incidents.
Dick quietly asked Donna to speak to the boy after the second occasion but was angry
after the third. Donna believed that Dick was trying to tell her how to bring up her
son and argued that it was the little girl's fault. She knew that this wasn't the case
and that her son had already been in trouble at school for bullying other children.
Nevertheless, she concealed both the truth and her shame by persisting in her false
interpretation of events. Dick and his wife wanted to drop the matter but Donna persisted
in ringing him up to demand an apology. Soon all communication ceased between them.*

*As the years went by, Donna dropped the pretence of the row being Dick's fault.
She felt ashamed that she had behaved as she had and finally acknowledged that she
was in the wrong. After her best friend's brother died of cancer, she realised how awful
it would be if she and Dick remained unreconciled and one of them died. She determined
that the bland exchange of family Christmas cards was a good time to write an apology
in the hope that contact would start.*

*It was hard for Donna to apologise as she was a normally defensive woman and
hated to show any sign of weakness. She had often mistaken aggression for assertiveness
in other relationships and sometimes wondered if her son had modelled his touchy
behaviour on her. Not surprisingly, her first apology was lukewarm: 'I'm sorry if you
took me the wrong way and got upset. I forgot how sensitive you were.' Also, not
surprisingly, Dick thought this risible. His reply was brief: 'Why can't you just say
sorry?'*

*Donna was furious at the reply; she had thought that Dick should have been so
delighted at her gesture that he would have accepted it with gratitude. She spoke about
the unacceptable apology to her friend who laughed at her indignation; she was told
that she had allowed her refusal to acknowledge the extent of her shame and remorse
to overcome her common sense. The next apology told Dick that she was really very
sorry, that he was not to blame in any way, that she would like to do something nice
for him and his wife, and that she promised to curb her excessive pride in the future
and hoped that they could have their old relationship back. In short, she managed to
hit the criteria (see above) set out by Petrucci (2002) and others for credible apology.
Dick accepted.*

Unlike Gerald (see p. 95), Donna did have the opportunity, despite her
prevarications, to make direct atonement to her brother before it was too late.
In both cases, however, it was only when the burden of guilt exceeded the
burden of shame that they were able to move forward at all. There are many
protestations that members of our societies lack shame and as many beliefs
that more shame would bring us back to a more moral place (e.g. Nun Ioanna,
1996, see p. 83). Yet Gerald's and Donna's predicaments turn a more complex
face to this argument: shame held them back but a growing experience of
guilt was helpful. Pattison (2000) firmly states a contradictory opinion to
that of Nun Ioanna:

Insofar as shame is a condition of exclusion, isolation and self-preoccupation, it is likely to exercise a positive rather than negative effect, diminishing possibilities for effective responsibility and action. This should be borne firmly in mind in the context of cries for more shame and shaming in society. Shame should be seen as a more primitive, a-social condition than guilt. It needs to be superseded by guilt if people are to live together in a way that enhances mutual life and well-being. What is required for society to be more moral, in the sense of being more respectful and other-regarding, is more guilt and less shame

(p. 129)

Shame, compassion and therapy

Donna was fortunate to have a good friend who accepted her and was prepared to be honest when honesty was needed. The friend provided just the feedback that Donna needed to break her habit of shame-denial and allow guilt to motivate genuine expression of remorse. Not all shame-bound people are so fortunate. They cannot transcend shame by themselves and perhaps do not have friends or family who are sufficiently close to help them find the best choice of decision to make. Without help, they may spend the rest of their lives in a painful and isolated state. Some of them, however, will seek help through formal professional channels and enter into some form of therapy that may or may not help them.

Pattison (2000) provides some insights into therapy for individuals under the shadow of chronic shame. He states (p. 165) that there are two main therapeutic types: informal self-help (e.g. as for Donna and her friend, see p. 97); and formal psychological and clinical interventions. His comments on popular self-help 'manuals' available on bookshelves do not inspire confidence in them, and, in any event, he doubts that chronically shame-bound individuals will raise their heads above the high parapets of their conceal-ment to reach out for such material. There is some support for this opinion given that there is a high rate of non-disclosure by clients in therapy. For example, Hook and Andrews (2005) used 85 men and women who had received treatment for depression to examine the relationship between shame-proneness, depression and non-disclosure in therapy. The subjects completed a questionnaire that assessed these clinical traits as well as reasons for non-disclosure. The results demonstrated that 54 per cent of the respondents admitted concealing depression-related symptoms and behaviours and/or other distressing experiences from the therapist. Hook and Andrews (2005) state that

Shame was the most frequently reported reason for non-disclosure overall, but was a more frequent reason for non-disclosure of symptoms than experiences. Similarly, shame-proneness was significantly related to non-disclosure of symptoms but not to non-disclosure of experiences. For participants no longer in therapy, non-disclosure of symptoms made a significant independent contribution to current level of depressive symptoms after controlling for demographic variables, worst depression, and shame- proneness

(p. 425)

It is necessary, however, for shame-bound individuals to emerge from the habit of concealment if they are ever to seek and benefit from therapy. Pattison discusses the process of 'externalisation' described by Bradshaw (Pattison, 2000, p. 164) that is highly psychodynamically oriented and begins with a shame-bound individual seeking out a group of non-judgemental people who will engage in honest non-shaming relationships. This is a potentially useful start point as such a group may help shame-bound individuals come to terms with their pain in the secure context of unconditional positive regard. Unfortunately, it is probable that few shame-bound individuals will take the extremely risky first step of engaging with a group even if they could find one that was genuinely non-judgemental. In addition, the next hurdle, that of disclosure, is at least as high. The probability of these individuals finding the confidence to disclose their shame is quite low; indeed, Tangney and her colleagues (1996) comment, 'public disclosure of one's shameful and guilty acts is undoubtedly awful' (p. 1266).

It is probably a mistake to believe that shame can always be treated as a primary presenting condition. In my professional experience, it is often masked by more conventional diagnoses, such as depression, anxiety and obsessive compulsive disorder. Some clients, particularly men, are referred for therapy because of anger and violence; others present with self-harm and self-loathing. Pattison (2000) suggests also that some therapists may be reluctant to confront shame issues for fear of invading their clients' privacy, yet nothing can be gained unless there is recognition of the shame, even if it is not labelled as such. Typically, psychodynamically oriented therapists retain a benign but detached relationship with clients. In my experience, many shame-bound people experience this as a superiority that is humbling of them and likely to increase their sense of shame. Some psychologists (e.g. Kaufman, 1992) suggest that in order to promote a non-shaming professional relationship, there should be a move towards a portrayal of friendly equality. In addition, it appears to me that it is important not to promote a goal of 'curing' shame. It is a fundamental aspect of human emotional life and few of us are lucky enough to escape its punishment. The goal should not be to eradicate shame but to learn how to cope with it and see it as an important warning of threat to well-being. Its emergence should not become an ominous defining moment in life from which there is only protracted self-condemnation and hopelessness but a signal that certain courses of action, if persistent, will lead to degradation and humiliation of the ideal self.

Cognitive behaviour therapy (CBT) has been used to assist shame-bound clients but often tangentially. In treating other difficulties, particularly depression that shame may be a partial cause of, I am aware that for some clients there have been benefits even when shame has not been acknowledged by either client or therapist. It is not normally desirable for interventions to have goals hidden from the client, but if this facilitates the alleviation of distressing symptoms through the promotion of desirable prosocial behaviour and the goals are framed purely in behavioural outcomes, then the practice seems justifiable.

A variant of CBT is compassionate mind training (CMT), a practice application of the school of compassion-focused therapy. This is described by Gilbert (2009) as

> an integrated and multimodal approach that draws from evolutionary, social, developmental and Buddhist psychology, and neuroscience. One of its key concerns is to use compassionate mind training to help people develop and work with experiences of inner warmth, safeness and soothing, via compassion and self-compassion.
>
> (p. 199)

The Buddha's teachings included detail about the functioning of the mind. These teachings have, over time, been refined and within the last few decades it has been recognised that they have predated the exposition of some of the principles used in modern psychology. Although there is a fundamental difference in that Buddhist principles veer away from modern assertions of the self and its functioning, there are significant points where their influence is helpful. For example, clinical psychologists have utilised Buddhist principles in both therapy and research. In particular, mindfulness practices have been incorporated in or used to influence various psychological interventions, including compassion-focused work (see Chapter 8). Other areas of involvement include the treatment of anxiety, depression, obsessive-compulsive disorder and drug addiction (e.g. Siegel, 2007).

Compassionate mind training (CMT) was developed for people suffering high levels of shame who typically find good self-warmth and self-acceptance problematic if not impossible (Gilbert and Procter, 2006). It is recognised that these people have a long history of such difficulties and have often experienced critical, shaming or otherwise traumatic circumstances. CMT is designed to help these clients overcome the impediment of chronic shame and become able to treat themselves more kindly and compassionately.

This form of therapy subscribes to an essentially behavioural approach in that there is a presumption that internal events such as thoughts and imagining can function just as external stimuli do in affecting different areas of the brain, so modifying 'internal behaviour' as well as external behaviour. Internal behaviours include thoughts, images, illusions, reflections, phantasies, delusions, hallucinations and intentions to act (e.g. Skinner, 1957). It is advocated that therapists clarify this concept for clients by referring to commonplace examples, such as how imagining some delicious food (internal stimulus) can stimulate a hungry response to much the same extent as actually seeing that food (external stimulus). From there it is possible for clients to understand that negative, critical and derogatory comments from another (external stimuli) can result in them experiencing undermined confidence, anxiety, low self-worth and poor performance. By the same token, clients' own fears of discovery (shame) can be presented as the internal stimuli for similar outcomes.

The main proponent of compassion-focused therapy is Paul Gilbert, Professor of Clinical Psychology, who refers to the Buddhist belief in the importance of compassion and to the therapeutic efficacy of self-compassion (Gilbert, 2009). Neff (2003), cited by Gilbert, also finds value in the Buddhist position. She states:

> when faced with experiences of suffering or personal failure, self-compassion entails three basic components: (a) self-kindness – extending kindness and understanding to oneself rather than harsh judgment and self-criticism, (b) common humanity – seeing one's experiences as part of the larger human experience rather than seeing them as separating and isolating, and (c) mindfulness – holding one's painful thoughts and feelings in balanced awareness rather than over-identifying with them. While these aspects of self-compassion are conceptually distinct, and are experienced differently at the phenomenological level, they also interact so as to mutually enhance and engender one another. It has already been argued that a certain degree of mindfulness is needed in order to allow enough mental distance from one's negative experiences that feelings of self-kindness and common humanity can arise.
>
> (p. 89)

Compassion is a vital ingredient of many complex personal–social interactions. It is expected of therapists in respect of their clients, just as it is of doctors and nurses in respect of their patients. Only recently has there been any scientific study of compassion, and the results have been surprising. For example, Lutz and colleagues (2008) found effects on neuropsychological measures, and Davidson and colleagues (2003) found influence on the immune function. Gilbert (2009) describes how a focus on compassion can assist shame-bound clients whose levels of shame and self-criticism interfere with responding to the CBT goal of shifting negative to positive cognitions. For example, Rector and colleagues (2000) report that some clients with high levels of self-criticism did less well with cognitive therapy although, 'The most striking finding was the degree to which successful treatment response to CT was associated with a significant reduction in self-criticism' (p. 581).

CMT is based on the belief that two basic systems regulate the experience of positive emotions: one associated with action and achieving, and the other with self-soothing and the experience of contentment (Gilbert and Procter, 2006). Clearly, the ability to self-soothe effectively is a potential regulator of the fear response to aversive experiences such as shame. Thus, CMT provides clients with the means of developing non-judgemental comprehension of why their self-criticism has reached such levels that they are immobilised by it and effectively distanced from normal personal–social functioning. Self-corrosive thoughts are replaced by self-soothing ones that encourage empathy for the fears and distress of clients, and promote self-reward rather than self-condemnation. As this time, there is little formal clinical evidence of the efficacy of CMT but initial findings are encouraging.

Summary

This chapter represents an attempt to explore the relationship between shame and guilt. There is interdisciplinary agreement that shame and guilt are differentiated negative emotions, although their operation sometimes appears as though they are a single spectrum emotion with self-directed shame at one end and behaviour-directed guilt at the other. There is, however, considerable cultural and religious variation in the conceptualisation of shame and a simplistic depiction of the difference is that Western cultures attach shame to wrongs, whereas Eastern cultures attach it to failing to do right. Dishonouring family, group and tribe figure largely outside of Christian cultures, and shame is more significantly attached to this dishonour than to undetected wrongdoing.

Over time, many people who are sorry for the harm they have caused through wrongdoing make a shift away from the urgency of concealing shame by moving towards outward directed guilt. This often implies empathy towards victims of wrongdoing and an evolving sense of remorse. When this leads to genuine attempts at reparation, such as sincere apology, the wrongdoer may be returned some measure of respect because of their acknowledgement of responsibility. Many experience a reduction in shameful feelings and diminished levels of self-criticism and self-vilification. In addition, victims of transgression benefit from the demonstrable respect that reparation brings. Obviously, a keyword in respect of remorse is 'genuine'. Feigned remorse can bring personal benefit in terms of some relaxation of the sanctions imposed by victims and society, but in such cases there is only an appreciation that the appearance of being sorry can bring rewards; shame and guilt have little or nothing to do with it. The next chapter examines this in relation to criminal offending.

The shift from shame to guilt to remorse may take a very long time. Events occurring after the wrongdoing may make direct reparation impossible; nevertheless, indirect reparations can have a similar soothing effect on previously shame-bound individuals who then become less likely to withdraw themselves from the company of others and worry about the risk of exposing their shame. Not all shame-bound individuals can, however, find the strength to risk exposure. Some may develop clinical disorders that lead them into treatment. Even then, they may maintain denial by continuing to conceal their shame and so fail to benefit. Others learn to treat themselves to a degree of compassion and benefit from the self-soothing this brings. Whatever wrongdoers experience in terms of shame, guilt and remorse, it is quite clear that the majority experience being sorry: sorry for their victims and sorry for themselves.

Chapter 5

Remorse and criminal offending

Introduction

Jack Abramoff was a highly successful American businessman, writer and lobbyist whose illicit activities of mail fraud and conspiracy earned him a six-year sentence. He commented that 'Words will not be able to ever express how sorry I am . . . , and I have profound regret and sorrow for the multitude of mistakes and harm I have caused.' His words convey the essence of remorse – sorrow and profound regret. His further words to the Florida court where he was tried add another dimension, that of hoping for forgiveness as he called on God and his victims, seemingly using the language of scripture as he did so: 'I am much chastened and profoundly remorseful. I can only hope that the Almighty and those whom I have wronged will forgive me my trespasses' (2006).

Warren Wiersbe, the American pastor and prolific writer of Christian and theological works, would find support for his views in these quotes. He states:

> We must correctly distinguish regret, remorse, and true repentance. Regret is an activity of the mind; whenever we remember what we've done, we ask ourselves, 'Why did I do that?' Remorse includes both the heart and the mind, and we feel disgust and pain, but we don't change our ways. But true repentance includes the mind, the heart, and the will. We change our mind about our sins and agree with what God says about them; we abhor ourselves because of what we have done; and we deliberately turn from our sin and turn to the Lord for His mercy.
>
> (Wiersbe, 2007, p. 149)

It seems to me that the essence of Wiersbe's opinion is probably correct – it may well be possible to identify states of evolving contrition in terms of the cognitive and affective processes he ascribes to the three Rs: regret, remorse and repentance. Such a separation is particularly valuable if we chose to introduce hypothetical constructs such as 'heart' and 'will' into the mix. Nevertheless, it does seem that an act of regret that goes no further than a wistful moment of self-questioning ('Why did I do that?') without prompting some reparation or even just a determination to behave better in future, is of little real value. If that is all there is to atonement for wrongdoing, then for what and for whom is the perpetrator feeling sorry? As Kathleen Mansfield, the short-story writer, opined, 'Regret is an appalling waste of energy; you can't build on it; it's only good for wallowing in'.

It is certainly the moral expectation of society that individuals who seriously violate the personal and property rights of others should be subject to criminal law. Beyond that, it also hoped that offenders would do the decent thing and express remorse. The severest execration of criminals is reserved for those who harm innocent people and show no remorse. Indeed, the desire to witness expressions of remorse has insinuated itself into the justice systems of several Western countries such that these expressions are evaluated throughout trials, sentencing and parole hearings. Despite the great epistemological problems that bedevil the assessment of an offender's level of remorse, many attempts have been made to justify the relaxation of punitive conditions as a consequence of the expression of remorse and some consideration is now given to the underpinning of this.

Genuine remorse, good acting and sentencing

I once questioned a man whose selfish exploitation had caused great harm to many vulnerable people and caused chaos in their families. He was asked if he would consider making an apology to his victims. His reply was that his father had never apologised for anything and neither would he. He was then asked if he would apologise for a hundred pounds. 'Certainly not,' he replied. What about a thousand pounds? He gave the same answer. Would an apology be worth a million pounds? 'Of course it would,' he replied without second thought, 'I'd put on a really good grovelling show for that'. When asked next, 'Would you feel truly sorry then?', he replied just as quickly, 'Absolutely not'. It would appear clear, therefore, that although the presentation of remorse may have a price, the genuine affective experience of it is beyond value.

Given that judgements about the credibility of offender remorse play an important part in the sentencing practices of many jurisdictions from Australia to the United Kingdom (e.g. Bagaric and Amarasekara, 2001), it is of considerable concern that there should be an accurate assessment of the presentations of remorse. As has been discussed, the presentation of remorse may lead to more favourable treatment if it is judged to be genuine. This cuts across most contexts of human interaction, including the prosecution of offenders. It might be expected that the formal nature of judicial procedures and depth of legal training would lead to more consistent assessment of the credibility of remorse than is found in the everyday lives of ordinary people who are either the presenters of remorse or its recipients. Indeed, it might be expected that analysis of remorse before the courts and the outcomes in terms of judgements and rates of recidivism might provide a firm bedrock on which an understanding of remorse assessment may be based. This chapter considers the role of remorse in criminal proceedings and the determination of its credibility.

The validity of remorse in criminal proceedings

Although the expression of remorse is a powerful influence on the future of damaged interpersonal relations for almost everyone throughout life, its validity in criminal proceedings appears to lack definition, rigour and acceptance. Proeve *et al.* (1999) concluded that the concept of remorse was not clearly understood and that there was little evidence as to whether contrition was associated with decreased recidivism. Bagaric and Amarasekara (2001) also commented on the fact that they found no evidence to suggest that contrite offenders were less likely to reoffend. They argued forcefully that it is not appropriate 'to give legal recognition to the virtue of forgiveness in the context of the sentencing inquiry' (p .376).

Although various writers have supported the necessity of taking account of remorse in legal proceedings (e.g. Bender and Armour, 2007; Tudor, 2008), others have taken a contrary position. For example, Lippke (2008) is opposed to the mitigation of sentences as a consequence of apparently remorseful behaviour. He argues strongly that the behaviour observed and interpreted as genuine remorse may be something quite different. He states:

> Many offenders will experience some guilt or shame at having been apprehended, charged, and convicted, yet these internal states are not the same as remorse in spite of their producing what may appear to be remorseful behavior. More unfortunately still, most adults will have long ago learned how to mimic remorse, as a way of countering and reducing the disapproval of parents, teachers, or other authority figures who enforce standards that children or young adults struggle to understand or accept. Individuals convicted of crimes will have quite powerful incentives to feign remorse whether they feel it or not, given the longer sentences they face if they do not behave as they are expected and encouraged to behave. As a result, their apologies or efforts to compensate victims cannot simply be interpreted as demonstrating lucid and genuine remorse.
>
> (p. 261)

This opinion does not argue that genuine remorse is non-existent within the arena of criminal proceedings, but asserts that it is too difficult to distinguish it, given the contextual circumstances, from feigned remorse or other behavioural antecedents of similar behaviour.

The context of offender remorse

The most common expression of remorse is apology, a statement made to victims that transgressors acknowledge both responsibility and regret for wrongdoing. It is commonly assumed that repair of damaged relationships is more likely to be achieved if transgressors take ownership of the misbehaviour that caused harm and ruined trust. It is expected that apology not only states that the offender feels sorry for the harm done, but also indicates that there will be no reoccurrence of the misbehaviour. If, however, the primary motivation for the apology is the repair of trust in the relationship, then there is a degree of risk. Apology is the admittance of guilt; the transgressor is acknowledging at least one instance of untrustworthiness, of betrayal and the breaching of a code of ethics that defined the mutually accepted boundaries of loyalty within the relationship. Such an admission may tip the outcome against resumption of trust. Balanced against that possibility, however, is the hope that a fervent intention to avoid future misbehaviour will persuade the victim to trust once again. As Kim and his colleagues (2004) commented:

> Thus, on a theoretical level, we can observe that the effectiveness of apology as a response to a trust violation depends on the notion that this response's benefits (due to potential redemption) would outweigh its costs (due to the confirmation of guilt).
>
> (p. 111)

This gamble is not restricted to the activities of wrongdoers and victims within personal relationships; virtually any violation of trust may result in similar schema. This includes alleged offenders involved in criminal proceedings who must evince credible remorse if they are to succeed in persuading the courts that they are reformed characters (or at least capable of reformation) and so worthy of lighter sentences. The similarity ends there, however, because in criminal proceedings the state is substituted for the victim and can apply significantly greater coercions in terms of punishments and rewards than can an individual victim. At stake for the alleged offender is ruination, loss of liberty, length of sentence or even death in countries that retain capital punishment. For example, Sundby (1998) comments:

> The interviews of jurors who served on a jury that imposed a sentence of death ('death jurors') strongly corroborated earlier findings that the defendant's degree of remorse significantly influences a jury's decision to impose the death penalty. Jurors not only identified the perceived degree of the defendant's remorse as one of the most frequently discussed issues in the jury room during the penalty phase, but the topic also pervaded the interviews themselves. Overall, 69 per cent of the death jurors who participated in the study (fifty-four of seventy-eight jurors) pointed to

lack of remorse as a reason for their vote in favor of the death penalty. Many of those jurors cited it as the most compelling reason for their decision. Moreover, it was a theme that arose in every one of the death cases; at least one interviewed juror in each of the nineteen cases raised lack of remorse as a factor that had influenced his decision to sentence the defendant to death.

(p. 1560)

Consequently, the decision to show remorse, even if it is genuinely experienced, is likely to be more strategic than ingenuous, deliberated rather than artless and covert rather than open. Weisman (2009) recognises that impression management[1] is a probable strategy used by defendants such that courts look beyond simple apology for evidence that expressed remorse is genuine. He states:

> The very expression – 'showing remorse' – suggests that, in conventional usage, it is through gestures, displays of affect, and other paralinguistic devices that remorse is communicated. Both the apology and the expression of remorse may rely on the same verbal formulae such as 'I am sorry for what I did', but the work of remorse is to call attention to the feelings that accompany the words even more than the words.
>
> (p. 51)

Thus, the words of remorse must be congruent with the non-verbal behaviour evident as they are uttered; for example, Weisman (2009) refers to 'such body glosses[2] as tears or broken speech as evidence of remorse' (p. 51). Sundby (1998) presents excerpts from interviews with death jurors that clearly indicate they take as much notice of the non-verbal communication of remorse as they do the words uttered and respond negatively where there is conflict.

It would appear, therefore, that simple oral confession before the court may be insufficient to prompt leniency. Indeed, Martel (2010) believes that confession has had a privileged status devolved from Christian ideology that is inappropriate. She states, 'concepts such as culpability, responsibility and remorse constitute relics of Christian influences on law' (Martel, 2010, pp. 422–3). It is noteworthy that Sundby (1998) enters the domain of religion when he comments that 'When the wrongful act is especially egregious, such as the intentional taking of human life, we view those who refuse to seek absolution[3] as outcasts who have forfeited their claim to live in society' (p. 1558). In any event, whatever the roots of confession may be in the context of criminal proceedings, Martel believes that it is only when confession is combined with the presentation of sincere contrition that it may 'acquire a "correctional" value for the offender, and a restorative value for the community' (p. 424).

The assessment of expressions of remorse in criminal proceedings

There has been no lack of guidance as to possible evidence of genuine remorse. For example, Bagaric and Amarasekara (2001) cite the report of the New South Wales Law Reform Commission that lists pleading guilty, cooperating with the police, apologising, and self-inflicted harm or attempt at suicide. Aside from the fact that the first three of these are, as Bagaric and Amarasekara point out, already mitigating factors, one can provide alternative explanations of these behaviours that have little or nothing to do with remorse. From the psychological viewpoint, such lists pose significant operational difficulties for the accurate assessment of remorse as there is no associated guidance by which the probability of alternatives to remorse attribution can be gauged. In any event, it is not clear from a scrutiny of court judgements where remorse or its absence has been influential, that any particular models or definitions of remorse have been used. This should not be taken to imply that there is no assessment of offenders' presentations of remorse and several research studies have investigated the practice. It does, however, raise questions of consistency and reliability.

Wood and MacMartin (2007) made use of discursive psychology[4] to examine sentencing decisions in 74 cases of child sexual assault to identify the practices involved in the assessment of the credibility of remorse presentation. They demonstrated that judges use a number of strategies to augment their assessments of the credibility of remorse presentations including text citation, appearance–reality contrasts, references to stake and interest, and other fact-construction devices. They also found, however, that there was variability in the selection of material and flexibility in how it is used.

This study revealed that considerable work went into the testing of remorsefulness, but Wood and MacMartin (2007) recorded that

> judges do not offer a definition of remorse, nor do they specify the nature of remorse (e.g., as cognition, emotion, etc.), although some do refer to feelings of remorse. Remorse is constructed grammatically (in noun or adjective form) rather than lexically as a quality possessed by or characteristic of an offender and may be viewed as a matter of degree. It may be seen to consist of multiple components (sorrow for one's actions, concern for the victim, a desire for rehabilitation). However, such components (or their expression) may alternatively be used as evidence for remorse . . . And it is with the evidence for remorse, with the construction of remorse or its absence, that the judges are principally concerned.
>
> (p. 346)

A plea of guilty is a mediator applied automatically, but that does not prevent it being rejected as evidence of remorse in that it may become evident that such a plea was merely recognition of inevitability. The study revealed, however, that judges were concerned with appearance–reality contrasts in that 'A contrast between appearance and reality is implicit in the qualification of remorse as genuine or sham' (p. 349).

Considerations of stake and interest concern the appraisal of why offenders undertake actions that are suggestive of remorse. For example, actions such as pleading guilty, apologising, entering therapy or other treatment and attempting restitution may all be motivated by self-interest in sentence reduction. In contrast, Proeve *et al.* (1999) suggest that admitting to crimes that were unknown to the police or unlikely to result in conviction may well be evidence of remorse. Analysis of the probable motives for remorse presentations is therefore vital. Other strategies for assessing the credibility of offenders' presentations include looking for evidence that there is a genuine concern for the suffering of their victims. Where there is evidence that a guilty plea has been made in order to spare victims further suffering, it is probable that remorse will be considered more credible. In addition, attention is paid to rehabilitation, albeit in ways that are variable. Wood and MacMartin (2007) state:

> Reference to an offender's rehabilitation (or willingness to enter rehabilitation) is used by some judges to support an assessment that the offender is remorseful, but the reverse argument is also made, that is, remorse can be offered as evidence that the offender is a good candidate for rehabilitation, which is one reason that remorse is considered to be important in sentencing.
>
> (pp. 353–4)

The study reported by Weisman (2009) took a very different tack but also demonstrated the detailed work that judges undertake to test the authenticity of remorse presentations. Weisman described the purpose of the study thus: 'this study addresses not how the presence of remorse influences the sentences meted out by judges and juries but rather the prior question of how remorse is made recognizable' (p. 49). From the viewpoint of a psychologist, Wiesman introduces an important characteristic of remorse that insinuates throughout his discussion – that is, feelings of remorse are seen to be involuntary, unwanted and painful. It is expected, therefore, that genuine remorse presented before judge and jury is unlikely to be a polished performance of impression management but rather spontaneous, awkward and troubled. The words uttered and the body language speak together of genuine contrition.[5] Weisman (2009) states: 'It is this epistemological privileging of feelings over words that contributes to the widespread belief in legal discourse that demonstrations of remorse reveal the core attributes of the person who has offended' (p. 51). This simplistic belief demonstrates again the necessity of a robust means of accurately sorting the genuinely remorseful offenders from the good actors.

Within this epistemological framework, Weisman's analysis of proceedings identifies three criteria that underpin the main accepted representations of genuine remorse: acknowledgement, suffering and transformation.

Of these, *acknowledgement* refers to the submission of an unqualified acceptance of personal responsibility for the offending in the way that the court has defined it. It is not acceptable to attempt to weaken the degree of personal agency and appear to split hairs over who did what and the seriousness of the impact on the victims. In respect of the latter caveat, Weisman states, 'the wrongdoer accepts without modification how judicial authority has constituted the act of misconduct' (p. 60). Failure of complete acceptance often leads to failed presentations, as the following example demonstrates.

Sabirah, a middle-aged woman, was impatient to get to a rugby match, to support her son. She was frustrated by a lack of parking spaces close to the pitch and deliberately parked across the driveway of a nearby house. This left it inaccessible to the house owners. Just as she was walking away from her car the house owner, also a middle-aged woman, drove up with her passengers and asked Sabirah to move it. Sabirah flew into a rage, threw the owner to the ground and kicked her hard three times. The elderly mother of the owner tried to intervene and was also kicked and punched. All this was witnessed by two other women still in the owner's car. They managed to restrain Sabirah and held her until the police arrived.

Sabirah was arrested and charged with various offences concerning the assault and the circumstances leading up to it. Her case was heard at the local magistrates court where Sabirah was allowed to speak to her plea of guilty. She stated that she felt ashamed and remorseful over the incident and that she wished to sincerely apologise for rising to the provocation so violently and for her part in causing any distress experienced. She expressed hope that their worships would accept this apology for her 'defensive behaviour that might have been excessive'. The court had already found that there was no provocation and that the only violence shown was that of the defendant who was alone responsible for the severe distress suffered by both victims. Sabirah's attempt to modify the opinion of the court about the circumstances did not amuse their worships, who were pleased to hand down a stiffer sentence than they might otherwise have done.

Suffering is the demonstration that offenders experience the painful emotion of shame over their wrongdoings; their self-esteem has been lowered by their misbehaviour and they recognise that they are lesser persons than they should be. It is regarded as important also that the remorseful offenders do not seek to portray themselves as victims of their own crime. Although offenders suffer indignity, losses and possible vilification as a consequence of their crimes, they should not express sadness about these privations. Instead, the offenders should be seen to suffer for the harm they have caused rather than any suffering they may have experienced as a consequence of their detention.

The third criterion, *transformation*, refers to the willingness of the wrongdoer to accept rehabilitation, to be prepared to engage in a process that will change those traits of their character that are associated with their misbehaviour. They must show a credible determination to reduce the probability of reoffending by accepting such conditions and activities that maximise the potential for change. Weisman provides detail on this criterion: 'What is offered as evidence of remorse is engagement with those identity-transforming institutions that are believed by the court to bring about these profound inner changes' (p. 59).

There is an additional caveat that concerns an over-arching acquiescent state of mind that is represented by the general tone of the remorseful presentation. Offenders must recognise that their presentations are made to a greater power than themselves; they must display appropriate subjugation. Thus, credible demonstrations of remorse are those that

> have as their common point of reference a posture of abjection and surrender by the offender before the authority of the law. Whether or not these manifestations correspond to actual feelings of shame or guilt, in the population of cases here considered, it is clear that, in extended contests, anything short of unconditional acknowledgment of wrongdoing coupled with severe self-condemnation will not lead to the conferring of the law's mercy.
>
> (Weisman, 2009, p. 66)

The good actors

These analyses of the assessment processes show that considerable thought on a case-by-case basis goes into judgement concerning the credibility of remorse. I am struck, however, by the variability of the process and the fact that the conceptualisation of remorse does not appear to follow a standard pattern that might, if akin to the diagnostic criteria for the behavioural manifestations of mental disorders, align the overt presentation of offenders to probability of authenticity. One has only to sample trial extracts and judgements from around the world to discover that this variability is considerable between judiciaries and even between courts in the same judiciary. The good actor would appear therefore to stand a reasonable chance of persuading a court of the sincerity of feelings that he does not possess but understands how to mimic.

Another potential advantage handed to the good actor is the wealth of trial extracts and judgements readily available through the Internet and spanning the judiciaries of most countries. These can provide unintended guidance on what to say and how to act remorsefully when saying it. Indeed, Weisman (2009) stated baldly 'juridical discourse constitutes not only when remorse should be demonstrated but how it should be demonstrated' (p. 65). The good actor could be scripted into a reward-winning performance that sees reduction in sentence or some other benefit without once experiencing the scourge of negative emotions that give rise to genuine remorse. Lippke (2008) is trenchant on the concern about remorse-based sentence reduction; he states:

> I believe that what one would most often find is that sentence reductions are handed out more or less indiscriminately to accused offenders who simply agree to plead guilty or who exhibit some remorseful behavior about what they have done. In other words, the gap between a theory that supports sentence reductions for remorseful offenders and contemporary legal practices remains a yawning chasm.
>
> (p. 268)

It would appear, therefore, that the formality of court processes cannot provide a firm bedrock on which an understanding of remorse assessment may be founded.

Finding God: religious conversion and remorse

I have assisted assessments of several prisoners on remand who have drawn to the attention of the courts that they have had a significant, life-changing religious experience. As a consequence, they have 'found God' and are no longer the weak sinners that they were. They expect their claims to be taken seriously, mostly in the hope that their sentences will be reduced.

Religious conversion, 'being saved', 'finding God', 'seeing the light' and other epithets for a supposedly life-defining experience are not as common as one may think. Nevertheless, they do occur and not all are feigned. In my experience and according to survey reports, the overwhelming majority of religious conversions are to a denomination of Christianity. Technically, religious conversion refers to a transfer from one religion to another; thus, the convert was already a believer but aligned to a different faith or branch of the same faith (e.g. Anglican to Catholic) before the conversion. In most cases, however, the convert had no religious allegiance or, indeed, any behavioural history indicative of a commitment to religiousness of spirituality in any form, prior to the conversion. From an entirely cynical viewpoint, Christianity is a good conversion destination. At its core is the belief that God's love redeems all sinners who repent. In contrast to other religions where acts of atonements are required, this might seem like a soft option for the offender who wants to claim a conversion that he or she does not truly experience. Despite this apparently easily claimed passport to redemption, it is clear that some offenders do experience sincere conversion and set about demonstrating convincing 'good works' in the environment of their incarceration. William Peyton, for example, had been sentenced to death for his brutal murder of two women and a 10-year-old boy. He claimed to have found God and became a committed Christian who befriended and supported other prisoners with their spirituality (see Simons, 2004). Likewise, Karla Faye Parker was also a death-row inmate who experienced a profound religious conversion and spent many years assisting fellow prisoners (see Price, 2006). Both these condemned prisoners were thought to have been genuinely committed to their new religious lives and attracted the fulsome approbation of prison staff and other prisoners.

Sadly, however, many claims to religious conversion are risible and convince no one. I recall one young man on remand whose description of a divine visitation was of a spirit resembling a demented Yoda. In most cases, the feigned conversion comprises little more than a breathless description of a moment of religious insight, a statement about making a new and godly life and remorse over whatever offence(s) led to arrest. Seldom is there any evidence that the offender has taken his or her new morality into the arena of charitable works.

A key factor in the appraisal of religious conversion is the belief that there is a close association between the new religiosity and genuine remorse. This appears to be held by all parties in criminal proceedings. Whether the conversion is genuine or feigned, there is an expectation that its demonstration will give added weight to any claim of remorse.

This expectation is, however, without much substance. Two important factors are influential. First, although Christianity and other religions require wrongdoers to experience remorse and repentance, there is no guarantee that this requirement will be applied to the particular behaviour that constitutes the offender's crimes. The acquisition of religion does not necessarily bestow upon offenders a fully formed belief that their behaviour requires remorse and repentance. They may continue to hold a belief that although their actions were criminal they were not immoral. For example, a man who allows his terminally ill child to die by withholding medication that would prolong a painful life may still not consider his action a reason for remorse and repentance. Murphy (2007) provides as another example that of a non-religious terrorist who converts to a fundamentalist pattern of beliefs and becomes even more convinced of the rightness of his actions.

A second reason for conversion failing to deliver remorse is associated with the belief that finding God is to commence a new life as a totally different person. The new person claims to have thrown off the slough of previous immorality and to have become munificent instead of exploitive, striving for peace instead of giving way to anger, and spiritual rather than temporal. The crimes of the old person are swept away by God's love and forgiveness and the new person need feel no guilt, shame or remorse for the actions of that person who no longer exists. Indeed, it could be argued that to persist in ruminating on past sins, as is to be expected in the genuinely remorseful state, is to run the risk of the new person fearing that God's love and forgiveness is forever withdrawn. This is the sin of despair that is regarded by some Christian authorities as unforgivable.

It would seem, therefore, that credible conversion need not bestow an overt and previously absent capacity for remorse, although without it religious conversion is unlikely to be reasonably presented as a mitigating factor. Despite the difficulties surrounding the validation of religious conversion, the probability that genuine conversion will lead to future experience of the negative emotions of shame, guilt and remorse and consequently to a life guided by strong moral precepts, suggests that it must be considered in mitigation. Simons (2004) states: 'an authentic religious conversion is legally, practically and morally relevant to capital sentencing, but only if it begins with repentance and culminates in atonement' (pp. 336–7). At least this self-monitoring requires that the convert should feel remorse for crimes committed, but it fails to provide sufficient detail to assess that this requirement is met. Murphy (2007) is more strident. Although he recognises that conversion and remorse are often presented together, he requires that shame should forge 'the resolve to become a new and better person' (p. 438). In addition, guilt should engender atonement whereby the offender comes to embrace the sacrifice, such as the loss of liberty, that is required to restore the moral balance that has been harmed through the offending. Furthermore, the repentance of the offender disowns the message to the victim that they are of low worth, fit only to be exploited for the offender's advantage.

Although religion has much to say about remorse and repentance, it does not have a monopoly on them. Atheists and agnostics experience them and recognise their value and place in a moral society. Life-long believers do not wear out the capacity to respond to these emotions or fall into the shadow of the new converts' shining zeal for atonement. In short, I do not accept that religious conversion adds anything to the mitigating properties of genuine remorse. It appears to provide little more than an alternative package enabling offenders to claim an immersion in piety, a cleansing rebirth and a clean slate. As the Christian theologian Karl Barth remarked, 'Faith is never identical with piety'. Apart from the dubious relevance of religious conversion, there remains the same practical problem that has been discussed in the previous section – the detection of acting out a feigned presentation of remorse in order to accrue some benefit. Murphy (2007) refers to 'the perpetual possibility of self-serving fakery on the part of wrongdoers' (p. 440), a frame of mind that has no communality with the valour shown by those who publicly express genuine remorse without thought for their own benefit. I am mindful of Molière's comment that 'There are pretensions to piety as well as to courage'; thus, those offenders who fail to convince others of their new-found religiousness are likely to lose all credibility. The next section deals with the assessment of pretension and those wrongdoers whose remorse owes more to faith in impression management than religious conviction.

Integrity or impression management?

I asked a young woman why she had told me that she was a committed Christian when I had not asked her about her religious life. She had said that she did a lot for a particular charity and went to church regularly. I thought none of this was likely to be true because, during an on-going psychometric assessment, she had just exceeded the ceiling scores on two separate 'lie scales' and achieved an exceptionally high 'fake good' score on a separate test.[6] She told me that she thought I ought to know these things about her to demonstrate that she was a good person who certainly would not abuse her child.

This young woman was responding according to the imperative of social desirability. This is the inclination held by some people to deny undesirable traits and make false claims of possessing desirable ones in order to create a better impression of themselves, usually for reasons of personal gain. The young woman in question was at risk of losing her infant son to the care system because of her neglect and emotional abuse of him. She hoped that my assessment of her would be positive if I was fooled into believing her lies. Unfortunately for her, I did not accept her claims and neither did the magistrates who ordered her child into care.

In this case the psychometric evidence of her test results was hardly needed to torpedo her attempts to create a positive myth about herself. That is not always true, however, and I and some of my colleagues have often expressed surprise at how criminal offenders and some defendants in civil proceedings have presented as very trustworthy people only to be 'exposed' as it were, by their responses on fake good scales. Simons (2004) finds that jurors are quite able to see through attempts to present false claims of religious conversion during murder trials, but I am not confident that this is the case across the range of offending. It has been my experience that when the views of jurors and officials coincide, then jurors are assumed to be perspicacious; when, however, the opposite occurs, then jurors are not so well regarded.

One of the most important reasons for the inclusion of 'fake good' or 'lie scales' into many types of psychometric questionnaires is to detect the possible confounding impact of socially desirable responding (SDR). In brief, when individuals' scores on these scales exceed statistically determined levels, then the credibility of their responding to trait and clinical scales must also be regarded as suspect. Clearly, such devices have a wide range of usefulness over many areas of human activity, including the assessment of offenders' self-reports where assessors have been aware for many years of the potentially confounding effect of SDR (e.g. Sackheim and Gur, 1979). There are several theories about the origins of SDR; for example, Furnham (1986) argued that it was a trait, whereas Walsh *et al.* (1974) opined from their work with children that social learning theory was a sufficient explanation.

Statistical analysis of SDR measures generally reveals two factors that constitute this style of responding; *self-deception* and *impression management* (e.g.

Paulhus, 1984). Self-deception is described as an unconscious defensiveness that inhibits thoughts and feelings that might harm the self. These are the kinds of mental events that individuals shy away from and try to think of something else that is not painful. In contrast, impression management is an entirely conscious attempt to manipulate the representation of the self to others. Mills and Kroner (2005) provide a comparison: '*Self-deception* occurs when a person believes a statement to be true of him- or herself even though it is not true, whereas purposely misrepresenting the truth to avoid negative evaluation is defined as *other-deception* (impression management)' (p. 71).

It has been assumed that offenders frequently dissemble when providing self-report data (e.g. Holden *et al.*, 1992). Their presumed intention would be to employ impression management to sway opinion in their favour. If this were invariably the case, then there would be little use for self-report measures in the prediction of recidivism. In fact, research evidence indicates that self-report is a reliable predictor of recidivism as well as institutional misconduct (e.g. Motiuk *et al.*, 1992; Mills and Kroner, 2003). In addition, several studies have shown that 'a self-report questionnaire to be at least as effective in predicting offender post-release outcome as other widely used actuarial instruments' (Mills and Kroner, 2005, p. 72).

These findings raise a contradiction that was identified by Mills and Kroner (2005). On one hand, conventional wisdom holds that offenders cannot be trusted to tell the truth about themselves, but on the other findings concerning their self-report responding is positively associated with recidivism. Furthermore, other findings indicate that antisocial offenders tend to have lower scores on measures of impression management. Mills and Kroner (2005) report, 'impression management is significantly and negatively associated with criminal risk and recidivism' (p. 72). In short, those offenders who answer the items relating to SDR honestly show the highest risk of future criminality.

This is a potentially discomforting finding because, for one reason, the inverse relationship implies that the less honest an offender is the more likely he or she is to behave acceptably. The relationship is awkward also in that there is no theoretical basis for predicting that impression management (IM) and criminal risk should be related at all or as strongly as the statistical findings indicate, particularly as it flies in the face of expectation. In seeking an explanation, Mills and Kroner suggest that the IM scale they used for the 2005 study contained items that related strongly to risk such that the scale 'is a proxy for risk, and this variance dominated the relationship that the IM scale has with other self-report measures' (p. 77). A further explanation offered by them is that the subjects in these studies are criminals convicted of serious crimes, whereas the test items related to minor offences. Indeed, they provide the example of one such offence as dropping litter. They suggest that the respondents were prepared to answer such items honestly because they perceived no threat to themselves by doing so. Mills and Kroner (2005) suggest that this may not be the case for middle-class, well-socialised people who might be tempted to deny even minor transgressions. They suggest also that seriously offending perpetrators may admit to minor transgressions in order to contribute to an illusion of truthfulness that might gain them credibility in clinical interviews where IM was their preferred response style. Presumably, that tactic may also be applied to their evidence in court.

Mills and Kroner (2005) have one further suggestion to explain the awkward finding of the inverse relationship between SDR and future criminal risk. The test used by them and others of SDR is the balanced inventory of desirable responding (BIDR), now renamed as the Paulhus deception scales (PDS; Paulhus, 1998). They state:

> The central limitation of this study is the reliance on SDR as represented by a single measure. Although the BIDR is widely used, it represents only one particular conceptualization of SDR. Different outcomes may be possible with other instruments, such as the Marlowe–Crowne scale . . .
>
> (p. 79)

There is good evidence that this may be correct. The Marlowe–Crowne social desirability scale (MCSDS) (Crowne and Marlowe, 1960) has probably been the most frequently used psychometric assessment of SDR across clinical, medical, occupational, research and other fields of study. Its validity and reliability have been researched on very many occasions, including its use for forensic assessments (Andrews and Meyer, 2003). In addition, its accessible readability for self-reporting subjects, ease of administration and relative cheapness has made it popular. Its use with different populations continues to be investigated with good results. For example, Tatman and colleagues studied the psychometric properties of the MCSDS with adult male sex offenders. They concluded that

> Results from this project would support the use of the MCSDS within a comprehensive evaluation battery, or as part of a structured interview process, to assess the degree to which sexual offenders are attempting to respond to interview questions or test items in a socially desirable manner
>
> (Tatman et al., 2009, p. 33)

The items of this scale are less likely also to confound those relating more specifically to recidivism.

A further possible explanation for Mills and Kroner's findings (2005) arises from the fact that the offenders used for these studies had already been tried and sentenced. Their main reason for the use of impression management strategies, that of trying for sentence mitigation, could well be absent. For example, Mills *et al.* (2003) made use of 124 male offenders, 77 of whom were newly released; a later study of Mills and Kroner (2006) made use of 172 volunteer-sentenced violent offenders. Ideally, results should be obtained from prisoners on remand, pre-trial, when the desire to create a good impression would surely be at its greatest. I am not aware of studies of subjects who have been assessed pre-trial on measures of both criminal risk and SDR. It is acknowledged that several studies have noted high rates of SDR in respect of offending behaviour pre-trial (e.g. Archer, 1999, for both male and female perpetrators of intimate partner violence), but at present there does not appear to be any published study that could be linked to the work of Mills and colleagues to further examine the awkward findings described above.

Psychometric assessment and socially desirable responding

It is easy for some perpetrators, whether they are criminal offenders, workplace gossips or transgressors against their intimate relationships, to pretend remorse and act out the abject misery of shame. They are helped by the fact that many people are not excellent judges of character and fall for good acts of feigned emotion. The average person distinguishes lies from truth with a little more than 50 per cent accuracy (e.g. Bond and De Paulo, 2006). Fortunately, psychometric instruments are available to improve the odds of correct assessment in formal situations where improved accuracy is important.

Often referred to as lie scales, many psychometric questionnaires have banks of items built into them that detect attempts at styles of impression management. For example, the Eysenck personality scales (EPS) include items such as 'Are *all* your habits good and desirable ones?' and 'As a child, did you do as you were told immediately and without grumbling?'. Responding 'Yes' to these and questions like them suggests that there has been falsification. It may appear that these two items are easily spotted and avoided, rather like a motorist spotting a speed camera and slowing down until the danger has passed behind. In fact, the number and sophistication of items makes it hard for the unsuspecting tester to avoid sufficient of them to make a decision to answer them truthfully and falsify responses to the clinical items.

The following shows a little of the range of areas where the detection of deception is possible. Most personality and related inventories have sophisticated scales for the detection of incorrect response styles. For example, the 344-item Personality Assessment Inventory (PAI) has four validity scales: Inconsistency (measuring the consistency of response to items with similar content); Infrequency (items used to detect if the testee is responding randomly or carelessly); Negative Impression (items investigating deliberate attempts to exaggerate unfavourable impressions or malingering), and Positive Impression (items evaluating the presentation of a very favourable impression and/or a reluctance to acknowledge minor personal flaws). A sister test of the PAI is the Interpersonal Behavior Survey (IBS). This has three validity scales:

the Infrequency scale of random responding, the Impression Management scale (as above), and the Denial scale that is a measure of a tendency to hesitate to acknowledge minor and commonly occurring personal weaknesses. This corresponds to the self-deception component of SDR.

Many specifically oriented psychometric self-report inventories include similar validity scales. For example, the Child Abuse Potential inventory (CAP) detects response distortions using three validity scales: the lie scale, the random response scale, and the inconsistency scale. These scales may be used in different pairings to provide three validity indices, namely, the faking-good index (positive IM), the faking-bad index (negative IM), and random response index. Elevation of any of these validity indices suggests that the item responses may not yield an accurate representation of the individual's abuse potential. The Parent–Child Relationship Inventory (PCRI) is a self-report inventory that examines the quality of parent–child interaction. It has two validity indicators: the Inconsistency indicator records random or inattentive responding, while the Social Desirability indicator tests for parental responses that are designed to misrepresent the quality of the parent–child relationship in an unrealistically positive manner.

The above are all self-report inventories. Some others report on the presentation of other people. For example, the Personality Inventory for Children (PIC, 1990) uses parents' responses to 420 items to derive a profile of their children's personality structure. SDR responding has a somewhat different context within this format. Where, for example, children or young people are being assessed because of delinquent or otherwise aberrant behaviour there may be a tendency for parents to overly accentuate their acceptable behaviour and minimise undesirable behaviour. This inventory is therefore equipped with a lie scale designed to investigate the potential exaggeration of virtue while minimising behavioural problems. Other parents may wish to emphasise particular symptom sets or simply respond randomly. The inventory has a frequency scale that evaluates random inconsistency and exaggerated deviant patterns. Finally, there is a defensiveness scale to detect a parent's attempts to be defensive about the extent of the problems their children present or experience.

My personal experience of carrying out pre-trial assessments includes many within the domain of child protection proceedings. Psychometric personality assessments were carried out routinely and these incorporate SDR scales, the results of which may be contrasted with self-reports obtained during interview. It is my experience that some of the perpetrators who intended to plead guilty expressed profound remorse but also had high fake good results. Many also believed their own propaganda and scored high on self-deception items. The following is illustrative.

Martin, a 24-year-old machine operator, eventually admitted to shaking his baby son so hard that he caused acute encephalopathy with subdural and retinal haemorrhages and some injuries to the child's neck and spinal cord. He admitted to only one incident but others were suspected given medical findings. He and his wife had been very supportive of each other, stating that neither would consciously injure any child. The fact that neither parent had confessed to this physical abuse cast serious doubt about the safety of either for future parenting. Their son entered foster care and they had only limited supervised access to him. Martin's confession came about largely because of the outcome of a psychometric self-report test battery that he had been given over several sessions.

The first test he had taken was the Personality Assessment Inventory (PAI, see below). His profile of scores was mostly within the normal range with some notable exceptions. The score on the Positive Impression scale was significantly elevated and indicated that Martin was consciously giving socially desirable answers to create a better impression of himself. This result cast doubt on the credibility of his responding generally.

In addition, his score on the scale recording somatisation was significantly high. This suggests an individual who reports frequent experience of various physical symptoms (e.g. headaches, pains, gastric discomfort) and rather vague worries about fatigue and ill health. Sometimes these are accompanied by depression or anxiety but not in Martin's history. His work record was marred by many absences and his doctor had not found any significant health issues. It was suspected that he malingered to avoid work on some occasions.

His score on the Resentment scale was moderately elevated. This suggests an individual who is easily slighted and responds by holding grudges towards others. A frequent tendency is to blame others for their misfortunes and to try to offload personal responsibility for unwanted events.

Martin was also asked to complete the Interpersonal Behavior Survey (IBS). This is a sister test to the PAI and investigates excesses and deficits of assertiveness and aggression evident within an individual's social responding. The IBS is equipped with a variety of validity scales that reflect test-taking attitudes that may adversely affect the credibility of responding. Martin's profile showed a significantly elevated result on the Denial scale, which suggested that he experienced some hesitancy in admitting to himself the experience of commonly occurring but socially undesirable feelings or weaknesses. In addition, his score on the Impression Management scale was also significantly elevated, a finding that suggested attempts to create a false impression of himself.

Two of the aggressiveness scales of the IBS were moderately but significantly elevated. The highest result was on the Hostile Stance scale that samples an antagonistic orientation towards others and a view of the social world that enables testees to justify some form of aggressive response in order to maintain or protect themselves. The second was obtained on the Disregard of Rights scale that examines the tendency to protect oneself by ignoring the rights of other people. These two scales are essentially measures of perceived self-importance and a willingness to respond aggressively to threat in order to preserve one's own circumstances, even at the expense of others. It is probable that these scores would have been higher and also other scales elevated to significance if Martin's tendency to socially desirable responding had been within normal limits.

These findings indicated that Martin had difficulties of anger management, responded aggressively to frustrations and was resentful of disturbances of or threats to his personal circumstances. He was prepared to disregard the rights of others in order to maintain the integrity of his circumstances.

The Child Abuse Potential Inventory (CAP) was also administered but Martin's score on the Lie scale was so elevated that it was invalidated. However, his responses to the Novaco Anger scale showed risk scores on scales reflecting poor anger regulation and weak inhibition of aggressive responding to frustrating events. The validity index of this test was elevated but not sufficiently to invalidate the test.

Martin's results on the Parent–Child Relationship Indicator (PCRI) again revealed an aberrant score on the Social Desirability scale. The five items of this scale are seldom endorsed in a positive direction and Martin's score fell just within the population whose responses are indicative of 'faking good'. All other responses had therefore to be treated with caution. Despite the attempt to present well on this inventory, one scale showed significant results that were of concern. This was the Involvement scale and is associated with the level of interaction with a child and an understanding of him or her. Weak scores suggest parents who do not seek out much interaction with their children and have little interest in them.

As a consequence of concern over the health issue arising from the PAI profile, Martin was given the Structured Inventory of Malingered Symptomatology (SIMS). This test is used for the detection of malingering across a variety of forensic and clinical settings. His results indicated an elevated probability of feigned symptomatology. This finding was set aside for separate investigation but obviously raised a further concern about Martin's willingness to present openly.

The findings of the battery were discussed with Martin who initially displayed considerable anger over the results, particularly with the evidence of impression management. He prevaricated at length over this aspect of the findings and demanded to be accepted as a truthful person rather than a liar. He stated that he had never lied in his life and thought of himself as one of the most honest people he knew in his age group. Much of his tirade revealed that he had come to believe his own self-statements even though they were manifestly wrong. During this angry and threatening diatribe he completely forgot the findings about poor anger management, response to frustration, disregard of others' rights and weakness of involvement with his son. When reminded of the whole set of findings he capitulated and accepted that the profile was correct. He stated honestly that it would probably have been worse if he answered the items openly. His admission of guilt followed swiftly. He had shaken his son when his wife was out leaving him with the baby who cried loudly for his mother. His wife became incensed that he had allowed suspicion to fall on her also. She stated that she was going to leave him, taking their son with her. Martin immediately professed great remorse and punctuated his statements of shame and guilt with crying, rocking back and forth and biting at his hands. He told her how good it was finally to confess and lift that burden 'of a moment of madness' from his shoulders. His fluid transition from injured innocence to abject misery left her speechless but not moved to forgiveness.

It is clear that this case does not show the apparently contradictory SDR and criminal risk findings that Mills and colleagues report (see p. 118). It supports the common-sense opinion that some offenders who show high SDR tendencies, particularly in respect of impression management, are likely to be attempting to present themselves as less risky for the future than they actually are. In addition, this case study introduces another facet of other-deception, that of malingering. The term malingering refers to the behaviour of pretending or exaggerating the symptoms of mental or physical illness for one or more of a variety of personal gains such as financial compensation; reduction of criminal sentences; avoiding work, school, or exams; attempting to obtain medication; or simply to gain sympathy. Rogers (2008) discusses the significant impact this behaviour has on response styles. Consistent research findings demonstrate that malingering is strongly associated with impression management (e.g. Kucharski *et al.*, 2007).

Summary

The presentation of remorse by perpetrators is associated with diminution of punitive responses towards them. Offenders who present remorse during their trials may receive lighter sentences if they are convincing and judges use a variety of sources of evidence to establish the credibility of expressed remorse. It is expected that what offenders state about their remorse should be congruent with their non-verbal communication; contrition must be displayed and judged to be serious. Observers must be sure that the wrongdoers really do feel sorry for their actions. Analysis of the criteria associated with the evaluation of remorse shows that offenders must acknowledge their crimes as defined by the courts, express suffering associated with shame and the pain caused to their victims rather than any personal privations associated with their arrest and also show evidence of transformation from criminality to atonement. Regrettably, however, the process of attributing remorse has been found to be inconsistent and not guided by an agreed operational definition. This may result in inappropriate early release for offenders who have merely feigned contrition and so continue to present a high risk of recidivism. Furthermore, it may contribute to the reasons why there appears to be little negative association between expressed contrition and recidivism.

Religious conversion is sometimes presented in support of claims of genuine remorse but there appear to be no effective tests of the credibility of such claims and opinion is divided as to whether such claims should be taken account of in sentencing decisions. It is noteworthy that the most credible published claims of conversion are those that are backed by independent observations of charitable actions presented over a substantial period of time.

Assumptions that offenders make use of impression management to persuade officials in the judiciary of their remorse and transformation do not appear to be fully supported by research. Analysis of the populations of offenders sampled show, however, that the subjects had already been sentenced and were, for the most part, in custody. This suggests that their motivation for faking good might be lower than if they were still at the pre-trial stage. Evidence suggests that psychometric investigation using self-report measures that incorporate scales of social desirability responding may assist in determining the authenticity of claims of transformation and remorse.

Chapter 6

Religion, spirituality and remorse

Introduction

There can be little doubt that religion is the subject of wildly divergent and extreme views with a full spectrum of opinion in between. A significantly positive and commonly held attitude is exemplified by Ralph Waldo Emerson who commented, 'Religion is to do right. It is to love, it is to serve, it is to think, it is to be humble.' A significantly discrepant attitude was expressed by Larry Flynt who commented, 'Religion has caused more harm than any other idea since the beginning of time. There's nothing good I can say about it. People use it as a crutch.' These opposed views of religion mirror the evolution of psychological theory. At one point the main thrust of psychological opinion was that religion was not good for people, even if it was not particularly bad for them. More recently, opinion seems to have veered toward a cautious positive view of involvement with religion; perhaps it may be good for you after all. Koenig (2009) summarises the general outcome of research findings thus:

> Religious beliefs provide a sense of meaning and purpose during difficult life circumstances that assist with psychological integration; they usually promote a positive world view that is optimistic and hopeful; they provide role models in sacred writings that facilitate acceptance of suffering; they give people a sense of indirect control over circumstances, reducing the need for personal control; and they offer a community of support, both human and divine, to help reduce isolation and loneliness. Unlike many other coping resources, religion is available to anyone at any time, regardless of financial, social, physical, or mental circumstances.
>
> (p. 285)

This chapter is not about the psychology of religion and its evolution, although inevitably the changing perspective over time must influence content. Instead, this chapter examines the relationship that religion and spirituality have with each other and lays a foundation for examining their impact on the response of individuals to wrongdoing from the perspective of both victims and offenders. Does religious affiliation and commitment make the presentation of genuine remorse more or less likely? Genuine remorse, used in this context, is that which leads to some form of atonement and even, perhaps, to forgiveness.

Previous chapters have suggested that genuinely religious people are more likely to experience shame, guilt and remorse, although those from authoritarian and fundamentalist persuasions may experience less of these negative emotions because their religious beliefs enable them to act in ways that cause harm in the name of their religion. It is the case also that non-religious people, including many who are opposed to the concept of religion, are capable of profound remorse. A tragic example is provided by the suicide of a middle-aged atheist who could not forgive himself after he killed a child who ran in front of his car. Although the parents never blamed him and he was not driving carelessly, he could not cope with his remorse and believed that the only atonement he could make was to take his own life.

Perhaps, therefore, there is something that transcends formal religion, that can impact on people across the religious/non-religious divide to bring out the moral imperatives of prosocial behaviour. It can be argued that spirituality is that transcendent force. If that is correct, then it is logical to argue that the experience of genuine remorse, that cuts across religious and non-religious belief structures, has much to do with spirituality. The following sections, therefore, consider the nature of religion and spirituality.

Religion and spirituality

Religion

A brief section in a single chapter cannot even scratch the surface of the labyrinthine theological, moral, philosophical, scientific and faith-based theories and opinions on the subject of religion. Religion has been a part of human existence from prehistoric times and the question 'What is religion? has been debated over thousands of years by thinkers from many civilisations and cultures. That debate goes on unresolved, and over the centuries, concepts of religion and spirituality have, in tides of opinion and rhetoric, advanced and receded to and from each other. If there is any agreement among these thinkers, it is only within the self-evident truth that there is considerable overlap; that religion and spirituality have shared domains of influence and even some interdependence. And yet it is also self-evident that there are many differences such that it is perfectly possible for individuals to have spiritual lives without attributing them to any religion.

Religion has been a dominant characteristic of all recorded civilisations and cultures. It remains incredibly diverse, ranging from simple belief in a naturalistic spirit world that permeates the functioning of primitive cultures to the complexity of modern religions that suffuse and influence politics and cultural expression across the developed world. Typically, religion is conceptualised as collections of beliefs about the nature, purpose and origin of human life and, to a lesser extent, the universe. Creation is attributed to a supernatural agency that has many names across and within cultures. Religious practices define the relationships humans have with this divine agency and, in many cases, to attendant holy, sacred and revered figures that appear throughout the histories of religions. Many religious people believe that we come from God and to God we will return once our lives have run their course.[1]

Although religiousness is a private experience in terms of how each religious individual relates to the divine, religions have public faces and platforms. These take the shape of formal ritual and other organised behaviour of observance and worship. Holy places provide the centres for mass congregational activity and pilgrimage. Clerical hierarchies maintain order, determine the content of religious teaching and dictate, more or less benignly, the format of belief. These structures are usually evident across all religions, whether they are internalised and transcultural or smaller, indigenous and culture-specific. Many play lip-service to each other, but there are few that are not proclaimed to be the one true religion by their adherents. As in most political structures, there are internecine strifes that diminish the communal good that organised religion can do.

The meaning of religion has varied significantly across time, place and culture. Typically, it is used to denote the relationship that human beings have with the divine however that may be conceptualised within specific cultures but universally accepted as that which is transcendent, greater than humanity, and usually associated with the creation and purpose of human existence. More recently, the meaning of religion has become associated with diversity within humanity that is characterised by distinctive beliefs, actions, commitments and ways of thinking and living together. This is religion as an immanent rather than transcendent feature of human life.

In terms of world religions, Islam emphasises transcendence whereas Buddhism emphasises immanence; Christianity, however, spans both with a belief in God being all around us and yet also within us (e.g. Nelson, 2009). People find his works in the miraculous saving of miners from entombment and the patient dedication of a loving mother for her profoundly disabled child. God is perceived to be omnipresent, omnipotent, infinitely just, holy and loving, and all knowing. God loves us but also God is the love within us.

Many adults might agree that their life experiences include those that are transcendent in that they are beyond comprehension, emotional and spiritual. These experiences go beyond the self-improvements that take people into new areas of skilled behaviour, feelings or understanding. Education and training can help in transcending our present state of knowledge and awareness, just as new social interactions can increase our emotional range and sensitivity. Such changes are examples of self-transcendence; they are within our grasp and control and they require no divine assistance. Other experiences, however, go beyond self-transcendence and often teach us that events occur that are well beyond our control and understanding. These experiences do not leave us unchanged and usually disturb the general and routine progression of our lives.

Ben, a life-long non-believer who joked that he had even been expelled from Sunday School, found himself visiting church after church to pray for his little son who was crippled by a weakening heart and having little hope of reaching his next birthday. All attempts to find a new heart had failed and Ben watched his child die slowly. He had had no faith in prayer, rejected the religion his parents thrust at him and espoused agnosticism. Yet, as he watched his son's life ebb away, he turned desperately to the possibility that his parents' faith had had some meaning. 'I kept thinking about the old adage that there are no atheists in foxholes so I suppose I jumped into the first one I found.'

Another child died and gave Ben's son the heart he needed just as he had become almost too weak to operate on. His life was saved by the thinnest of margins. Ben said, 'I cannot write this off to chance. I cannot simply go back to the humdrum of my old life. Even if it was just coincidence it cannot feel like that to me. I have no doubt; someone or something tilted the scales our way.'

It is clear that the experience of and response to many transcendent events places them beyond psychological enquiry that is dependent on the logical progression of scientific method. Transcendence goes beyond logic such that its nature becomes a matter of faith rather than proof. Some religious people, theists, share a belief that transcendence is evidence of the personal nature of God. Others, non-theists, acknowledge transcendence but do not believe that there is any evidence therein of a personal quality. Buddhism typifies this stance.

An alternative to a focus on transcendence is one on immanescence that conceptualises religion as a distinctive type of human activity. For example, Smart (1998), when considering varieties of Indian religion and early Hinduism, posits a number of dimensions of religious activity that span the world's major religions. The first concerns Ritual and Practice such as prayer, meditation and worship. The second is the Experiential and Emotional Dimension and concerns the empowering feelings brought to religious practices to give them the vitality and potency that prevents them from becoming simply arid acting-out without point or relevance. The Narrative and Myth Dimension provides the stories underpinning religions. These are the narratives and myths for the preservation of truths and integration of the 'structure' of religions. Within these are issues about life and death, creation, parables that teach vital moral lessons, and descriptions of the central figures such as the life of the Prophet Muhammad, the burning bush and Moses, the enlightenment of Buddha and the resurrection of Jesus. Included within this dimension are the material substance of religions such as scriptural texts, relics and icons.

Placing the substance of religion into a structure requires the activity of the Doctrinal and Philosophical Dimension. This enables the religious teachings to be presented in intellectually coherent arrangements. From these the Ethical and Legal activities are derived; those that provide rules for human behaviour and that may have been revealed within a supernatural context.

The Social and Institutional Dimension enables religions to be embodied in external form. This may be a simple grouping of worshippers or it may refer to the full complexities of the mosque, synagogue, church or sangha. This is the dimension where religion may be seen to work among its adherents. Finally, Smart refers to the physical symbols of religions, be they incredibly ornate structures as in the Eastern Orthodox and Catholic churches, eschewed by Calvinists as idolatrous from their elegantly simple churches, or natural features that have especial significance (e.g. the Mount of Olives, Ayers Rock, the River Ganges, Mount Sinai).

The activities associated with these dimensions are seen by Smart to delineate religions and provide bedrock for the beliefs of their adherents. As Smart points out, however, this schematisation of religion could equally be applied to secular movements such as Marxism and humanism, but argues that this is not appropriate as such movements portray themselves as antireligious. Almost by semantic slight of hand, such movements are accepted as providing a world view by contributing 'a basic set of assumptions and way of thinking about self, the world and our place in it' (Nelson, 2009, p. 6). This is true for humanism that, in its unadulterated form, espouses the basic good and worth of humanity in much the same way as Christianity, for example, asserts the love of God and its power to do good on Earth.

A further attempt to present religion as an activity attributes it to culture in that it can be conceived of as a complex facet of adapting to and living in a particular social context. This allows individuals to adopt the constructs of their culture that describe and make sense of the world (Nelson, 2009). One advantage of viewing religion as a human activity is that it is then possible to investigate it using functional analysis, a commonly used tool of the psychological study of behaviour. This analysis enables the study of religion in terms of what it does for its adherents. This may be more important than a substantive analysis that is concerned primarily with examination of the content of a religion and the structure of its beliefs. Berger (1974) argues, however, that functional analysis of religion encourages movement away from transcendence and enables a quasi-scientific legitimisation of its avoidance. He advocates a return to substantive analysis in order to counter this. Neither form of analysis can deal with the degree of ardour participants display in practising their chosen religion. Both functionality and belief may be very different across the continuum from zealots at one end to the ambivalently half-hearted at the other. In addition, aspects of any given religion may have greater meaning for some adherents than others. Since most religions span both immanence and transcendence, it is quite possible that those who attach great significance to religious ritual and traditions will look more towards their religion's transcendency. Those who care more for the influence of their religion on the way they live their lives will pay more heed to immanence and less to ritual.

There would appear to be no definition of religion that is entirely satisfactory. The obvious similarities with the world views of secular movements and the range of preference of adherents concerning which aspects of their chosen religion they particularly cleave to makes a formal and embracing definition an unlikely aspiration.

Spirituality

Originally, 'spirituality' was the term used to provide a dividing line between the holy lives of religious officiates and the more worldly lives of the laity. In the recent past, however, it was strongly linked to Spiritualism, the belief in psychic phenomena and attempts to contact the dead. More recently still, it has become a preferred term used in a general manner to demarcate the experiential and personal characteristics one has in relation to the transcendent and sacred domains of life (e.g. Nelson, 2009). This may seem to many as being religion without the rituals and structure of communal worship. Zinnbauer and colleagues warn against attempting to strenuously differentiate between religiosity and spirituality. After a detailed review of the meanings and significance attributed to both, they caution,

> The polarization of religiousness and spirituality can yield only a limited understanding of the two constructs. For example, opposing "institutional" religion to "personal" spirituality ignores the fact that virtually every major religious institution is ardently concerned with spiritual matters . . . In fact, the primary objective of religious organizations is to bring individuals closer to God . . . or to whatever is defined as the transcendent. Certainly some groups may be more effective at this task than others, and some groups may have lost sight of this goal, but the search for the sacred[2] remains the most fundamental of religious missions.
>
> (Zinnbauer et al., 1999, p. 903)

It is inevitable, therefore, that there is a significant overlap in meaning and description. Indeed, some theologians have argued that spirituality is the experience of individuals whose lives are enriched by religion. Ingersoll (1994) reviews descriptions of spirituality; some include the theme of a journey towards communication and union with God. Other descriptions suggest that spirituality is an attitude that emphasises creative choice making, energy and a powerful force for living. Most imply an approach to living that is directed towards the transcendent.

Harry Aponte (1998) expresses similar views in relation to the spiritual base of psychotherapy. He states,

> I use the term spirituality . . . broadly, referring to the meaning, purpose and values in people's lives. As a therapist who is trying to understand people and help them navigate through the pain, conflicts and mysteries of life, I am looking for what drives their lives. Spirituality, for me, is how they understand life, where they want to go with it, and the standards by which they measure and judge life. It is the pursuit of money, sex and power or the idealization of poverty, chastity and humility, and everything in between and combinations thereof. It lies in the god of the belly or in the transcendent God of religion. It is what drives and/or we believe should drive our lives. For most of us it is complex, conflicted and fragmented. Its roots are everywhere in our lives: our cultural heritage, racial identity, politics, everyday philosophical views and our religious convictions. Spirituality as the explanation, drive and measure of life operates everywhere: in our institutions, our personal relationships and in our psyches. The world of therapy, like its subject – the living of life – is imbued with spirituality of every shape, colour and texture.
>
> (pp. 37–8)

Ingersoll (1994) provides a schematisation of spirituality that employs seven dimensions: meaning, conception of divinity, relationship, mystery, experience, play and integration. These are now considered briefly.

Meaning   Citing Frankl, Ingersoll (1994) refers to an innate human 'will to meaning that manifests itself as a search for an ultimate meaning for the individual life' (Ingersoll, 1994, p. 101). In general, the often over-used meaning in this context appears to refer to the learnt outcome of those experiences that individuals believe enhance the quality of their lives. Included within these experiences is the perception of beauty and other forms of aesthetic appreciation. To this I add Maslow's drive towards self-actualisation that is a motivation for personal growth associated with the desire for self-transcendence through new learning and experience (Maslow, 1971).

Conception of divinity   It is axiomatic that an individual's spiritual life must include a curiosity about the nature of that which transcends human existence. Whether this is thought of by individuals to be the Divine or the Sacred or the Force from Star Wars makes little difference. Ingersoll (1994) categorises these conceptualisations under four headings. Theists relate to a single primary being or force. Atheists deny any concept of divinity; they eschew belief in any deities and are sceptical of the supernatural. Pantheists believe in an absolute being or force that pervades everything, including themselves. Finally, individuals who subscribe to pantheism believe the force or being not only moves through everything but also transcends all things. These descriptions are not rigid and Ingersoll takes care to point out that variations occur, according to gender, temperament and the nature of personal relationship.

Relationship   This dimension concerns the ways in which individuals relate to their conceptualisation of the divine, if they have one, and to other people also. Much of what is written on this aspect of spirituality appears to me as lacking descriptive rigour, but the general theme is the individual's awareness of a non-corporeal linkage between self, other people, natural phenomena and a transcendent being or force such that this awareness assists in making life worthwhile and meaningful.

Mystery   This refers to the ambiguity or ineffability of the spiritual; the indistinct boundary between the real world and that of the transcendent. It is beyond the compass of language to describe the interface of everyday living with the spiritual life of individuals in that realm where they are comfortable with the indefinable and an inability to discover fact or reason.

Play   It is supposed that spirituality has a playful dimension where the individual's reality succumbs to a pleasurable experience beyond daily living. It is seen as the rejuvenation or refreshment of aesthetic qualities that may otherwise be suffocated by daily necessities and routines.

Experience   The experience of spirituality is regarded as vibrant and sometimes ecstatic 'peak experiences' as Maslow (1971) referred to them. He believed that these peak experiences could exert an influence on the ideals in the secular world and stimulate desire for greater meaning. Nevertheless, one's spirituality is not entirely filled with peak experiences; aesthetic qualities can be found also in the experience of the mundane and humdrum events of everyday life. This theme is echoed in several major religions where ritualistic behaviours are designed to nurture these experiences. Ingersoll (1994) comments that experiencing the sacred characteristics of the ordinary is fundamental to theological concepts.

Integration   This is probably the most important of all the dimensions. It enables the other dimensions to function as a synergy, allowing individuals to connect their religious experiences, beliefs and practices with their everyday experiences such that the combination moves towards transcendence.

There are several other organisational frameworks of spirituality in the literature. LaPierre (1994), for example, provided a structure for spirituality comprised of a number of spiritual categories of activities: a search for meaning in life; an encounter with transcendence; a sense of community; a search for ultimate truth, or highest value; a respect and appreciation for the mystery of creation and a personal transformation.

The religion–spirituality connections

The brief consideration of the meaning of religion and spirituality above provides no embracing definition for either, separately or together. Many reviews of the literature (e.g. Zinnbauer *et al.*, 1999; Hill *et al.*, 2000) lead one to the conclusion that it is impossible to provide descriptions of concepts that mean different things to different people, different cultures, different disciplines and different styles of enquiry. As Hill and colleagues state: 'Indeed, if any belief or activity that provides individuals with a sense of identity or meaning . . . is defined as a religion or spiritual endeavor, then this field literally knows no bounds' (Hill *et al.*, 2000, p. 71). The association of religion and spirituality with a search for the sacred at least limits meaning and activities associated with them to a core facet, which if absent, rules out other activities that help people to find significance in their lives.

It is clear, however, that both spirituality and religion share similar characteristics that reflect seeking the existential and striving for trans-cendence. Both activities are associated with the sacred but need not be associated with the organisation and formality of religion. This makes clear that while religion cannot be separated from spirituality, the latter does not require religion in order for individuals to have a spiritual life. Indeed, as Vaughan *et al.* (1996) suggest 'spirituality, unlike religion, does not require obedience to a particular set of beliefs or prescribed dogma' (p. 500). In a similar vein, Sussman *et al.* (1997) comment that whereas spirituality concerns transcendental processes that supersede ordinary existence, religion requires the adoption of a set of beliefs that are organised and institutionalised. It may be stated, therefore, that spirituality encompasses religion, leaving open the doors for non-religious people to seek the sacred alongside those who adhere strongly to their particular religions. Partaking in practices or activities that are thought of as religious expressions cannot be considered as spiritual unless they involve the sacred. Saucier and Skrzypinska (2006) have demonstrated that spirituality and tradition-oriented religiousness are independent dimensions and should not be considered as a unitary phenomenon. This study used 325 adult Americans who responded to questions about religious denominational affiliation and items tapping expressions of spirituality. Other scales were used to evaluate impression management, eccentricity, collectivism, conformity, magical thinking, authoritarianism and associated variables. They concluded that subjective spirituality and tradition-oriented religiousness are highly independent and are associated with different correlates among personality variables.

This independence does not mean that there is no sharing of characteristics. Indeed, there are points of congruity that occur over a wide area of psychological study. An appreciation of these helps to locate the mediators of shame, guilt and remorse such that the experience of being sorry for wrongdoing can be related to the spiritual and religious lives of transgressors.

Religion, spirituality and development

The growth and development of conscience was considered in Chapter 1. This was shown to be a developmental process with each stage contributing to a greater and more sophisticated reasoning about moral issues and events. Religion and spirituality are also developmental phenomena that parallel general development across the life span. Some developmentalists consider that these aspects of human growth may be so integral that they provide a unique perspective on general development. For example, Elkind (1964) distinguished children's spontaneous religion from their acquired religion. He stated: 'The child's spontaneous religion consists of all those ideas and beliefs that he has constructed in his attempts to interpret religious terms and practices that are beyond his level of comprehension' (p. 40). Acquired religion, however, consists of those

> religious ideas and beliefs that the child acquires directly from adults either through imitation or through instruction. A child's recitation of the standard definition of theological terms or of particular prayers would thus reflect acquired rather than spontaneous religion.
>
> (p. 40)

Elkind shows that the growth of spontaneous religious beliefs follows normal patterns of Piagetian cognitive developmental growth from concrete to formal operational thinking. Barrett (2000) states:

> children easily adopt ideas about gods, ghosts, Santa Claus and other agents possessing supernatural properties, and use ordinary conceptual resources for reasoning with these concepts. Furthermore, many of the properties that set religious entities apart from natural agents might actually be easily accommodated by children's less developed conceptual systems.
>
> (p. 29)

Hill et al. (2000) note also the shared relevance of religion and spirituality in psychological development across diverse cultures.

Cognition, religion and spirituality

Given the developmental context of religion and spirituality, it is not surprising that they are related to cognitive events. This understanding opens up new avenues for the investigation of religion and spirituality. Barrett (2000) states:

> The new cognitive science of religion was motivated by a dissatisfaction with the vagueness of previous theories of religion, and thus their inability to be empirically tested, as well as by a desire to extend the psychological scholarship concerning concepts and causation. It differs from previous approaches to the study of religion by insisting that much of what is typically called 'religion' may be understood as the natural product of aggregated ordinary cognitive processes.
>
> (p.29)

Previously, McCallister (1995) opined that psychological religious and spiritual events are explicable in terms of contemporary cognitive theory. In support of the importance of cognitive function as a primary factor, Hunsberger *et al.* (1996) found that there were significant cognitive differences between high and low Christian fundamentalists. They stated:

> low fundamentalists were more likely to question the underpinnings of religion, while high fundamentalists' doubts seemed to focus on concerns that others are not living up to religious ideals or that adjustments should be made within the church, rather than doubts about God or religion per se.
>
> (p. 201)

Not surprisingly, there is some disquiet among theologians that religious experiences may be made explicable, and thereby reduced to cognitive events bounded by cognitive theory. Slingerland (2008) has, however, defended the use of the tools and knowledge of the natural sciences from the charge of reductionism. He argues that 'reductionism is ultimately an empty term of abuse – any explanation worthy of being called an explanation involves reductionism of some sort' (p. 375). It is not obvious why religious belief and commitment should be lessened or reduced in significance by an understanding of the cognitive development and processes that give rise to it, but people may believe that such understanding could mitigate against the transcendent striving of religiosity. Perhaps the fear arises from a perception of intellectual elitism exemplified by Bertrand Russell's comment, 'Religion is something left over from the infancy of our intelligence; it will fade away as we adopt reason and science as our guidelines' (1953, p. 109).

Religion, spirituality and affect

Being sorry about transgression involves both cognition and emotions. Religion and spirituality are, as discussed above, evident as cognitive experiences, but their associations with affect are also as significantly linked to emotional expression. For example, Zinnbauer and Pargament (1998) described the role of affect in respect of religious conversion. Perceived life-stress prior to conversion was subjectively judged to be lower after it and converts also reported that they experienced greater personal adequacy and competence after their conversion.

Ros had three periods of inpatient treatment as a consequence of stress-induced anxiety disorder. She had been sexually abused by an uncle during early adolescence and the severe post-traumatic effects of this had not been resolved. Her tolerance of minor conflicts, frustrations and other common stressors was low such that her functioning became maladaptive and bizarre.

During her third period as an inpatient she worked with a young Christian psychiatric nurse who talked to her about her spiritual and religious life. Ros explained that she had no religion and if there was a god she would be angry at him or her for allowing the years of abuse. Patiently, however, the nurse helped Ros realise that she did have leanings towards spirituality. She had often looked for something beyond her immediate existence and sought evidence that there was more humanity and beauty in the world than she had been used to. She had looked for innocence in the peace of the countryside and the beauty of natural phenomena. She spent some time studying still life and pastoral art and turned to poetry and classic literature to find evidence of human talent to balance against human debasement. Gradually, she began to think there was a force of creation, an influence well beyond the capabilities of human beings. Ros began to attend church services with the nurse and was introduced to a theologian who spoke with her about transcendence rather than religion. She had felt calmed and began to understand that she had, like all other decent people, a worthy place in the world.

It is also the case that the manner by which emotional arousal is assessed cognitively is significant as a determining factor of the expression of religious and spiritual events (Hill, 1995). Fuller (2006) believes that several emotions are particularly associated with developing cognitive structures. He is particularly aware of the influence of the emotion of wonder and is influenced in this by the work of Plutchik. He states:

> wonder would be grouped not with 'emotions of avoidance' but rather with 'emotions of enhanced rapport' such as joy, amazement, or interest. Various researchers have suggested, for example, that the emotion of joy motivates approach and belongingness – traits shared with the emotion of wonder. The emotion of interest, meanwhile, is also linked with wonder in that it motivates attention and thereby promotes greater awareness of the environment.
>
> (pp. 366–7)

After reviewing its nature and influence Fuller opines, 'wonder is at least one principal source of adult spirituality' (p. 365). However, following their study of elders, Schlehofer *et al.* (2008) concluded that those who identified themselves as spiritual rather than religious might miss out on a variety of benefits in times of need. These include benefits of community affiliation associated with religion that appear to be greater for religious people in times of need.

Religion, spirituality and personality

There is a long history of understanding that religion, spirituality and personality have an integral association. Abraham Maslow, the founder of humanistic psychology, has already been mentioned in relation to his concept of 'peak experiences', particular transpersonal and ecstatic states that are often flavoured with euphoria, harmony and a feeling that there are connecting strands to all things. He stated that respondents described these experiences as revelatory and possessing mystical, ineffable or religious significance (Maslow, 1970). At a more prosaic level, psychometric studies point to a significant relationship between personality variables recorded by self-report and observer-report instruments and religiosity. Typically, the findings suggest strongly that individuals who express traditional, church-centred religious beliefs and practices are generally responsible, well-controlled, sociable and tender-minded. In particular, there is a well-demonstrated positive relation between religiousness and the Big Five measures of Agreeableness and Conscientiousness (for example, see Saroglou, 2002, for review).

Further research demonstrates that the link between personality variables and religiosity/spirituality is one that unfolds developmentally. For example, Wink and colleagues (2007) made use of observer-based schedules in a longitudinal study and reported:

> In late adulthood, religiousness was positively related to Conscientiousness and Agreeableness, and spiritual seeking was related to Openness to Experience . . . Conscientiousness in adolescence significantly predicted religiousness in late adulthood above and beyond adolescent religiousness. Similarly, Openness in adolescence predicted spiritual seeking in late adulthood. The converse effect, adolescent religiousness to personality in late adulthood, was not significant in either model. Among women, adolescent Agreeableness predicted late-life religiousness and adolescent religiousness predicted late-life Agreeableness; both these effects were absent among men.
>
> (p. 1051)

A study by Salsman *et al.* (2005) examined the variables of optimism, social support, religiousness and spirituality. Salsman and colleagues made use of the descriptive dichotomy of intrinsic and extrinsic religiousness provided originally by Allport to define the religiousness variable. Intrinsic religiousness comprises faith 'as a supreme value in its own right. It is oriented toward a unification of being, takes seriously the commandment of brotherhood, and strives to transcend all self-centered needs' (Allport, 1966, p. 455). Extrinsic religiousness is, however, 'strictly utilitarian; useful for the self in granting safety, social standing, solace and endorsement for one's chosen way of life' (p. 455). In short, intrinsic religiousness has transcendence at its core, whereas extrinsic religiousness looks mostly to the temporal and need not owe anything to spirituality.

The purpose of the study by Salsman and colleagues was to investigate whether optimism and social support influenced the relationship between religiousness and adjustment, and between spirituality and adjustment. The latter variable was examined in terms of levels of distress and life satisfaction. It was found that the relationship between intrinsic religiousness and life satisfaction, and between prayer fulfilment and life satisfaction was mediated by both optimism and social support. The researchers also found that

> the relationship between religiousness and adjustment varied depending on how religiousness was operationalized and whether positive versus negative adjustment indicators were used. That is, intrinsic religiousness and prayer fulfilment were associated with greater life satisfaction, but extrinsic religiousness was not associated with life satisfaction. These findings were significant even after accounting for covariates (age, gender, ethnicity, social desirability). Results suggest religiousness and spirituality are related but distinct constructs and are associated with adjustment through factors such as social support and optimism.
>
> (Salsman *et al.*, 2005, p. 522)

These findings support the opinion that personality variables have much to do with individuals' openness to the affirmation of transcendence in their lives and the satisfactions that this may bring. Despite the expediency of extrinsic religiousness, there may be little to be gained from it in terms of life satisfaction. It is reasonable to suggest that intrinsic religiousness has much to do with life satisfaction and spirituality, and the absence of the latter leaves the presentation of religiousness as a flawed and hollow extemporisation.

Religion, spirituality and social benefits

Religion and spirituality are associated with benefits to society both nationally and internationally. It is noteworthy that people of different faiths come together to provide aid and support to the victims of earthquakes, war, famine and disease, and at times of great distress and disaster generally. People from multifaith communities often combine to establish ways and means of improving their shared environment, to assist their young people, combat drug dealing and provide care systems for the needy. I have been touched by examples I have witnessed of great religious divides being ignored when a need arises. A simple example springs to mind.

One Saturday on a London street I saw a young man dressed as an Hasidic Jew struggle with a roll of carpet and a bag of shopping. His load was slipping precariously and he was seconds away from dropping everything. I moved forward to help him but was beaten to it by another young man wearing a Moslem taqiyah prayer cap. The load was saved. Both men laughed and spoke kindly to each other. They seemed completely oblivious to the huge gulf between their cultures as they went their separate ways. Down the same street were a mosque, synagogue and chapel, all within a few hundred yards of each other. People wandered in and out of them and paused to chatter to each other outside the small supermarket that provided a focus for them all, irrespective of their different faiths.

Most major religions encourage their adherents to act charitably, support the health and welfare of others, and assist vulnerable people. In addition, prayer and meditation are advocated to help heal illness and improve the lot of distressed people. Bainbridge (1989) suggests that violent crimes and other forms of deviancy are significantly reduced simply by the close presence of visible religion such as churches, mosques and synagogues. He concludes, however, that while religion has an inhibiting effect on some deviant acts (e.g. violent crime), it does not on others (e.g. suicide). It is important to note, however, that the religious rejection of deviancy is congruent with the norms of the local culture for the effect to be influential (Hill *et al.*, 2000). The social benefits of religion and spirituality are embedded in their social and psychological grounding. Organised religion is inevitably expressed in a social context and, in my experience, groups may form to investigate their ideas on spiritual matters, particularly in respect of transcendency. Of especial interest to the experience of remorse and the expression of atonement are the behavioural expectations and guidance provided by religious observance. Most major religions provide their adherents with instruction on how atonement should be made, whether this is through penance or restitution.

Religion, spirituality and protective factors

There are several other similarities between spirituality and religion but those described briefly above are of particular significance to considerations of remorse. Previous discussion has indicated that remorse is motivated by the negative emotions of shame and guilt, and that it involves cognitive processing (i.e. the sequential workings of conscience) and often finds expression within a socio-psychological behavioural context (e.g. some form of atonement). In addition, personality variables influence propensity to remorse, without which atonement is either impossibility or a sham arising from the intention of minimising negative feedback from victims and their supporters. Given that religion and spirituality are also influenced by these variables, it is probable that remorse and its expression are influenced by them as well. It is therefore relevant to consider what religion and spirituality actually bring to people in terms of guidance and other benefits. A particular area of interest is that of mental health. Shame, guilt and remorse are, as discussed previously, linked to anxiety and depression. Do religion and spirituality offer any mental health benefits that in turn make it more possible for individuals to manage their negative emotions that emanate from wrongdoing?

Religion, spirituality and mental health

There has been considerable research into the effects of religion and spirituality (often abbreviated to RS) on mental health. Some of this research has differentiated the variable of spirituality, albeit most is associated with religious observance. In general, the outcomes have revealed that RS has positive influences on mental health, although that is not uniformly the case. Koenig (2009), for example, concluded that religious belief and practice 'are often intricately entangled with neurotic and psychotic disorders, sometimes making it difficult to determine whether they are a resource or a liability' (p. 283). It is, however, noteworthy that the positive effects of spirituality on mental health 'apply across boundaries and religions' (Baetz and Toews, 2009, p. 292).

There are some caveats associated with the consideration of the effects of RS on mental health. A substantive one is satisfactorily described in terms of the distinctions made by Allport (1966) between intrinsic and extrinsic religiousness. This has already been mentioned in the previous section but further description may be helpful here. In essence, adherents who practise an extrinsic religiosity do so for largely egotistical purposes; they gain positive self-reinforcement from reassurance, insulation from self-doubt, social activities with other adherents and self-aggrandisement. Those who have intrinsic religiosity are genuine seekers of transcendence and usually find their reason for being in the core beliefs of their faith. In my experience, these intrinsically motivated individuals practise spirituality through religious observance.

There is a marked contrast between these different forms of religiousness in respect of mental health. For example, intrinsic religiousness is associated with lower levels of depression in comparison with extrinsic religiousness. Smith *et al.* (2003) made use of a meta-analytic study across 147 independent investigations of the relationship between religiousness and depressive symptoms. They found a modest but significant negative correlation between religiousness and depression that supports the opinion that religiousness acts as a protective factor associated with fewer symptoms. More detailed analysis, however, revealed a contrast between intrinsic and extrinsic religiousness in that the protective factor was more likely to be offered by the former, whereas extrinsic religiousness is more likely to be associated with heightened depressive symptoms.

These findings and others reviewed by Smith *et al.* (2003) confirm the expectation that the spiritual aspects of faith offer greater protection than a religious observance that is either imposed and/or motivated by self-interest without faith. There are some interesting explanations for this arising out of consideration of the possible mechanisms that underpin the association of religiousness with mental health. One example, drawn from the work of Kenneth Pargament, concerns the coping measures adopted by religious people. He and his colleagues introduced the concept of religious coping measures (see Chapter 3) as a set of coping styles including self-directing, deferring, collaboration and surrender (Pargament *et al.*, 1988). Subsequently, other researchers have modified these somewhat (e.g. Zondag and van Outen, 2010). In essence, Pargament's research leads him to opine that religious beliefs that are intrinsically motivated, internalised and espouse a secure faith in God are linked positively to mental health. Conversely, religions that are authoritarian, accepted without question or examination, and are only tentatively mediated by belief in God are negatively associated with mental health. Spirituality, transcendency, admiration of the natural world and the place of humanity within it, combine with both public and personal religious behaviour (worship, prayer, etc.) to augment the potency of positive coping through the positive emotions of gratitude, compassion, forgiveness, hope and optimism.

Horning *et al.* (2011) make the point that most of the research on coping has ignored non-religious groups. Their own research was designed to make comparisons between religious and non-religious (atheist and agnostic) groups on a variety of measures. The measures enabled the assessment of relationships between well-being and religiosity, social support, locus of control and meaning of life in respect of older adults (+55 years, mean age +65.6 years). These participants presented a range of beliefs from high to low religious observance, atheistic and agnosticism and were examined in relation to coping behaviours. The results revealed that the groups did not differ significantly on satisfaction with social support, locus of control and well-being. The highly religious participants did experience greater belief in meaning of life than the atheists and a greater number of social supports in comparison with the non-religious participants. The religious groups significantly endorsed religious coping styles in contrast to the others. The atheist participants were more likely to endorse substance use to help them cope and additionally made use of humour to assist coping to a significantly greater extent than the religious participants. It is of significance that religious coping did not offer a significantly greater sense of well-being than non-religious coping.

On a different tack, James and Wells (2003) take a cognitive-behavioural approach to religious beliefs. They propose that a mental model for the appraisal of events during the life course is provided by a schema comprised of religious beliefs. They suggest that

> A religious belief system may be beneficial by enabling individuals to find meanings in stressful life events that are otherwise difficult to explain. The content of the generic beliefs held would influence the content of situational stress appraisals and so affect an individual's response.
>
> (pp. 365–6)

The attribution of religious beliefs to life events characterised by high stress could provide meaning, predictability and a perception of control. The strength of belief is proportional to the degree of mental health benefit, even if this belief is opposed to religion or is equally strongly in favour of it. Thus, extrinsic religiousness that is motivated mainly by expediency has little benefit to bestow in times of trouble. Circumstantial evidence for this cognitive-behavioural position comes from the observation that religious behaviours (e.g. meditation, prayer and communal worship) reduce self-focus and anxiety, while increasing self-regulation and calming. Thus, Wachholtz *et al.* (2007) state:

> Research has demonstrated that R/S (Religion/Spirituality) coping correlates with feelings of spiritual support, spiritual connection, peace, calmness, and decreased anxiety and results in an improvement of mood. More positive mood has been correlated with decreased sensitivity to pain and increased ability to withstand the impact of negative situations.
>
> (p. 316)

Flannelly *et al.* (2010) used a sample of 1,306 American adults to investigate the association between specific pairs of beliefs about God (Close and Loving; Approving and Forgiving; Creating and Judging) and psychiatric symptoms. Their findings revealed that the belief that God was Close and Loving had beneficial effects on mental health. None of the other pairs of beliefs investigated had any significant association. Conversely, other findings also yield support from the perspective of increased negative conditions for mental health. For example, Baetz and Toews (2009) state: 'Religiously motivated behaviours that increase self-focus and worry are associated with intrusive thoughts, thought control and undoing and poorer mental health' (p. 294).

It is clear, however, that religious/spiritual coping does have some significant relationship with the experience of mental health symptoms. As stated previously, depression and anxiety are particularly associated with guilt and shame. Remorse is associated with religion/spirituality. It is relevant, therefore, to consider the impact of RS coping on depression and anxiety.

Depression   The majority of studies of the association of religion with depression indicate that religious people are less prone to depression. Some studies reveal that remission rates are better for religious people who become depressed and other studies suggest that religion-based psychotherapies were associated with more rapid improvement than non-religious intervention (see Koenig, 2009). The large meta-analytic study of Smith *et al.* (2003) has been mentioned above. The results indicated a small negative correlation between religious involvement and depression.

Religious behaviour, taking the form of communal worship, prayer and reading scripture, is also associated with a 'protective' facet in respect of depression. For example, Koenig (2009) evaluated inpatients with and without depression. He found that

> Depressed patients were significantly more likely to indicate no religious affiliation, more likely to indicate spiritual but not religious, less likely to pray or read scripture, and scored lower on intrinsic religiosity. These relations remained robust after controlling for demographic, social, and physical health factors. Among the depressed patients, severity of depressive symptoms was also inversely related to religious indicators.
>
> (p. 286)

The negative association between religiosity and depression does not always hold. It appears to be particularly true for older participants in the relevant studies but is perhaps not evident among younger people. For example, Sorenson *et al.* (1995) studied emotional well-being among unmarried teenage mothers using prenatal and postnatal interviews. They found that 'Young mothers with no particular faith (and Protestants) appear to have experienced the lowest levels of depression. Participating in religious activities during pregnancy is actually associated with greater distress . . .' (p. 75). It is also the case that different branches of the same religion can exert different levels of 'protection' in mental health terms. For example, in relation to Christian adherents, Alferi and colleagues worked with Roman Catholic and Evangelical Hispanic women who had been recently diagnosed with breast cancer. Their religious coping strategies and levels of emotional distress pre-surgery were investigated and also for the year following surgery. The Evangelical women with higher levels of religiousness showed lower levels of distress, whereas the opposite was true for Catholic women. It was suggested that the Evangelical women's emphasis on faith, acceptance and being saved for eternity was more helpful to them than the Catholic women's greater emphasis on confession, judgement and absolution from guilt (Alferi *et al.*, 1999).

The findings discussed above suggest that intrinsic religiousness does have a protective value in respect of depression. Those people who have a genuine belief that they portray through religious observance seem to experience less of the vicissitudes of depression than those without such belief. Religion is not, however, a panacea and the more authoritarian it is or the more extrinsic its value to adherents, the less support it brings. It appears that in some instances it can cause more distress and be associated with higher levels of depression. It is probable that this has much to do with the additional burden of guilt that it may foster. The following may be an example of this.

I have often thought that one of the greatest tyrannies that can be inflicted on kindly people is the unrelenting need of others. Ruth, a caring middle-aged Jewess of good standing in her community, might well agree in her quiet moments of reflection.[3] Her ageing parents required more and more of her as she tried to share out her time between work, her children, husband and them. Although never overtly demanding, they made clear that she should give them priority and were apt to remind her of the fifth commandment, 'Honour thy father and mother.'[4] Ruth was well aware that this commandment did not just mean that children must obey their parents while they are growing up. She fully appreciated that her faith required her to ensure their well-being as far as she was able. Nevertheless, their insistent requests and polite criticism left her feeling exhausted, demeaned and clinically depressed. It was suggested to her by elders in her community that perhaps she should consider giving up her career in order to be able to spend more time with those of her family who needed her.

Fortunately, one highly respected elder pointed out that their faith did not prescribe how much time Ruth should spend with her parents or that she should have to do things for them that they were capable of doing for themselves. He also reminded her that they, as parents, had a continuing duty to be mindful of her welfare and this did not include forcing an overly stringent interpretation of scripture upon her.

Anxiety   Although not so marked, it appears that religious practice can exert a protective force against the impact of anxiety. Religious behaviours do exert calming effects and although the meditation practices of Eastern religions, particularly from the Buddhist traditions, spring most readily to mind, other religions have calming and reassuring practices also.

The associations between religion and anxiety are complex and vary across the life course. A longitudinal study conducted by Wink and Scott (2005) has been particularly helpful in clarifying the associations for people in late adulthood in respect of their fears about death and dying. Wink and Scott studied 155 participants who had been born between 1920 and 1929. They had been studied as children and then during their 30s, 40s, 50s or early 60s and into late adulthood. The study employed a variety of psychometric measures, including material for fear of dying, fear of death, religiousness and belief in an afterlife. It is axiomatic that fears of death and dying would be an issue for participants in late adulthood,[5] whereas they would probably been less affected by such fears earlier in their lives.

The results were revealing. The authors state that they found no linear relationship between fears of death and dying, and religiousness:

Individuals who were moderately religious feared death more than individuals who scored high or low on religiousness. Fear of death also characterized participants who lacked congruence between belief in an afterlife and religious practices. . . . firmness and consistency of beliefs and practices, rather than religiousness per se, buffers against death anxiety in old age.

(Wink and Scott, 2005, p. 207)

As for depression, religious adherence is not always beneficial or even merely neutral. Koenig (2009) cites research on women newly diagnosed with gynaecological cancer, revealing that those who felt God was punishing them or was powerless to help them or had deserted them, had significantly greater anxiety. Pargament and colleagues carried out a two-year longitudinal study of 268 elderly inpatients in respect of their religious coping, and spiritual, psychological and physical functioning. They concluded:

Generally, positive methods of religious coping (e.g. seeking spiritual support, benevolent religious reappraisals) were associated with improve-ments in health. Negative methods of religious coping (e.g. punishing God reappraisal, interpersonal religious discontent) were predictive of declines in health. Patients who continue to struggle with religious issues over time may be particularly at risk for health-related problems.

(Pargament et al., 2004, p. 713)

It is hard to avoid the conclusion that intrinsic religiousness confers benefits for mental health through its overarching spirituality combined with consistent religious behaviour such as prayer, worship rituals and reading scripture or associated literature. Extrinsic religiousness that is entered into for self-centred reasons, and lacking spiritual content, is associated with negative effects that may contribute further distress or augment it. The following provides an example.

Twin brothers Simon and Ian ran their father's transport business when he retired. They lived in the same street, their children went to the same school and they worshipped at the same church.

Simon regarded himself as an ordinary member of the congregation and was happy to celebrate his faith with his fellow members. He also prayed at every opportunity, giving thanks for his comfortable life, his loving family and friends. He also used arrow prayers[6] whenever he saw something that reflected the beauty of God's works or was worried about a specific situation. Simon's health was good and he felt relaxed and at peace with himself. He gave spontaneously to charities, helped any employee fallen on hard times and looked after elderly neighbours. In every observable way Simon showed intrinsic religiousness.

Ian was not content to be an ordinary member of the congregation. Even at school he had been something of a social climber, seeking out friendships with the children of wealthy families. As an adult, he recognised the material benefits of befriending 'the right people' and it was true that the family business had done well as a result. Ian tackled his religious life on the same basis; he became a member of various church and parish committees and was sure to take part in prestigious ceremonies, meeting bishops and royalty, engineering international links and visits, fundraising and campaigning in high- profile matters when local politics and church came together. His life became increasingly frenetic and remorselessly ground him down. Simon commented that Ian had many missions but little religion. Inevitably, Ian's physical and mental health collapsed and his empire building went with it. He sought solace in faith but was shocked to discover that Simon was right; he had lost his core faith and could not believe that what little belief was left had any power to help him recover. In every observable way Ian had shown extrinsic religiousness.

Religion, spirituality and well-being

Other aspects of well-being may be derived from religion and spirituality, apart from those protective factors in respect of depression and anxiety described above. These are discussed briefly in this section. The focus is on benefits from intrinsic religion rather than temporal benefits that accrue from the more superficial adherence to extrinsic religion. That, too, has its benefits but these are somewhat analogous to those gained by joining a country club in order to improve social standing and have little to do with spirituality.

Physical health

There is little doubt that there is a positive association between religion and physical health. The evidence has been accumulating over a long period that religiosity has a protective effect at both individual and group level, and some researchers believe that this effect is mediated by other intervening factors, including various bio-behavioral and psychosocial mechanisms (e.g. Chatters, 2000). Some research links the effects of stable marriage with those of religious observance to provide protective factors in respect of physical health (e.g. Waite and Lehrer, 2003). Whatever the mechanisms may be, it is increasingly clear that genuine religious faith and observance has a significant positive impact on health, even to the extent of being associated with improved longevity.

Longevity and mortality   Spirituality and religious observance effects on mortality rates have been subject to thorough research. Nelson (2009) reviews much of this work and notes that frequent church attendance and subjective religiosity are associated with increases of longevity of up to seven years and reductions in mortality rates of up to 25 per cent. Nelson comments that these improvements are similar to the impact on health of giving up smoking. Although the size of the effect is reduced for those studies that have examined participants who have had terminal illness such as cancer (e.g. Strawbridge *et al.* (1997), it is noteworthy that the association is evident even among religious participants in increasingly secular Europe. Nelson (2009) states:

> Interestingly, variables related to health seem to differ between religious and secular samples. For instance, the giving or receiving of help and the presence of bigger, more active social networks have a stronger connection to health among the more religious.
>
> (p. 313)

Illness   A growing accumulation of research studies reveal an association between religious involvement and improved outcomes over a variety of physical health/illness measures. Evidence of positive effect has been found in relation to cerebral vascular events, heart disease, cancer, hypertension, gastrointestinal disorder and cognitive decline. Maselko and colleagues were able to demonstrate a positive relationship between religious observance and pulmonary function among a sample of elderly participants (Maselko *et al.*, 2006), a finding that indicates a positive health effect across the life course. Interestingly, there is some intimation that there is a differential impact in respect of how authoritarian the religious affiliation of choice may be such that members of stricter denominations display an advantage (Waite *et al.*, 2003).

Educational and economic benefit

Freeman (1986) reported a positive association between churchgoing and school attendance for inner-city black adolescents. Regnerus (2000) reported that active participation in religious events was associated with improved test results and raised educational expectations among public school students in their tenth grade. Barro and McLeary (2002) also found there is a positive effect of religiosity on educational attainment. This would lead to improved opportunities to access the open labour and vocational training markets and promote economic growth. They also reported that 'economic growth responds positively to the extent of some religious beliefs but negatively to church attendance. That is, growth depends on the extent of believing relative to belonging'. This suggests that intrinsic religiousness is linked to a strong work ethic.

Children and parenting

Religion appears to have multiple benefits for the development and socialisation of children. Stability of family structure is more likely where parents observe religion and stronger family ties are evident (e.g. Pearce and Axinn, 1998) Additionally, the majority of relevant studies suggest that children fare better when they grow up in intact families. Conversely, for example, Cherlin (1999) concluded that growing up in a non-intact family could be associated with problems, both short- and long-term, that impacted on the children's mental health. Consequently, if shared religion assists parents in keeping their family intact, then it must be of benefit to the children. Volling *et al.* (2009) found that where parents believe that parenting is a manifestation of God (i.e. the sanctification of parenting), their management is positively related to affirmative socialisation and the use of praise and induction strategies for behaviour management. Their children tended to have higher scores for moral conduct. Some studies, however, suggest that where parents are members of very conservative Christian denominations or hold fundamentalist views on the Bible, their use of physical chastisement is likely to be greater than for moderate parents (e.g. Mahoney *et al.*, 2001). There are, however, positives for those with conservative religiosity. For example, even though conservative Protestants place great emphasis on obedience and may subscribe to an opinion that corporal punishment is acceptable, it is the case that they are more likely to eschew shouting at children and also are more likely to use frequent praise and display affection warmly (e.g. Bartowski *et al.*, 2000).

Religious participation among children and young people is associated with a range of positive associations. A number of studies document the effects of children's own religious participation, showing that young people who grow up having some religious involvement tend to display better outcomes in a range of areas. Such involvement has been linked to a lower probability of substance abuse and juvenile delinquency (Donahue and Benson, 1995), a lower incidence of depression among some groups (Harker, 2001), delayed sexual debut (Bearman and Bruckner, 2001), more positive attitudes toward marriage and having children (Waite and Lehrer, 2003), and more negative attitudes towards unmarried sex and premarital childbearing (Marchena and Waite, 2001).

Contraindications

It is clear that the bulk of research findings suggest that religion generally has a positive influence on the well-being of adherents. It is a source of social support, facilitates integration into a like-minded community and is associated with healthy activities and moral lifestyles. It is also associated with empathy, fellowship and the spiritual wealth that is the reward of personal faith. For most sincere, genuine religious individuals, a belief in the afterlife lessens their fear of dying and robs death of its sting. Sadly, however, religious observance is associated also with some negative influences. For example, although religious observance is negatively associated with domestic violence, there is evidence that some varieties of religious dissimilarity do increase the risk of partner abuse. The study by Ellison *et al.* (1999) led them to conclude that 'men who hold much more conservative theological views than their partners are especially likely to perpetrate domestic violence' (p. 87).

The theme of extreme religious conservatism is echoed also in research on terrorist violence. Although religious fundamentalism is an improbable single cause of terrorism, Rogers and colleagues believe that it may reflect interpersonal and group dynamics that are important antecedents, as well as poverty, discrimination and growing gaps between groups in relation to socioeconomic factors. Religion also appears to play an important role by providing the rhetoric that is associated with suicide bombers and other terrorist attackers. Rogers and his colleagues suggest that 'It is possible to suggest a constellation of extrinsic religiosity, authoritarianism and prejudice, and early experiences of punishment play a role in influencing the likelihood of participation in terrorist groups and terrorist activity' (Rogers et al., 2007, p. 262).

It is noteworthy also, and not unexpected, that extrinsic religiousness has been shown to be associated with intolerance. It is also the case that adherents revealing intrinsic religiousness but who are attached to some religions that espouse prejudice in respect of specific out-groups may also express prejudicial views about those groups, sometimes without recognising the gap between their intrinsic religiosity and the rhetoric of their church. Hunsberger and Jackson (2005) summarise the complexity of these issues:

> Religious persons and groups do many helpful, cooperative, and tolerant things in our world; there are surely many non-prejudiced religious persons as well as prejudiced nonreligious persons on this planet; and the frequently reported positive associations between religion and prejudice are often specific to certain definitions of religion or religious orientation, targets of prejudice, and group and cultural contexts. In spite of this, we cannot ignore the religion-prejudice links found in research . . .
>
> (p. 821)

Religious orientation, guilt and remorse

So far, this chapter has examined the concepts of religion and spirituality, and dealt briefly with the connections between them and possible mechanisms that mediate their effects on individuals. Some of the consequences of religious and spiritual beliefs for the lives of adherents have been examined and a loose conclusion may be drawn that, in many important ways, individuals who do attach importance to transcendence, either through the formality of religious observance or an informal but genuine acceptance of spirituality, are likely to experience benefits. Some of these benefits are protective factors that influence mental and physical health, relationships and positive coping strategies, while others assist with behavioural regulation and moral lifestyles. The latter two are of relevance to a consideration of the relationship that religion/spirituality has, if any, to the experience and mediation of the negative emotions of guilt and remorse, those being the most associated with feeling sorry and blameworthy, and experiencing a desire for the forgiveness of wrongdoing.

The distinction between intrinsic and extrinsic religiousness (Allport, 1966) has been utilised in previous sections as a means of describing orientation to religion. It may also be useful when considering how religious observance may influence the feeling of being sorry for wrongdoing and the mediation of guilt and remorse. These distinctions are briefly summarised here for the sake of convenience.

Individuals possessing an intrinsic religiousness are generally thought of as 'genuine'. They are completely committed to their religious/spiritual beliefs, and they practise living within the guidance and standards of their religion. However, those whose orientation is extrinsic use religion to gain entry into influential in-groups that offer social status, mutual benefits and support, group ritual worship and increased self-worth. These aspirations are not thought to reflect a genuine spirituality, although they may result in scrupulous overt religious behaviour. It is quite obvious that these distinctions can be used in a pejorative manner to discriminate against religious individuals who appear not to 'practise what they preach' in favour of those who do. Indeed, Cohen et al. (2005) state that writers have uncritically accepted the superiority of intrinsic over extrinsic religiousness. Nevertheless, Allport's distinction remains useful as a point of departure for research on a variety of issues, including those of guilt and remorse. In general, the reported themes associated with intrinsic and extrinsic religiousness hold also for guilt and remorse. Predictably, individuals who practise intrinsic religiousness experience less guilt than those with extrinsic religiousness (Maltby, 2005).

This relationship is not uniform, however. For example, Richards (1991) carried out a study using 264 undergraduate students to investigate the relationships between religious orientation and mental health. Psychometric measures included religious orientation and devoutness, existential well-being, psychological separation from parents and depression, shame and guilt. It is of particular relevance to this discussion that subjects within an intrinsic religiosity group showed scores to be positively associated with guilt despite experiencing higher religious well-being. There was no significant difference between these subjects and those who were in the less devout extrinsically religious group for depression, shame and existential well-being. These findings suggest that the intrinsic orientation group were more likely to experience guilt and, by association, remorse because, perhaps, they were more sensitive to wrongdoing than the less religious subjects. This does not appear to be entirely congruent with the findings of Meek et al. (1995) who investigated the relationship between religious orientation, individual guilt experiences and forgiveness, and subjective well-being. Subjects imagined three scenarios in which they were offenders and their guilt levels were recorded. Compared to intrinsically religious subjects, extrinsically religious subjects experienced higher guilt levels. They also reported a lower probability of repeating the offence and less satisfaction about getting away with it. In addition, they also professed a higher probability of confession. All subjects reported increased guilt levels after telling someone else about the offence, and experienced a reduction in guilty feelings after contemplating making a confession. Additionally, extrinsically oriented subjects were less able to report self-forgiveness and the experience of God's forgiveness than intrinsically oriented individuals who, according to Meek and colleagues, were prompted by a heightened guilt response to be 'likely to forgive themselves and feel forgiven by God . . .' (p. 196).

Maltby (2005) suggests 'extrinsic religious individuals may be unable to deal effectively with guilt, and that retention of guilt may be unhealthy for these individuals' (p .79). Similarly, Meek et al. (1995) suggested that extrinsically oriented religious individuals are more prone to the negative effects of guilt than intrinsically oriented individuals: 'Extrinsics are less protected by beliefs of forgiveness and, therefore, may be more likely to convert their guilt feelings to emotions of depression, anxiety, hostility, and so on' (p. 196). This negative outcome is contrasted with benefits accrued by intrinsically religious people. They comment that

> Guilt and religious orientation are also associated with confession. Across all scenarios, intrinsics were more likely than extrinsics to confess their misdeed. This suggests that intrinsics' confessions may be more related to internal factors, and less influenced by external events.
>
> (p. 196).

They draw attention to the finding that confession is associated with important emotional and physical benefits (e.g. Pennebaker et al., 1987) that extrinsically religious people are less likely to experience.

The possibility that people with extrinsic religiosity are more likely to experience difficulties when dealing with guilt and consequently the remorse that often emanates from it, suggests that their religious observance is a setting condition for any mental health difficulties that may develop. In addition, this outcome may assist in understanding why there are inconsistencies in the relationship between the negative emotion of guilt and the styles of religious observance. It may be simplistic to suggest that those individuals with extrinsic orientation are less able to interpret and mediate their guilt without harm to themselves; nevertheless, the following is illustrative of this possibility.

Sharif was a 33-year-old accountant for a moderate-sized engineering company. There was one other accountant who was his junior. Sharif knew that he was not particularly religious but he did attend his local mosque, engaged in most of the communal acts of worship and sought out senior people to ensure that he gained their approval.

At the same time, he was steadily embezzling small amounts of money from the company in order to pay for a drug habit and a fairly libidinous lifestyle in a city nearly a hundred miles from his home. The theft could not go on forever and Sharif made plans to evade detection by laying a false trail that pointed towards careless work carried out by his junior colleague. Unfortunately for him, this young man was clever enough to spot the discrepancies before the trail was established and reported them to senior management. Sharif was devastated at his undoing and became terrified that he and his family would be dishonoured. The shame induced by this possibility was overwhelming but rather than acknowledge guilt and admit to his activity, Sharif pretended that the errors on his part were due to poor concentration because of stress arising from the fact that his mother was terminally ill with cancer. This happened to be true, but Sharif had not been overly solicitous until the threat of detection became real. He then presented as a caring, anxious son who dutifully attended to his mother. His sympathetic managers accepted his excuses and he was able to keep his job.

Sharif found, however that his guilt remained with him. This was not shame about his theft or the intention to implicate his junior colleague, neither was it associated with his use of his mother's illness as a means of impression management. Instead, his shame was associated with the near dishonour within his community of nearly being caught. He became so anxious at the thought of dishonour that he sought intervention.

The converse argument can be made to the effect that individuals with genuine beliefs who express intrinsic religiousness are better able to interpret shame, guilt and remorse such that their mediation of these negative emotions is less likely to be as self-damaging (e.g. Fischer and Richards, 1998). Tangney et al. (2007) review evidence that unresolved shame is strongly associated with serious psychological symptoms, including depression, anxiety, low self-esteem, eating disorders, PTSD and suicidal ideation (see also Chapter 4). Guilt is less significantly associated with psychological symptoms unless 'fused' with shame (Tangney et al., 2007, p. 352).

By delineating religious involvement from religious orientation Dezutter et al. (2006) provide additional research detail to clarify the association of religiosity with the negative emotions of remorse. They used 472 participants drawn from a variety of sources, including choirs, sports clubs and youth movements, as well as student residences and churches. They were given questionnaires recording religious involvement, religious orientations and social-cognitive approaches to religion. Psychological distress (personal feelings incorporating both shame and guilt) and psychological well-being (self-esteem and satisfaction with life) were assessed also.

The results revealed that both religious attitudes and religious orientation had a significant effect on psychological well-being and psychological distress. Differences of religious attitude and orientation were more influential than differences of religious involvement, which appears therefore to be a more superficial aspect of religiosity. Church attendance and salience of belief had little impact on psychological well-being and psychological distress. In addition, the results were congruent with previous studies (e.g. Maltby and Day, 2003) in that mental health indicators were related positively to intrinsic and negatively to extrinsic personal orientation.

The general thrust of results from research studies in the area of religious orientation and individuals' response to negative emotions places some importance on the role religiousness might have in respect of the treatment of individuals whose response is inimical to their mental health and psychological well-being. It is important, therefore, to consider how such individuals might best be supported by therapeutic endeavours.

Religion and intervention

In my experience, many religious people are reluctant to accept psychological intervention; some believe that they are being punished for not being good enough and for letting God down. Others are fearful that their fellow congregationalists will find out that their faith has not been strong enough to sustain them in times of trouble and some worry that their beliefs will be thought of as a major part of their problem. Still others have an intuitive grasp of the fact that psychologists and other therapists are probably less likely to be religious and so will not understand the importance of faith. I am aware also that some religious clients hide the fact of their religiosity from therapists and so risk an erroneous understanding of their difficulties. My colleagues who practise psychotherapy alert me to another difficulty, one that is also raised by Worthington and Aten (2009, citing Thurston, 2000) who state:

> many religious clients, especially those with more theologically conservative beliefs (Thurston, 2000), have sought and even demanded, therapy tailored to include religious concepts (e.g., sin, soul, karma, dharma, five pillars of Islam, salvation, reincarnation, the laws of Moses), themes (e.g., grace, forgiveness), and even practices (e.g., prayer or use of scripture). Overall, clients who fit into this category are seeking a psychotherapy approach tailored specifically to their beliefs and values.
>
> (p. 125)

My colleagues cannot assist these clients as they are unable to meet these requirements. Unfortunately, there is sometimes a dearth of trained therapists who also hold similar beliefs as these clients. Worthington and Aten (2009) discuss the difficulties for clergy when they have to do their best to meet the counselling needs. Although not subscribing to particular religious denominations, some therapists are sensitive to spiritual issues across diverse faiths. This seems to work reasonably well for clients who are not aligned to particular religions or do not follow very traditional and unquestioning beliefs. Those with highly religious beliefs are unlikely to view this as satisfactory and will resist involvement with the therapy on offer, preferring to try to deal with their difficulties within the guidance offered by their faith. Worthington and Aten (2009) refer to these clients as having a 'zone of toleration' (p. 126) and will work with therapists whose belief system appears to fall within it. It has been suggested that religious clients view and interpret their world through the lens of their religion that defines this zone and are comfortable working with someone who appears to share it. Wade, *et al.* (2007) carried out a thorough evaluation of the effectiveness of religiously tailored Christian therapies. They state:

> The results of the current study suggest that clients who seek and receive explicitly labeled Christian therapy, as well as those who seek and receive secular therapy, tend to feel close to their therapists and perceive therapy to be effective. Those clients who have strong religious commitments respond particularly well when therapists use discernible religious interventions. Clients and their therapists in Christian agencies representing several regions of the United States generally believed that religiously tailored interventions were appropriate in therapy and were comfortable with their use.
>
> (p. 102)

Worthington and Aten (2009) raise an important practice issue concerning the initial meeting of therapists with highly religious clients who may ask a direct question about the therapist's faith. The common practice of reflecting back questions and comments may well cause irritation and a suspicion that the therapist is withholding information about themselves that might be an anathema to the client. One of my psychotherapist colleagues recalls an abrupt end to an initial session when a client declared loudly that only those who do the Devil's work need to hide the truth of their faith. He was of the opinion that many highly religious clients do not reject therapists who do not share their faith or the strength of their faith out of bigotry. Instead, they need to be assured that the therapist has, through personal experience, a firm understanding of their belief-centred coping strategies. These clients do not want to develop insights into new ways of living and coping with stress; instead, they want to reaffirm their faith and strengthen the coping benefits derived from it. This opinion is partly congruent with one of the oldest models of coping and religious intervention available. The work of Kenneth Pargament in respect of religious coping strategies has been referred to previously (e.g. Pargament, 2002). In essence, he believes that religious people under stress initially use therapy to strengthen their existing coping strategies and so absorb stressors without making fundamental changes to their convictions (e.g. Pargament *et al.*, 1988).

It is not always immediately obvious that clients have problems that relate to their spirituality and coping strategies. Shyness, a reluctance to admit to strong religious belief in an increasingly secular society, lacking the words for spiritual expression, or rejection of a belief system that has been damaging, may lead to some obfuscation of the presenting problem and its context. Delaney and colleagues (2009) acknowledge the difficulties of knowing how to begin; they suggest:

> Open questions are a good place to start, as these challenge clients to reflect and to explore. Answering an open question requires not only content, but also some processing and organization of information. The therapist therefore learns not only facts, but also something of how the person organizes meaning. These questions can be asked during a clinical interview or in an initial session as the therapist begins to piece together the patient's narrative. Examples of open questions to begin exploration of this area are:
>
> * Whom or what do you believe in, have faith in?
> * What do you imagine God is like?
> * How do you understand your purpose in life
> * What things in your life have you regretted?
> * When in your life have you felt truly blessed?
> * When has it been hard for you to forgive someone?
> * In what ways is it important for you to deepen your spiritual life?
>
> (p. 190)

Such direct questioning grates against the non-directive principles of some of my psychotherapist colleagues but others are aware that the mind-set of many conservative and deeply religious clients is oriented towards the structured guidance that is a major characteristic of their religious observance. If they are assured that the questioning or any other part of the therapeutic process is not an assault on their faith then they may be pleased to be given an opportunity to deal openly with the therapist and be sure that the context of their difficulties is made explicit.

Delaney *et al.* (2009) have other guidance to offer. They suggest that the initial questions suggested above can lead to further follow-up questions that can assist the client in providing more detail of their spiritual life and how it interacts with the therapeutic process. This could include asking questions about how their religious beliefs and traditions relate specifically to their presenting problems. For example, after detailed follow-up questions, a client who could not progress beyond feelings of guilt for experiencing unconsummated sexual attraction to her sister's husband was able to stop persistently and obsessively thinking about adultery, an unforgivable sin in her faith, and think instead about how she had obeyed her faith and her own marriage vows by not acting on those thoughts. In addition, it is often good practice with highly religious clients to deal directly with specific questions they may ask about spiritual uncertainties. Reflecting back such questions with comments asking why their question is important to them seems to miss the point that their spirituality is as vital to them as breathing. It is potentially unhealthy to leave them in a state of desperate uncertainty when the therapist could answer the question from their own experience or, alternatively, find someone who can (e.g. theologian, clergy). It is the case, therefore, that therapy with highly religious clients can involve both careful listening and equally careful responding. Various commentators suggest that therapists should ask permission to respond to questions from their own experience (e.g. Delaney *et al.*, 2009).

Strategies employed in religious-oriented therapies may contain a mix from different religious practices. Thus, practices such as confession, atonement, giving and seeking forgiveness, prayer and meditation are used according to need. Not all therapists using such strategies are particularly religious; indeed, many secular therapists are prepared to work with clients' religious beliefs and practices that they do not share. Propst (1996) suggested that there is an interaction between the cognitive change emphasis of CBT and religious perspectives. She believes that cognitive change processes are deliberately engaged in both cognitive therapy and Christian spiritual formation. Such emphases may not be restricted solely to Western theisms and could also be present in the content of other religious traditions. Nevertheless, it is particularly evident that the synergy is strong between cognitive behavioural therapy (CBT) and Christianity. An oft-quoted study investigating CBT with depressed volunteers (Propst *et al.*, 1992) evaluated the use of this therapy with both religious and non-religious therapists. Treatment success initially favoured the outcomes associated with the non-religious therapists, but there were no significant differences at three-month and two-year follow-ups, and all treatment outcomes were better than for a waiting-list control group.

Summary

While it is clear that religion and spirituality have many points of communality, it is also clear that it is entirely possible to lead a deeply spiritual life without having much reference to any formal religion. Although religion remains a factor of more or less importance to the majority of people on the planet, there is no evidence that religiousness places a higher premium on the imperative of morality or other moderators of personal–social behaviour than does spirituality. Indeed, whereas it is not necessary for individuals to proclaim any of the formal (organised) religions in order to seek transcendence, it is necessary for them to acknowledge their spirituality. This acceptance has an impact on their behaviour regulation in that it prohibits harming others and prompts the negative emotions of shame and guilt when transgressions occur.

Religion and spirituality appear to have a common basis in normal child development in that young children seem quite able to accommodate the required supernatural concepts by utilising their normal processes of conceptual development. The formalities, beliefs and rituals of organised religion are then acquired from direct teaching, a process that grafts on the 'man-made' structure and formality of religious practice to children's developing spirituality. Inevitably, psychological study has found cognitive theory to be successful in explaining some of the aspects of religious and spiritual beliefs. A major outcome of this line of enquiry has identified that moderate believers who are low in fundamentalist attitudes question the underpinnings of religion when it seems appropriate to do so, whereas fundamentalists allow no doubts or questions but seek instead to question the commitment of those who do.

There are significant personality variables associated with religiousness and spirituality. Conscientiousness and Agreeableness are positively related to religiousness and Openness to Experience is associated with spirituality. The differentiation between extrinsic and intrinsic religiousness has proved very useful. In worldly terms, extrinsic religiousness is self-directed and can improve temporal rather than spiritual opportunities. Intrinsic religiousness, however, is associated with well-being, optimism, life satisfaction, reduction of isolation and the provision of a community of support that is both divine and human. The negative emotions of shame and guilt are significantly associated with depression. In general, religiousness and spirituality offer protective factors in respect of mental health but there are contraindications in that extrinsic religiousness is considerably less beneficial. In addition, fundamentalism and authoritarian religions are negatively associated with mental health. It is also the case that religious coping with stressors do not offer a significantly greater sense of well-being than non-religious coping. In short, it appears to be overarching spirituality that confers benefits rather than formalised religious beliefs.

Intrinsic religiousness and spirituality is associated with protection against negative emotions in that the experience of guilt is greater for those who practise extrinsic religiousness. Other findings suggest that extrinsically religious people are more likely to claim self-forgiveness and the experience of God's forgiveness because perhaps they seek to diminish the intensity of being sorry for wrongdoing. It is probable that these individuals are more likely to experience difficulties is coping with guilt and remorse without help. It is noteworthy that religious factors are of great significance to the provision of therapy, a subject that is considered again in Chapter 8.

Chapter 7

Forgiveness

Introduction

Forgiveness is a complex subject for psychologists. Mostly, they understand it to be a gift made available by individuals to others who have harmed them. Both victims and offenders may benefit; indeed, Hope (1987) described forgiveness as 'a key part of psychological healing' (p. 240). Although victims understand that they can justifiably seek revenge or reparation, many choose instead to extend compassion and even love to those who have wronged them. They respond positively to the remorse and repentance expressed by the perpetrators and may offer a possibility of improved relations. George Eliot (Mary Ann Evans) attempted to capture the intensity of forgiveness following repentance in her words, 'Would not love see returning penitence afar off, and fall on its neck and kiss it?' Although the forgiving response may not be quite as florid as suggested by her words, the essence of forgiveness is encapsulated by them.

Forgiveness may be treated as any other human psychological function using standardised tests and other frequently used methodologies. At this level of involvement psychologists can determine the personalities of those who ruminate vindictively rather than forgive and those who are prepared at some point to release their transgressors from shame, guilt and remorse through the gift of forgiveness. The same methods can determine who is likely to feel sorry for their wrongdoings and seek forgiveness, and those who believe their own arrogant propaganda of narcissistic virtue.

There is, however, another dimension to forgiveness. People associate it with goodness, holiness and religion; they attach it to whichever belief in the sacred they subscribe to. Across cultures and religions forgiveness is a transcendent, spiritual and inspirational phenomenon. It has been the subject of centuries of philosophical debate and sublime works of art. Sadly, it has stimulated uplifting sermons at the same time as thousands of young people had been conscripted to the battlefields of vengeful nations. The thought of forgiveness can arouse guilt of wrongs done years before and cast a pall over every joy and pleasure. Such is the power of forgiveness that it can evoke misery when it is refused and elation when it is received. From early times, heaven has awaited those souls blessed by forgiveness following repentance, whereas the pits of hell await the unredeemed and the unforgiven.

As discussed in Chapter 2, forgiveness is not always associated with excusing the wrongdoer, neither does it guarantee a return to the state of a relationship as it was before the harm was done (e.g. Enright *et al.*, 1992). When the victims do allow a return to the previous state of the relationship, they are said to exercise *decisional* forgiveness. Where, however, they choose simply and only to let go of the negative emotions caused by the harm done and give up thoughts of revenge, then they are said to exercise *emotional* forgiveness (Nelson, 2009). Under such circumstances the relationship does not return to the pre-harm state. For some victims either the extent of multiple transgressions, the frequency of betrayal or the superficiality of remorse makes forgiveness a Sisyphean task. They remain with unresolved complex negative emotions such as fear, humiliation and anger. This complex of negative emotions has been referred to as a state of *unforgiveness* by Worthington and Scherer (2004) who state: 'Delayed negative emotions – resentment, bitterness, hostility, hatred, anger, and fear (the combination of which is unforgiveness) – may derive from rumination' (p. 386), a blight on well-being that was discussed in Chapter 3.

Although the interpersonal forgiveness of a perpetrator by the victim(s) is not the only form of forgiveness,[1] this form is the subject of this chapter. Damage done to interpersonal relationships is the ubiquitous and most frequent form experienced during the lives of most people, who may suffer or perpetrate it several times throughout their life course. Forgiveness, contingent on genuine perpetrator remorse, is the age-old and most important nostrum for the healing of such damage and the restoration of accord between perpetrator and victims (e.g. Eaton and Stuthers, 2006). In respect of marital relations, Fincham and colleagues state: 'Perhaps not surprisingly, spouses report that the capacity to seek out and grant forgiveness is one of the most important factors contributing to marital longevity and marital satisfaction' (Fincham *et al.*, 2004, p. 72). In addition, the act of forgiveness may bring an end to a frustrating waste of living. Hope (1987) believes that 'By choosing to forgive the past we need not feel deprived and unfulfilled, and we do not expend our energy in the process of seeking vindication' (p. 241).

Given that genuine forgiveness is an act of transcendence over the understandable inclinations of the wounded victim to seek revenge, it is not surprising that major religious and spiritual authorities espouse and sanctify it. Christianity, for example, places great importance on forgiveness, even when it has not been preceded by acts of repentance. Many religions not only inform adherents that forgiveness is vital, they also provide guidance on the positive emotions that should be sought and the procedures that are appropriate (Tsang *et al.*, 2005). It is quite possible, therefore, that victims experience a moral imperative to forgive even when, perhaps, they would rather not. It is appropriate to enquire why, from the perspective of religion, children and young people could develop a forgiving disposition instead of a desire for vengeance. One opinion is that it evolves from a strong sense of receiving divine forgiveness. Forgiveness perceived to have been given by God is thought to stimulate gratitude and motivate individuals to demonstrate dispositional forgiveness of wrongdoing by others (Roberts, 1995). Accordingly, believers become forgivers as a consequence of their joyous and grateful response to the gift of God's grace.[2] It is also believed that people can learn forgiveness by following the models provided by God and Jesus, and meditating, praying and worship (Phil 2:12–13). By the same token, it is believed that believers can become more forgiving as result of God's response to the prayers of others for them. Other sources of development are considered to be influential; Lampton and colleagues (2005) state:

> People can also become more forgiving because they develop an orientation toward virtues in general ... universities and churches can promote forgiving by promoting an environment that explicitly values forgiveness by preaching, teaching, and providing experiential opportunities that explicitly promote forgiveness.
>
> (p. 279)

Whether or not religious doctrine has a direct and significant mediating influence on the negative emotions of victims, it is appropriate to consider forgiveness as it is conceptualised within the belief structures of major religions.

Religion and forgiveness

It has long been understood that people function reasonably comfortably during their everyday lives on the basis of a set of personalised beliefs, constructs and theories that they find useful in predicting the events to which they should respond and the most successful ways of doing so. These events may be as simple as organising their supermarket shopping or as complex as dealing with the fractiousness of other people. They make plans, establish goals, enjoy themselves and regulate their social behaviour according to the representations they establish of their world. These representations are comprised of meaning systems that Epstein (1994) suggests develop in order to satisfy four equally important basic needs that steer our behaviour. These basic needs are distilled from a variety of descriptions of human functioning. These are the needs to:

1   maintain the maximisation of pleasure and the minimisation of pain (e.g. Freud, 1959);
2   meet the requirements of interpersonal relatedness (e.g. Bowlby, 1988);

3   maintain stability and coherence (e.g. Rogers, 1959); and
4   enhance self-esteem (e.g. Allport, 1961).

From the 1970s Epstein (1973) has merged these four needs into his Cognitive-Experiential Self-Theory (CEST) of personality. Behaviour is viewed as a compromise between these needs, each providing checks and balances against the others. In Epstein's opinion, all individuals construct their own theory of reality in order to maximise the meeting of these needs in such a manner that their lives are as satisfying as possible.

Religion is an important meaning system within this framework of constructs for many individuals and will, therefore, influence important behaviours, including forgiveness, through the individual's beliefs, emotions, actions and goals. For example, I find that most religions encourage a belief in striving for justice and fairness in the world, an end to bigotry, the support and welfare of vulnerable people, the protection of innocence and the freedom to live pleasantly without harming others. The deeply personalised interpretations of religious meaning systems add to the social cognitive benefits of other non-religious meaning systems held by individuals to help them fashion a means for understanding and predicting the social world they function in.

Unlike other meaning systems, however, those of religion are based on doctrine about the sacred. No matter how robustly they might guide individuals through everyday living, their essence is holy and transcends the temporal. As such, they attain such a unique significance and reverence for most committed believers that they may be superimposed on all other meaning systems held by them. Silberman (2005) states: 'The connection to the sacred can be fully manifested . . . in each of the components of the meaning system, namely, beliefs, contingencies, expectations, and goals, as well as in prescriptive postulates regarding emotions and actions' (p. 646).

Beliefs   At the personal level religious doctrine may mediate idiosyncratic beliefs about the characteristics of the self, of other people, and the nature of the world people have created. Religious belief almost certainly will influence thinking about piety and preparation in this life for whatever may come after it. Many highly religious individuals in my experience utilise doctrine to formulate beliefs about contingencies: thus righteous people, including themselves, should receive the rewards of their piety, whereas sinners will be punished. At the extreme end of the reward–punishment dichotomy individuals may link up into in-groups sharing the same beliefs, leaving everyone else in an out-group that is beyond redemption. Such in-groups can become harmful, not necessarily in such flagrant terms as terrorism, but in respect of their hostility and divisiveness towards others who do not share their beliefs.

Paul and his wife Sally moved with their two young children into rented temporary accommodation on the edge of the city where Paul's promotion had taken them. They were Methodists and generally attended Sunday services. Sally unwittingly made an error when she asked a neighbour where the nearest Methodist church was. The family was immediately regarded with suspicion and a small group from the local Catholic church became quite vitriolic about Methodists generally. Quite quickly Sally found that no one would speak to her outside the local school and her children were bullied once or twice until the teachers stepped in. The local shopkeeper asked her not to come into the shop otherwise he would lose trade. Sally was told that she should go and live with her own. Fortunately, their next move took them into a warm and friendly secular community.

Not all communities of like-minded believers are as toxic as the above example. Indeed, most major religions are prescriptive of beliefs concerning benevolence, compassion and forgiveness (e.g. Rye *et al.*, 2001a). As a consequence, forgiveness can be presented as sanctified and a means of religious coping (e.g. Pargament and Rye, 1998).

Emotions   The emotions evoked by religion are potentially very powerful, particularly those that arise from the sensation of being near to a wonderful spiritual force. In addition, the act of communal worship is often associated with a feeling of great joy and the reduction of sadness and despair. Doing good or improving one's piety may likewise be associated with joy and great satisfaction. The power of these emotions to bring about changes in oneself and others is considerable and opens up opportunities of coping with adversity (e.g. Pargament, 1997).

Several positive emotions predispose individuals to forgive transgressors. Compassion and empathy are also at the forefront of these and frequently ease the road to forgiveness. For example, McCullough *et al.* (1997) carried out a study of the relationship between the motivation of empathy and the act of forgiveness. The results enabled them to conceptualise 'interpersonal forgiving as an empathy-facilitated set of motivational changes that is structurally and functionally similar to the relationship between empathy and altruistic motivation to help people who are in need . . . '(p. 333).

Actions   Most religions provide guidance on appropriate actions, such as displaying charity and compassion, as well as proscription of maladaptive behaviour (e.g. Pargament, 1997). Spiritual behaviours such as praying and meditation are advocated for believers, but sadly the perversion of doctrinal guidance may lead to the apparent sanctification of acts of violence such as religious terrorism (e.g. Silberman, 2003) and torture (e.g. Fontana, 2003) when inappropriate but persuasive spiritual role models gain sway over the moral behaviour of individuals.[3] On a pro-social level, however, most major religions are also specifically prescriptive of the act of forgiveness[4] and supply many examples or models of such acts.[5]

It is to be expected, therefore, that the religious meaning systems crafted by individuals throughout their life course will influence how they understand and practise forgiveness. Tsang *et al.* (2005) believe that the combination of beliefs, emotions and actions give rise to goals of forgiveness by increasing motivation for engaging transgressors with a more forgiving disposition. This basic combination of psychological factors is reflected in the forgiveness-related prescriptions of the world's major religions.

Christianity and forgiveness

Christian doctrine places forgiveness squarely within its core faith. The Lord's Prayer is arguably the most important ritual for the laity and within it is the plea to 'forgive us our sins, as we forgive everyone who sins against us' (Luke, 11:4). Although Mark does not include the Lord's Prayer, he strongly supports the act of forgiveness: 'And when you stand praying, if you hold anything against anyone, forgive him, so that your Father in heaven may forgive you your sins' (Mark, 11:25).

God and Christ provide the ultimate models of forgiveness (Marty, 1998). The manifestation of God the Son in the human form of Jesus provided a different context for the evolution of forgiveness than had been the case for faith bounded by the Old Testament. In essence, God's forgiveness of human transgression was channelled through the sufferings of Jesus and became unconditional. Repentance was no longer a precondition for forgiveness but was instead an initiation into practising membership of the Kingdom of God.

Christian scripture provides explicit significance and guidance on interpersonal forgiveness. Despite the early concept of the washing away of original sin by baptism, later theological authority recognised the continuing sinfulness of humans and adjured adherents to continue to seek forgiveness from God and from each other. Indeed, the giving and receiving of interpersonal forgiveness came to be regarded as a vital exercise for living in God's Kingdom (e.g. McCullough and Worthington, 1999). Forgiveness concerns the experience of compassion for transgressors and releasing them from their wrongs. Christians are exhorted to forgive just as God has forgiven them. Various passages from Christian scripture are quite firm on this, making it a requirement. For example, Luke (6:37) states: 'Do not judge, and you will not be judged. Do not condemn, and you will not be condemned. Forgive, and you will be forgiven.' Despite the stringency of this requirement, Christianity does not demand reconciliation or repentance (Rye *et al.*, 2001a).

Most Christians believe forgiveness comes from God such that remorse and forgiveness of others are vital ingredients of their practice. Despite this, however, there are doctrinal differences about the process of forgiveness.

Christian scripture states that Jesus gave the right and power of forgiveness to his apostles. Mark quotes Jesus as saying, 'And I will give you the keys of the Kingdom of Heaven. Whatever you forbid on earth will be forbidden in heaven, and whatever you permit on earth will be permitted in heaven' (Matthew, 16:19). Similarly, John quoted, 'If you forgive anyone his sins, they are forgiven; if you do not forgive them, they are not forgiven' (John, 20:23). Catholic doctrine gives that authority to its bishops and priests as successors of the apostles. Thus, the Catholic and Orthodox churches exercise the formal forgiveness of sins through the sacrament of Reconciliation (Confession) whereby a priest dispenses a penance and grants forgiveness, thereby reconciling the penitent with the Church.

The Protestant doctrine takes a very different stance. During the Reformation of the sixteenth century, Protestants abhorred the corrupt practice that many Catholic priests practised of selling 'indulgences' to the wealthy in order to reduce the penalties of sin. They rejected the Roman Catholic Church's sacrament of Penance, denied its claim to apostolic succession, and most particularly rejected its authority to forgive sins. The Protestant stance on forgiveness was based on the strict following of scripture such that whereas the Church may be instrumental in encouraging people to repentant, the power to forgive belonged to God and Christ alone.[6]

Judaism and forgiveness

Judaism conceptualises forgiveness in some similar ways to Christianity. A core belief is that God is forgiving and that people should imitate his kindness, to 'walk in all his ways, and to cleave unto him' (Deuteronomy, 11:22). Not only should people aspire to imitate God, it is God's Law that they should practise forgiveness as is clear from the book of Leviticus: 'Thou shalt not avenge, nor bear any grudge against the children of thy people, but thou shalt love thy neighbour as thyself' (Leviticus, 19:18). Also in common with Christianity, Judaism views forgiveness as the reversal of wrongdoing and the forgiveness of transgressors enables them to regain their relationship with those they offended against (e.g. Dorff, 1998). In addition, Judaism requires that followers forgive those who transgress against them because God has forgiven them.[7] Unlike Christianity, however, forgiveness is not freely given as there are prior conditions. Forgiveness is obligatory[8] provided that the wrongdoer not only expresses genuine remorse and compensates the victim, but also makes a solemn commitment not to reoffend.[9] Under these circumstances, forgiveness must be given[10] and some authorities teach that the failure to forgive is as bad as the original offence. This means that in Judaism, unlike Christianity, wrongdoers cannot get forgiveness from God for wrongs they have done to others. Despite the act of forgiveness, however, it is still not necessary for the victim to offer reconciliation.

Islam and forgiveness

Islam also prizes forgiveness, as is apparent from many verses within the Qur'an – for example, 'Hold to forgiveness; Command what is right; . . . If a suggestion from Satan assails thy mind, seek refuge with Allah for He heareth and knoweth all things' (Qur'an, 7: 199–200). Indeed, one of the appellations of Allah is *Al-Ghafoor*, meaning the Oft-forgiving or Forgiving One. Muhammad is also regarded as a role model of forgiveness within Islam. He is presented within the Hadith[11] as an example of someone who would forgive others for their ignorance, even those who might once have thought of themselves as his enemies.

At a simple level and rather like Judaism and Christianity, Islam stresses the importance of forgiveness by individuals in order that Allah can forgive them their own sins. The key to forgiveness of offenders is their repentance; Ayoub (1997) states: 'Repentance may be regarded as the cornerstone of the religious life of both the individual and society' (p. 90). Islamic belief stresses that God not only forgives us but that He loves the repentant person.[12] God's capacity for forgiveness of penitent wrongdoers is boundless as is made clear in the Qur'an: 'O My worshippers, who have sinned excessively against themselves, do not despair of the Mercy of Allah, surely, Allah forgives all sins. He is the Forgiver, the Most Merciful' (Qur'an, 39:53). It is also taught that being forgiven contributes to happiness in this life.

Not all sins are forgivable, however, and the Qur'an is clear that God will not forgive idolatry. The Qur'an states firmly, 'Idolaters should not inhabit the mosques of Allah bearing witness against themselves with disbelief. Those, their deeds have been annulled, and in the Fire they shall live forever' (9.17). In addition, the Qur'an forbids violent behaviour except in defence of one's religion, life and property. Sadly, fundamentalists have greatly exceeded Qur'anic permission for defensive violence. In particular, references to defence of the faith[13] have been the source of overly aggressive responses and unjustifiable violence. Vociferous debate on interpretation continues and, during its disputation, there will doubtless be many acts of violence committed vengefully in the name of Allah. This, despite the teaching of the Qur'an that believers are those who 'when angered, forgive' (Qur'an, 42.37).

The instructions given for the expression of remorse and request for forgiveness bear many similarities with those of other religions. There are three requirements when asking God for forgiveness:

1 Stating the wrongdoing and admitting responsibility for it.[14]
2 Promising faithfully not to repeat the wrongdoing.
3 Asking for God's forgiveness.

Hinduism and forgiveness

Forgiveness, in the Hindu religion, is one of the paths of *dharma* or righteousness. Failure to forgive in a present life is thought to lead to negative events in a future life. Forgiveness is one of the qualities of soul that include control of the mind, austerity, purity, sincerity, mercy and non-violence. Displaying these qualities is the way to salvation (Klostermaier, 1994, p. 252). Temoshok and Chandra (2000) explain that forgiveness for practising Hindus is the absence of anger when confronted with wrongdoing by others. In common with other major religions, some theistic versions of Hinduism do provide models of Divine forgiveness for the guidance of adherents. At the core of the concept of forgiveness is the belief that all individuals have the capability to forgive because each of us has divinity within us.

Buddhism and forgiveness

Forgiveness within the Buddhist tradition is included within the requirement of compassion and forbearance. This includes the releasing of anger directed at transgressors. Forbearance is a more inclusive and broader concept than forgiveness because it deals with the endurance of hardships experienced from all other sources and not only the impact of transgression. It is concerned with the prevention of suffering, while compassion is concerned with the relief of suffering. Buddhist scriptures counsel that forbearance calms the raging heart and helps with the avoidance of evil.

Uniquely, the Buddhist tradition does not separate victims from wrong-doers. Given the central tenet that all things are connected, victims and wrongdoers are united such that there cannot be forgiveness in the traditional Western sense as there is no discrete transgressor to be forgiven. However, the Buddhist concept of *karma* teaches that good actions earn good consequences and evil actions have evil consequences. The refusal to give up anger and resentment at another's transgression is viewed negatively and would result in the unwelcome consequence of being resented by others in the future (Rye *et al.*, 2001b). Higgins (2001) states, 'Buddhist notions of forgiveness do not arise from the benevolence and goodness of a transcendent God but from one's awareness of the interconnectedness of all things' (p. 9).

Is there a religion–forgiveness discrepancy?

It is clear from the brief summary above that the world's major religions all place great positive emphasis on forgiveness. One would expect, therefore, that adherents to these religions would show high levels of forgiveness-related activity in their dealings with wrongdoers, particularly those who were genuinely sorry for their harmful behaviour and experience genuine remorse. Certainly, it is the case that religious people do espouse the virtues of forgiveness, but there appears to be a gap between this espousal in the abstract and the manifestation of forgiveness in terms of overt behaviour. Indeed, evidence has been presented (e.g. McCullough and Worthington, 1999) that religious involvement seems to have little influence on transgression-specific forgiveness. To begin to understand why this might be (or appear to be), it is desirable to consider the evaluation of both *dispositional* forgiveness and *transgression-specific* forgiveness.

Dispositional forgiveness and religiousness

McCullough and Worthington (1999) demonstrated that dispositional forgiveness could be measured from self-report items recording the importance that individuals place on forgiveness and their opinions about how forgiving they believe they are. Variables including religious orientation, feeling close to God, and frequency of prayer and church attendance are linked to attitudes and behaviour associated with individuals' view of how forgiving they are. In addition, self-report on the degree to which individuals are influenced by a higher power may be included. Edwards and colleagues (2002) state:

> The strength of an individual's religious faith is the extent to which he or she is influenced by this relationship with a higher power. Though religious faith often is associated with frequency of attendance at services and involvement in religious activities, many people have high levels of faith without engaging in traditional practices or rituals.
>
> (p. 148)

Thus, some self-report questionnaires also seek information about the social support and guidance offered by religious involvement. For example, Plant, Vallaeys, Sherman and Wallston (2002) included items such as 'I enjoy being around others who share my faith' and 'I look to my faith as providing meaning and purpose in my life' (p. 368) in their short version of the Santa Clara Strength of Religious Faith Questionnaire (Plante and Boccaccini, 1997). Edwards *et al.* (2002) found a moderate positive correlation between results on the Santa Clara questionnaire and the Heartland Forgiveness Scale. Their results lent support to the hypothesis that 'individuals with higher scores on the strength of religious faith measure also see themselves as more forgiving as suggested by responses on the forgiveness scale' (p. 151).

In addition, it is notable that moral reasoning about forgiveness is associated with religiosity. Thus, Enright *et al.* (1989) demonstrated that participants in their study who were rated as more sophisticated on a six-stage model of reasoning about forgiveness[15] tended to be among those with strong religious beliefs. Tsang *et al.* (2005) cited the 1977 study of Shoemaker and Bolt who found that when Christian students were asked how Christians should live, only 'loving' was ranked ahead of 'forgiving'. It is clear, therefore, that these religious people found forgiveness to be of great importance to them.

It is also clear that religious people have a self-image that includes the disposition to forgive. Thus, when Gorsuch and Hao (1993) carried out a factor analytic study of forgiveness using over a thousand participants, they concluded that 'Consistent with traditional Christian teachings, Protestants, Catholics, evangelicals, and the more personally religious generally reported more forgiving responses than Jewish, no/other religious preference, non-evangelical, and the less personally religious respondents' (p. 333). This provides further evidence that individuals who perceive themselves to be very religious also see themselves as being more forgiving than those who express less strong religious commitment.

Transgression-specific forgiveness and religiousness

A claim to believe in forgiveness and to work hard to be forgiving may well be an aspiration that is not always observed once in the face of wrongdoing. A trait that one merely aspires to does not make it real when grave hurt is experienced. This seems to be the case given findings of the religious-forgiveness discrepancy mentioned above. Tsang *et al.* (2005) state: 'The existence of this religion-forgiveness discrepancy is especially disturbing because religious doctrines purport to encourage compassion and forgiveness' (p. 790). An individual's true capacity for forgiveness becomes evident when they show forgiveness, having experienced specific wrongdoings that have been inflicted on them.

A valuable tool for the investigation of this and other issues of forgiveness is the Enright Forgiveness Inventory (EFI) (Subkoviak *et al.*, 1995). The EFI is an objective measure of the degree of forgiveness people grant to others who have hurt them deeply and unfairly. The inventory consists of 60 items divided into three subscales of 20 items, each of which are further divided into 10 positive items and ten negative items. These subscales record Positive and Negative Affect, Positive and Negative Behaviour, and Positive and Negative Cognition. In addition, five final items access construct validity of responding.

Subkoviak *et al.* (1995) used the EFI in conjunction with a measure of self-reported religiousness in order to determine the strength of the relationship between transgression-specific forgiveness and religiousness. In contrast with the strong relationship between dispositional forgiveness and religiousness, the correlation obtained was only weakly positive (r = .09). There was only a slight elevation of EFI scores for people of any religion, suggesting that although they may consider themselves to be forgiving, in reality they are unlikely to be much more so than people who have no strong religious commitment or none at all. Rackley (1993), cited by McCullough and Worthington, also made use of the EFI to examine the relationship between marital satisfaction, forgiveness, and religiosity. His results revealed 'that among 170 married individuals, self-reported forgiveness for one's spouse for a particular transgression . . . was not significantly associated with a multi-item measure of religious involvement' (McCullough and Worthington, 1999, p. 1150).

A variety of explanations for the religion-forgiveness discrepancy have been extended (see, for example, McCullough and Worthington, 1999). Of these, the most apparently obvious is the influence of social desirability. In essence, religious people know that they should be compassionate and forgiving and consequently are more likely than non-religious people to demonstrate dispositional forgiveness. When, however, they are put to the test by suffering the harmful actions of wrongdoers, they are not much more forgiving than those with little or no religious commitment. As McCullough and Worthington (1999) put it, 'The spirit is willing, but the flesh is weak' (p. 1152). The possible impact of social desirability on claims of being forgiving has received some support from findings of a significant positive correlation between social desirability and forgiveness measures. For example, Rye *et al.* (2001a) reported a slight but significant positive correlation between forgiveness scores from the Enright Forgiveness Inventory and social desirability scores from the Marlowe–Crowne Social Desirability Scale. It has to be noted, however, that the Subkoviak *et al.* study (1995) did not find a relationship with social desirability.

Following the suggestions of McCullough and Worthington (1999), Tsang *et al.* (2005) put forward two possible explanations of the religion–forgiveness discrepancy: an explanation based on the psychometric characteristics of the measurements used and a rationalisation explanation.

Psychometric issues   It has been argued (e.g. Epstein, 1986) that single items of behaviour, no matter how thoroughly and objectively measured, usually are too restricted in terms of their generality and too low in reliability to produce substantive and revealing correlations with measures of traits. Consequently, they are incapable of demonstrating either stability or generality in behaviour. This has important ramifications for the study of personality and for stable traits such as forgiveness. It is arguable, therefore, that the aggregation of forgiveness-specific behaviour may show a higher and more representative correlation with self-reported religiousness than single measurements of forgiveness behaviour.

In addition, Tsang *et al.* (2005) investigate the possibility that methods employed to investigate transgression-related forgiveness could result in contamination by recall and encoding biases. They state:

> Transgression-specific forgiveness is usually measured by having participants freely recall a past transgression, and then complete a questionnaire about the transgression event. These free recall procedures may introduce error. If we assume that forgiven offenses are more difficult to recall than unforgiven offenses, then a more forgiving individual might have a difficult time recalling a transgression during a forgiveness study. In contrast, a less forgiving individual would more easily recall a salient transgression. Yet, both individuals may end up recalling situations that have been forgiven to approximately equal extents, making it seem like they are equally forgiving people, when, in fact, they are not.
>
> (p. 791)

The error introduced might result in the diminution of the correlation between forgiveness behaviours with other variables, including religiousness. This could result in a false portrayal of non-religious people being as adroit at forgiveness as religious people when they are not.

Tsang *et al.* (2005) subjected these two potential distortions of the transgression-specific, religion-forgiveness relationship to investigation. They carried out three studies that varied according to the degree of restriction on the type of specific transgression they recalled and aggregated across multiple responses. The results suggested that 'When forgiveness is assessed using restrictive recall procedures and aggregate measures of forgiveness, a small positive relationship between religion and transgression-specific forgiveness emerges' (p. 801). They acknowledge, however, that their study, along with most others of forgiveness and religiousness, depend entirely on the self-report of forgiveness and suggest that research using behavioural measures is needed in order to obviate the confounding effects that self-report may produce. Nevertheless, their study does indicate that the psychometric limitations of the research methods typically used may attenuate what appears to be a small trend among religious people to be more forgiving than non-religious people in respect of transgression-specific forgiveness.

Rationalisation   However, dubious psychometrics cannot be the only explanation of the religion-forgiveness discrepancy. It is acknowledged that the correlation between transgression-specific forgiveness and religiousness is small, accounting for only about four per cent at best of the variance in the study by Tsang and her colleagues. As they point out, the relationship should be much stronger given the emphasis that world religions place on forgiveness and compassion. They rue the fact that 'In many places, individuals who consider themselves to be devout followers of their religions actively work to maintain centuries-old stances of bitterness and hate toward their enemies' (Tsang *et al.*, 2005, p. 795) and list many long-standing bloody conflicts between peoples in the promotion of their religions. In common with others, Tsang and colleagues comment that often religion appears to ferment revenge rather than forgiveness. They suggest that the rationalisation explanation for the religion-forgiveness discrepancy is that religious meaning systems are sufficiently open to idiosyncratic interpretation to allow them to be used to justify vengeful as well as forgiving behaviour. This appears to be at the core of radicalisation, a term that sadly has at the start of the twenty-first century become synonymous with violent Islamic fundamentalism. Silber and Bhatt (2007) include within their report on 'homegrown' radicalisation, a comment that embodies the distortion of a peaceful religion into a celebration of violence:

> As Muslims in the West seek to determine their appropriate response to the perceived 'war on Islam' many look for guidance for action from their

religion. The jihadi-Salafi interpretation paves a path to terrorism by its doctrines, which suggest that violence is a viable and legitimate means to defend Islam from perceived enemies, even if means attacking one's own government and/or sacrificing your own life.

(p. 18)

This description is at the extreme end of the rationalisation of religion but it makes clear that circumstances can bend religious practice away from its core belief and espousal of forgiveness into a vindication of an unforgiving and vengeful stance. Adherents do not, however, give up their religion and still respond with high scores on assessments of religiousness. Under these circumstances, it is clear that the religious–forgiveness relationship will become attenuated. Tsang *et al.* (2005) present three assumptions that underpin the explanation of the religion-forgiveness discrepancy in terms of the rationalisation of religion.

The first is the recognition that religions do not provide their adherents with only one meaning system. Rather multiple meaning systems are generally available and can be called into service as circumstances suggest but all under the overarching general doctrine. Paloutzian and Smith (1995) suggest that situational schema for a variety of responses exist within the religious life of individuals. None, however, are all-embracing; they have specific boundaries 'and exist within a more narrowly proscribed domain' (p. 21). Paloutzian (2009) emphasises the fluidity of religious beliefs in his comment:

> we must live with murky variations of concepts and categories that can initially seem clear and simple, such as "forgiveness". In life, forgiveness is a process that people have to work through over time, and victims can exist in any number of places during that process.

(p. 74)

The second assumption is that behaviour is less likely to be motivated by higher order ethical, moral and religious values than by whatever motivation is predominant at the time. What an individual hopes for at the time a response is necessary is more likely to sway selection of behaviour than cool reflection upon doctrinal teaching. Paloutzian (2009) believes that where a person has reached in the forgiveness process is dependent on where they are located along various continua, including:

1   the degree to which the emphasis is on feelings *versus* behaviors;
2   if the emphasis is on feelings, the degree to which the person is encouraged to generate feelings of forgiveness *versus* identity and accept his or her feelings whatever they might be;
3   the degree to which the process is comprehensive in the scope of offences that it covers;

4   the degree to which the process is closer in time to beginning *versus* ending;

5   the degree to which the process has come to resolution or closure;

6   the degree to which its outcome is positive *versus* negative;

7   the degree to which it is or was public *versus* private.

(p. 75)

As is clear, there are no obvious references to religious or other doctrinal belief systems; these continua are process oriented and situationally motivated. In my opinion, these continua lead to decision points to Forgive or Not-forgive that are largely independent of the specificity of religious belief. The following provides a simple example.

Glen, a managing director, decided that it was not possible to forgive his normally loyal personal assistant for giving sensitive business information to her journalist boyfriend. He claimed, 'I'd have liked to (forgive) because I'm a good Christian, but the rest of the board would think I'd gone soft.'

The third assumption is that if individuals' proximal motivations conflict with their religious or moral principles, then they may decide to rationalise their behaviour in order to fit with the relevant principles. This process is sometimes referred to as *moral rationalisation* and is the use of cognitive strategies by individuals to convince themselves and others that their seemingly dubious actions actually fall within proper moral standards. Tsang (2002) states:

> The occurrence of moral rationalization is a normal and prevalent psychological phenomenon and can be involved in small unethical acts, such as cheating on taxes, as well as large atrocities such as the Holocaust. An explanation of evil that incorporates moral rationalization posits that people can violate their moral standards because they have convinced themselves that their behavior is not immoral at all.
>
> (p. 26)

This process is rather like cognitive dissonance when individuals are forced to try to align conflicting ideas and do so by changing their attitudes, beliefs, and actions (Festinger, 1957). Tsang (2002) considers evil doing in the context of moral rationalisation in some detail and comes to the rather chilling conclusion that

> the explanation of evil resides not simply in evil situations or evil people but in a complex interplay between situational factors and normal psychological processes. Moral rationalization plays an important role in allowing an individual to autonomously engage in immoral behavior while

still seeing the self as moral. The individual then engages in more and more extreme behavior, until small unethical acts escalate into large atrocities. Because of moral rationalization, large-scale evil and small breaches of morality are, on a certain level, qualitatively similar.

(p. 48)

Tsang *et al.* (2005) report a pilot study into their rationalisation model, designed to investigate whether endorsement of different religious meaning systems was related to forgiveness of a recent transgressor. The subjects were thirty-eight young Christian psychology students who were asked to respond to three psychometric questionnaires. Forgiveness was measured by a revised version of the Transgression-Related Interpersonal Motivations Inventory (TRIM) (McCullough *et al.*, 1998) to which had been added a new scale recording Benevolence. Rationalisation was recorded through the use of two religiousness scales: an augmented version of the Dimensions of Religious Commitment Scale (Glock and Stark, 1966) and a series of items recording participants' concept of God. The results were multifaceted but suggested that individuals may use religious meaning systems to rationalise forgiving and unforgiving attitudes. Tsang and her colleagues (2005) concluded that

it is difficult to conclude the direction of causality. On one hand, a rationalization explanation posits that retributive and forgiveness motivations cause individuals to access different parts of their religious meaning systems. However, it is also possible that differences in people's religious meaning systems influence their propensity to forgive. Future research with larger numbers of participants and controlled experimental manipulations will aid in uncovering the mechanisms of moral rationalization in religion and forgiveness

(p. 800)

As far as I am aware, no such study has been published at the time of writing but I await the results of one with enthusiasm. It seems clear, however, that moral rationalisation is a significant factor within the context of the religion-forgiveness discrepancy, but it is also apparent that individuals are not passive automatons to the dictates of their religious meaning systems. They may also actively shape those systems to conform to their immediate motivations, thereby finding it not only possible but also coherent to espouse forgiveness at the religious dispositional level while concurrently rationalising unforgiveness (or even vengeance) at the behavioural level of response to transgression-specific harm done to them.

Investigation of self-forgiveness has some input of value to add to this. It seems probable that psychological mechanisms that enable victims of wrongdoing to proselytise about the virtues of forgiveness at the same time as practising unforgiveness may be similar to the mechanisms that enable wrongdoers to find justifications of their own harmful behaviour. Campana (2010) reported that disingenuous self-forgiveness arises from egotism, narcissism and a sense of entitlement and is 'related to reluctance to accept responsibility' (p. 15).[16]

If religion is not a consistent determinant of transgression-specific forgiveness what then are those determinants that link a disposition to forgive and situational factors to forgiveness in specific instances of inter-personal transgression? A recent study by Ahadi (2009) provides some answers. A total sample of 344 students was used. Their responses to the TRIM (see p. 174), items concerning closeness of relationship and 43 items that measured transgression-related contextual factors were subjected to factor analysis. The results revealed a number of unique factors that predicted forgiveness of specific offences. These were the offended party's disposition to forgive, the value placed by the victim on their relationship with the wrongdoer, the positive post-transgression actions of the wrongdoer (expressions of remorse) and level of expectation that the wrongdoer would repeat the offence. More specifically, pre-transgression measures of closeness and value of the relationship determined the value placed by the victim after the transgression but did not predict forgiving the wrongdoer after the offence. Post-transgression measures, however, suggest that a change in the relationship occurs after the wrongdoing and it is the re-evaluation of the relationship that is important to the decision whether to forgive. Post-transgression factors became more important than pre-transgression closeness. The actions of the wrongdoer after the offence were important, as was a perception that the offence was non-malicious. Convincing assertion that the wrongdoing would not be repeated was important, as was the adjudged level of severity of the offence.

There seems to be little need for an individual to be religious in order for these factors to function except that the initial disposition to forgive may well have a basis in religion. It should be remembered that there is a consistently strong positive relationship between dispositional forgiveness and religiousness, and this may be the starting point for many religious people as they ponder a decision whether to forgive or not. Otherwise, the religion-forgiveness discrepancy has little significance in relation to the information and feelings that victims process as they come to their decision. Is a claim that they are motivated by their religious beliefs indicative of hypocrisy on the part of religious people when they chose to forgive or simply a demonstration of their human frailty when they chose not to?

Ayden, a retired engineer, had a pragmatic view of the conundrum religious people experience when they really do not want to forgive someone but their beliefs state they should. 'I'm glad that I'm not religious. If someone harms me in some way I weigh up all the facts available including who did what, why and whether it was out of character. If I want to forgive them, I do; if I don't want to, then I won't. I don't have to worry about being out of some step with some doctrine or make excuses for my decision. What's the point of having free will if you can't exercise your own judgement?

Forgiveness and apologies that fit

It would appear that religion is not a major promoter of forgiveness for specific interpersonal transgression. In contrast, as has been mentioned previously, contrite apology is strongly associated with forgiveness and the repair of relationships (e.g. Eaton and Struthers, 2006). It is axiomatic, however, that not all apologies from remorseful individuals succeed in winning forgiveness. Many apologies bounce off injured, hurting and angry victims like sea spray from a granite cliff. Others appear to be superficial and unconvincing, whilse some are so clumsily fashioned that they miss their target. Struthers *et al.* (2008) describe the possible problems that arise when attempts at apology fail. They comment that

> the benefits of an apology may backfire when transgressors intended to harm the injured party. When saddled to purposefully harmful acts, transgressors who apologize may be perceived, suspiciously, as self-interested, untrustworthy, and as having an ulterior motive . . . rather than, normatively, as empathic, genuine, and trustworthy. In this case, apology might, paradoxically, limit the possibility of forgiveness even further because the victim fails to adjust his or her initial harsh impression of the transgressor to a more favorable one and instead adjusts to a pejorative one.
>
> (p. 984)

Paradoxically, however, the investigation of why some apologies are successful and others are not, provide clues about the process of forgiveness itself within intimate relationships.

An important part of this process concerns the components of remorseful apology and the constructs held by victims about what they require in an apology (Fehr and Gelfand, 2010). Until relatively recently research has tended to examine only the dichotomy of Apology/No Apology when investigating the effectiveness of apology in respect of forgiveness. For example, Frantz and Bennigson (2005) hypothesised that later rather than earlier apologies may be more effective in conflict resolution. Their view was that late apology might allow victims some time to ventilate their emotional response to transgression and so feel better understood as victims. Later apology might therefore help victims to become more ready to accept apology and so more able to take part in conflict resolution. Their research study substantiated this hypothesis and they suggested that the delay in apology enabled transgressors 'hear' the impact of their behaviour on the victims' emotions and acknowledge that impact. They suggest links to the psycho-therapeutic notion of unconditional positive regard. However, their study did not evaluate the components of the apologies made, being more concerned with the timing of the apologies and the 'voice' of the victim. The simple dichotomisation is not restricted to apologies; it appears in other forms of communication associated with unfavourable events. Thus, for example, Shaw *et al.* (2003) found that within organisations explanations were viewed more positively when they were presented as excuses rather than as justifications of unfavourable outcomes. They did not, however, 'codify or model the contents of the accounts themselves' (Fehr and Gelfand, 2010, p. 38).

The simple dichotomisation does not allow for a clear appreciation of why some apologies work and why others do not. Second, it cannot take into account that in the real world victims differ significantly one from the other in terms of their opinions of the severity of the wrongdoing that harmed them and what they might expect from an apology. In addition, the overly simplistic experimental concept of apology cannot reliably inform intervention that could use carefully tailored apology to affect therapeutic organisational goals.

Recent research on the effective components of apology has focused on the importance of victims' self-construals that link apology to forgiveness. Self-construals concern how individuals perceive their relationships with other people. They have been implicated as having functional significance across cognitions, emotions and behaviour. For example, Cross *et al.* (2002) stated that the self is thought to be largely defined in terms of connections to significant others, referred to as 'independent self-construals' (p. 399). Self-construals also appear to influence how people perceive conflict. Gelfand *et al.* (2001) found that there are culture-specific construals of conflict that mediate the way in which individuals from different cultures perceive the same conflict. In general, people from individualistic cultures (such as the UK and USA) perceive conflict in such a way that they prefer adversarial strategies to achieve resolutions. In addition, those people having robust independent self-construals believe they are unique and self-directed. Their objectives are usually self-oriented and they expect that their provisions and services to others will lead to an exchange of benefits. They are competitive and cooperate with others when it is advantageous to do so, but their actions are seldom determined by consensus. Indeed, Wagner (1995) stated, 'Individualists look after themselves and tend to ignore group interests if they conflict with personal desires' (p. 1995).

By contrast, individuals from collectivist cultures (e.g. Japan) respond to conflict very differently in that they prefer mediation and negotiation. Whereas individualistic people tend to look for a blameworthy individual in interpersonal conflict, those from collectivistic cultures tend to construe conflict as being the product of both parties' behaviour. Those people with the collective self are more directed towards groups and social affinities. These individuals identify strongly with the groups they belong to and their actions are often focused on the enhancement of these groups. Group-norms and rules take precedence over self-directed actions. Johnson and Chang (2006) state, 'the self is defined in terms of group membership. As such, individuals tend to internalize the goals and norms of their group and derive satisfaction when they successfully fulfill their social roles and obligations' (p. 551).

Individuals with highly relational self-construals hold strongly to a belief in connectedness with other people. They believe that they are defined by their relationships; their actions are directed at maintaining and improving their relationships, and they possess complex cognitive networks concerning relationships. Cross *et al.* (2002) state:

> In the relational-interdependent self-construal, representations of significant others and relationships share the self-space with other attributes, such as abilities, traits, and goals . . . . Persons with a highly relational self-construal will think and act in ways that support and maintain this self-view. They will tend to emphasize their connectedness to others and behave in ways that promote and strengthen existing relationships.
>
> (p. 400)

Conceptualisations of self-construals refer to a three-part model reflecting different dimensions of the self. Gelfand and her colleagues (2006) describe these as:

> (1) the individualistic dimension of the self, which refers to the self as an independent, autonomous, and agentic entity; (2) the relational dimension of the self, which refers to the extent to which people regard themselves as emotionally connected to other individuals; and (3) the collective dimension of the self, which refers to the self in relation to a group or collective. The latter emphasizes group affiliation, in-group norms, and statuses defined by collectives
>
> (p. 432)

Fehr and Gelfand (2010) hypothesise that for forgiveness to be successfully evoked by an apology its contents, or components, should be congruent with the construals held by the recipient. Some attention is now given to the nature of these components.

Components of apology   There has been a focus on components of apology from the domains of psychiatry and sociology, but less so from psychology. Five components have been thought of as predominant in terms of the construction of a convincing apology (e.g. Schmitt *et al.*, 2004). These are: (1) admitting fault; (2) admitting harm done; (3) expressing remorse' (4) requesting forgiveness, and (5) offering compensation. Of these five, Fehr and Gelfand (2010) focus on three in particular, suggesting that 'victims who emphasize the independent, relational, and collective self-construals will be most likely to forgive their offenders following offers of compensation, expressions of empathy, and acknowledgments of violated rules/norms, respectively' (p. 38).

In this context, *compensation* concerns the restoration of the situation prior to the wrongdoing. This need not be as simple as the replacement of a window shattered by a rogue cricket ball; it may well be the restoration of status when a victim has been left feeling like a person of no worth, fit only to be abused by the betrayal of the relationship that was once thought to be of mutual importance. In some cases, it may not be clear what specific compensatory actions could be taken to restore matters, in which case an open offer may have to suffice ('Please let me know what I can do to make amends'). An apology having no offer of compensation may lack substance; there should be some visible cost to the transgressor.

In Richard's case the apology he received from Sally for claiming credit for the excellent work he had done was her confession to their manager that she had wrongly allowed him to think that it was her initiative rather than Richard's. In Richard's presence she explained that she had had no part in designing the successful operation and had only helped in carrying it through. Richard deserved the credit and not her. This was satisfactory in Richard's estimation as it restored his status of creative thinker within the department and provided a useful fillip for the annual bonus he was hoping for.

The second component, expression of empathy, is centred on the relationship that was damaged. The transgressor shows awareness and remorse for the pain and suffering imposed on the victim by the offence. In addition, these expressions may signify that the quality of the relationship is still of great importance to the transgressor. This communication is vital if the transgressor hopes that the relationship can be continued. There are both emotional and cognitive elements to these expressions of empathy; not only does the transgressor empathise with the pain and suffering, but also shows understanding of the victim's opinion of what happened and accepts that there was a betrayal. Offenders may also augment their expressions of empathy with self-castigation and requests for forgiveness (e.g. Schlenker and Darby, 1981).

Steve confessed to his wife Anne that he had been unfaithful to her with an old girlfriend who had briefly come back into his life. He made no excuses for his behaviour and acknowledged that a combination of lust and alcohol had been sufficient for his act of betrayal. He also acknowledged that he had hurt her badly and had no right to expect that he could regain her trust. More specifically, he recalled a promise that he had made to her before their wedding that he would not be disloyal to her. He said that he could not forgive himself for breaking that promise as he had made it spontaneously without any pressure from her. This broken promise had hurt Anne more than anything and the fact that he recalled it helped her to believe that his empathy for her might just be genuine.

The third component concerns the violations of the norms and rules that govern behaviour and exclude the offending behaviour. These violations are more obvious where they concern the direct flouting of an organisation's rules or codes of conduct. For example, a soldier could go absent without leave or a politician may falsify his or her expenses. Both of these contravene specific rules laid down by the armed forces and government respectively. There are also implicit rules and norms within interpersonal relationships that concern the ways in which individuals should behave in order not to betray the trust of the other(s) or demean them. Where victims are particularly harmed by the violation of these informal yet vital relationship rules, it is appropriate that the transgressor acknowledges the breaches that have occurred.

Mark had been brought up in a succession of foster homes after his mother was found to be unfit to care for him. He spent six years from aged ten to sixteen in the last of these where he was the perpetual butt of jokes and sarcasm about his mild stammer. These came from both foster parents and their own children; they had all got into the habit of laughing raucously at his attempts to communicate and even wanted him to entertain their friends by reciting lines that were particularly difficult for him. Not surprisingly, his confidence fell badly and he had little self-esteem.

Mark married Toni who understood when he told her about this treatment of him and she promised never to make fun of him in the same way. Unfortunately, she had too much to drink at a party and started to laugh at him with her friends. He left quickly in shame and embarrassment with her shouting after him that she was only joking. Later she apologised profusely to him and made clear that she knew she had broken the simple rule that was so important to him and had demeaned him in front of a houseful of guests. She told him that she understood how her behaviour could have damaged the fragile confidence he had gained over the years since he left the foster home.

Individual responses to the components of apology   Fehr and Gelfand (2010) examined the direct effects of the apology components on forgiveness. They argue that as individuals respond differently to the same stimuli, it is probable that they would respond differently to the same apology components. Their individual self-construals would be probable antecedents to those responses. Their influence on the perception, processing and response to information would apply to the reception of an apology as they would to any other relationship-related information. As Fehr and Gelfand (2010) state: 'When specific attitudes or beliefs are particularly central to the self, individuals tend to interpret the world through the lens of these views and pay particular attention to information that is consistent with them' (p. 39). They suggest, therefore, that when apologies are congruent with the self-construals of victims, they are more likely to be considered favourably. It is possible to consider how the three aspects of self (i.e. independent, relational and collective selves) would influence responses to apology components.

Given the strength of their individualistic and competitive belief structure, victims who have independent self-construal might well attend closely to apologies that reflect damage to their autonomy and rights. They are more probably concerned with components of apology that offer some compensation or action to restore their equality with the transgressor. Components relating to an empathetic understanding of how hurt they feel as a consequence of the offence would be of significantly less importance. Not only do offers of compensation restore what has been lost, but also provide tangible evidence that the confrontation has gone in their favour; they have captured the high ground of the moral competition with the offender. Under some circumstances the apology component of offered compensation may also satisfy concerns over the fair distribution of resources. As Johnson and Chang (2006) point out, 'In organizational settings, work outcomes, such as pay and benefits, are especially important for employees with strong individual self-concepts, as these outcomes represent visible standards for comparison' (p. 551).

In the example of Sally's admission of guilt to Richard above, the nature of the apology restored Richard's reputation within their department and also made clear to their line manager that it was he who was capable of initiative and creativity. In that particular instance at least, Richard was not only a victim but also something of a hero initiator. He had won the high ground morally and occupationally, a much better prize than an apology for hurt feelings.

The victim with strong collective self-construals may feel that the offender has violated the rules and norms of the valued group where the group may be two partners in an intimate relationship or more people in an occupational or friendship context. This victim will be less concerned with empathetic responses and offers of compensation but more attracted to acknowledgement that the cohesion of the group has been threatened by this violation: 'Together we stand, divided we fall.' A remorseful acknowledgement that the wrongdoing vitiated the rules also shows that the offender possesses a degree of approval of them and thereby confirms their continuing credibility and importance to the victim. In addition, victims will want to be assured that the rule-breaking action will not be repeated and look for evidence in the expression of remorse that offenders understand this (Gold and Weiner, 2000, p. 299).

Those victims with robust relational self-construals will look for the empathetic component in apology. Compensation and acknowledgement of rule violation are of lesser significance than acceptance of harm done. Johnson and colleagues (2006) state: 'individuals are motivated by the welfare of the specific other, and appropriate role behavior regarding a specific person determines self-worth' (pp. 176–7). Statements expressing an understanding that the victim has every right to feel pain and suffering demonstrate that the victim is allowed a 'voice' to describe the sense of betrayal and emotional harm that was done by the transgressor.

These considerations led Ferh and Gelfand (2010) to formulate three specific hypotheses:

1   Victims with strong independent self-construal will respond more positively to apologies that contain the component of compensation offers.
2   Victims with strong collective self-construal will respond more positively to apologies that contain the component of acknowledged violation of rules/norms.
3   Victims with strong relational self-construal will respond more positively to apologies that contain empathetic expressions.

To test these hypotheses Fehr and Gelfand constructed an apology component scale based on 15 items that reflected adequate representations of each of the three apology components. These 15 items were subjected to a validation procedure and were rated on a five-point scale (1 = Strongly Disagree to 5 = Strongly Agree). The three apology components were represented by 5 items each and were confirmed as adequate by statistical analysis. Self-construal was measured using the Levels of Self-Concept Scale (LCS) (Selenta and Lord, 2005, cited by Fehr and Gelfand, 2010).

These two scales were taken by 175 undergraduate students over two sessions with a separation between sessions of nearly one month. The results 'provided clear evidence that perceived importance of different apology components is directly related to victims' self-construals' (Fehr and Gelfand, 2010, p. 41). Thus, victims with predominant self-construals of one type did find the associated apology component significantly more attractive than the other two components. A second study established that this relationship was not significantly affected by different levels of harm severity associated with the offence. The self, therefore, made decisions about apologies that confirmed to internal representations of what apologies should contain and was not diverted from this process by increased severity of harm.

Forgiveness, power and commitment

We have seen above that the offender who feels sorry enough to apologise should take care to make sure that the apology is focused on the particular beliefs and constructs of the recipient. The probability of forgiveness, and perhaps even reconciliation, rises as the apology more closely fits the victim. There is, however, another important dimension to forgiveness that the offender may not be able to do much about. This is the dimension of victim power.

It is rare to find strong intimate relationships where both partners have the same degree of 'power' as each other. Generally, in my experience, one of them may be deferred to over some important aspects of the functioning of the relationship. Sometimes one partner has more control over material resources than the other; perhaps one partner decides the social engagements or where the couple has their home. This is not a gender-specific phenomena; the man does not always wear the trousers.

Power can be a formal aspect of a relationship; thus, a manager has position-power over his or her staff, although he or she may be more or less respected according to their perceptions of his personal and/or expert power (e.g. Yuki and Falbea, 1991). Some people have power referred to them because they are so well respected that others are content to defer to them whereas other people are simply bossy and exert power over those who are more vulnerable. Whatever the source of power may be, it can be regarded as an individual's perceived ability to control resources and direct the behaviour of others. Thus, Keltner and colleagues state:

> We define power as an individual's relative capacity to modify others' states by providing or withholding resources or administering punishments. This capacity is the product of the actual resources and punishments the individual can deliver to others . . . Resources and punishments can be material (food, money, economic opportunity, physical harm, or job termination) and social (knowledge, affection, friendship, decision-making opportunities, verbal abuse, or ostracism). The value of resources or punishments reflects other individuals' dependence on those resources.
>
> (Keltner *et al.*, 2003, pp. 265–6)

It is often assumed wrongly that power in interpersonal relationships is invariably abused, that power corrupts and is used selfishly. There is some support for this jaundiced viewpoint. Keltner *et al.* (2003) reviews many of the negative findings about 'powerful' people. They tend to favour stereotypic and negatively biased information about people regarded as inferiors. They tend to be rude in conversation, fail to turn-take and act more aggressively than less powerful individuals and sometimes abuse people by bullying and harassment. Often their behaviour is blatantly self-seeking. However, while these abuses may be true on occasion. there is growing evidence that power is functionally associated with consistent goal-directed orientations and proactive commitment. Indeed, Smith and colleagues have demonstrated that a lack of power is disruptive of goal maintenance whereas empowerment of individuals can lead to improved performance (Smith *et al.*, 2008). It is probable, therefore, that the powerful partners in damaged relationships may be forgiving because that is a sensible strategy for helping to mend the relationship after transgression if they consider it worth repairing.

Formal or statutory authority does not usually define power in most intimate relationships. An exception to this occurs when in some orthodox religions women are perceived as subservient to men. Where both partners in a relationship share the same faith, then, no matter what his faults may be, the man is granted power by virtue of his gender only. In general terms, however, and in more permissive cultures, power often goes to the partner who has most experience of it in other walks of life (e.g. Karremans and Smith, 2010).

It is this variety of power that is considered here, rather than the absolute power given by formal decree or other imposition. In my experience, it is a form of power that almost titrates out of the processes of daily living as the partners in the relationship function together.

In addition, power need not be defined by dependency. It is clearly the case that a vulnerable partner with no alternatives to go to in the event of his or her leaving the relationship has less power than the other partner. This referral of power by circumstance does not necessarily make for adroitness in the use of the power so fortuitously gained. Unless something goes wrong in the relationship, the 'powerful' partners may never know of the strong position they are in. Once again, it is the awareness of power and the experience of using it that is the telling factor when transgression threatens the cohesion of the relationship. The core trend among powerful people is that they are significantly more goal-directed than people with less experience of power and they act purposively and persistently towards the resolution of their goals. For example, Guinote (2007) showed that

> having power decreases procrastination and facilitates goal-consistent behavior. Compared with powerless individuals, powerful individuals prioritized their focal goals. They devoted their undivided attention to the pursuit of these goals and responded more in a goal-consistent manner compared with powerless individuals.
>
> (p. 1084)

Not surprisingly, therefore, people with high power who are also committed to responding to the needs of others are more likely to behave responsibly, attentively and responsively to them (Chen et al., 2001). Thus, they use their experience of power to boost prosocial and other-oriented goals.

Relationship commitment   Intimate relationships differ one from another in part according to the degree of commitment the partners hold towards them and this appears to have a bearing on the probability of forgiveness. One dimension of commitment concerns the degree of effort a partner may be prepared to make in order to preserve and develop the relationship. Sadly, only one partner may be highly motivated to maintain the relationship, while the other experiences ambivalence. When both are strongly committed to the relationship they are more likely to share goals concerning its longevity, whereas in low-commitment relationships partners tend not to have such other-oriented goals; instead, they concentrate on their personal needs and act for their partners only after they have received some benefit from them (e.g. Karremans and Smith 2010).

Chen et al. (2001) found that experienced powerful individuals who were communally focused showed greater activity in respect of prosocial goals. This effort would include that expended for the maintenance of important relationships. It is reasonable to hypothesise, therefore, that such people would be more likely to forgive as to be unforgiving would mitigate against the meeting of relationship-maintenance goals. In addition, research has demonstrated that experienced power is an important factor in the suppression of thoughts, emotions and motivations that inhibit goal-directed activity (e.g. Smith and Trope, 2006). Karremans and Smith (2010) suggest that this may help to suppress the ruminations that tend to block forgiveness. Partners with only low commitment, be they 'powerful' or not, would be more likely to work towards self-oriented goals and not be highly motivated to preserve the relationship. Research findings are largely congruent with these expectations. For example, Zechmeister and Romero (2002) suggested that one of the motivations energising forgiveness is a desire to preserve the relationship by discarding victim status and being angry at the offence rather than the offender.

It is possible to suggest, therefore, that experienced powerful individuals who are highly committed to an intimate relationship are more likely to forgive their partners for hurtful offences. After linking the behavioural traits associated with experienced power and commitment, Karremans and Smith (2010) hypothesised that high levels of experienced power would facilitate forgiveness, particularly in respect of relationships characterised by high commitment. They employed three studies that made use of both experimental and correlational designs for hypothetical offences as well as incidents of forgiveness for actual previous offences. The results bore out the hypothesis that experienced power in high commitment relationships was associated with forgiveness. Their findings supported the view that individuals with high experienced power were more able to suppress the ruminations that militate against forgiveness in intimate relationships and might otherwise maintain feelings of aggressiveness towards individuals (e.g. McCullough et al., 2001b). Karremans and Smith (2010) suggest that an alternative explanation could be supported by the results, whereby high levels of forgiveness may simply suppress the tendency to aggressive rumination generally.

Summary

Forgiveness is not the dewy-eyed heart wrench portrayed in romantic comedies; it is frequently hard-headed and decisive. Contrary to popular belief, it is not always the rekindling of a relationship that existed before betrayal, but is the decision of a victim not to endure the painful hurt and persistent ruminations that arise from transgressions. Although the offender may no longer face condemnation and the revenge of a vengeful victim, he or she may not necessarily expect to get back to the comforting bosom of the relationship that once was.

Victims may exercise decisional forgiveness and allow the relationship to continue without ever forgetting the harm done or may simply exercise emotional forgiveness to release themselves from the negative emotions that blight their lives while they are in a state of unforgiveness. Many look for religious or spiritual guidance to assist their decision-making. The significance of forgiveness within the beliefs and practices of most of the world's major religions is considerable. Religions provide moral teaching about forgiveness and guidance of its process. Sadly, not all the guidance is clear and allows for the distortion of idiosyncrasy and rampant fundamentalism. In addition, by espousing its virtues robustly religious teachers make forgiveness seem like a veritable commandment to devoted adherents such that they feel obliged to forgive at a time when the wounds of their betrayal are still raw and they might rather not.

Part of the power of religions to benignly compel forgiveness is the linkage drawn between empathetically motivated altruism for those people in need because of poverty, sickness, warfare and other disasters, and those people whose needs for forgiveness are defined by the discomfort of their remorse. There is, however, an apparent discrepancy between the acceptance by religious people of the duty to forgive (dispositional forgiveness) and their alacrity to do so in respect of specific harm done to them (transgressional forgiveness). Whereas several studies show that strongly religious people claim that they believe in the need for forgiveness and strive to practise this, other studies reveal that in the face of actual transgression the probability of forgiveness is below expectation. One study revealed that religious people are no more likely to forgive specific transgressions than people who have no religion.

Attempts to demonstrate that the discrepancy was illusory and merely the product of procedural problems failed to account for the size of the discrepancy despite some psychometric difficulties being identified. A further possible explanation was that religious meaning systems are sufficiently broad to allow a belief in vengefulness under some circumstances as well as forgiveness. This is one factor that lies at the heart of radicalisation and reflects a rationalisation that may mediate the probability of transgression-specific forgiveness. This effect was not found, however, to account for the size of the discrepancy either. Thus, being religious does not always promote forgiveness for specific transgressions. As for non-religious people, it is quite probable that the transgression event so alters the relationship between victim and offender that a re-evaluation of the correctness of forgiveness is undertaken. In consequence, it is probable that religiousness is not as strong a predictor of transgression-specific forgiveness as it appears it should be given its strong association with decisional forgiveness.

A more powerful influence on the probability of forgiveness is a contrite apology from the offender that includes remorse for the harm done, an understanding that the 'rules' of the relationship have been violated, a desire to make some form of restitution, and a promise to behave better in the future. In addition, when the apology is tailored to fit the self-construals of the victim, then the probability of forgiveness is improved further. Thus, victims with strong independent self-construals respond more positively to offers of recompense. Those with strong collective self-construals respond better to apologies that acknowledge violation of the rules that govern behaviour within the relationship. Victims with strong relational self-construals are more influenced by expressions of empathy for the harm done. Accurate appeal to a victim's self-construals is able to more credibly demonstrate that the offender is truly feeling sorry and not just saying so disingenuously.

Victim power is a further variable that influences the probability of forgiveness. It appears that if the victim in a damaged relationship is the one with the greatest power, perhaps by being more worldly or experienced from occupational responsibilities, and if that individual is very committed to the relationship, then he or she is more likely to forgive the offender by regarding the transgressional behaviour as the problem rather than the offender. Such individuals are more likely to consider forgiveness rather than tolerate the persistent aggressive ruminations associated with unforgiveness.

Chapter 8

Remorse, empathy, forgiveness and therapy

Introduction

I have met many people who, despite the painful wounds they have had inflicted on them by the experience of betrayal within their intimate relationships, vehemently eschew suggestions that they would benefit from therapeutic help. Their strident opinions on counselling and other treatments find resonance with the views of Allan Bloom, the philosopher, classicist and academic, who stated: 'There are great industries of psychotherapy that address our difficulties in "relationships" – that pallid, pseudoscientific word, the very timidity of which makes substantial attachments impossible. One has to have a tin ear to describe one's great love as a relationship.' One can have a degree of sympathy for this opinion that the tired word 'relationship' fails to capture the deep sense of belonging that individuals experience from an intense intimate rapport with another person. It is understandable also that such a man as he, chronically disenchanted with his contemporary society and firmly of the belief that commercial goals had become more highly valued than love, should look sceptically on the struggles of psychotherapists to help clients 'fix' their relationships. Yet it may well be the Herculean effort that many couples put into the 'fixing' of their damaged lives together that confounds such a view and places their love above displays of meretricious emotionality. Some of the content of this chapter extends material introduced in Chapter 3 and is supportive of therapeutic endeavour in respect of remorse and forgiveness.

I start with the simple fact that narratives of counselling, psychotherapy and confession yield countless examples of transgressors who long to put matters right and find the means to repair the relationships they have damaged. Sadly, however, in shrinking away from thoughts and actions that bring them face to face with shame, they block opportunities for going forward to express their remorse and prepare the apologies or other acts of contrition that might lead to forgiveness and the restoration of a previously loving relationship. If therapy in whatever form can help them summon their courage and take the first steps to moving from merely being sorry to actually showing their sorrow, then that is a small but vital triumph of humanity. The desire for forgiveness dominates the thoughts of many perpetrators who are genuinely ashamed of the harm they have caused. Therapy not only can promote forgiveness of the perpetrator, but also assist in the healing of the victim and the repair of the damaged relationship. This transcendent benefit is important in Buddhist teachings where the mindset of well-being is characterised by calmness, friendliness, compassion, the renouncement of ill will, the abandonment of self-centredness and the practice of forgiveness.

Shame became a massive stumbling block for David who, in his mid-fifties, had developed a severe addiction to gambling. He lost almost all the retirement funds that he and his wife Mary had painstakingly built up. They both had full-time work, David as an independent accountant and Mary as the manager of leisure centre. She had trusted him to invest their money carefully and thought that all was well. She had had no idea that he was gambling and was unaware of the erosion of their funds.

David knew how much retirement meant to her as she often chattered happily about the hobbies she wanted to take up and the places she wanted to visit. He described her as 'brokenhearted rather than angry. She told me that I had betrayed both of us'. Both knew that they would have to work for years longer than they had planned and could never expect the same opportunities in their retirement that he had frittered away on one failed bet after another. David desperately wanted Mary's forgiveness but could never bring himself the greater intensity of shame and guilt that would arise from approaching her. His retreat from this pain caused him other problems because he could see that his abject failure to openly acknowledge the damaged he had caused left her even more hurt, as though what he had done to her was not even worth an apology.

David would agree that he did not just want to be forgiven by Mary; he *needed* to be forgiven by her. He also made a link between forgiveness and love during one of his sessions when he said, 'If Mary forgave me, I would know that I hadn't entirely lost her love. It's only now I realise I don't need gambling but I do need her love.' His insight is congruent with the opinion of Aponte (1998) who believes it is 'unconditional love that can be the wellspring of an unconditional forgiveness' (p. 56). Perhaps David understood that if Mary was able to truly forgive him, despite the severity of his betrayal, then her love for him was unconditional.

David and Mary did accept therapy as a couple. He had become very low of mood as increasingly he could not distance himself from his shame and guilt. A particular incident forced him to fully acknowledge what he had done. This occurred when Mary was forced to explain to their daughter that she and David would be unable to give the young woman the support for university fees that had been planned. David heard Mary's fumbling attempts to explain the situation without attributing blame to him. He was angry at how ashamed this made him feel and he blurted out rather coldly to their daughter what had happened and then marched out of the house without any word of the regret that he felt.

David's primary motivation for accepting therapy was to seek forgiveness; Mary's was to get help to overcome the feelings of worthlessness that David's apparently dismissive behaviour had created. Eventually, when the depths of his distress became evident, she found that she could not only empathise with David's suffering but also that she could not be worthless if she had the power to forgive him, whether or not she chose to do so. Thus, forgiveness was very important for them both, but in Mary's case the right to grant it or withhold it was essential to her well-being.

The fact that Mary had a choice was beneficial to her and David also. They understood that choice making about forgiveness was deliberate and conscious. Forgiveness without thought, given carelessly, had little prospect of being genuine or long-lasting. It would have the characteristics of a shallow cliché – 'I forgive you because I'm a nice person and it's the right thing to do'. For Mary, to choose to forgive David, she must intend to do so. Forgiveness would be a product of her will alone and enduring as a consequence.

In order for her to make her decision, Mary wanted to know what good would come of her choice. Would David simply heave a mental sigh of relief and then go back to his old selfish behaviour? Would she feel any better about herself if either she forgave or decided to withhold forgiveness? Could forgiveness help her to trust him again and motivate him to make some form of recompense? She worked through these questions during one-to-one sessions with the therapist and eventually she did forgive David after she listened to his carefully considered apology. He understood that she was a person for who relational factors were vitally important (see relational self-construals, p. 187) and stressed that he knew he had hurt her badly and effectively devalued her in their relationship. He stressed that he understood that she had every right to be enraged by this and that his treatment of her place in their relationship was every bit as wrongful as losing their money. He understood also that she had a right to tell him how she felt and the right to reject not just his apology but him also. He stated that he wanted to make recompense when she decided what form this should take and that, in the meantime, he would work very hard to try and restore their circumstances.

The example of David and Mary's therapeutic work on forgiveness can be understood in relation to the three main dimensions of forgiveness described by Lagaree and her colleagues (2007). They state:

> The dimensions are (a) essentiality: the importance, applicability, and healing potential of forgiveness, (b) intentionality: forgiveness as a decision or a discovery, and (c) benevolence: the role of compassion for the offender in forgiveness and who forgiveness is for.
>
> (p. 195)

These are considered in terms of David and Mary's case.

Essentiality   There is some dispute among therapists as to whether forgiveness is essential to successful therapeutic outcome or a block to the resolution of angry feelings and recovery from harm. It seems clear from most perspectives, however, that forgiveness is essential to the repair of damaged relationships. Whether it is also vital to personal healing for victims is less clear, but the balance of opinion suggests that it is (e.g. Lagaree *et al.*, 2007). Some comments about this virtuous human behaviour owe more to fervour than to scientific enquiry; even so, experience of working with families does lend support to Hope's comment (1987):

> Forgiveness is a concept deeply embedded in our Judeo-Christian culture, so fundamental that it is little noticed in the background of our awareness. It is proposed that the process of forgiveness is a key part of the psychological healing process, but that it is rarely recognized as such; instead the talented psychotherapist intuitively practices and models forgiving attitudes in the course of the therapeutic encounter and teaches clients to "work through," "let go," or "accept" the wounds and shortcomings of the past. By clarifying the concept of forgiveness it can be seen that learning to forgive is an important and perhaps core element in the therapeutic process.
>
> (p. 240)

In addition, the converse of the consequences of withholding forgiveness can be catastrophic, as is made clear by DiBlasio's observation (2000):

> Where unforgivingness exists, clients compound their problems because cognitive and emotional energy is misdirected into resentment that prevents healing. A breakdown in some aspect of the emotional, psychological, physical, spiritual, and interpersonal functioning can result. The result is that a second order of dysfunction is laid over the original offense; that is to say, the victims become their own offenders as they become absorbed in unresolved bitterness. In addition, resentment and bitterness can block objective understanding by the betrayed spouse to his or her own contributions to the interpersonal difficulty.
>
> (p. 151)

Clinical experience suggests that enduring reconciliation demands forgiveness, but even if reconciliation is not possible because the victim does not want it, forgiveness still brings an end to the hurting caused by betrayal; it enables a new beginning unburdened by vengeful ruminations and protestations of harm done. Clinical narratives reveal a further benefit of the goal of forgiveness in therapy; that is, its general 'goodness of fit'. Ferch (1998) reviewed the contemporary literature of the use of forgiveness in therapeutic work associated with the impact of perpetrator behaviour on the lives of victims. He found multiple references to individual group and family counselling 'regarding experiences such as emotional, physical, and sexual abuse; extramarital affairs and various contexts of relational distrust, discord and conflict' (p. 262). He cites also studies relating to severe trauma; relieving debilitating emotions such as bitterness, anger and depression; and interventions in respect of addictions.

David and Mary's difficulties were such that the pursuit of forgiveness was essential even if Mary chose to withhold it. It was essential as a focus of David's positive shift away from the blocking effects of shame and movement towards the expression of remorse. Working towards an appropriate apology gave direction to David's efforts. Mary's need was for the positive exploitation of power given to her by being the victim of David's unacceptable and disloyal behaviour. Working towards forgiveness was essential in order for her to find a healing outlet for the negative emotions that David's behaviour had engendered.

Intentionality This second dimension has been studied in relation to whether forgiveness comes directly as the result of a conscious decision or is 'discovered' as part of a broader strategy to deal with corrosive, angry and bitter feelings by reducing anger and encouraging compassion (e.g. Lagaree *et al.*, 2007). Some therapists have considered that forgiveness is an act of will that can arise fully formed almost instantaneously and not necessarily with emotional readiness. For example, DiBlasio (2000) utilises cognitive behaviour therapy and observes that the cognitive event of deciding to forgive may be the spur to positive emotional change. Other therapists (e.g. Enright and Fitzgibbons, 2000) regard this as a simplistic conceptualisation and argue that forgiveness is more than a unitary cognitive phenomena; Hill (2010) argues that forgiveness 'is more a discovery via understanding and empathy than an act of will' (p. 169).

Did Mary suddenly reach a decision to forgive or did she discover it as part of her own journey from negative to positive emotions? Did David's carefully framed apology suddenly shift her from rumination and anger to a plan to forgive, or was she already at a stage of emotional readiness to divine the sincerity and value of his remorse? In common with a seemingly frequent pattern of clients' responses, Mary appears to have come to forgiveness as a by-product of her own healing process (e.g. Simon and Simon, 1990). Once discovered, however, Mary's individual sessions were manifestly oriented towards what might be the connotations and consequences for her of forgiving David. There is little doubt that she had decided to forgive and that the actual act of communicating that forgiveness was intentional.

Benevolence This third issue largely concerns the issue of who benefits from forgiveness. It is probable that not only do perpetrators benefit from receiving mercy, compassion and possibly the restoration of a damaged relationship, but also victims may benefit from the cessation of negative emotions such as rage, bitterness, a desire for vengeance and feelings of worthlessness. Such outcomes may be thought of as the benevolence component of forgiveness.

This appears to be the dominant position within therapeutic circles (e.g. Lagaree *et al.*, 2007) and is typified by the thoughts of Enright and the Human Development Study Group (1996) who consider that benevolence and compassion can assist both victims and perpetrators to find their common intrinsic worth as human beings. The same group also comment that if victims work solely to reduce their negative emotions concerning the offence against them, the result will be only a 'cold neutrality' with the perpetrators, not forgiveness (Enright *et al.*, 1991, p. 494). They consider that forgiveness with benevolence forms a paradox in that when victims give up their emotional centering on self and the injury experienced in order to offer the boon of forgiveness, then the victim will experience the benefit of healing also. Tsang *et al.* (2006) go further in that they find that the benevolence qualities of forgiveness appear to facilitate later closeness and commitment in the damaged relationship. This suggests that the quality of benevolence as a dimension of forgiveness is strongly implicated in the increased probability of reconciliation.

The acceptance of the importance of benevolence in forgiveness is not universal. Some researchers and therapists make use of conceptualisations of forgiveness that include neither considerations of possible reconciliation nor of changes to positive feelings towards perpetrators. Generally, they veer towards conceptualisations that are restricted to the release of negative emotions, particularly of vengeful feelings, blame attribution and anger. Thus, Ferch's review of the literature led him to give a general opinion: 'Current counselling understandings of forgiveness, then, point to forgiveness as a unique opportunity for clients to be free of deeply embedded emotions that may restrain healing' (1998, p. 262). In addition, Gordon and colleagues (2004) accept that forgiveness may arise when partners pursue an improved understanding of themselves and each other, stating,

> Forgiveness means that negative affect no longer dominates their lives or controls their actions toward their partners and that this event has been resolved to such an extent that the injured partner no longer carries its negative effects into other relationships.
>
> (p. 216)

What of Mary and David? Did Mary's gift of forgiveness to David include benevolence? It seems fairly certain that it did. David understood that although his behaviour was not forgotten or in any way that his slate was wiped clean, he had not lost Mary's love. Their relationship could survive despite the damage done to it. David understood that Mary no longer harboured a wish to be avenged; instead, she wanted him to show his worth by doing his best to repair their finances and rescue something for their retirement. Mary also experienced benevolence; she no longer ruminated about feelings of worthlessness and accepted the harm done was about David's weakness, not hers. It was her choice to forgive him and her power to do so was a form of self-affirmation.

Forgiveness and empathy

It is often said that when we really stop to evaluate a situation in which we have been subject to a transgression of relationship we find we have more in common with the perpetrator than we may be comfortable with. That acknowledgement, when it is relevant in any given case, may sow a seed of forgiveness, which Worthington (1998) states, 'is the natural response to empathy and humility' (p. 64). This reasoning is based on a succession of realisations; first, that all humans are fallible; second, the offender is human; last, oneself is just another fallible person. In my experience, of many narratives of relationship betrayal, this reasoning is sharpened considerably when the victim realises that what the offender did and got caught doing was something similar to that which the victim might have liked to have done him or herself if the risk of detection had not been a deterrent. This is not a facile attempt at claiming that offenders are no worse than those they harmed, only that private reflective analysis and self-knowledge may tip the scales against the portrayal of a completely innocent victim whose shrill demands for justice are perhaps a little too extravagant.

Empathy, however, is not always possible or even desirable; some harmful transgressions may be too extreme or if the transgressor wields such power that a failure to at least go through the motions of forgiveness may be a source of further harm. When forgiveness is given just to avoid further pain from a dominant offender it is 'collusive forgiveness' in the words of Walrond-Skinner (1998, p. 12) and harm and injustice remain to rear up again and again.

Jo was terrified of her partner, Rod, who frequently abused alcohol and became violent. He attacked Jo on several occasions and then punched her six-year-old daughter, Kelly. He was instantly contrite and asked Jo to forgive him. When she was slow to respond he became very angry and frightened her: 'I told you I was sorry, didn't I? What do you want – blood?' Hurriedly, she told him she did forgive him and that she knew he wouldn't do it again. This forgiveness was collusive and for her own safety, it became the first link in a chain of collusive abuses that led eventually to Kelly's hospitalisation.

It is obviously asking too much of very vulnerable and powerless victims, or those too young to have the social development of mature empathy for others to experience humility in acknowledgment of fallibility. They are in no position to experience humility when, in many cases, they have been regularly ground down by powerful offenders to the point that their self-esteem is virtually non-existent. To expect such victims to formulate forgiveness from empathy and humility is futile and dangerous because it merely places additional stress on them. Yet, it is my experience that often physically abused wives and emotionally abused children are cajoled into statements of collusive forgiveness, perhaps to maintain family honour or the reputation of a respected person in the community or simply to get life back to normal as soon as possible. This begs the question: is it really possible for a vulnerable person to truly forgive those offenders who hold them in thrall?

Where, however, greater equality exists between transgressor and victim it is suggested that the discovery of empathy and humility is a potent factor in not only diminishing negative emotions but also pointing the way towards forgiveness and, perhaps, reconciliation also. Hill (2010) speaks of an empathetic-discovery process that 'seems to encompass a willingness to embrace the negative emotions that are invariably involved in our relational wounds and wounding, particularly the emotion of shame' (p. 173). It is possible therefore that forgiveness need not be an intentional act; indeed such intention does not guarantee success, a victim may not succeed in forgiving no matter how hard the struggle to do so. Hill (2010) suggests that the process of acknowledging empathy and humility in respect of a transgressor may lead not just to the release of negative emotions, but also to a surprising discovery that forgiveness has occurred anyway. This is congruent with conceptualisations arising from the behaviour of transgressors who, being ashamed of themselves and feel sorry for the harm they have caused, begin to express remorse and frame apology in a fashion that best fits the characteristics of their victims (see Chapter 7). As we have seen, getting the components of apology right improves the probability of forgiveness. Perhaps this is due to a catalytic effect on the victim that facilitates a psychological reaction to the offender revealing the mutual humanity of both offender and victim. This could enable or accelerate the process of letting go the negative emotions associated with the offence.

Aaron learned about the infidelity of his young wife, Jamie, from a work colleague. Jamie admitted that she had sex on two occasions with an old army boyfriend who contacted her when he came home on leave. Initially, Jamie's attitude was dismissive. She acknowledged what she had done, said it would not happen again and then refused to discuss it further. On several occasions when Aaron persisted, Jamie simply left the house and went shopping with her mother or friends. Aaron found this cold attitude as demeaning and corrosive as the infidelity. He felt that Jamie was rejecting him and demonstrating that their relationship had little value for her. He discussed this with his sister who helped him stiffen his resolve to get a divorce.

Aaron told Jamie that he wanted a divorce. Her reaction was startling; she became very distressed and blurted out a very confused mix of apology, self-recrimination and strong desire to repair their relationship. Her abject misery was so acute that Aaron was convinced that it was not an act. The aloof and dismissive Jamie was gone and the new one was almost incoherent with grief and self-loathing. Over a few days Aaron found his anger and protestations of injured innocence wilting as he watched his wife buckle under the weight of shame and guilt. He found he could empathise with her vulnerable, hopeless state and had sufficient humility to admit that no one is free of human frailty.

They had four sessions of couple therapy and Jamie had other individual sessions. She needed to know what to do with her shame, in her words, 'Put it to good use for Aaron's sake'. Her therapist helped her craft a careful apology based on the components of recompense, expressions of empathy and acknowledgement of the violation of the expectations of the relationship (see Chapter 7) and focused on what Aaron would find most meaningful given his self-construals. Jamie then asked for forgiveness and a little later Aaron was surprised to discover that he had already forgiven her and that it was about time to tell her so. Gradually a desire for reconciliation took hold.

This study is of further interest in that Aaron not only discovered forgiveness rather than set out to be forgiving; he also described the experience as 'outside myself'. He felt that passage from vengeful feelings and angry ruminations to reasserting his strong positive feelings for Jamie had taken him beyond what he had thought himself capable of. It was not surprising to find that Aaron was, in a fairly chaotic way, a very spiritually aware young man. His observation that the process of forgiveness had taken him 'outside' himself suggests a degree of spiritual transcendence. This is congruent with findings that such transcendence is positively correlated with dispositional humility and forgiveness (e.g. Powers *et al.*, 2007). It fits also with Piedmont's description of spiritual transcendence as 'the capacity of individuals to stand outside of their immediate sense of time and place to view life from a larger, more objective perspective . . . On this broader, more holistic perspective, individuals recognize a synchronicity to life and develop a sense of commitment to others' (Piedmont, 1999, p. 988).

Empathy, forgiveness and relationship quality

Depth of empathy and the readiness to forgive have much to say about the quality of intimate relationships. As we have seen, in respect of individuals, forgiveness is more likely if they are amenable and low in neuroticism and narcissism (McCullough *et al.*, 2001). Forgiveness is also more likely when the transgression occurs within an intimate relationship where the partners are committed to it and each other and when the victim shows empathy for the offender (McCullough *et al.*, 1998). In addition, victims who do not attribute blame to their offending partner (Fincham, 2000) and quell the temptation to ruminate persistently about the offence (McCullough *et al.*, 2001) are also more likely to show forgiveness within intimate relationships. Also, as we have seen, where transgressors show how sorry they are through genuine and well-delivered apologies and accounts of mitigation (McCullough *et al.*, 1998), forgiveness is more probable.

When forgiveness occurs within a damaged relationship an improvement often results such that there is a restoration of positive regard, positive interaction and affection. This is not a definite outcome; as Fincham (2000) comments:

> Reconciliation involves the restoration of violated trust and requires the goodwill of both partners. Thus, reconciliation entails forgiveness, but forgiveness does not necessarily entail reconciliation. Similarly, where harm-doing has resulted in the breakup of a relationship, forgiveness may, though it need not, lead to reunion, but reunion, unlike reconciliation, does not necessarily entail forgiveness.
>
> (p. 7)

These findings concern forgiveness in intimate relationships generally. Some researchers have considered marital relations specifically with interesting results. Fincham *et al.* (2004), for example, investigated forgiveness in married couples in their third year of marriage in order to examine whether forgiveness is associated with better conflict resolution. Their results identified retaliation, avoidance and benevolence as forgiveness dimensions whereby husbands' retaliatory or avoidance motivation reduced conflict resolution and wives' benevolence predicted better conflict resolution. Fincham and colleagues suggest that forgiveness is good for marital relationship quality; it is associated with less ineffectual argument, reduced psychological aggression and better communication (Fincham *et al.*, 2004). A number of studies have shown that attributions and emotional empathy for the victimised spouse have a direct bearing on marital forgiveness. Higher marital quality is associated with more benign attributions and these are, in turn, associated with forgiveness (Paleari *et al.*, 2005).

Paleari *et al.* (2005) have made the point that most forgiveness research was restricted by its dependence on cross-sectional data. In order to investigate this, the variations, if any, of forgiveness with the variables associated with it, studies should be made of more than one occasion. This would enable causal connections to be explicated with greater conviction. The study reported by Paleari and colleagues was the first to examine whether the documented cross-sectional association between marital quality and forgiveness is sustained over time or if it alters for better or worse (Paleari *et al.*, 2005). This relationship may be influenced by repeated offences.

The layperson's approach might be that repeat offending within an intimate relationship would reduce the probability of repeated forgiveness and be associated with worsening relationship quality. Frank was definitely of this opinion after his wife, Susan, was discovered to be maintaining an extra-marital relationship on two further occasions after expressing apparently sincere remorse and promising her future fidelity. Susan continued to be very remorseful and, in mitigation, claimed that she found she had little control over her emotions for her lover. Frank tended to believe this because he knew that she had been very easily led by others into less serious difficulties. Nevertheless, her repeated promises to reform began to sound hollow and Frank found himself unable to remain in the marriage and also unable to forgive.

This inability to forgive Susan worried him almost as much as the prospect of divorce as he continued to love her. He was fully aware that he could forgive her and still go through with the divorce but, in his words, 'The milk of my human kindness has curdled; not just for her but others as well. I've grown intolerant and wrapped up in my own woes to the point where I can feel little sympathy for anyone. The next step is total selfishness.'

Frank was a committed Christian with a long history of regular charity work. His embittered new self felt alien to him and distressed him greatly. Not only was his present and probable future life tainted but he had come to feel that the quality of his marriage had always rested on a sham. He was diagnosed with depression and underwent cognitive behaviour therapy.

Frank's experience is congruent with an expectation that whatever factors reduce the propensity to forgive also degrade marital quality. In this gross sense, therefore, the positive correlation between forgiveness and marital quality was maintained over time.

The study reported by Paleari and colleagues made use of 119 husbands and 124 wives from long- and medium-term marriages. Data was obtained on two occasions, separated by six months. Social-cognitive variables of forgiveness (offended spouses' emotional empathy and ruminations) and relationship variables (quality of the relationship in which the offence took place) were recorded. The results showed 'that rumination and empathy independently predicted concurrent marital forgiveness. Forgiveness in turn predicted concurrent marital quality. Finally, reciprocal direction of effect emerged between forgiveness and marital quality over time' (Paleari *et al.*, 2005, p. 368). Thus, the outcomes indicate that rumination and emotional empathy are related to concurrent forgiveness and this in turn influences the quality of the relationship. Spouses who show high empathy towards the offender and suffer less corrosive rumination are more likely to be forgiving and benevolent. They also experience their marriage as more satisfying.

There were some gender differences in these associations that are congruent with previous findings. First, husbands appear to have a stronger association between emotional empathy and forgiveness than wives such that they are less likely to be unforgiving. Second, there was a stronger relationship between rumination and unforgiveness among wives. Research evidence (e.g. Collins and Clark, 1989) had already indicated that victims who hold negative attributions towards transgressors are more likely to ruminate on the offence and experience vengeful feelings.

The longitudinal data provided interesting information. Those spouses who showed more benevolence and are less unforgiving experience significantly greater marital satisfaction even over that which they had six months previously. It is surmised that the effect of forgiveness, being associated with marital quality, produces an increase on the earlier level. In addition, the researchers noted that

> Spouses in initially satisfied marriages later manifest fewer ruminative thoughts about the offence . . . Independently of their earlier level of forgiveness, it appears that spouses who are more satisfied with their marriages are more benevolent and less unforgiving towards the partner 6 months later because they ruminate less about the offence.
>
> Paleari et al., 2005, pp. 375–6)

It is noteworthy that McCullough *et al.* (2007) also reported on longitudinal studies using student subjects to show that increased rumination fuelled by anger at transgressors was associated with within-persons reductions in forgiveness.

A further finding of significance concerns the stability of forgiveness for both husbands and wives. It is generally thought that dispositional forgiveness is a relatively stable trait that should remain steady across multiple offences. These results suggest that married couples do not always operate in that way; instead, they appear to take account of the specific nature of the offence before becoming forgiving or unforgiving. Paleari and colleagues state, therefore, that, 'Our results suggest that conceptualizing forgiveness as a stable trait that does not vary across multiple offences might not reflect the way forgiveness actually unfolds in specific domains, such as marriage' (2005, p. 376). It is not clear whether these findings would be similar for non-marital relationship quality or if they are particular to marriage partners. If the latter, one may then ask what distinguishes married partners from non-married partners who at some point have made a deep commitment to each other and their relationship. If a religious connotation is a primary distinguishing characteristic, then it is reasonable to predict that religion becomes an important consideration for therapeutic intervention when therapy is sought.

Religious people and therapy

Despite the increasing secularity of marriage, Duba and Watts (2009) claim that the majority of married couples identify with a particular religion. Around the world codes of ethical practice, therapists and other offering therapeutic services require clients' religions to be recognised and discriminatory practice cannot be condoned. Despite this and, as has been suggested previously, religious clients are often wary of seeking therapeutic services from psychologists who, as a group, are known to have low levels of religious belief and affiliation (Ecklund and Scheitle, 2007). Adherence to non-discriminatory practice should mitigate against any negative influence from non-religious practitioners and, in my experience, this is less of a problem than the differential motivations and religiosity of the partners comprising religious couples. The fact that a married couple are both Catholics does not mean that they have an equal strength of faith or are prepared to take part to the same extent in religious ceremonies and rituals. There is no guarantee either that such differences are always tolerated amicably. No matter what religion or denomination a married couple may share, there is no reason for them to both be intrinsically motivated by their faith such that it is of central significance to both their lives and identities. One may be while the other may be extrinsically motivated; being seen at church may be more important than what it stands for. Such variations in religiousness between married couples may be the cause of continuing stress and other external stressors may considerably augment problems that religion may be the source of.

Despite this, as has been discussed previously, research does indicate that shared religion brings benefits to marital satisfaction. It is associated with degree of commitment, conflict resolution, sexual adjustment and intimacy (e.g. Brimhall and Butler, 2007). The beneficial qualities of religiousness as a defining characteristic of an intimate relationship cannot be ignored when therapy is sought.

Many married couples are clear about how God or their religion impacts on their lives. A study by Goodman and Dollahite (2006) was carried out by interviewing Jewish, Muslim and Christian married couples about their perceptions of how God and their religion directly influenced their marriages. A variety of influences were revealed, of which some were motivational of actions leading to improvement of their marriages. Others suggested that God was a model of unconditional love, mercy and forgiveness. In addition, God was seen to provide guidance, stability, unity and help in overcoming distress. Clearly, given the mix of complex positive and negative influences, it is particularly important that therapists determine how religious and/or spiritual beliefs impact on each married couple that presents for therapy. Not only do particular religions, sects and denominations create rules and norms for their behaviour, but also their joint and individual levels of religiosity mould and imprint their lives. One area of particular stress arises when the strongly religious requirement of forgiveness runs counter to the feelings of an angry and hurting victim.

Fadwa and her husband, Jamil, were devout Muslims and she accepted the role that the Qur'an laid out for dutiful wives. She accepted that Jamil's understanding of Surah 4:34[1] such that he could admonish her, withdraw from intimate behaviour and even beat her if he became particularly displeased with her behaviour. Fadwa did her best to maintain their home impeccably and often went without in order to purchase things that he enjoyed.

She discovered that Jamil made use of prostitutes when his work took him away from their home community to places where he was not known. When she confronted him with this and told him how hurt she was, he laughed and told her that the women were of no account and he held her far higher in his estimation than them. His view was that she had no reason to feel hurt and that, in any event, it was her duty to forgive him.

Fadwa felt unable to forgive Jamil and wanted to seek the guidance of their religious adviser. She no longer felt herself bound to his wishes and believed he had betrayed their faith and their marriage.

On a positive note, however, when marriages are in severe difficulties Duba and Watts (2009) observe that 'most couples are encouraged by their affiliated faith doctrine to seek acceptance and support . . . while making sincere efforts towards reconciling' (p. 212). They provide a series of questions that therapists could address when considering how they can best integrate religion into their theoretical approaches. Among these are the questions:

> Are the core beliefs (or values) of my theoretical approach compatible with the couple's religious beliefs? Is the theoretical language similar to what the couple might hear in church or in other religious settings (e.g. about the source of depression or obsessions; about hope in the future; the meaning of life; forgiveness and interpersonal conflict)?
>
> (p. 215)

This has particular relevance to those therapists who have significant religious beliefs of their own. Bilgrave and Deluty (1998) investigated the matching between the religious beliefs and therapeutic orientations of clinical and counselling psychologists. They found positive correlations between orthodox Christian beliefs and cognitive-behavioural orientations and Eastern beliefs with humanistic, existential orientations. It is possible that there may be some confounding difficulties between these approaches such that, for example, Christian therapists may veer away from humanistic approaches. In respect of Judaism, the authors reported that 'Psychologists who self-designated as Jewish tended to indicate that their practice of psychotherapy did not influence their religious beliefs; they also tended to claim that their religious beliefs did not influence their therapeutic practice (Bilgrave and Deluty, 1998, p. 345). One possible explanation given was of 'a possible tendency in Jewish therapists – perhaps out of a keen awareness of their minority status – to carefully separate their religious beliefs from their professional practice, especially, perhaps, when treating Christian clients' (p. 345).

Even within a religion, different sects or denominations may be sufficient to create incompatibilities. For example, staunchly Catholic councellors may find it difficult to work with Protestant clients over some presenting problems. This is a case in point.

Sarah, a loving mother of two young children under four years and long-time practising Church of England Christian, experienced depression, guilt and grief after having an abortion. She had felt compelled to undertake this procedure because of severe financial strictures and the needs of her young family, but afterwards she became very distressed and questioned her integrity as a mother and as a Christian.

Her doctor's letter of referral for counselling followed Sarah's wishes to meet a female counsellor who was a Christian willing to respect her faith. The referral also described the cause of Sarah's distress but did not provide the non-medical antecedents of the abortion. She was referred to a counsellor who was a practising Catholic with orthodox attitudes to abortion. During the course of the initial session Sarah recounted the circumstances of her decision-making and the consequences. She was told then that the counsellor did not feel able to assist because she was a devout Catholic and might not be able to work around her own opinions on abortions in general that were not carried out for reasons of medical necessity.

Sarah acknowledged that this was said in a kindly manner and was in no way an expression of disapproval. The counsellor was helpful in immediately finding a male counsellor with more pluralist faith who worked well with Sarah. Inevitably, however, the passive rejection caused Sarah additional distress and further self-deprecating rumination that made it harder for her to achieve self-forgiveness.

Therapy within the social contexts of empathy and forgiveness

Hill (2010) reminds us that most people do not live in isolation. They live and develop within a variety of contexts and are part of complex relationships. Empathy and forgiveness are human traits that are honed by enduring circumstances and relationships also function within the same contexts. They develop with use and the proficiency of their deployment is largely determined by the responses of others. Gender, race and culture are major influences from the broader environment, while attachment experiences are powerful influences from the narrower context of close relations such as immediate family (Hill, 2010). As has been previously touched on, secure attachment facilitates the development of empathy. Without empathy, individuals cannot proficiently gauge the emotions of others and remain unable to utilise emotional intelligence in their interpersonal behaviour. The capacity for caring and sympathy remains undeveloped and consequently these roots of forgiveness wither and perish.

Although the concept of emotional intelligence is not without its critics (e.g. Roberts *et al.*, 2001) it is a useful concept to help understand the processing of emotional information. The debate as to whether it is, in the traditional sense, a type of intelligence is protracted and beyond the scope of this book. Nevertheless, measures of emotional intelligence have been found to have concurrent validity with cognate measures such as empathy (e.g. Mayer *et al.*, 1999). There is substantive evidence that secure attachment is positively associated with the development of emotional intelligence (e.g. Kafetsios,

2004). In terms of child development, Hill cites evidence that emotional intelligence is a good predictor of how well children will function in life. Those with well-developed emotional intelligence tend to respond better to stress, calm themselves more efficiently, perform better academically, show less challenging behaviour and have better relationships with others (Hill, 2010). Conversely, children who suffer attachment deficits show poor emotional intelligence and do less well in relation to the achievement of life success (Hall *et al.*, 2004). Thus, children whose attachments have been of poor quality or dysfunctional are unlikely to develop effective emotional intelligence and may lose the opportunity to acquire the empathetic qualities required for forgiveness. Under such circumstances therapeutic endeavour that focuses on forgiveness and reconciliation will probably not succeed because the victim is unlikely to experience an empathetic link to the transgressor. In my experience, therapeutic goals for the reduction and release of negative emotions attributable to the offence may be more realistic despite being somewhat more limited in scope.

Robert came from a severely dysfunctional background of emotional neglect, parental discord, multiple partners and addiction. His mother said often that she had loved him and his two sisters but she was unable to show this consistently in any recognisable form of adequate parental caregiving. Robert was taken into care at the age of nine years and had nine changes of foster carer before he left the care system at age 16 years. Throughout much of his childhood and early adolescence he was on the cusp of a diagnosis of reactive attachment disorder. Fortunately, the last foster carers he had were, over three years, able to reach through his challenging behaviour and gradually help socialise him. They were distressed, however, that he could not show affection, reciprocate emotions or sympathise with the hurts suffered by other children. He finally left their home with a gruff 'bye' and walked away, never once looking back. Later, however, he cried because he missed them very much.

He gained employment and eventually married Kim, a girl from the same factory he worked in. Their relationship seemed to mutually satisfy them but Kim left Robert to live with another man until, after two weeks, she realised that she had made a mistake and tried to repair her relationship with Robert. She expressed remorse, begged forgiveness and pleaded for reconciliation. Robert was devastated by her actions but seemed immune to her pain. All he wanted from the counselling he received was to cast out his own sense of rejection, stop all the intrusive thoughts that constantly clouded his mind and regain his lost confidence so he could enjoy himself again. He acknowledged that he still loved Kim but he was quite unable to understand that she was truly remorseful or might again be trustworthy.

Grief, empathy and forgiveness

If therapy can successfully go beyond the limited goal of relieved negative emotions there has to be some dialogue about the nature of the harm done by the betrayal of the victim's intimate relationship. The transgressor can probably understand readily that what he or she did hurt and angered their partner and be appropriately sorry for having caused that hurt. This is seldom the full spectrum of the harm that has been caused; most victims not only experience the pain of betrayal, they also experience grief over the quality of the relationship that has been lost. The warmth, comfort and security of the relationship that sustained and nurtured them have been destroyed. As with the sundering of a protective shield a new and harsh environment surrounds the victim; one where isolation, dismissal and rejection form a landscape of pain and grief.

It is axiomatic that for therapy to be successful the twin strains of loss and grief are inseparable and both have to be identified and tackled. Forgiveness becomes more possible if an empathetic, relational experience shared between victim and offender is sought as a task for therapy. It is only through dialogue that the complexity of the hurt may be explored and accepted by both transgressors and victims, whereupon the discovery of forgiveness can properly begin. For many couples, the only safe place for them to explore their relationship, damaged as it is by anger, pain and grief, is in a therapeutic context.

Terry did not want to know how much time he had invested in wanting Alice dead. Once he found out about her affair he found himself travelling through an awful place of desolation and anger, thinking alternately how he hated her so much he wanted to spit in her face and loving her so much he ached to have their marriage back as it had been. He wondered constantly why they stayed together and knew it was not just for the sake of their two children. For her part, Alice hung on to the marriage just as fiercely but she never knew who was going to come home from work on a day-by-day basis. Would it be the loving husband trying to be forgiving or the grieving, moody, resentful man who constantly looked for something to argue about.

Alice was openly remorseful, deeply ashamed and unable to believe what she had done. She wept a lot, prayed often and refused to offer any excuse for her behaviour. Instead, she said that she was the only one to blame and that Terry had given her no reason at all to betray their marriage. Later, he accepted that his replies to her were cruel and deeply ignorant. He said that all she had to do each day was look after the home, take care of their children, look after her father and drink coffee with her idle friends. He concluded, therefore, that she had had the affair because she was bored. Their talking through the problems never went further than that.

Terry was not a cruel man; he was very hurt and in grief over the loss of a relationship that had nurtured and sustained him for nearly twenty years. He felt that his seemingly secure place in their world had been illusory. Once it had been stripped away he felt exposed and vulnerable. He had revelled in family life and treasured the warmth it gave him. Terry worked very long hard hours to give his family a comfortable existence and make sure that Alice could be the full-time homemaker and mother she wanted to be. He thought she understood why he came home exhausted after a twelve-hour day and was often too tired to do much more that rest before he had to start again the following day.

Alice and Terry did go to a counsellor whose main objective in the opening sessions was to give each of them a voice for their feelings. Terry indignantly spoke about grief, hurt, betrayal and the indignity of coming for counselling when he was just an innocent victim. He talked about his hard work, its reward of disloyalty and how his image of family life seemed like a barren wasteland. Alice was unwilling to talk about her feelings; instead, she focused on her wrongdoing and blameworthiness. She talked of sin and the violation of her marriage vows, how sorry she was for the harm she had done and her selfishness in wanting some warmth for herself. It took Alice a long time to speak of her loneliness and stress; how it was difficult for her to make ends meet despite Terry's good income, of how hard it was to hear her teenage daughter saying how she could never bring her friends to the house when her grandfather was a senile embarrassment, and how heartbreaking it was that her beloved father could no longer recognise her.

Terry heard this and knew it to be true. At first he was angry, feeling that the moral force of his victimisation had been swept from under his feet; he demanded to know why Alice had not asked for his help. She then showed her first flash of annoyance by asking why he hadn't seen the obvious and when he would have been available to help her anyway. She told him, 'You didn't need to have an affair, your work is your mistress.' During further sessions Terry was able to say that he had used his work as a buffer against the problems at home. Eventually, he came to believe that he was the first to betray their marriage; he had opted out of all the difficult bits and took part only in the good.

This vignette provides an example of how a secure therapeutic process enables victim and offender the structure they need to explore each other's feelings free from the cloying trap of acrimony they engage in privately. Terry would never have 'heard' Alice without that structure and might have remained unmindful of his wife's needs for support and acknowledgement. Indeed, he might have stayed mired in his grief and carried around the burden of his victim status for a very long time, while his marriage withered to a sad husk of its former state. Hill (2010) believes that 'Providing a therapeutic environment where personal history can be explored, injuries and wounds shared, and empathy encouraged can usher in a resolution process that facilitates forgiveness as discovery' (p. 180).

Mindfulness and therapy

Terry's nadir arrived when he could no longer ignore his wife's voice and hide it behind the white noise and fallacy of his self-awarded status as considerate, supportive, and unselfish husband and father. In order to become mindful of Alice's loneliness and hurt, he had to shed the delusions in which he had wrapped himself and accept the reality of life as Alice experienced it. Once he had achieved that, he was able to form a better partnership with her and together face challenges in a more pragmatic and healthy way.

Mindfulness has become an important component of some therapeutic intervention, as has been mentioned briefly in Chapter 4. It is appropriate here to consider this further as it directly linked to a religious practice as well as to the reduction of faulty constructs, beliefs and ruminations.

Mindfulness

According to the teaching of Buddha, mindfulness (also referred to as awareness) is a spiritual faculty of great significance to the goal of enlighten-ment. It is the process that prevails over delusion, leaving the mind with a clear comprehension of whatever is on-going in the present. It is the seventh element of the noble eightfold path, which may be thought of in terms of cognitive psychology as a progression in the positive change of thought and behaviour. Mindfulness should be sought across a variety of influences: bodily functions, sensations and feelings, objects of consciousness (perceptions and thoughts), and consciousness itself.

Mindfulness-based therapy

Psychologists have turned their attention to mindfulness and many view it as a major adjunct to therapeutic process. Shapiro and colleagues define mindfulness as 'the process of intentionally attending moment by moment with openness and nonjudgmentalness' (2006, p. 378). A psychological application of mindfulness is mindfulness-based cognitive therapy (MBCT). This builds on a stress-reduction approach based on mindfulness and developed by Kabat-Zinn (see Hathaway and Tan, 2009 for details). This form of cognitive therapy aims is designed to facilitate the recovery of clients suffering with anxiety or depressive disorders by enabling them to perceive their problematic experiences (negative thoughts, feelings and sensations) in a more positive manner. Segal et al. (2002) consider that mindfulness creates a new mental approach that helps clients

> recognize and disengage from mind states characterized by self-perpetuating patterns of ruminative, negative thoughts . . . This involves moving from a focus on content to a focus on process, away from cognitive therapy's emphasis on changing the content of negative thinking, toward attending to the way all experience is processed.
>
> (p. 75)

Segal et al. (2002) discuss the shift of mind into the 'being mode' that allows negative thoughts and feelings to be considered as 'passing events in the mind that arise, become objects of awareness, and then pass away' (p. 74). This requires the individual to experience the transitory discomfort of these feelings and not immediately try to replace them ('doing mode') with more pleasant feelings. This process involves a greater and more adaptive tolerance of discomfort.

Hathaway and Tan (2009) suggest that a combination of mindfulness with cognitive treatments help clients learn to improve vigilance of the signs that significant mood swings are likely. This improved awareness enables the engagement of mental resources that would usually support negative events such as rumination. It is argued that, given improved mindfulness, clients can avoid the repetition of depressive thinking that is stimulated during times of lowered mood. This is referred to as decentering and some practitioners of MBCT believe it may produce the shift to positive mediation evident in successful cognitive therapy instead of a change in the content of negative thinking.

Hathaway and Tan (2009) record the important outcomes that clients may acquire from MBCT, including

> concentration, engaging and maintaining attention on a particular focal point, awareness/mindfulness of thoughts, emotions/feelings, bodily sensations, being in the moment, decentering, acceptance/non-aversion, non-attachment, kindly awareness, letting go, being versus doing, non-goal attainment, no special state to be achieved, and becoming more aware of how a problem manifests physically. Mindfulness training teaches clients to welcome their experiences, even those that have been troubling, instead of avoiding them.
>
> (p.161)

It is reasonable to consider the possible relevance of this therapeutic work with offenders, who are perhaps unable to move on from ruminating about the shame of their wrongdoing to expressions of remorse and apology, and victims who are unable to move beyond persistent ruminations about how badly they have been treated.

In MBCT, clients learn several things: concentration, engaging and maintaining attention on a particular focal point, awareness/mindfulness of thoughts, emotions/feelings, bodily sensations, being in the moment, decentering, acceptance/non-aversion, non-attachment, kindly awareness, letting go, being versus doing, non-goal attainment, no special state to be achieved, and becoming more aware of how a problem manifests physically.

Mindfulness training teaches clients to welcome their experiences, even those that have been troubling, instead of avoiding them. This is done initially by increasing one's awareness of one's body and the sensations that it encounters (e.g., tightness of certain muscles when stressed). According to Segal and colleagues (2002), relapse occurs when patterns of maladaptive thinking are reactivated by the experience of sad moods. These patterns are thought to be automatic. As such, mindfulness training increases the client's ability to have greater awareness of their mode of mind and to disengage from unhelpful modes that perpetuate sadness and depressive thinking.

The authors posit that there are two modes of being. The doing/driven mode tends to be triggered when there is a discrepancy between what people wish for or expect and the reality of what is present. In this mode, a person may feel dissatisfied and tends to focus on the discrepancy, possibly leading to rumination. In contrast, the being mode is characterised by a sense of allowing without the need to expect or to evaluate one's experience. Thus, the client is able to be in the here and now where the feelings do not trigger automatic modes of doing or thinking that are geared towards changing feelings of dissatisfaction.

There is evidence that mindfulness-based therapy does influence various positive psychological states positively. For example, Keng *et al.* (2011) concluded after an extensive review that benefits included increased subjective well-being, reduced psychological symptoms, better behavioral regulation and lowered emotional reactivity. Chambers *et al.* (2008) used non-clinical novice meditators who took part in a ten-day intensive mindfulness meditation retreat. There was also a comparison group who did not take part in mindfulness training. The experimental subjects were given self-report scales recording mindfulness, rumination and affect. They were also given performance tasks examining working memory, sustained attention and attention switching. The results demonstrated that completion of the mindfulness training was associated with 'significant improvements in self-reported mindfulness, depressive symptoms, rumination, and performance measures of working memory and sustained attention, relative to a comparison group who did not undergo any meditation training' (pp. 303–22). Oman and colleagues (2008) examined the effects of mindfulness-training on stress levels and forgiveness. Their results indicated that the training was associated with lowered stress, increased forgiveness and reduced rumination.

Terry, from the study above, did not undergo mindfulness training in any formal sense but the therapeutic sessions did cause him to focus on the reality of all his feelings and experiences of family life. He had to attend to these feelings and not shy away from those that were aversive to him. He was not allowed to concentrate only on those experiences that were pleasant and positive. He began to attend to all the daily events of family life and his own responses to it. As he did this he ruminated much less on Alice's affair and understood that it represented her escape from intolerable stress rather than a deliberate betrayal of him. His growing awareness of the pressures she faced and of his own avoidance behaviour led him to understand that he had betrayed Alice as surely as she had betrayed him. His awareness of the circumstances that were the antecedents to the affair and the continuing pressures that their family faced inevitably led him to the conclusion that he must change and become the involved husband and parent he had pretended he was.

Summary

Between the remorse of a wrongdoer and forgiveness from their victim lies empathy; empathy for the victim's pain and empathy for the wrongdoer's self-disgust, shame and guilt. Sometimes an external agent is required to utilise this empathy and encourage both the halting steps towards the act of contrition and the hesitant act of forgiveness. This agent may be a therapist whose intervention is required to initiate effective responses from offender and victim. Three major dimensions appear to be relevant to the understanding of forgiveness in the context of therapeutic change: *essentiality*, its importance and healing potential for a damaged relationship; *intentionality*, whether forgiveness is given after a conscious decision or discovered as changes unfold in feelings for and from the offender; and *benevolence*, the compassion experienced for the offender whose own shameful pain becomes exposed as the victim's flood of pain and outrage ebbs away and leaves room for some appreciation of the offender's remorse. It appears that damaged relationships cannot be repaired without genuine remorse on the offender's side and the essential response of forgiveness on the victim's. Even if reconciliation is not contemplated by the victim, forgiveness is still required if there is to be an end to the hurt of betrayal and a cessation of vengeful ruminations. The benevolence of forgiveness is helpful, if not vital, if both victims and offenders are to rediscover their self-worth.

For some victims, part of their beginnings of empathy for those who have harmed them may be a painful realisation of their own fallibility. Private reflective self-analysis may suggest reasons to find greater understanding from one's own behaviour as to why a transgression occurred. This can improve victims' receptivity of the expression of remorse and lead to a surprising discovery that forgiveness had occurred without it being a conscious decision but rather, in some cases, a transcendent event occurring beyond the victims' awareness. This process must be distinguished from that of 'collusive forgiveness' where victims accede to forgiveness simply to avoid further harm from offenders who browbeat them into acceptance of a false portrayal of remorse. In contrast, it is noteworthy that genuine remorse followed by genuine forgiveness often results in improved relationship quality. Partners who show high empathy towards offenders benefit by suffering significantly fewer corrosive ruminations and experience greater relationship satisfaction.

There are gender differences in association with this finding in that husbands show a stronger positive association between empathy and forgiveness than wives, whereas wives are more prone to rumination and unforgiveness. Both husbands and wives who show benevolence and are less unforgiving experience greater marital satisfaction than they had known prior to the transgression. This suggests a kind of shared post-forgiveness epiphany. The degree of satisfaction experienced initially has also a positive bearing on subsequent benevolence and lower unforgiveness because of reduced rumination about the offence.

Shared religious beliefs also bring benefits to the experience of marital satisfaction and cannot be ignored in therapeutic interventions. These beliefs often shape the shared lives of the couple, but a religious commitment to forgiveness accepted by both partners adds an extra burden of stress when the feelings of a hurting vengeful partner cannot readily be reconciled with this commitment. Consequently, the need of religious couples for their beliefs to be treated properly by therapists can lead to significant difficulties, particularly when therapists have different religious beliefs. Sometimes it is not possible to reconcile the differences and some couples may then be prepared to accept the input of a non-religious therapist who is willing to accept and respect their faith.

A major success of therapeutic intervention occurs when partners in a damaged intimate relationship become able to 'listen' to each other and become mindful of the other's reality. This may be a hard task for some individuals who are too used to listening only to their inner voices talking to them about their own versions of reality and whatever pain and distress they are experiencing. Often, they come to believe that their own views are the only truth and freeze out the quiet voice of their partner who sees life differently. The therapeutic change from self-delusion to awareness has been linked to Eastern religious teaching in the form of mindfulness-based cognitive therapy. Victims may become able, through increased mindfulness, to observe the evidence, if it is there at all, that the wrongdoers are feeling genuinely sorry for their behaviour.

Although considerable research on efficacy is required it does appear from present results that the outcomes of this therapeutic process are indicative of lowered stress, reduced rumination and increased forgiveness.

Chapter 9

The weight of the soul

Introduction

Pastor Stoddart[1] was a great believer in preaching a good dose of hellfire, in giving his congregation a strong sniff of brimstone. No doubt he would have been well pleased to have caused many cases of hadephobia (morbid fear of hell) among his flock of American frontiersmen and women in order to keep them in check. He preached stridently about the threat of hell and expressed his views baldly: 'Many Men are in a deep Sleep, and flatter themselves as if there was no Hell, or at least that God will not deal so harshly with them as to damn them' (1723).

The threat of hell has been used for thousands of years to keep sinners fearful and regretful of their wrongdoings. Whatever mechanisms may encourage religious wrongdoers to feel sorry for their actions, many may only be prompted to confession by fears of punishment in the afterlife however they may conceive it. For example, some people who are given a diagnosis of a serious illness experience a period of religious struggle (e.g. Fitchett *et al.*, 2004) that is often associated with fear of dying and the hereafter.

Gina, a Catholic lady approaching her eighty-first birthday, became increasingly fearful and overtly anxious. She was persuaded with some difficulty to talk about her fears and confided to her daughter that she was terrified of being judged as a sinner fit only for hell in the afterlife. Gina refused, however, to explain why she held this belief until considerably later, by which time her fears often caused her to shudder and weep.

She was aware that she had caused a lot of harm over the years to a number of people by gossiping about them. Sometimes her gossip had strayed into the realms of imagination when she was short of facts. One of her victims had lost his job, another lost her reputation by being tarred as a thief and an engaged couple had gone their separate ways after talk of infidelity. Gina had done nothing to minimise the damage, as she was afraid that her own reputation would suffer and no one would trust her again. A heart attack brought her face to face with her own mortality and her fear of the Judgement became acute. She was well aware of the solution to her difficulty and, with a lot of support from her daughter, she made her confession.

Despite the reluctance to openly admit to wrongdoing during the life course it is my experience that people who know they have broken moral or religious codes of conduct frequently anticipate some form of existential punishment, usually in an afterlife, and many may also believe that their contentment in this life is largely undeserved as they have unconfessed transgressions weighing down upon them. The avoidance of these predicaments is the stuff of sermons and Pastor Stoddart could call upon the Bible to reinforce his preaching. For example, he could summon up Luke who quoted the words of Jesus: 'But I will show you whom you should fear: Fear him who, after your body has been killed, has authority to throw you into hell. Yes, I tell you, fear him' (Luke 12:5). Likewise, Stoddard's Islamic contemporary could have made his own congregation fearful with words from the Qur'an: 'And whoever opposes the Messenger after guidance has become clear to him and follows other than the way of the believers – We will give him what he has taken and drive him into Hell, and evil it is as a destination' (Qur'an 4:115). Part of this chapter considers the links between fears of the life hereafter in the context of remorse for wrongdoing that has remained unalleviated for years, put aside whenever possible, but always on the edges of perception and memory, and becoming more prominent as the end of the life course approaches. The bite of conscience that developed from infancy is not lessened by age and can add its burden to anxieties about dying.

The carrot and the stick

Many of the major world religions have successfully employed a 'carrot-and-stick' approach to wrongdoing. Its simplicity seems akin to a style of management applied by many parents to young children with a penchant for mischief – be a good person and, after death, be rewarded (in heaven); be an unrepentant bad person and, after death, be punished (in hell). Preachers like Stoddart thought it was their duty to spare their flock the terrors of hell in the afterlife by, literally, putting the fear of damnation into them in this. The promotion of dreadful punishments for the unforgiven sinner goes back at least to the time of the ancient Egyptians. The Preface comments on the age-old belief about the weight of the soul that was at the core of the religious life of that civilisation.

Who, however, in these cynical times still believes in such anachronistic concepts as heaven and hell? Apparently, many still do (e.g. Greeley and Hout, 1999; Lester et al., 2001; Exline, 2003) and their numbers may be growing (e.g. Papyrakis and Selvaretnam, 2011). The question as to why this should be has received considerable research interest and some pundits suggest that Terror Management Theory (TMT) offers a viable explanation. The basis of this theory is that during the socialisation of childhood, the vitally important security provided by care-taking adults is gradually replaced by legal and cultural authorities, religious meaning systems and other belief structures, including deities. These secular and spiritual authorities expect certain attributes and behaviour to be evinced by individuals and provide rewards and punishers to assist compliance. Deities tend to be modelled on parental figures that are congruent with stereotypic portrayals of early childhood care-taking adults. These deities are not, however, always benign; as Bering states: 'Deities are also judgers and punishers because in a world full of tragic, scary events, a deity who does not dole out punishment is not plausible' (Bering, 2006, p. 475).

Belief in the afterlife

It is axiomatic that in order to believe in heaven and hell or to have some similar belief structure, an individual has to have a belief in an afterlife or some form of existence after death. Although many individuals have a significant and spontaneous interest in the future (often referred to as Future Time Orientation), it is noteworthy that the same individuals also show significant interest in the possibilities of an afterlife, a future time for them beyond the end of earthly life (e.g. Öner-Özkan, 2007). It may be reasonably believed that religious doctrines provide the mainsprings of such beliefs. Carl Jung is well known for his commentary on the significance of religion and for his opinion that many of the primary concepts of religions may be interpretable as structures developed from within the human psyche. In respect of Christianity and Buddhism, he thought that the meaning of human existence is consummated at its end. It was his view that most religions could be thought of as complex systems of preparation for death (see Jung, 1972). Nelson (2009), when considering the positive and comforting characteristics of belief in life after death, commented that 'Afterlife beliefs make death a meaningful event, reducing questioning or blaming God which is associated with less well-being' (p. 304). Some people experience anger towards God that evokes anxiety and others hold God responsible for negative events in their lives such as cruelty, severe harm or loss (E.g. Exline et al., 2011). It is also the case, however, that belief in the afterlife is significantly associated with anxieties about death, the hope for the pleasures of heaven are tempered by the fears of hell. Death anxiety is a common experience for many religious people and several studies indicate that a variety of personal and other characteristics mediate the intensity of anxiety. Thus, older adults with physical health problems, those with a history of psychological distress, weak religious faith, lower life satisfaction and resilience, all tend to show greater anxiety about death. Institutional living (e.g. in nursing homes) is also associated with greater anxiety than is the case for those living independently. Adult Caucasians have anxieties about the process of dying, while people of African descent tend to worry more about being buried alive and the condition of the body after death. Younger people also have fears about the deteriora-tion of the body after death and are concerned about being helpless, in pain and lonely. Older people, however, are more likely to be concerned about loss of their autonomy and the existence and nature of an afterlife. The experience of early loss and bereavement in childhood or adolescence is associated with fears about loss of their social identity and the impact of their deaths on family and friends. Those whose experience of important loss has come later in life are more likely to be fearful of the annihilation of the body and confrontation with the unknown (see Neimeyer *et al.*, 2004).

In addition, people who are moderately religious tend to suffer greater death anxieties than those who are either very religious or atheists (e.g. Wink and Scott, 2005). There is also differentiation between individuals with intrinsic religiousness from those with extrinsic religiousness. Ardelt and Koenig (2006) reported on a study designed to examine the differences between these two forms of religious orientation in respect of healthy older individuals and those in hospice care. The results indicated that those in hospice care tended to turn positively towards religious materials irrespective of content and so were more likely to reveal extrinsic religious orientation than the healthy group. In common with the findings of other studies (e.g. Wink and Scott, 2005), those with extrinsic religiosity showed greater death anxiety than those with intrinsic religious orientation. Ardelt and Koenig (2006) commented:

> Extrinsically religious persons are likely to be exposed to the doctrines and teachings of their church, but if they have not committed their lives to God or a power greater than themselves, they might be more aware of the fact that their lives are not morally perfect than nonreligious individuals. Hence, their extrinsic religious orientation might do more harm than good by increasing their fear of punishment after death and decreasing their approach acceptance of death.
>
> (p. 209)

There are several other sources of death anxiety as individuals reach an age or circumstance when they have reason to consider the end of their lives. Many fear leaving vulnerable members of family who rely on them, others fear the end of their creativity and tasks left undone, and some worry about if or how they will be remembered. Sadly, some will worry that they have not met the levels of achievement that their parents expected of them and death will rob them of the opportunity of ever doing so.

Mansur was such a person. His father had always expected him to go to university, train as a doctor and become as famous a specialist as had his oldest cousin. It had been very important to his father that Mansur brought respect to the family and he thought that meant Mansur must compete successfully with his brother's children. Mansur was well aware that should be interpreted as a requirement to do better than the top achiever in that family.

Mansur had no wish to be a doctor and he was no academic. His educational standards were average and his aspiration was to go to horticultural college. This was a grave disappointment to his father, although nothing was ever said about failure. It remained as a permanent sadness between them until his father died. Mansur worked for many years successfully in horticulture but he always felt guilty about failing his father. After he retired he became very anxious and increasingly fearful about his own death. Counselling was arranged for him through his religious community and the therapist was able to help Mansur accept that his father's problems within his own sibling relationships were his alone and had nothing to do with Mansur's own achievements as a decent and moral man who, within the codes of his own faith, had nothing to fear from the afterlife.

Florian and Kravetz (1983) provide a useful multidimensional model of the overt expression of the fear of personal death. This is comprised of three components relating to the intrapersonal, interpersonal and transpersonal consequences of death. Of these, the *intrapersonal component* includes fears about the expected consequences of death on the mind and body of the deceased. A major fear within this component is that the self will be annihilated completely, that there will be no extension of awareness of self after the event of death. In addition, there are fears that there will be no further opportunities to realise one's potential and important personal goals would be left unmet. The *interpersonal component* includes anxieties about the impact of one's death on important attachment relationships. Worrying issues about the fading of one's social identity after death may arise from concerns about being forgotten or unloved alongside more altruistic anxieties about the subsequent welfare of family members and friends. Lastly, the *transpersonal component* emanates from beliefs held by the individual about the transcendental aspects of death. These may include fear of the unknown nature of death, the possibility of adverse judgement and subsequent punishment in an afterlife.

A number of studies have confirmed that each of these components is associated with quantitative differences between persons differentiated by a variety of factors, including level of religious commitment and loss of significant others and (e.g. Florian and Kravetz, 1983; Florian and Mikulincer, 1997; Lazar, 2006). The transpersonal component of death anxiety is of particular relevance here because it incorporates fear of punishment in the hereafter. For example, Lazar (2006) reported a modest association between death anxiety and belief in divine order. People who are motivated by a belief in divine order want to behave properly, relate well to God, achieve a sense of purity and holiness, and receive an eternal reward (Lazar *et al.*, 2002). Fear of punishment in the hereafter is also associated with the motivational belief in divine order (Lazar, 2006). The desire for an eternal reward and fear of punishment in the hereafter brings this discussion back to the ubiquitous 'carrot-and-stick' teaching of religious doctrine, particularly for those who approach the end of their lives with unresolved feelings of sorrow for wrongdoing.

Afterlife conceptualisation within major world religions

Not all religious societies place the punishment of sins within the hereafter. For some, the sins of this world are punished in this world, usually by visitations of ill fortune such as poverty, illness, the loss of beloved family or friends and other calamitous events. Angry ancestors may also send their judgements on the living in the form of earthly punishments. For the most part, however, punishment for wrongdoing is supernatural, after death, often sanguineous and eternal. The agents of this eternal punishment are likewise supernatural (e.g. demonic) and remorseless in their infliction of pain (Bering, 2006). This section presents a brief summary of beliefs in the nature of the afterlife as portrayed by some of the world's major religions. These are the doctrinal structures of life after death that adherents respond to as the end of their lives approach. Although some of the after-death destinations and circumstances differ,[2] it is quite clear that that there are significant similarities – in particular, the promise of rewards for good living and the threat of punishments for unconfessed sins.[3]

Judaism   Put simply, when people die, their disembodied souls may, after a period of detoxification to remove the taint of wrongdoing in the physical world, enter into the Divine Presence. This entry is influenced by the extent of Torah learning and good deeds done during earthly life. Every year on the day of passing the soul moves to another level closer to God. The process of cleansing or purification of souls is Gehinom, which some regard as a form of hell.

The Talmud contains a number of views of the afterlife. In essence, after a person dies, his or her soul is brought to judgement. Those people who have lived pure lives, largely uncontaminated by the taint of the physical world, may pass directly into the World to Come. The majority, however, must go through a process of refinement enabling souls to acquire wisdom as their earthly errors are considered. For some believers, this is a period of punishment; for others, it is a time of re-education. In either case, the Jewish concept of afterlife does not have eternal damnation and punishment as a core tenet. Even virtuous Gentiles may be allowed into the World to Come. Eternal punishment is kept for those wicked and malevolent leaders who lead others into great evil.

Maimonides, who is popularly considered to be one of the greatest Jewish philosophers, taught against the notion of physical resurrection. In his opinion, mankind has two kinds of intelligence – one that is influenced by somatic and physical variables during earthly life, and one that is immaterial and influenced by a universal spiritual intelligence. This is acquired from the efforts of each soul to achieve an understanding of the absolute and pure nature of God. Once attained, this understanding confers immortality and immunity from misfortune and the temptation to sin.

Overall, therefore, there seems to be some flexibility of afterlife conceptualisation in Judaism and one might form the opinion that the afterlife is left largely in God's hands. Nevertheless, the 'carrot-and-stick' principle is still evident within the intellectualisation of the nature of the afterlife.

Islam   The Qur'an is descriptive of Islamic heaven and hell:

> The parable of the Garden which the righteous are promised! Beneath it flow rivers: perpetual is the fruits thereof and the shade therein. Such is the End of the Righteous; and the End of Unbelievers is the Fire (Hell). The joys of Heaven are unlike the joys of earthly existence; they do not fade away or become cloying. Instead they are pure and everlasting. The reference to the shade of the garden encompasses coolness, shelter, protection and security. This may be contrasted with the fires of hell, which afflict the unbelievers with the fierceness of great heat.
>
> (13:35)

As in other religious beliefs, heaven has several levels. The highest and greatest is the seventh where God can be seen and where all things are possible. However, even the lowest level of heaven offers a life that is one hundred times better than anything that may be experienced during earthly life.

Life on earth is nothing other than a test to determine how, through belief, reverence for life and good deeds one can worship Allah and be assigned to an ultimate destination in the levels of heaven. Having reached heaven, the God-fearing will be happy, never experiencing negative emotions, wear costly clothes, luxuriate on gilded couches, bask in the warmth of family and parents, wives and children, and enjoy sumptuous banquets. Those who fail to live properly during their lives fall into the pits of hell and are apt to become fuel for its fires.

Christianity   Typically, during medieval times heaven was envisaged as a dwelling place for God, the angels, and the good and pious after death. It was thought to be a physical place sited above the Earth where God and the angels watched over humanity. The 'heavens' was a synonym for 'the skies', and the stars were lights shining down from heaven. God chooses to live in heaven with his believers who are resurrected there in new and incorruptible bodies. Death was believed by many to be a remedial process coming after the Fall when Adam and Eve disobeyed God and brought original sin to humankind. Through death, humankind could avoid living in sin for an eternity separated from God's love.

By contrast, hell is the final destination of those who have been judged unfit to join God and his believers. Instead, they are punished after the last judgement by being banished to hell. There are several different versions, depending on which Christian church one belongs to, of what constitutes the saving of souls from hell, but all include the acceptance of Jesus Christ as their Saviour. The most commonly accepted statement of faith within Christianity is the Nicene Creed that opens with affirmation of the belief 'in one God, the Father, the Almighty, maker of heaven and earth, of all that is, seen and unseen . . .' and ends with a clear and unequivocal conviction about the afterlife, stated as, 'We look for the resurrection of the dead and the life of the world to come'.

Buddhism   The carrot-and-stick theme is less obvious in this faith. The realms of heaven are temporary abodes, from which one experiences rebirth into a number of planes of existence. This earthly world is only one realm or path en route to Nirvana, the state of enlightenment. This is the ultimate goal and the means by which the cycle of rebirth is brought to an end. Hell exists among the realms that are subdivided into varying degrees of pain and pleasure. The realms of hell are the lowest of the realms of rebirth and, of these, the Avici hell is that of endless suffering. Placement in the realms of hell are dependent on evil doing and individuals are destined to remain in them until retribution is complete or their evil karma (sum of their actions throughout their states of existence) has dissipated.

Hinduism   Once again, heaven is presumed to exist above the earthly plane. It is the home of gods and beatified mortals. The generic term for the six phases of heaven is Good Kingdom and it is a paradise of pleasure. People who sin go to hell where they are subjected to punishments judged by Yama, the god of death, to be appropriate to the severity of the wrongs done. The list of punishments includes burning with fire, scalding with boiling oil and instruments of torture. Once shriven by pain, individuals may be reborn.

Strength of belief in the afterlife

Given that fear is a powerful motivator of avoidance behaviour (e.g. Öhman, 2000) and given the assumption that mature people have the learning and skills to produce such behaviour, it is reasonable to expect that those who have religious faith will respond with their best endeavours according to the carrot-and-stick teaching about the afterlife corresponding to their faith. One would expect the threat of punishment in the afterlife to be a significant influence on their behaviour in this life. It is appropriate to enquire what proportion of the population has a belief in the afterlife and might be influenced by the prospect of judgement after death. Such individuals may well be strongly prompted to feel sorry for wrongdoing as a consequence even if more existential factors had not influenced them. Belief in the afterlife is often held in positive ways and may provide comfort to individuals who are close to death themselves or who have loved ones who are dying. A belief in heaven may be particularly comforting and fulfil an emotional need (Exline, 2003). Dixon and Kinlaw (1982) reported that most people who believed in an afterlife also believed that their own afterlife would be positive.

However, this does not prevent significant concerns about the possibility of hell, which is associated with anxieties concerning death, even among young college students (e.g. Exline and Yali, 2007). Thorsen and Powell (1988) carried out a survey of 599 adolescents and adults using a death anxiety scale. The greatest anxiety expressed by over 80 per cent of the elderly people sampled was concern about whether there is an afterlife and, if so, what the next world would be like. The authors considered this to be an understandable and reasonable concern for people approaching their lives' end, but the same anxiety was common among much younger people also. Exline (2003) comments: 'although research has tended to focus on the bright side of the afterlife, many Americans consider the existence of Hell to be a real – and threatening – possibility' (p. 156). Exline's own study of the belief in heaven and hell among North American Christians examined differences of belief across denominations (Exline, 2003). Data was available from over 700 Catholics and over 1,500 Protestants with a mean age of 47 years (range 18–89 years). In the sample, 59 per cent was female and the majority identified themselves as white. The results revealed that not only did the majority of North American Christians believe in life after death, but they also believed in heaven and hell. Thus, 62 per cent believed that hell does exist and 74 per cent believed that heaven exists. Protestant Christians maintained a slightly higher rate of belief in heaven and hell than Catholics, but these two groups did not differ significantly in respect of belief in life after death. Fundamentalist Protestants showed greater belief in heaven and hell than less fervent Protestants and Catholics. In relation to religious activity, the results showed that, regardless of denomination, stronger beliefs in an afterlife, heaven and hell were associated with greater religious participation.

With regard to younger people, the survey conducted by Lester and colleagues using American undergraduates (mean age + 23.8 years) found that over 90 per cent of the sample surveyed believed in an afterlife. Among those, it is noteworthy that they also believed that God owned their lives. Their beliefs about the nature of the afterlife were quite complex: 'The most common beliefs were that one is reunited with family and friends, that the afterlife is comforting, that there is Heaven and that the transition is peaceful, all believed by more than 90 per cent of the students (Lester *et al.*, 2001, p. 113). Other beliefs were less comfortable, including that the majority of people believed that there will be a time when God judges them and decides whether they will go to heaven or hell, a decision that is determined by how their earthly lives had been lived. The students also believed that forgiveness should be requested before death.

What happens in the afterlife?

It is clear that a substantial proportion of the population believes in an after-life, but their opinions on the nature and circumstances of that life appear to vary from religion to religion, from denomination to denomination, and also from individual to individual within the same religious group. It is apparent, however, that many religious people believe they have reason to fear punishment in the hereafter for whatever reason. For example, Ghorbani *et al.* (2008) found a highly significant correlation between Afterlife Motivation and Fear of Punishment in Hell in respect of a sample of Iranian Muslims. This seems to reflect a desire for nearness to God associated with a hope that he would not punish believers with hell but would instead reward them with heaven.

Florian and Kravertz (1983) found from a factor analytic study that the potential for punishment in an afterlife (however it may be conceived) represents a strongly fearful concern for the religious group sampled such that they scored highly on the punishment in the hereafter factor. The same group did not score significantly on the self-annihilation factor that is associated with the belief that after death the self ceases to exist. Not surprisingly, atheists score highly on this factor and consequently do not concern themselves with items associated with the punishment in the hereafter factor. In conclusion, Florian and Kravertz (1983) caution that the 'relations between different aspects of fear of personal death and extent of religious belief may not be monotonic and may differ across different religious belief systems' (p. 606).

It is noteworthy that a study by Hamama-Raz *et al.* (2000) found that fear of punishment in the hereafter was a major concern to religious physicians. Their sample consisted of 233 Jewish-Israeli physicians from a range of medical specialities. It was found also that neither religious nor non-religious physicians had particularly discrepant fears concerning self-annihilation after death and nor were there differences according to medical specialisation. This suggests that the physicians with a fear of punishment did not owe this fear to the fact that they worked in specialisations where there were particularly high rates of patient death.

Burris and Bailey (2009) further examined the nature of afterlife beliefs and differentiated them between religious faiths. Their undergraduate sample of believers included Protestant and Catholic Christian, Jewish, Muslim, Hindu, Buddhist faiths, and individuals professing a personal religion. Agnosticism and atheism were also represented within the sample. These students were given the researchers' own After Death Belief Scale that records five variations of belief: annihilation, disembodied spirit, spiritual embodi-ment, reincarnation and bodily resurrection. If an individual believes that consciousness does not survive after death, it must be accepted that the self has experienced annihilation, and there can be no identity and no physi-cality. Those who believe that consciousness does survive death may consider that this is as a disembodied spirit without physicality or sense of identity.

Individuals who believe that not only consciousness but also memory and sense of identity survive death will relate to the concept of spiritual embodiment. Others may believe in a third form of survival, reincarnation, where consciousness is preserved in a new physical form bereft of memory and identity. Finally, a fourth belief may be held, that of bodily resurrection, where consciousness and identity are preserved within a new physical body.

The results of particular interest here concern the differences between religions and between religious and non-religious participants. In general terms, the pattern of afterlife beliefs were predictable given the major characteristics of the religious and non-religious groups. Thus, atheists held strongly to annihilation of the self at death and rejected other possibilities for some form of survival of the self. Agnostics had a similar but somewhat less certain opinion. Hindus and Buddhists professed to a belief in resurrection of some corporeal form, whereas Protestant, Catholic and Muslim adherents veered more towards an afterlife of spiritual embodiment, as did those who had a personal religion. Less predictable was a finding that Christians did not show a high level of endorsement for bodily resurrection; this is surprising given the importance of that belief as expressed in the major Christian creeds. Not only do these refer to belief in the resurrection of the body and the life everlasting, they also describe the resurrection of Christ and his role in the judgement of the dead.[4] In addition, adherents to all religions were more likely than the non-religious groups, particularly atheists, to believe that what they did in life would affect what would happen to them in the afterlife. One might suggest that, no matter how religious teaching deals with the relationship between behaviour during life and afterlife experiences, there is a belief that at the doctrinal core there is a 'carrot-and-stick' approach.

This does not mean that a fear of punishment in the afterlife is the primary motivation of religious activity. Instead, all major faiths would endeavour to dissuade believers from such a negative involvement in worship.[5] Nevertheless, the findings of the various studies outlined above do show the fear of punishment to be a powerful influence. It is inevitable that wrongdoing in life will be associated with feelings of being sorry and anxiety as the prospect of dying becomes more urgent with age or other circumstance.

Dying: shame, guilt and the pain of being sorry

Satterly (2001) reminds us that for many dying is a spiritual matter and explains that people in hospices may experience both religious and spiritual pain as they approach the end of their lives. It would seem that a major reason for this profound experience is being sorry for previous wrongdoings that have caused harm to others. Religious and spiritual pain are associated with the concept of 'total pain' developed by Cecily Saunders, a leading and much revered specialist in palliative care. Total pain includes physical, psychological, social, emotional and spiritual distress (see Clark, 1999, for a review). The study of pain has linked several disciplines over the last half century and it is commonly recognised that many people experience not only physical pain as they approach the end of their lives, but religious and spiritual pain as well.

Religious pain appears to be rooted in guilt and fear arising from individuals' belief that they have failed to live up to the expectations, values and creeds of their faith. Increasingly, as they age or suffer terminal illness, they begin to appraise their life course against the parameters set for their behaviour by the teachings of their religion. As has been described above, the fear of punishment in the afterlife to which they subscribe fastens on to the guilt that their adverse self-judgement imposes. Some religious people who have been taught guilt and shame from an early age, may need to recall only minor infringements of their religion's code of conduct to fall into a pit of guilt from which they see little hope of escape.

Anne had been strictly brought up in the Roman Catholic faith. Her parents were dogmatic even to the extent that their parish priest had counselled them against the perils of being over-zealous. The convent boarding school she attended was run by nuns who Anne, parodying John Knox, described as 'a monstrous regiment of women'.

As Anne's terminal illness reached its last stages she became very fearful of being judged too sinful to enter heaven and sent for eternal punishment in hell. The dreadful deed she had never confessed was, at the age of 12 years, the theft of another girl's hair slide. Apparently, this girl had wealthy parents (by Anne's standards) who had given their daughter a lovely hair slide that 'shimmered like pearl'. Anne coveted this object so much (a terrible sin in itself) that she stole it from the girl's bag. The loss of the slide was put down to carelessness and Anne was never suspected. Despite this, she was too ashamed and frightened to wear the slide and smashed it to pieces before throwing it away. She never confessed this sin and had gone through life dreading the outcome. Anne felt much more than being sorry, she felt terrified. Fortunately, a hospice nurse patiently encouraged her to make a full confession.

Doubtless, Pastor Stoddart would be pleased with the outcome for this deeply anxious, fearful and terminally ill woman who had been taught from an early age to fear the wrath of her God and suffered the religious pain of failing to live up to the standards her parents and teachers had inculcated into her. Bering (2006) describes the generality of this process as

> Children are made into moral agents easily through socialization and social control mechanisms, as they are assigned blame and learn to blame others and especially themselves. The panhuman experience is that parents are the carriers of morality, as they convey to their children a fantasy of a world ordered into right and wrong, reward and punishment. The moral universe we all inhabit was developed in early childhood in our private consciousness, and it may be projected on the universe.
>
> (p. 465)

Other people experience religious pain as a consequence of more serious transgressions than Anne's. Criminality, desertion, child abuse, adultery and social abortion figure significantly as guilt-inducing wrongdoing. In my experience, the failure to reconcile these sins through confession made to a religious authority is the primary source of guilt and fear.

Barry's parents had not been strongly religious but he had been brought into a strict High Church community through a marriage that gradually nourished his rudimentary belief structure. His wife predeceased him without ever knowing that he had married her bigamously, having deserted his first wife and their two children when he had lived abroad. As he grew older the weight of this desertion pressed down harder on him. He felt very ashamed of the way he had abandoned his first family and guilty that he had fooled his loving second wife into believing in a fiction of marriage. After her early death he began to believe that his sinful behaviour was in some way responsible, that she was punished for his mendacity. Given his increasing feelings of guilt, Barry developed a growing fear that he would be punished in the afterlife according to the teachings of his faith. His mood became increasingly depressed and eventually he was medicated and entered into psychotherapy whereupon he finally became able to deal with his pain and fears.

Satterley (2001) makes the point that the idiosyncratic experience of religious pain does not have to make sense to observers, only to its sufferers. Ultimately, the crucial factor that determines the intensity of that pain is not the absolute content of religious doctrine but the way that the individual has come, through whatever processes, to interpret it. Parts of this book have examined how these processes might be established and a later section of this chapter will return to these. At this point, it suffices to place the idiosyncratic beliefs of individuals derived from their interpretations of wrongdoing and doctrines at the heart of the extent of their religious pain. This pain may lead to the experience of being very sorry for wrongdoing, an emotion spiced by the fear of punishment after death. For some people, this fear has a powerful impact on their daily life, preventing enjoyment and robbing them of peace. They become the source of their own punishment. Some, like Anne (see above and below), may make an attempt to rid themselves of this pain and fear by making a confession.

Anne was finally persuaded to make the full confession she had been too ashamed to manage despite her regular attendance at church. She derived great reassurance and reduction of anxiety from this act and her fear of dying diminished accordingly. She thought deeply about the process of confession and attended thoroughly to each stage.

First, she carried out a rigorous preliminary examination of her life course as a Christian by using Christian teachings, scripture and requirements as the yardsticks of judgement about her conduct. In essence, she wanted to make sure that the theft of the hair slide was not symptomatic of some deeper malaise infecting her religious moral code. The fact that she had responded to envy by stealing and then to shame by destroying the evidence of her crime suggested a deeper vein of sinfulness; a rejection of God's commandments on a more fundamental level than that of a simple impulsive and opportunistic act. She carefully examined other instances of wrongdoing (for which she had assiduously made confession) and tried to find evidence of some persistent flaw of unrepentant wickedness. Anne believed that she had been scrupulous in this examination and was greatly relieved not to find such evidence.

This first step of examining her conscience enabled her to begin her confession with a clear understanding of the grave sin, as she believed it to be, as well as the venial sins[6] that she had experienced since her last confession. She knew exactly what she was confessing and apologising to God about. Within this clarity, Anne had also been able to acknowledge the anxious circumstances of her present life as the precipitating context of the confession of the transgression from years ago. She experienced catharsis and also the commonly reported lifting of a burden as she described how she felt about her behaviour of long ago.

Finally, Anne was able to recite the act of contrition in which penitents make their sincere apologies to God, promise to do penance and to improve their future conduct. Given her circumstances at the last stage of a terminal illness, future conduct meant little in purely behavioural terms. For Anne, however, it was a solemn declaration that she held steadfastly to the Christian code that she had followed unwaveringly for all of her adult life.

During childhood, Christianity, as for all other of the world's major religions, teaches the means through which penitents may be cleansed of the guilt of wrongdoing. How this process is interpreted may vary from person to person, but their goals are generally the same: the genuine expression of guilt and remorse, a willingness to carry out some form of penance and a promise to try to do better in the future, all within the light of their faith and in the sincere hope of forgiveness.

If guilt is the fuel of religious pain, then shame serves that function for spiritual pain. Whereas religious pain can arise when individuals acknowledge that they have failed to live up to standards set by the doctrine, creeds and dogma of their religion, spiritual pain can arise when individuals believe they are deficient or corrupt within themselves such that they have failed the relationship they have with the divine, the transcendent source of their lives. Satterly (2001) acknowledges that attempts to define spiritual pain are fraught with difficulty.[7] This is, at least in part, a consequence of the complex problems of satisfactorily defining spirituality (see Chapter 6), but it seems apparent that spiritual pain can arise from an individual's understanding that he or she has, in some way, failed to live up to their potential for transcendence, for a life beyond the pursuit of basic physical needs and the goal of self-actualisation (Maslow, 1971). My own conversations with some people I believe to have been in spiritual pain suggest that they regard this as a betrayal or a loss of their true selves because wrongdoing in pursuit of base goals has led them away from the self that could have been. Millspaugh (2005) comments that loss of self may produce a state of disorientation and confusion 'leaving one unable to construct purposes or meaning resulting in a profound detachment and an unarticulated sense of emptiness beyond despair' (p. 921).

It is my experience that the unresolved transgressions that produce the sorrow of spiritual pain are similar to those that are associated with religious pain. Indeed, the concept of 'total pain' allows for all sources of pain to be experienced by individuals. Thus, it is hardly surprising that a person should rue their transgressions in terms of failing the behavioural standards of their church as well as the contamination of their personal spiritual lives. The fear of punishment in the afterlife, however, is most particularly associated with religion (e.g. Lazar, 2006). Satterly (2001) notes that spiritual pain is mostly associated with being sorry for becoming a 'bad person' or feeling that 'something is wrong with me' (p. 34), a common experience associated with the negative emotion of shame. Although some people may be helped to believe that God will forgive them and find them worthy, they may never achieve self-forgiveness and so remain unworthy in their own estimation.

Judy's great secret sin was a sexual relationship she had as a teenager with a considerably younger cousin. She described him as 'unbearably sexy' and spoke of spending her days 'lusting after him. She admitted to cajoling, flattering and deceiving him into believing that she loved him and that making love was her way of proving it. He was heartbroken when she found a boyfriend of her own age and brushed him aside. There were no serious repercussions for her, but he was left heartbroken, confused and unable to trust anyone who was nice to him. He took a long time to recover and begin to enjoy normal peer relations again. Judy knew she had harmed him but simply tried to laugh it off whenever they met as though it was of no great importance, simply 'Part of our growing up'. Her cousin died young in a traffic accident and she knew then that she would never have the opportunity to acknowledge with him what had happened.

Judy had no religious beliefs but her studies had convinced her of the search for transcendence as a meaningful goal. She attempted to live modestly and with consideration for others; she was well thought of within her community and known for charity projects. Judy believed that she had become 'damaged goods and that she could never realise the potential she had had for achieving goodness in this life. She was never able to forgive herself and stated, 'God may forgive me but I never will'. She knew this burden of sorrow was hers to carry for the rest of her life.

Judy is an example of the fact that it is not only the very old or those close to death whose sorrow at the harm they did to others becomes lodged in their consciousness as religious or spiritual pain. Many basically good and decent people are unable to believe positively in themselves and find self-forgiveness. Being sorry is a life sentence for them.

The unforgiving self

Few of us can get through life without causing harm to others despite our fervent wish it was otherwise. That truism has been recorded by an army of writers, theologians, scientists and others over hundreds of years. Paul Eddington, CBE, the famous British actor, said, when terminally ill,

> A journalist once asked me what I would like my epitaph to be and I said I think I would like it to be 'He did very little harm.' And that's not easy. Most people seem to me to do a great deal of harm. If I could be remembered as having done very little, that would suit me.

The harm done can be accidental or intentional. Sometimes the transgressions are not intended to harm but are insufficiently hidden to avoid detection and subsequent damage. Thus, serial adulterers may never wish to harm their spouse but end up doing so by being caught. The behaviour of some others is so herostratically brazen, almost as though notoriety is a major goal and rampant wrongdoing is merely a vehicle to achieve it.

Betrayals of interpersonal relationships are, as have been considered earlier, a common cause of anxiety and harm. The memory and effects of these may rebound down through decades. Thus Hansson et al. (1990) reported that, among a sample of adults over 60 years of age, 14 per cent reported that they had betrayed people close to them and been betrayed by 19 per cent of the people in their social networks. The authors state that, in many cases, the betrayal events had taken place much earlier in the subjects' lives, but had continued to exert a significant negative impact throughout the years. The social networks included partners, spouses, work colleagues, friends and family. The nature of betrayal in respect of intimate relationships usually revolves around emotional and/or sexual behaviour that is contrary to the established rules of the relationship betrayed.

As Whisman and Wagers (2005) point out, these rules may vary from couple to couple depending on the freedom and openness of their relationship. Nevertheless, emotional and sexual infidelity remain among the most common forms of betrayal. However, this behaviour may be defined, and the impact of guilt and shame may well endure for the remaining life of the guilty parties who find it impossible to forgive themselves (e.g. Ingersoll-Dayton et al., 2010). The impact of these old betrayals is significant on older adults who have reached a point where they may begin to review their lives. Unresolved emotional issues, shame, guilt and painful memories become associated with remorse and a feeling that they are not acceptable, even to themselves. Persistent and ruminative thoughts rob them of peace of mind and may lead to despair and depression (e.g. Ingersoll-Dayton and Krause, 2005). In my experience, some religious people try hard to understand how they came to betray and harm others when such actions went deeply against the grain of their own characters and moral codes. Often they find that the motivations of their betrayals were base and selfish, and they cannot hide from the lash of their own conscience.

For example, Neil looked back at the betrayal of his marriage through sexual infidelity some 40 years previously. He had tried to persuade himself that he had fallen in love with each of the other women involved but had to conclude that he was motivated only by lust. This did not sit well with his strict religious creed. He became persistently ruminative about his sins and eventually reached the point where self-loathing overwhelmed him and he sank into depression, experienced suicidal ideation and developed a morbid fear of punishment in the life hereafter. His faith told him that because he was sincerely repentant God would forgive him through Jesus Christ. Sadly, he could not forgive himself and neither did he feel that he should.

The relationship between unforgiveness and mental health is well established and Ingersoll-Dayton and colleagues (2010) extend this by demonstrating the mediating role of rumination in respect of depression in later life. The 'cold emotion' of unforgiveness (Worthington and Wade, 1999) incorporates emotions that are far from cold: bitterness, hatred, loathing and resentment. They dominate victims' ruminations about wrongdoers and wrongdoers' ruminations about their own wickedness. Self-unforgiveness directs these feelings against the self, often as a consequence of shame and guilt arising from one's own transgressions. The opposite side of this particular coin is self-forgiveness and that can be attained after 'a shift from fundamental estrangement (self-unforgiveness) to being at home with one's self in the world' (Bauer *et al.*, 1992, p. 153). Inability to forgive oneself is associated with lack of forgiveness by one's victims (e.g. Ingersoll-Deyton and Krause, 2005) and also with a feeling of being forsaken by God, of being too sinful to be forgiven by God.

Emma knew that she had betrayed her older sister, Sandra, many years ago when she had lied about her to their mother about who had stolen money from the elderly lady. Emma had needed the money to settle her son's debts but could not face having to ask for it and having to admit that her son was a gambling wastrel. Emma's mother had assumed it was Sandra who, when still a teenager, had once stolen a small sum of money from her. Emma simply encouraged her mother to maintain her suspicions and the elderly lady died believing that Sandra was still a thief. Sandra was distraught that her mother died with this opinion of her.

Sandra also died before Emma had done anything about the situation. She had listened many times to Sandra's misery as she went over her mother's mistaken belief in her guilt. Emma tried to persuade herself it was for the best as Sandra had been guilty of stealing from her mother and also her son had turned his life around and done well. It was not until Emma developed an inoperable brain tumour and approached her own death that she fully acknowledged the enormity of what she had done. She begged God for forgiveness but had little hope that she could receive it and therefore knew she could never forgive herself. In conversation with her best friend, she revealed her fear of punishment in the hereafter and hoped that the pain she suffered from the tumour would in some way mitigate the pain she expected after the Judgement.

Certainly, Emma's plight suggests that a belief that she had irrevocably offended God was the primary cause of her inability to forgive herself. Evidence from some research studies suggests that this difficulty is shared by many others who never lose their feelings of sorrow for the harm that they caused. For example, Hall and Fincham found that conciliatory behaviour directed at a higher power was related to a decrease in self-forgiveness. They suggest that appealing to a higher power may inhibit self-forgiveness because, possibly, the individuals concerned believe in a vengeful God rather than a forgiving one, or alternatively, that the need to seek forgiveness from a higher power, illuminates their guilt and shame arising from transgression and might serve 'to emphasise one's culpability for the offence or index a form of penance' (Hall and Fincham, 2008, p. 197).

The power of persistent rumination about betrayal to maintain shame and guilt may last a lifetime. Self-forgiveness remains impossible under such circumstances and resulting depressive symptoms are probable within the population of older adults. Choi and Jun (2009) suggest that

> most people are likely to take some personal responsibility for the regrets about family relationship issues and behavioral commissions and omissions, and the associated guilt and remorse may generate more intense negative thoughts and emotions, which may contribute to depressive symptoms.
>
> (p. 215)

Ingersoll-Dayton and colleagues (2010) found in their study of 965 men and women aged 67 years and older that 'feeling unforgiven by God was related to an inability to forgive oneself. This inability to forgive oneself was related to a tendency to ruminate which, in turn, was associated with symptoms of depression' (p. 446). They comment also 'by not forgiving themselves, older individuals may experience a downward spiral characterized by rumination and symptoms of depression' (p. 446).

Thus, being able to forgive oneself augments the experience of being profoundly sorry for transgressions that have harmed others. Compounding these difficulties is a persistent tendency to ruminate about the harm done and sometimes also about a terrible disquiet that the individual could ever had behaved in such an unacceptable way or that the offending behaviour was even within the individual's repertoire. Such blocks on forgiveness arise perhaps because individuals do not understand the frailties of humanity and believed that their lives should have been spent erradicating such imperfections. As Halling (1994) comments,

The journey of self-forgiveness does not end as long as one is alive, for to be alive is to be fallible, to provide material for forgiveness. It may even be a journey that remains partly unacknowledged. But the road to freedom moves both through compassion for oneself and for the other. It is ironic that forgiveness, which is not so much a matter of effort as of letting go, is so difficult for us to approach.

(p. 112)

Feeling sorry: a summary

It is appropriate now to summarise the psychological processes and factors that create the feeling of being sorry for a harm done to others. To reiterate, the harm referred to is that done to interpersonal relationships by acts of betrayal.

The main driving force is that of conscience: the amalgam of moral emotions, moral reasoning and moral conduct. There is no morality without conscience and empathy for others is its fuel. Conscience is a fundamental part of human development and occurs from infancy at roughly the same ages and stages independently of race and culture. Among the several factors influencing the development of conscience are temperament and the lessons of socialisation provided by parents and other important caretakers. With regard to the latter, most major religions share with psychology an emphasis on the need for parents to provide models of moral behaviour. In general, religious guidance lays stress on authoritative and nurturing parenting, as does developmental psychology. Whereas scriptural material does not comment significantly on the perils of authoritarian parenting, the emphasis found in such material on the duty of kindness to children negates the styles of parenting that research in developmental psychology has shown to be inimical to good socialisation. Indeed, evidence suggests that authoritarianism within religious belief and practice is associated with reduced empathy and benevolence, particularly for people outside the believers' in-groups. Although religion and psychology have reasonably congruent views on the nature of beneficent parenting, there is little evidence that religious people are more (or less) moral than those without religion.

Religious teaching, belief and practice are closely aligned to the general thrust of psychological teaching that betrayal of interpersonal relationships by acting outside the 'rules' of those relationships is harmful to both betrayed and betrayer. Infidelity, for example, can severely damage intimate relationships irrespective of marital status. Victims suffer rejection, loss of self-esteem, outrage that precious trust has been violated and grief over the loss of support and companionship. Offenders experience shame, guilt and regret; eventually, the feeling of being profoundly sorry for the harm done finds expression in remorse. Whereas religions offer significant punitive observations on betrayal of marriage, psychology is not moralistic but certainly highlights probable negative outcomes of the effects of these negative emotions.

Outcomes may include persistent ruminative thoughts of vengeance on the part of victims and these are associated with mental health difficulties, particularly depression. Likewise, unremitting shame is, for offenders, also associated with mental health difficulties, loss of self-esteem and withdrawal from social situations where shame may be exposed. Vengeance is condemned by most major religions with some caveats of interpretation that are seized upon by extremists who are susceptible to 'scriptural literalism'. Psychological studies find that personality factors such as psychoticism and narcissism are associated with vengefulness and authoritarian religious beliefs, and provide bulwarks against feeling sorry about harm done.

When feelings of being profoundly sorry lead to expressions of genuine remorse, then amelioration may come with forgiveness by the victim. Apologies may be effective in diminishing trends of vengeance and negative rumination. Most religions provide guidance on the value of repentance and acts of contrition. These are generally congruent with the outcomes of psychological studies that have identified the characteristics of apology that are most strongly associated with forgiveness and the probability of reconciliation. It is noteworthy that whereas most major religions espouse the value of forgiveness (some making it a duty), not all require reconciliation. Likewise, psychological reports note the beneficial influence of forgiveness for both victims and offenders but do not present reconciliation as an inevitable consequence of forgiveness.

Sorrow expressed as a remorseful acknowledgement of the harm done and trust broken is often construed as sincere. Genuine remorse is usually the product of shame and guilt that are most helpfully regarded as separate negative emotions. There are cultural differences in the way in which shame is interpreted. Eastern cultures perceive it to be the failure to do right, whereas Western cultures attach it to wrongs done. Shame in some cultures and religions is significantly associated with dishonour brought to family and community rather than to undetected wrongdoing. However it is interpreted, a movement away from shame and concealment of the wrongdoing towards guilt is the first step towards an empathetic response to the victim. When this occurs wrongdoers may feel a reduction in the intensity of their shameful feelings and the degree of their self-vilification. Major religions and psychology espouse confession of wrongdoing as the best way of regaining a sense of personal worth through forgiveness.

Feigned remorse brings no such rewards no matter what short-term gains may be obtained in terms of, for example, reductions of punishments (e.g. prison sentence) or diminutions of other people's bad opinions or threats. Whatever emotions may be experienced, feeling genuinely sorry is unlikely to be among them. Criminal offenders may feign remorse after claiming religious conversion but this may be no more than a product of impression management for the majority of claimants. Those who claim conversion and then demonstrate empathetic behaviour, perhaps through charitable works, may be sincere. Their expressions of remorse might be genuine and motivated by new-found religious beliefs. It appears, however, that they are in the minority of conversion claimants.

The majority of the world's adult population claims to have some degree of religious belief. There is significant overlap between religiousness and spirituality in that both are associated with transcendence. Spirituality appears to be the overarching phenomena and there is little evidence that religiousness leads believers to a greater grip on moral behaviour than spirituality alone. Religiousness and spirituality are associated with the inhibition of transgressions against others and the elicitation of shame and guilt when such transgressions occur. Exceptions arise when religiousness is extreme and allows no questioning of religious beliefs that are in conflict with more liberal and empathetic approachs to human behaviour.

Distinctions are made between intrinsic and extrinsic religiousness. The former is a genuine belief in the transcendence of religiosity and the divine. It is associated with benign empathetic functioning, including a capacity for forgiveness. Extrinsic religiousness is primarily associated with the trappings of religion and may often be motivated purely by temporal influences including self-interest. Extrinsic religiousness is associated with persistent shame and its avoidance, often resulting in mental health and stress-related difficulties. Being sorry for transgressions has more far-reaching and aversive consequences for people who practise extrinsic religion than for those who hold genuine and sustaining intrinsic beliefs.

Forgiveness also raises some degree of differentiation among religious people. Whereas most of them subscribe to the desirability of forgiveness and claim a disposition to forgive, psychological studies reveal that the frequency of forgiveness related to specific (actual) transgressions is significantly lower than that predicted from the level of dispositional forgiveness. Thus, the disposition to be forgiving does not always transfer from a good intention into an act of forgiveness when actual transgressions occur. Although the extent of the discrepancy has included an artifactual elevation by methodological problems in some of the research, this has not been sufficient to account for the size of the discrepancy. As a consequence, it appears that religious people are not significantly more likely to forgive an offender than their non-religious contemporaries. Under some circumstances, however, unforgiven wrongdoing leads religious people into morbid fears of punishment after death. Those whose faith provides forgiveness through confession may be relieved of a terrible burden at the end of their life course.

Genuine offender remorse is a more powerful initiator of forgiveness. When feeling sorry for transgression is translated from shame into guilt and an act of remorse, then forgiveness becomes more probable. Apology is a common form of making remorse overt and apologies that take account of the victim's self-construals are more likely to be successful. Chapter 7 gives examples of such apologies.

On occasion, both offender and victim require some skilled therapeutic assistance to support their interaction and to facilitate the presentation of genuine remorse. This process can lead to a realisation that forgiveness is not only possible but also desirable. Where forgiveness is an essential catalyst for healing and potential repair of the damaged relationship and, in addition, the victim experiences compassion for the impact of shame and guilt on the offender, then forgiveness may be granted as a definite decision or is sometimes discovered as having occurred as part of the therapeutic process.

In many cases for married couples, the act of forgiveness can lead to long-term improvements in the state of marital satisfaction even pre-transgression. Having shared religious beliefs facilitates this outcome. Not all instances of forgiveness lead, however, to reconciliation no matter how successfully remorse, religious beliefs and reparation come together. The hurt, angry and betrayed feelings of many victims may be too great to counter no matter how sorry the offender may be.

Coda

Feeling sorry for wrongdoing is an emotional experience. There are no simple emotions; at times it appears to me that attempts even to label them as though each stands alone in some panoply of emotionality are fraught with difficulties and caveats. All emotions are complex psychological phenomena and being sorry for harming others in our personal relationships is no exception. It would be duplicitous of me to claim that the contents of this book do any more than skim over a subject such as this, intertwined as it is with issues of early development, parenting, socialisation, conscience, empathy, religious teaching, spirituality, rewards and punishers, morality and ethics, confession, the fear of being found out and terrors concerning the hereafter. Feeling sorry has many major constituents. Shame, as has been shown in the vignettes, seldom remains at a steady level of influence. It appears to grow in strength from something that thoughts can be diverted from into a shadow that blocks out every vestige of pleasure life can offer. Guilt also seldom stays quiescent – whether through ageing or growing pangs of conscience, it expands from a dull ache into a canker of remorse. Too little guilt and one's selfishness knows few restraints; too much and all perspective is lost about just how wicked one truly is. There is also the power of conscience – it is more than Plato's rational facility for recognising good and more than Aristotle's virtuous clamp on self-indulgence. It is the moral essence of our being that passes judgement and can only be silenced by a great effort of will. It is not fooled by specious excuses or extinguished by convenient platitudes. Religious doctrine (certainly Christian) asserts that conscience is part of our moral agency based on free will despite the punishments it inflicts. Perversely, therefore, we choose to punish ourselves with a scourge of our own making that we cannot shut off without great difficulty.

Remorse may lead to confession – another human behaviour of great importance to religions. This is the process by which the isolating, secretive and concealing traits associated with shame are weakened by sharing the transgression with someone else such as a priest or counsellor. It is the case, however, that intrinsically religious people are less likely to show serious interpersonal transgressions and are also more likely to espouse forgiveness. It is also true that couples who share the same religious beliefs are more likely to forgive such transgressions with an intact relationship. Despite these positives, there are also negatives. Religious belief characterised by authoritarianism is often unquestioning, intolerant, arrogant and sociable only with in-group members. Scriptural literalists sometimes hold aggressive beliefs that they may use to justify behaviour that is abhorrent to moderate believers and non-religious people. Some extremist religious leaders may slant interpretation of sacred material to purvey a hate-filled denunciation of other religions, races and cultures, promising, as they do so within their diatribes, extravagant rewards for martyrs. Feeling sorry for one's actions does not encompass all mankind under such circumstances and such preachers make a mockery of the generally benign and peace-loving religions they distort through the lens of their vain-glorious and narcissistic personalities.

The major religions are not particularly associated with an increased probability of a prosocial response to wrongdoing. People who claim to be non-religious are as likely to show shame, guilt, remorse and forgiveness as any other. The formality of religion is not as potent a force for good as spirituality. Those who have no formal religion but have belief in a spiritual existence are no less likely to behave effectively in the face of interpersonal harm than those who adhere to a formal religion.

This espousal of spirituality rather than religion is a growing phenomenon and is associated with an unchurched mysticism detached from religious institutions. Psychology has been accused of promoting this movement by portraying itself as a religion where the self is presented as requiring a form of worship in terms of developing its own self-esteem, potential for growth and success, and being part of a transcendental domain that owes little or nothing to the doctrines of religions or their accoutrements. Roots for this have been cited in Western and Eastern philosophies, and more than one claim has been made that if Buddhism came to the West it would be called psychology. Not surprisingly, this trend has been subject to criticism[8] and identified as a harmful secular religion. Whether or not this is valid, there seems little support for an argument that formal religion has much more to offer than contemporary interpretations of psychological findings in relation to the complex array of emotional and cognitive variables that underpin offender and victim responses to transgression within interpersonal relationships.

The case has been made, however, that for a long time psychologists failed to enter into an equal and unbiased dialogue with religion, that assumptions were made incorrectly and with insufficient evidence. The general consensus, perhaps led by Freud, was that religion was bad for you and to be avoided. The lack of evidence for such distain was an embarrassment to a discipline that called itself a science. Now, as we have seen, religion is mostly good for moderate and open-minded believers who aspire to a moral life that transcends everyday humdrum materialism and seeks the divine.

Nelson (2009) states that religion is more than psychology. Nevertheless, psychology is also more than religion in some aspects. Religion benefits from the unique individuation of psychology that is based on strict methods of study and analysis. Whereas faith needs no proof for it to influence people, individuals do benefit from scientifically supported means of understanding and, when necessary, modifying their behaviour. In addition, psychology has provided religion with insights into child development. It gives reasons why most people are imbued with a moral code that is founded on conscience, whereas others have lacked the opportunities or the models to learn how to feel sorry for wrongdoing and understand why. Also, while religion has a vast repository of material concerning the human condition, psychology has the means to analyse it effectively and generate testable hypotheses to the benefit of both. Perhaps ultimately psychology might reveal how people's aspirations for transcendency may be best achieved while religion offers them the doctrinal support they seek as they make the spiritual journey throughout their life course.

One area where religion and psychology have come together is in pastoral psychology, a union that is of particular relevance for both sorrowful and remorseful offenders and their victims. Pastoral counselling is an important part of this whereby psychology provides a structure and theoretical backdrop to support religious tradition. This application is not an additional purveyor of religious teaching, neither is it necessarily carried out by religious people from the clients' faith groups. Instead, those who work with the clients do so with an understanding of the religious traditions that the clients have faith in. The dialogue between religious authorities and counsellors is not about the nature of God's forgiveness, but how that may be manifested in the cognitive, emotional and behavioural changes required to assist the clients.

Religions, it seems, can take a punitive authoritarian stance about the behaviour of their adherents without meaning to. Psychology can help, for example, by suggesting that victims and offenders, who are not ready, should not be coerced into forgiveness or acts of remorse by religious authorities using scriptural material as an imprimatur for hasty action. Psychology should warn against the forgiveness of offenders that leaves victims more threatened and vulnerable, and perhaps without the sympathy from others that is accorded to victim status. Some victims are simply not ready to forgive, because their pain and anger remains too great. Patton (2000) suggests that the health risks of anger are not the physiological hazards of that emotion but lie in failure to find emotional resolution within a reasonable time. No matter how sorry the offenders feel and no matter how genuine their remorse, not all victims are ready to hear it and it victimises them again if they are obliged to forgive by those they trust to support them. Forgiveness is motivated in part by a feeling of sorrow for the perpetrator. Readiness to forgive arrives with that feeling, which can be profoundly spiritual and aligned to religious teaching; that forgiveness is divine and part of the victim's relationship with God.

Both religion and psychology share similar views on our appreciation of personal wrongdoing. Katchadourian (2010) talks of us accepting moral responsibility for our thoughts and deeds. Feeling sorry for our transgressions should not be a stimulus for casting around to find someone else to blame. There is no profit for us, no matter how shame-prone we may be, in seeking to divest ourselves of the bad choices we made that ended up by causing harm. We are the victims of our own moral violations and the only sorrow that we feel should be for others. Ultimately, we can only become reconciled with our conscience if we remove the barriers of selfishness and egotism that stand in the way of acknowledging what we have done and why we did it. Excuses are manifestations of the frailties of character that lead to the denial of personal responsibility. Ultimately it is not the behaviour of others or exogenous circumstance that puts the weight on our souls, but our own shame and guilt. This is an intensely personal dilemma and, rather like G.K. Chesterton, I am of the opinion that we have to be certain of our own morality because ultimately we must suffer for it.

Notes

Preface: the weight of the soul

1 The assessment of adult bullying is the subject of Randall, P.E. (2001), *Adult Bullying: The assessment of victims and perpetrators*, London: Routledge.
2 For example, see Shackelford, T.D., Buss, D.M. and Bennett, K. (2002), Forgiveness or breakup: Sex differences in responses to a partner's infidelity. *Cognition and Emotion*, 16, 299–307.
3 Abuse by passive collusion typically occurs when an adult is aware or suspects that abuse is occurring but does nothing to halt it. I note the media descriptions of 'passing by on the other side' taken from the parable of the Good Samaritan in reference to the passive collusion of members of clergy allegedly aware of abuse committed by colleagues.
4 See, for example, Mammen, O.K., Kolko, D.J. and Pilkonis, P.A. (2002) Negative affect and parental aggression in child physical abuse. *Child Abuse & Neglect*, 26, 407–24.
5 Behavioural traits such as cheating are increasingly studied within the field of Evolutionary Psychology. This is the study of human psychological adaptations to changing physical and social environments, particularly relating to changed brain structure, cognitive functioning and behavioural differences among individuals. David Buss provides an excellent discussion; see Buss, David M. (2008) *Evolutionary Psychology: The New Science of the Mind*. Boston, MA: Allyn & Bacon.
6 See, for example, Drigotas, S.M. and Barta, W. (2001). The cheating heart: Scientific explorations of infidelity. *Current Directions in Psychological Science*, 10, 177–80.
7 Murphy, J.G. (2007) Remorse, apology and mercy. *Ohio State Journal of Criminal Law*, 4, 423–53.
8 I use the term 'religion' in the exoteric sense of being associated with its public face of doctrine and formal worship rather than the esoteric sense relating to personal experiences of the divine.
9 For example, see Simons, M.A. (2004) Born again on death row: Retribution, remorse and religion. *Catholic Law*, 43, 311–78.
10 Care has been taken with all this material to follow the principles of ethical practice in order to preserve confidentiality.
11 The fallacy of 'two wrongs make a right' has been researched over a wide range of disciplines from child development to business ethics. For example, see Kavka, G.S. (1983) When two 'wrongs' make a right: An essay on business ethics. *Journal of Business Ethics*, 2, 61–6.

1 The stirrings of conscience

1 The concept of valence is sometimes used within this context. Valence refers to whether the experiences of thoughts, feelings or behaviours are negative, neutral or positive. Their strength refers to the intensity and intrusiveness at which they are experienced.
2 Chapter 9 contains some material about the impact of conscience at the end of the life course.
3 For example, 'It is for the father to provide for them (children) and clothe them with kindness' (Qur'an, 2.233).
4 Hoffman referred to this as 'other-oriented induction'.

2 Interpersonal relationships and betrayal

1 'Do unto others as you would have them do unto you' (Matthew 7:12).
This is elaborated by the further words of Jesus in Luke's Gospel:

> Give to everyone who asks of you. And from him who takes away your goods do not ask them back. And just as you want men to do to you, you also do to them likewise. But if you love those who love you, what credit is that to you? For even sinners love those who love them. And if you do good to those who do good to you, what credit is that to you? For even sinners do the same. And if you lend to those from whom you hope to receive back, what credit is that to you? For even sinners lend to sinners to receive as much back. But love your enemies, do good, and lend, hoping for nothing in return; and your reward will be great, and you will be sons of the Most High. For He is kind to the unthankful and evil. Therefore be merciful, just as your Father also is merciful.
>
> (Luke 6:30–36)

2 Emotional infidelity is generally thought to arise from an extra-relationship 'affair of the heart' that is centred on emotional intimacy but excludes sexual infidelity. Where this breaches the norms of the supposedly monogamous relationship, it is thought that the expression 'emotional infidelity' is appropriate.

3 Interpersonal relationships, religion and vengeance

1 I note that as of early August 2011, the young woman has dropped her demand that her assailant should be blinded although the Iranian Court was said to have had the sentence carried out if she had not agreed to exercise clemency.
2 Restorative justice is needs-led in relation to both victims and offenders and these take precedence over the desire of the community to give severe and possibly damaging punishments. Victims are given an active voice in the proceedings and offenders are required to take responsibility for their actions through sincere apology, and making restoration through, for example, community service, entering vocational training schemes, undergoing therapeutic programmes such as anger management and fulfilling requirements set by agency staff such as probation officers.
3 Justitia is the Roman goddess of justice. She is represented by the internationally known statue of a blindfolded lady holding the scales of Justice in her left hand and a double-edged sword in the right.
4 Trait anger is a general tendency to react angrily to perceived situations.
5 Finally, with regard to the large study of Jorm and Christensen (2004), it is noteworthy that they also found similar age and gender effects to those of previous studies. In addition, higher educational levels of subjects were associated with both high and low religiosity.

6 It has been argued that non-pathological narcissism is nothing more than exuberantly high global self-worth (e.g. Tracy *et al.*, 2009); a claim well known to me when legal professionals have sought to defend their narcissistic clients' excessive aggressive responses to social rejection or other slights.

7 These Web pages contain some useful material on the manifestation of narcissism and how this may impact on ordinary and unsuspecting people who have little knowledge of it. The particular quote above was found online at: www.halcyon.com/jmashmun/npd/traits.html

8 This was found online at http://jmm.aaa.net.au/articles/8554.htm

9 Negative religious coping is associated with experiences of spiritual discontent, feeling abandoned by God or being punished by God, dissatisfaction with clergy and/or the Church, questioning the power of God to help, etc. (e.g. Koenig *et al.*, 1998).

10 The modified version of REACH has six components: D, Defining forgiveness; R, Recalling the hurt in a nonthreatening context; E, building Empathy for the perpetrator; A, encouraging Altruistic responses to the hurt; C, Commitment to forgiveness, and H, Holding on to forgiveness.

11 John 3:16 states: 'For God so loved the world that He gave His one and only Son, that whoever believes in him shall not perish but have eternal life.'

12 Surah 25:71 states: 'And whosoever repents and does righteous good deeds, then verily, he repents towards Allah with true repentance.'

13 The ethical codes for researchers and practitioners would forbid such a lackadaisical approach under any circumstances. For example, the *Code of Ethics* of the British Psychological Society states that psychologists should: 'Respect individual, cultural and role differences, including (but not exclusively) those involving age, disability, education, ethnicity, gender, language, national origin, race, religion, sexual orientation, marital or family status and socio-economic status' (BPS, *Code of Ethics and Conduct*, p. 10).

4 Shame, guilt and remorse

1 'More than in measure' implies that the reward of the good doers will be greater than would be proportional to their qualities. For them is the supreme reward of being set near to Allah.

2 The Face is a term for the personality, the real inner self, which will be illuminated and purged by the Light of Allah. All imperfections would be erased and shame dispelled.

3 Smedes recalls hearing voices in church. One tells him that God requires him to be perfect before he could be acceptable. Another tells him that 'I was flawed, worse than imperfect, and all in all a totally unacceptable human being'. Fortunately, he was reassured by a third voice telling him that 'by the grace of God I could be forgiven for my failure (Smedes, 1993, p. 78).

4 Levirate marriage is described in Deuteronomy 25:5–10. Verse 5 states:

> If brethren dwell together, and one of them die, and have no child, the wife of the dead shall not be married abroad unto one not of his kin; her husband's brother shall go in unto her, and take her to him to wife, and perform the duty of a husband's brother unto her.

5 The extended family makes up an individual's group, and the collection of all of the relatives constitutes the tribe. This context defines the parameters of the individual's honorable actions. As long as the individual conforms to the group expectations the group will unquestioningly offer support and protection against people from outside the group.

6 Dr Hamady states, 'He who has done a shameful deed must conceal it, for revealing one disgrace is to commit another disgrace', (1960, p. 37).

7 This is the law of Qisas (retaliation) and is applicable only to murder. No capital punishment is applicable to other crime, including manslaughter. Indeed the Qur'an is clear that the remission of retaliation 'by way of charity, it is an act of atonement for himself' (S5:45).

8 Metalanguage is a form of language or set of terms enabling the analysis of another language, referred to as the 'object language'.

5 Remorse and criminal offending

1 From the field of social psychology, impression management is a goal- directed process whereby people attempt to influence the perceptions of other people about a context or event that is important to them.

2 The term 'body glosses' refers to non-verbal behaviours that augment communication. They include non-verbal apologies that are thought to be effective in conveying a message of sincere contrition in a variety of settings (e.g. Wolfinger, 1995).

3 Absolution: an ecclesiastical declaration of the forgiveness of one's sins.

4 The domain of discursive psychology is in human interactions that occur naturally. It treats verbal interaction as social action and is an analysis of text and talk that focuses on psychological phenomena that are interactive, constructed and attended to. Evaluation can be formulated using phrases and idioms, responded to by the recipient and treated as the expression of a particular position.

5 Unless, of course, the defendant is a very good actor.

6 These scales consist of series of items (questions) that provide a probability of unreliable responding to the tests being taken. Some people being assessed will attempt to 'get a better score' by deliberately falsifying their answers. The importance of this attempt is obvious in, for example, alleged child abusers attempt to diminish their risk levels by endeavouring to cheat on a test of child abuse potential.

6 Religion, spirituality and remorse

1 For a somewhat less prosaic expression of this sentiment that has brought comfort to millions, see *Intimations of Immortality*, William Wordsworth (1807).

2 Sacred is defined here as relating to the numinous (i.e. having a significant spiritual, religious, mystical or supernatural essence) or God, and in many Eastern religious traditions, to the Ultimate Truth or Reality.

3 Buddhist scripture suggests that it is the suffering of others that makes kindly people suffer beyond endurance rather than their own suffering.

4 In Talmudic sources, the most important and first source of charity and social support is considered to be the family. Children have a biblical obligation based on the fifth commandment to look after their parents. There are several biblical references including 1 Timothy 5:8: 'If anyone does not provide for his relatives, and especially for his immediate family, he has denied the faith and is worse than an unbeliever.'

5 See also Chapter 9.

6 Arrow prayers are short prayers that one sends up to heaven at any time and any place. These are usually just a few words in length such as, 'Lord, thank you for the beautiful flowers I've just seen', 'Lord, please help me get my family safely home'.

7 Forgiveness

1 Other forms include self-forgiveness, forgiveness by nation states of previous acts of war, criminal sentence reduction, etc.

2 Paul's letter to the church at Philipi states:

> In all my prayers for all of you, I always pray with joy because of your partnership in the gospel from the first day until now, being confident of this, that he who began a good work in you will carry it on to completion until the day of Christ Jesus (Phil. 1:4–6, New International Version).

3 Religion has, of course, no monopoly over terrorism and torture, each of which can emerge just as readily from dysfunctional secularism.

4 For example, in Christianity the rule is made clear: 'Bear with one another and, if anyone has a complaint against another, forgive each other; just as the Lord has forgiven you, so you also must forgive', Colossians 3:13.

5 For example, the parable of the prodigal son, Luke, 15: 11–32.

6 For there is one God; there is also one mediator between God and humankind, Christ Jesus, himself human', 1 Timothy 2:5.

7 Rabbi Andrew Goldstein and Rabbi Charles Middleburgh (2010, p. 24) provide a rather splendid prayer that depicts the understanding and practice of forgiveness from the Jewish perspective:

> O God of forgiveness, I hereby forgive all those who have hurt me, all those who have wounded me whether deliberate or inadvertent, whether by word or deed. May no one be punished on my account. As I forgive and pardon those who have wronged me may those whom I have hurt forgive and pardon me whether I acted deliberately or inadvertently, whether by word or deed.

8 'If someone who has wronged you asks for your forgiveness you should not refuse it. As long as you are forgiving to others you will find forgiveness yourself.' Midrash.

9 The caveat is important; Dorff (1998) states: 'if the offender never admits wrongdoing . . . no forgiveness can legitimately be demanded of the victims, even if the offender has served a prison term or some other form of punishment' (p. 46).

10 The Mishneh Torah states:

> It is forbidden to be obdurate and not allow yourself to be appeased. On the contrary, one should be easily pacified and find it difficult to become angry. When asked by an offender for forgiveness, one should forgive with a sincere mind and a willing spirit.
>
> (Teshuvah 2:10)

11 Early Islamic literature recounting the life of Muhammad.

12 'Your Lord knows very well what is in your hearts. If you are good, He is forgiving to those who are penitent' (Qur'an, 17:25); 'Allah loves those who turn to Him in repentance' (Qur'an, 2:222).

13 The Qur'an states:

> Will you not fight against those who have broken their oaths and conspired to expel the Messenger? They were the first to attack you. Do you fear them? Surely, Allah has better rights that you fear Him, if you are believers.
>
> Fight them, Allah will punish them with your hands and degrade them. He will grant you victory over them and heal the chests of a believing nation,
>
> (9.12–13)

14 Where the wrongdoing harmed another person or was committed against them, then there should be an admission to the victim as well as to God. Recompense should be given and forgiveness requested.

15 This is similar to Kohlberg's (1976) six-stage model of moral reasoning.

16 The vignette in Chapter 3 concerning the adulterous affair of Rhona with her sister's husband provides an example of a narcissist who forgave herself on superficial grounds and tried to off-load all responsibility for the harm done on to the husband.

8 Remorse, empathy, forgiveness and therapy

1 This is possibly one of the most controversial verses of the Qur'an and it has been used by those opposed to Islam to portray it as cruel and abusive of women. In addition, it has been used by cruel husbands to excuse their degrading and violent treatment of their wives. One translation is as follows:

> Men are the protectors and maintainers of women because Allah has given them more (strength) than the other, and because they support them from their means. Therefore the righteous women are devoutly obedient, and guard in (the husband's absence) what Allah would have them guard (the husband's reputation and property and her virtue). As to those women on whose part ye fear disloyalty and ill-conduct, admonish them (first), (next) refuse to share their beds, (and last) beat them (lightly); but if they return to obedience, seek not against them means (of annoyance) for Allah is Most High, Great (above you all).
>
> Surah 4:34

9 The weight of the soul

1 Solomon Stoddart was pastor of the Congregationalist Church in Northampton, Massachusetts. He became a major religious leader and was well known for his denigration of any form of extravagance and also for urging the preaching of hell fire and the Judgement.
2 For an amusing and well-researched description of the afterlife by religion, see the *Pocket Guide* by Jason Boyett (2009).
3 For a succinct description of cultural and interfaith differences of end of life rituals, see Kemp and Bhungalia (2002).
4 'On the third day he rose again; he ascended into heaven, he is seated at the right hand of the Father, and he will come to judge the living and the dead.' From the Apostles' Creed, *Common Worship*, Church of England.
5 The female Sufi mystic and Muslim Saint of Basra, Rābi'a al-'Adawiyya al-Qaysiyya, disparaged both stick and carrot as reasons for worship:

> O Allah! If I worship Thee in fear of Hell, burn me in Hell; and if I worship Thee in hope of Paradise, exclude me from Paradise; but if I worship Thee for Thine own sake, withhold not Thine Everlasting Beauty!

6 Venial sins are those that are not regarded as depriving the soul of divine grace, in contrast with grave or mortal sins that do unless absolved and forgiven.
7 Millspaugh (2005) delineates components of spiritual pain in the form of concern over predictions of particular losses: the loss of being and loss of relationships, the loss of self, the loss, the loss of purpose, and the loss of control.
8 Vitz (1994) argues that psychology has become an anti-Christian secular religion that may be hostile to the traditions of most formal religions and harmful to both individuals and society in general.

References

Ahadi, B. (2009) Situational determinants of forgiveness. *Research Journal of Biological Sciences*, 4, 651–5.

Akhtar, S.J. (1989) Narcissistic personality disorder: Descriptive features and differential diagnosis. *Psychiatric Clinics of North America*, 12, 505–30.

Aksan, N., Kochanska, G. and Ortmann, M.R. (2006) Mutually responsive orientation between parents and their young children: Toward methodological advances in the science of relationships. *Developmental Psychology*, 42, 833–8.

Alferi, S.M., Culver, J.L., Carver, C.S., Arena, P.L. and Antoni, M.H. (1999) Religiosity, religious coping, and distress: A prospective study of Catholic and Evangelical Hispanic women in treatment for early-stage breast cancer. *Journal of Health Psychology*, 4, 343–56.

Allen, E.S., Atkins, D.C., Baucom, D.H., Snyder, D.K., Gordon, K.C. and Glass, S.P. (2005) Intrapersonal, interpersonal, and contextual factors in engaging in and responding to extramarital involvement. *Clinical Psychology: Science and Practice*, 12, 101–30.

Allport, G.W. (1937) *Personality: A Psychological Interpretation*. London: Constable.

Allport, G.W. (1961) *Pattern and Growth in Personality*. New York: Holt, Rinehart & Winston.

Allport, G.W. (1966) The religious context of prejudice. *Journal for the Scientific Study of Religion*, 5, 447–57.

American Psychiatric Association (2000) *Diagnostic and Statistical Manual of Mental Disorders*, 4th edn (DSM-IV-TR). Washington, DC.

Andrews, P. and Meyer, R.G. (2003) Marlowe-Crowne Social Desirability Scale and short form C: Forensic norms. *Journal of Clinical Psychology*, 59, 483–92.

Aponte, H. J. (1998) Love, the spiritual wellspring of forgiveness: an example of spirituality in therapy. *Journal of Family Therapy*, 20, 37–58.

Aquino, K., Grover, S.L., Goldman, B. and Folger, R. (2003) When push doesn't come to shove: Interpersonal forgiveness in workplace relationships. *Journal of Management Inquiry*, 12, 209–16.

Archer, J. (1999) Assessment of the reliability of the Conflict Tactics Scales: A meta-analytic review. *Journal of Interpersonal Violence*, 14, 1263–89.

Ardelt, M. and Koenig, C. (2006) The role of religion for hospice patients and relatively healthy older adults. *Research on Aging*, 28, 184–215.

Arnett, J., Ramos, K. and Jensen, L. (2001) Ideological views in emerging adulthood: Balancing autonomy and community. *Journal of Adult Development*, 8, 69–79.

Ashton, M.C., Paunonen, S.V., Helmes, E. and Jackson, D.N. (1998) Kin altruism, reciprocal altruism, and the Big Five personality factors. *Evolution and Human Behavior*, 19, 243–55.

Ayoub, M. (1997) Repentance in the Islamic tradition. In A. Etzioni and D.E. Carney (eds) *Repentance: A Comparative Perspective*. New York: Dryden, pp. 96–121.

Azar, F. and Mullet, E. (2001). Interpersonal forgiveness among Lebanese: A six-community study. *International Journal of Group Tensions*, 30, 161–81.

Baetz, M. and Toews, J. (2009) Clinical implications of research on religion, spirituality, and mental health. *Canadian Journal of Psychiatry*, 54, 292–301.

Bagaric, M. and Amarasekara, K. (2001) Feeling sorry? – Tell someone who cares: The irrelevance of remorse in sentencing. *Howard Journal of Criminal Justice*, 40, 364–76.

Bainbridge, W.S. (1989) The religious ecology of deviance, *American Sociological Review*, 54, 288–95.

Banziger, S., van Uden, M. and Janssen, J. (2008) Praying and coping: The relation between varieties of praying and religious coping styles, *Mental Health, Religion & Culture*, 11, 101–18.

Barbee, A., Cunningham, M., Druen, P. and Yankeelov, P. (1996) Loss of passion, intimacy, and commitment: A conceptual framework for relationship researchers. *Journal of Personal and Interpersonal Loss*, 1, 93–108.

Barber, L., Maltby, J. and Macaskill, A. (2005) Angry memories and thoughts of revenge: The relationship between forgiveness and anger rumination. *Personality and Individual Differences*, 39, 253–62.

Baron, J. and Miller, J.G. (2000) Limiting the scope of moral obligations to help: A cross-cultural investigation. *Journal of Cross-Cultural Psychology*, 31, 703–25.

Baron, R.A., Neuman, J.H. and Geddes, D. (1999) Social and personal determinants of workplace aggression: Evidence for the impact of perceived injustice and the Type A Behavior Pattern. *Aggressive Behavior*, 25, 281–96.

Barrett, J. L. (2000) Exploring the natural foundations of religion. *Trends in Cognitive Sciences*, 4, 29–34.

Barro, R.J. and McCleary, R.M. (2002) Religion and political economy in an international panel, unpublished manuscript. Harvard University.

Bartowski, J. P., Wilcox, B. and Ellison, C.G. (2000) Charting the paradoxes of evangelical family life: Gender and parenting in conservative Protestant households. *Family Ministry*, 14, 9–21.

Baucom, D.H., Gordon, K.C., Snyder, D.K., Atkins, D.C. and Christenesen, A. (2005) Treating affair couples: Clinical considerations and initial findings. *Journal of Cognitive Psychotherapy*, 20, 375–92.

Bauer, L., Duffy, J., Fountain, E., Halling, S., Holzer, M., Jones, E., Leifer, M. and Rowe, J.O. (1992) Exploring self-forgiveness. *Journal of Religion and Health*, 31 (2), 149–60.

Baumeister, R. F., Stillwell, A. and Wotman, S.R. (1990) Victim and perpetrator accounts of interpersonal conflict: Autobiographical narratives about anger. *Journal of Personality and Social Psychology*, 59, 994–1005.

Baumeister, R.F., Stillwell, A. and Heatherton, T.D. (1995) Personal narratives about guilt: Role in action control and interpersonal relationships. *Basic and Applied Social Psychology*, 17, 173–98.

Baumeister, R.F., Exline, J.J. and Sommer, K.L. (1998) The victim role, grudge theory, and two dimensions of forgiveness. In E.L. Worthington, Jr (ed.) *Dimensions of Forgiveness*. Philadelphia, PA: Templeton Foundation Press, pp. 79–104.

Baumrind, D. (1966) Effects of authoritative parental control on child behavior. *Child Development*, 37, 887–907.

Bearman, P.S. and Bruckner, H. (2001) Promising the future: Virginity pledges and first intercourse. *American Journal of Sociology*, 106, 859–912.

Becker, D., Sagarin, B.J., Guadagno, R.E., Millevoi, A. and Nicastle, L. (2004) When the sexes need not differ: Emotional responses to the sexual and emotional aspects of infidelity. *Personal Relationships*, 11, 529–38.

Bellah, C.G., Bellah, L.D. and Johnson, J.L. (2003) A look at dispositional vengefulness from the Three and Five-Factor Models of personality. *Individual Differences Research*, 1, 6–16.

Bender, K. and Armour, M. (2007) The spiritual components of restorative justice. *Victims and Offenders*, 2, 251–67.

Ben-Ze'ev, A. (1997) Emotions and morality. *Journal of Value Inquiry*, 31, 195–212.

Berger, P.L. (1974) Some second thoughts on substantive versus functional definitions of religion. *Journal for the Scientific Study of Religion*, 13, 125–33.

Bering, J. (2006) The folk psychology of souls. *Behavioral and Brain Sciences*, 29, 453–98.

Berkowitz, M.W. and Grych, J.H. (1998) Fostering goodness: Teaching parents to facilitate children's moral development. *Journal of Moral Development*, 27, 371–92.

Berry, J.W., Worthington, E.L., Jr, O'Connor, L.E., Parrott, L. and Wade, N.G. (2005) Forgivingness, vengeful rumination, and affective traits. *Journal of Personality*, 73, 183–225.

Berscheid, E. and Peplau, L.A. (1983) The emerging science of relationships. In H.H. Kelley *et al.* (eds) *Close Relationships*. New York: W.H. Freeman and Company, pp. 1–19.

Betzig, L. (1989) Causes of conjugal dissolution: A cross cultural study. *Current Anthropology*, 30, 654–76.

Bibas, S. (2006) Forgiveness in criminal procedures. *Ohio State Journal of Criminal Law*, 4, 329–48.

Bilgrave, D.P. and Deluty, R.H. (1998) Religious beliefs and therapeutic orientations of clinical and counseling psychologists. *Journal for the Scientific Study of Religion*, 37, 329–49.

Blair, R.J.R. (2006) The emergence of psychopathy: Implications for the neuropsychological approach to developmental disorders. *Cognition*, 101, 414–42.

Blocher, W. and Wade, N.G. (2010) Sustained effectiveness of two brief group interventions: Comparing an explicit forgiveness-promoting treatment with a process-oriented treatment. *Journal of Mental Health Counseling*, 32, 58–74.

Bond, C.F. and DePaulo, B.M. (2006) Accuracy of deception judgments. *Personality and Social Psychology Review*, 10, 214–34.

Boschen, T.L. (2001) Shame and guilt in religious fundamentalism. *Journal of Christian Ethics*, 7, 21–9.

Bowlby, J. (1988) *A Secure Base*. New York: Basic Books.

Boyett, J. (2009) *Pocket Guide to the Afterlife: Heaven, Hell, and Other Ultimate Destinations*. San Franciso, CA: Jossey Bass.

Branden, N. (2001) *The Psychology of Self-Esteem*. San Francisco, CA: Jossey-Bass.

Brimhall, A.S. and Butler, M.H. (2007) Intrinsic vs. extrinsic religious motivation and the marital relationship. *American Journal of Family Therapy*, 35, 235–49.

Brown, R.P. (2004) Vengeance is mine: Narcissism, vengeance, and the tendency to forgive. *Journal of Research in Personality*, 38, 576–84.

Burris, C.T. and Bailey, K. (2009) What lies beyond: Theory and measurement of afterdeath beliefs. *International Journal for the Psychology of Religion*, 19, 173–186.

Carlsmith, K.M., Darley, J.M. and Robinson, P.H. (2002) Why do we punish? Deterrence and just deserts as motives for punishment. *Journal of Personality and Social Psychology*, 83, 284–99.

Carlson, D.C. (1982) Vengeance and angelic mediation in Testament of Moses 9 and 10. *Biblical Literature*, 101, 85–95.

Case, B. (2005) Healing the wounds of infidelity through the healing power of apology and forgiveness. *Journal of Couple & Relationship Therapy*, 4, 41–54.

Case, R.B., Moss, A.J., Case, N., McDermott, M. and Eberly, S. (1992) Living alone after myocardial infarction: Impact on prognosis. *Journal of the American Medical Association*, 267, 515–19.

Casey, K.L. (1998) Surviving abuse: Shame, anger, forgiveness. *Pastoral Psychology*, 46, 223–31.

Chakrabarti, A. (2005) The moral psychology of revenge. *Journal of Human Values*, 11, 31–6.

Chambers, R., Lo, B.C.Y. and Allen, N. (2008) The impact of intensive mindfulness training on attentional control, cognitive style, and affect. *Cognitive Therapy and Research*, 32, 303–22.

Chatters, L.M. (2000) Religion and health: Public health research and practice. *Annual Review of Public Health*, 21, 335–67.

Chen, S., Lee Chai, A. Y. and Bargh, J.A. (2001) Relationship orientation as a moderator of the effects of social power. *Journal of Personality and Social Psychology*, 80, 173–87.

Cherlin, A.J. (1999) Going to extremes: Family structure, children's well-being, and social science. *Demography*, 36, 421–28.

Chiaramello, S., Sastre, M.T.M. and Mullet, E. (2008) Seeking forgiveness: Factor structure, and relationships with personality and forgivingness. *Personality and Individual Differences*, 45, 383–8.

Choi, N. and Jun, J. (2009) Life regrets and pride among low-income older adults: Relationships with depressive symptoms, current life stressors and coping resources. *Aging and Mental Health*, 13, 213–25.

Clark, D. (1999) 'Total pain', disciplinary power and the body in the work of Cicely Saunders, 1958–1967. *Social Science & Medicine*, 49, 727–36.

Clifford, D. (2002) Resolving uncertainties? The contribution of some recent feminist ethical theory to the social professions. *European Journal of Social Work*, 5, 31–41.

Cohen, S. (1988) Psychosocial models of the role of social support in the etiology of physical disease. *Health Psychology*, 7, 269–97.

Cohen, A., Hall, D.E., Koenig, H.G. and Meador, K.G. (2005) Social versus individual motivation: Implications for normative definitions of religious orientation. *Personality and Social Psychology Review*, 9, 48–61.

Cohen, A., Malka, A., Rozin, P. and Cherfas, L. (2006) Religion and unforgivable offenses. *Journal of Personality*, 74 (1), 85–118.

Collins, J.E. and Clark, L.F. (1989) Responsibility and rumination: The trouble with understanding the dissolution of a relationship. *Social Cognition*, 7 (2), 152–73.

Corr, P.J. (2008) Reinforcement sensitivity theory (RST): Introduction. In P.J. Corr (ed.) *The Reinforcement Sensitivity Theory of Personality*, Cambridge: Cambridge University Press, pp. 1–43.

Costa, P.T. and McCrae, R.R. (1992) Four ways five factors are basic. *Personality and Individual Differences*, 13, 653–65.

Cota-McKinley, A.L., Woody, W.D. and Bell, P.A. (2001) Vengeance: Effects of gender, age, and religious background. *Aggressive Behavior*, 27, 343–50.

Cross, S.E., Morris, M.L. and Gore, J.S. (2002) Thinking about oneself and others: The relational-interdependent self-construal and social cognition. *Journal of Personality and Social Psychology*, 82, 399–418.

Crowne, D.P. and Marlowe, D. (1960) A new scale of social desirability independent of psychopathology. *Journal of Consulting Psychology*, 24, 349–54.

Darley, J.M., Carlsmith, K.M. and Robinson, P.H. (2002) Incapacitation and just deserts as motives for punishment. *Law and Human Behavior*, 24, 659–83.

Darwin, C. (1872) *The Expression of Emotions in Man and Animals*. New York: Philosophical Library.

Davidson, R.J., Kabat-Zinn, J., Schumacher, J., Rozencrantz, M., Muller, D., Santorelli, S.F., Urbanowski, F., Harrington, A., Bonus, K. and Sheridan, J.F. (2003) Alterations in brain and immune function produced by mindfulness meditation. *Psychosomatic Medicine*, 65, 564–70.

Day, J.M. (2010) Conscience: Does religion matter? Empirical studies of religious elements in pro-social behaviour, prejudice, empathy development, and moral decision-making. In W. Kroops, D. Brugma, T.J. Ferguson and A.F. Sanders (eds) *The Development and Structure of Conscience*, Hove: Psychology Press.

Delaney, H.D., Forcechimes, A.A., Campbell, W.P. and Smith, B.W. (2009) Integrating spirituality into alcohol treatment. *Journal of Clinical Psychology*, 65, 185–98.

DeSteno, D., Bartlett, M.Y., Baumann, J., Williams, L.A. and Dickens, L. (2010) Gratitude as moral sentiment: emotion-guided cooperation in economic exchange. *Emotion*, 10, 289–93.

DeYoung, N.J. (2009) A comparison of college students with narcissistic versus avoidant personality features on forgiveness and vengeance measures. ETD Collection for Purdue University, West Lafayette, IN: Purdue University Press.

Dezutter, J., Soenens, B. and Hutsebaut, D. (2006) Religiosity and mental health: A further exploration of the relative importance of religious behaviors vs religious attitudes. *Personality and Individual Differences*, 40, 807–18.

DiBlasio, F.A. (2000) Decision-based forgiveness treatment in cases of marital infidelity. *Psychotherapy*, 37, 149–58.

Dickerson, S.S., Gruenaewald, T.L. and Kemeny, M.E. (2004) When the social self is threatened: Shame, physiology, and health. *Journal of Personality*, 72, 1191–216.

Dixon, R.D. and Kinlaw, B.J.R. (1982) Belief in the existence and nature of life after death: A research note. *Omega – Journal of Death and Dying*, 13, 287–92.

Dollahite, D.C. and Lambert, N.M. (2007) Forsaking all others: How religious involvement promotes marital fidelity in Christian, Jewish, and Muslim couples. *Review of Religious Research*, 48, 3, 290–307.

Donahue, M.J. and Benson, P.L. (1995) Religion and the well-being of adolescents. *Journal of Social Issues*, 51, 145–60.

Dorff, E.M. (1998) The elements of forgiveness: A Jewish approach. In E.L. Worthington (ed.) *Dimensions of Forgiveness*, Philadelphia, PA: Templeton Foundation Press, pp. 29–55.

Duba, J.D. and Watts, R.E. (2009) Therapy with religious couples. *Journal of Clinical Psychology*, 65, 210–23.

Dunne, M.P., Martin, N.G., Pangan, T. and Heath, A.C. (1997) Personality and change in the frequency of religious observance. *Personality and Individual Differences*, 23, 527–30.

Dupree, W.J., White, M.B., Olsen, C.S. and LaFleur, C.T. (2007) Infidelity treatment patterns: A practice-based evidence approach. *The American Journal of Family Therapy*, 35, 327–41.

Duriez, B. and Soenens, B. (2006) Religiosity, moral attitudes and moral competence: A critical investigation of the religiosity–morality relation. *International Journal of Behavioral Development*, 30, 76–83.

Eaton, J. and Struthers, C.W. (2006) The reduction of psychological aggression across varied interpersonal contexts through repentance and forgiveness. *Aggressive Behavior*, 32, 195–206.

Ecklund, E.H. and Scheitle, C.P. (2007) Religion among academic scientists: Distinctions, disciplines, and demographics. *Social Problems*, 54, 289–307.

Edwards, L.M., Lapp-Rincker, R.H., Magyar-Moe, J.L., Rehfeldt, J.D., Ryder, J.A., Brown, J.C. and Lopez, S.J. (2002) A positive relationship between religious faith and forgiveness: Faith in the absence of data? *Pastoral Psychology*, 50, 147–52.

Eisenberg, N. (2000) Emotion, regulation, and moral development. *Annual Review of Psychology*, 51, 665–97.

Elkind, D. (1964) Piaget's semi-clinical interview and the study of spontaneous religion. *Journal for the Scientific Study of Religion*, 4, 40–6.

Ellis, A. (2000) Can rational emotive behavior therapy (REBT) be effectively used with people who have devout beliefs in God and religion? *Professional Psychology: Research and Practice*, 31, 29–33.

Ellison, C.G. (1991) An eye for an eye? A note on the southern culture of violence thesis. *Social Forces*, 69, 1223–39.

Ellison, C.G., Bartkowski, J.P. and Anderson, K.L. (1999) Are there religious variations in domestic violence? *Journal of Family Issues*, 20, 87–113.

Emmons, R.A. and McCullough, M.E. (2003) Counting blessings versus burdens: An experimental investigation of gratitude and subjective well-being in daily life. *Journal of Personality and Social Psychology*, 84, 377–89.

Engel, B. (2001) *The Power of Apology: Healing Steps to Transform All Relationships*. New York: John Wiley & Sons.

Enright, R.D. and Fitzgibbons, R.P. (2000) *Helping Clients Forgive: An Empirical Guide for Resolving Anger and Restoring Hope*. Washington, DC: American Psychological Association.

Enright, R.D. and Human Development Study Group (1991) Five points on the construct of forgiveness within psychotherapy. *Psychotherapy*, 28, 493–96.

Enright, R.D. and Human Development Study Group (1996) Counseling within the forgiveness triad: On forgiving, receiving forgiveness, and self-forgiveness. *Counseling and Values*, 40, 107–25.

Enright, R.D., Santos, M.J. and Al-Mabuk, R. (1989) The adolescent as forgiver. *Journal of Adolescence*, 12, 99–110.

Enright, R.D., Eastin, D., Golden, S., Sarinopoulis, I. and Freedman, S. (1992) Interpersonal forgiveness within the helping professions: An attempt to resolve differences of opinion. *Counseling and Values*, 36, 84–103.

Epstein, S. (1973) The self-concept revisited, or a theory of a theory. *American Psychologist*, 28, 404–16.

Epstein, S. (1986) Does aggregation produce spuriously high estimates of behavior stability? *Journal of Personality and Social Psychology*, 50, 1199–210.

Epstein, S. (1994) Integration of the cognitive and the psychodynamic unconscious. *American Psychologist*, 49, 709–24.

Exline, J.J. (2003) Belief in heaven and hell among Christians in the United States: Denominational differences and clinical implications. *OMEGA – Journal of Death and Dying*, 47, 155–68.

Exline, J. J. and Yali, A. M. (2007) Heaven's gates and hell's flames: Afterlife beliefs of Catholic and Protestant undergraduates. *Research in the Social Scientific Study of Religion*, 17, 235–60.

Exline, J. J., Park, C.L., Smyth, J.M. and Carey, M.P. (2011) Anger toward God: Social-cognitive predictors, prevalence, and links with adjustment to bereavement and cancer. *Journal of Personality and Social Psychology*, 100, 129–48.

Eysenck, H.J. (1967a) *The Biological Basis of Personality*. Springfield, IL: Thomas.

Eysenck, H.J. (1967b) Dimensions of personality: 16, 5 or 3? Criteria for a taxonomic paradigm. *Personality and Individual Differences*, 12, 773–90.

Eysenck, H.J. and Eysenck, S.B.J. (1991) *Eysenck Personality Questionnaire –Revised (EPQ-R)*. London: Hodder & Stoughton.

Eysenck, J.J. and Eysenck, M.J. (1985) *Personality and Individual Differences: A Natural Science Approach*, New York: Plenum Press.

Fehr, R. and Gelfand, M.J. (2010) When apologies work: How matching apology components to victims' self-construals facilitates forgiveness. *Organizational Behavior and Human Decision Processes*, 37–50.

Feldman, S.S., Cauffman, E., Jensen, L.E. and Arnett, J.L. (2000) The (un)acceptability of betrayal: A study of college students' evaluations of sexual betrayal by a romantic partner and betrayal of a friend's confidence. *Journal of Youth and Adolescence*, 29, 499–523.

Ferch, S.R. (1998) Intentional forgiving as a counseling intervention. *Journal of Counseling and Development*, 76, 261–70.

Ferguson, T.J. and Stegge, H. (1998) Measuring guilt in children: A rose by any other name still has thorns. In J. ByBee (ed.) *Guilt and Children*, San Diego, CA: Academic, pp. 19–74.

Feshbach, N.D. (1975) Empathy in children: Some theoretical and empirical considerations. *The Counseling Psychologist*, 25–30.

Festinger, L. (1957) *A Theory of Cognitive Dissonance*. Stanford, CA: Stanford University Press.

Fincham, F.D. (2000) The kiss of porcupines: From attributing responsibility to forgiving. *Personal Relationships*, 7, 1–23.

Fincham, F.D., Beach, S.R. and Davila, J. (2004) Forgiveness and conflict resolution in marriage. *Journal of Family Psychology*, 18, 72–81.

Finkel, E.J. and Rusbult, C.E. (2002) Dealing with betrayal in close relationships: Does commitment promote forgiveness? *Journal of Personality and Social Psychology*, 82, 956–74.

Fischer, L. and Richards, P.S. (1998) Religion and guilt in childhood. In J. Bybee (ed.) *Guilt and Children*. London: Academic Press, pp. 139–55.

Fitchett, G., Murphy, P.E., Kim, J., Gibbons, J., Cameron, J.R. and Davis, J.A. (2004) Religious struggle: Prevalence, correlates and mental health risks in diabetic, congestive heart failure, and oncology patients. *International Journal of Psychiatry in Medicine*, 34, 179–96.

Fitnes, J. (2001) Betrayal, rejection, revenge, and forgiveness: An Interpersonal Script Approach. In M. Leary (ed.) *Interpersonal Rejection*. New York: Oxford University Press.

Flannelly, K.J., Galek, K., Ellison, C.G. and Koenig, H.G. (2010) Beliefs about God, psychiatric symptoms, and evolutionary psychiatry. *Journal of Religion and Health*, 49, 246–61.

Florian, V. and Kravetz, S. (1983) Fear of personal death: Attribution, structure, and relation to religious belief. *Journal of Personality and Social Psychology*, 44, 600–7.

Florian, V. and Mikulincer, M. (1997) Fear of personal death in adulthood: The impact of early and recent losses. *Death Studies*, 21, 1–24.

Fluehr-Lobban, C. (1994) *Islamic Society in Practice*. Gainesville, FL: University Press.

Fontana, D. (2003) *Psychology, Religion, and Spirituality*. Oxford: Wiley-Blackwell.

Frantz, C.M. and Bennigson, C. (2005) Better late than early: The influence of timing on apology effectiveness. *Journal of Experimental Social Psychology*, 41, 201–7.

Freedman, E.M. (1997) The case against the death penalty. *USA Today*, 125, 48–51.

Freeman, R.B. (1986) Who escapes? The relation of churchgoing and other background factors to the socio-economic performance of black male youths from inner-city tracts. In R.B. Freeman and H.J. Holzer (eds) *The Black Employment Crisis*, Chicago, IL: University of Chicago Press, pp. 353–76.

Freud, S. (1959) *Beyond the Pleasure Principle*. New York: Norton.

Frick, P.J. and Ellis, M.L. (1999) Callous-unemotional traits and subtypes of conduct disorder. *Clinical Child and Family Psychology Review*, 2, 149–68.

Frick, P.J. and White, S.F. (2008) Research Review: The importance of callous-unemotional traits for developmental models of aggressive and antisocial behavior. *Journal of Child Psychology and Psychiatry*, 49, 359–75.

Friedman, H.H. (2006) The power of remorse and apology. *Journal of College and Character*, 7, 1–14.

Fuller, R. (2006) Wonder and the religious sensibility: A study in religion and emotion. *The Journal of Religion*, 86, 364–84.

Furnham, A. (1986) Response bias, social desirability, and dissimulation. *Personality and Individual Differences*, 7, 385–400.

Gaylin, W. (1979). *Feelings: Our Vital Signs*. New York: Harper & Row.

Gelfand, M.J., Major, V.S., Raver, J.L., Nishii, L.H. and O'Brien, K. (2006) Negotiating relationally: The dynamics of the relational self in negotiations. *Academy of Management Review*, 31, 427–51.

Gelfand, M.J., Nishii, L.H., Holcombe, K.M., Dyer, N., Ohbuchi, K. and Fukuno, M. (2001) Cultural influences on cultural representations of conflict: Interpretations of conflict episodes in the United States and Japan. *Journal of Applied Psychology*, 86 (6), 1059–74.

Ghorbani, N., Watson, P.J. and Shahmohamadi, K. (1997) Afterlife Motivation Scale: Correlations with maladjustment and incremental validity in Iranian Muslims. *International Journal for the Psychology of Religion*, 18, 22–35.

Gibbs, J.C., Basinger, K.S., Grime, R.L. and Snarey, J.R. (2007) Moral judgment development across cultures: Revisiting Kohlberg's universality claims. *Developmental Review*, 27, 443–500.

Gilbert, P. (2009) Introducing compassion-focused therapy. *Advances in Psychiatric Treatment*, 15, 199–208.

Gilbert, P. and McGuire, M.T. (1998) Shame, status, and social roles: Psychobiology and evolution. In P. Gilbert (ed.) *Shame: Interpersonal Behavior, Psychopathology, and Culture*. New York: Oxford University Press, pp. 99–125.

Gilbert, P. and Procter, S. (2006) Compassionate mind training for people with high shame and self-criticism. A pilot study of a group therapy approach. *Clinical Psychology and Psychotherapy*, 13: 353–79.

Gilligan, C. (1982) *In a Different Voice*. Cambridge, MA: Harvard University Press.

Glass, S.P. and Wright, T.L. (1985) Sex differences in type of extramarital involvement and marital dissatisfaction. *Journal of Sex Roles*, 12, 1101–20.

Glock, C. and Stark, R. (1966) *Christian Beliefs and Anti-Semitism*. New York: Harper & Row.

Gold, G.J. and Weiner, B. (2000) Remorse, confession, group identity, and expectancies about repeating a transgression. *Basic and Applied Social Psychology*, 22, 291–300.

Goldstein, A. and Middleburgh, C. (2010) *High Days and Holy Days: A Book of Jewish Wisdom*. Norwich: Canterbury Press.

Gonzales, M.H., Haugen, J.A. and Manning, D.J. (1994) Victims as "narrative critics": Factors influencing rejoinders and evaluative responses to offenders' accounts. *Personality and Social Psychology Bulletin*, 20, 691–704.

Goodman, M.A. and Dollahite, D.C. (2006) How religious couples perceive the influence of God in their marriage. *Review of Religious Research*, 48, 141–55.

Gordon, K.C., Baucom, D.H. and Snyder, D.K. (2004) An integrative intervention for promoting recovery from extramarital affairs. *Journal of Marital and Family Therapy*, 30, 213–32.

Gorsuch, R.L. and Hao, J.Y. (1993) Forgiveness: An exploratory factor analysis and its relationships to religious variables. *Review of Religious Research*, 34, 333–47.

Gray, J.A. (1970) The psychophysiological basis of introversion–extraversion. *Behavioral Research and Therapy*, 8, 249–66.

Greeley, A.M. (1991) *Faithful Attraction*. New York: Tor.

Greeley, A.M. and Hout, M. (1999) Americans' increasing belief in life after death: Religious competition and acculturation. *American Sociological Review*, 64 (6), 813–35.

Greenspan, P. (1993) Guilt as an identificatory mechanism. *Pacific Philosophical Quarterly*, 74, 46–59.

Guerra, V.M. and Giner-Sorolla, R. (2010) The Community, Autonomy, and Divinity Scale (CADS): A new tool for the cross-cultural study of morality. *Journal of Cross-Cultural Psychology*, 41, 35–50.

Guinote, A. (2007) Power and goal pursuit. *Personality and Social Psychology Bulletin*, 33, 1076–87.

Haidt, J. (2000) The positive emotion of elevation. *Prevention & Treatment*, 3, 1–5.

Haidt, J. (2003) Elevation and the positive psychology of morality. In C.L. Keyes and J. Haidt (eds) *Flourishing: Positive Psychology and the Life Well-Lived*. Washington, DC: American Psychological Association, pp. 275–89.

Haidt, J., Koller, S. and Dias, M. (1993) Affect, culture, and morality, or is it wrong to eat your dog? *Journal of Personality and Social Psychology*, 65, 613–28.

Hall, J.H. and Fincham, F.D. (2008) The temporal course of self-forgiveness. *Journal of Social and Clinical Psychology*, 27 (2), 174–202.

Hall, S.E.K., Geher, G. and Brackett, M.A. (2004) The measurement of emotional intelligence in children: The case of Reactive Attachment Disorder. In G. Geher (ed.) *Measuring Emotional Intelligence: Common Ground and Controversy*. New York: Nova Science Publishers, 199–217.

Halling, S. (1994) Embracing human fallibility: On forgiving oneself and forgiving others. *Journal of Religion and Health*, 33, 107–13.

Hamady, S. (1960) *Temperament and Character of the Arabs*, Twayne Publishers: New York.

Hamama-Raz, Y., Solomon, Z. and Ohry, A. (2000) Fear of personal death among physicians. *OMEGA – Journal of Death and Dying*, 41, 139–49.

Hansson, R., Jones, W. and Fletcher, W. (1990) Troubled relationships in later life: Implications for support. *Journal of Social and Personal Relationships*, 7, 451–63.

Harker, K. (2001) Immigrant generation, assimilation, and adolescent psychological well-being. *Social Forces*, 79, 969–1004.

Harris, C. (2002) Sexual and romantic jealousy in heterosexual and homosexual adults. *Psychological Science*, 13, 7–12.

Hartling, L.M., Rosen, W., Walker, M. and Jordan, J.V. (2000) *Shame and Humiliation, From Isolation to Relational Transformation*. In *Work in Progress*, Stoner Center for Developmental Services, Wellesley, MA: Wellesley College.

Hathaway, W. and Tan, E. (2009) Religiously oriented mindfulness-based cognitive therapy. *Journal of Clinical Psychology*, 65, 158–71.

Helwig, C.C. (2006) The development of personal autonomy throughout cultures. *Cognitive Development*, 21, 458–73.

Hennessy, D.A. and Wiesenthal, D.L. (2002) The relationship between driver aggression, violence, and vengeance. *Violence and Victims*, 17, 707–18.

Hennessy, D.A. and Wiesenthal, D.L. (2004) Age and vengeance as predictors of mild driver aggression. *Violence and Victims*, 19, 469–77.

Hess, M.B. (1997) A portrait of shame (Genesis 3: 8–15). *Christian Century*, 21–28 May, p. 509.

Higgins, R. (2001) Mindful suffering. *Christian Century*, 24–31 October, p. 9.

Hill, E.W. (2010) Discovering forgiveness through empathy: implications for couple and family therapy. *Journal of Family Therapy*, 32, 169–85.

Hill, P.C. (1995) Affective theory and religious experience. In R.W. Hood, Jr, (ed.) *Handbook of Religious Experience*. Birmingham, AL: Religious Education Press, pp. 312–52.

Hill, P.C., Pargament, K.I., Hood, R.W., Jr., McCullough, M.E., Swyers, J.P., Larson, D.P. and Zinnbauer, B.J. (2000) Conceptualizing religion and spirituality: Points of commonality, points of departure. *Journal for the Theory of Social Behavior*, 30, 51–77.

Hoffman, M.L. (1970) Moral development. In P.H. Mussen (ed.) *Carmichael's Manual of Child Psychology*, Vol. 2. New York: Wiley & Sons, pp. 261–360.

Holden, R.R., Kroner, D.G., Fekken, G.C. and Popham, S.M. (1992) A model of personality test item response dissimulation. *Journal of Personality and Social Psychology*, 63, 272–79.

Hook, A. and Andrews, B. (2005) The relationship of non-disclosure in therapy to shame and depression. *British Journal of Clinical Psychology*, 44, 425–38.

Hope, D. (1987) The healing paradox of forgiveness. *Psychotherapy*, 24, 240–44.

Horning, S.M., Davis, H.P., Stirrat, M. and Cornwall, R.E. (2011) Atheistic, agnostic, and religious older adults on well-being and coping behaviors. *Journal of Aging Studies*, 25, 177–188.

Hotard, S.R., McFatter, R.M., McWhirter, R.M. and Stegall, M.E. (1989) Interactive effects of extraversion, neuroticism, and social relationships on subjective well-being. *Journal of Personality and Social Psychology*, 57, 321–31.

Hunsberger, B., Alisat, S., Pancer, S.M. and Pratt, M. (1996) Religious fundamentalism and religious doubts: Content, connections and complexity of thinking. *The International Journal for the Psychology of Religion*, 6, 201–20.

Hunsberger, B. and Jackson, L.M. (2005) Religion, meaning, and prejudice. *Journal of Social Issues*, 61, 807–26.

Ingersoll, R.E. (1994) Spirituality, religion, and counseling: Dimensions and relationships. *Counseling & Values*, 38, 98–111.

Ingersoll-Dayton, B. and Krause, N. (2005) Self-forgiveness: A component of mental health in later life. *Research on Aging*, 27 (3), 267–89.

Ingersoll-Dayton, B., Torges, C. and Krause, N. (2010) Unforgiveness, rumination, and depressive symptoms among older adults. *Aging & Mental Health*, 14, 439–49.

James, A. and Wells, A. (2003) Religion and mental health: Towards a cognitive-behavioural framework. *British Journal of Health Psychology*, 8, 359–76.

Jang, S.A., Smith, S.W. and Levine, T.R. (2002) To stay or to leave? The role of attachment styles in communication patterns and potential termination of romantic relationships following discovery of deception. *Communication Monographs*, 69, 236–52.

Jennings, D.J. (2003) The transgressor's response to a rejected request for forgiveness. Thesis submitted in partial fulfilment of the requirements for the Master of Science at Virginia Commonwealth University, Psychological Studies Institute.

John, O.P. (1990) The "Big Five" factor taxonomy: Dimensions of personality in the natural language and in questionnaires. In L.A. Pervin (ed.) *Handbook of Personality: Theory and Research*. New York: Guilford Press, pp. 66–100.

Johnson, D.J. and Rusbult, C.E. (1989) Resisting temptation: Devaluation of alternative partners as a means of maintaining commitment in close relationships. *Journal of Personality and Social Psychology*, 57, 967–80.

Johnson, J.L. and Butzen, N.D. (2008) Psychoticism as a predictor of Vengefulness, Forgiveness and Religious Commitment. *Journal of Psychology and Christianity*, 27, 329–36.

Johnson, J.L., Kim, L.M., Giovannelli, T.S. and Cagle, T. (2010) Reinforcement sensitivity theory, vengeance, and forgiveness. *Personality and Individual Differences*, 48, 612–16.

Johnson, R.E. and Chang, C. (2006). "I" is to continuance as "We" is to affective: The relevance of the self-concept for organizational commitment. *Journal of Organizational Behavior*, 27, 549–70.

Johnson, R.E., Selenta, C. and Lord, R.G. (2006) When organizational justice and the self-concept meet: Consequences for the organization and its members. *Organizational Behavior and Human Decision Processes*, 99, 175–201.

Johnson, S. L., McKenzie, G. and McMurrich, S. (2008) Ruminative responses to negative and positive affect among students diagnosed with bipolar disorder and major depressive disorder. *Cognitive Therapy and Research*, 32, 702–13.

Jones, E. and Gallois, C. (1989) Spouses' impressions of rules for communication in public and private marital conflicts. *Journal of Marriage and the Family*, 51, 957–67.

Jorm, A.F. and Christensen, H. (2004) Religiosity and personality: Evidence for non-linear associations. *Personality and Individual Differences*, 36, 1433–41.

Jung, C.G. (1972) The Soul and Death. In *Collected Works of C. G. Jung*, Vol. 8, 2nd edn. Princeton, NJ: Princeton University Press, pp. 404–15.

Kafetsios, K. (2004) Attachment and emotional intelligence abilities across the life course. *Personality and Individual Differences*, 37, 129–145.

Kaprio, J., Koskenvuo, M. and Rita, H. (1987) Mortality after bereavement: A prospective study of 95,647 widowed persons. *American Journal of Public Health*, 77, 283–7.

Karremans, J.C. and Smith, P.K. (2010) Having the power to forgive: When the experience of power increases interpersonal forgiveness. *Personality and Social Psychology Bulletin*, 36, 1010–23.

Karremans, J.C. and Van Lange, P.A. (2005) Does activating justice help or hurt in promoting forgiveness? *Journal of Experimental Social Psychology*, 41, 290–7.

Katchadourian, H. (2010) *Guilt: The Bite of Conscience*, Stanford, PA: Stanford General Books.

Kaufman, G. (1992) *Shame: The Power of Caring*, 3rd edn. Rochester, VT: Schenkman Books.

Keltner, D., Gruenfeld, D.H. and Anderson, C. (2003) Power, approach, and inhibition. *Psychological Review*, 110, 265–84.

Kemp, C. and Bhungalia, S. (2002) Culture and the end of life: A review of major world religions. *Journal of Hospice and Palliative Nursing*, 4, 235–42.

Keng, S., Smolski, M. J. and Robins, C.J. (2011) Effects of mindfulness on psychological health: A review of empirical studies. *Clinical Psychology Review*, 31, 1041–56.

Kenrick, D.T. and Sheets, V. (1993) Homicidal fantasies. *Ethnology and Sociobiology*, 14, 231–46.

Kerr, D.C.R., Lopez, N.L., Olson, S.L. and Sameroff, A.J. (2004) Parental discipline and externalizing behavior problems in early childhood: The roles of moral regulation and child gender. *Journal of Abnormal Child Psychology*, 32, 369–83.

Kim, P.H., Ferrin, D.L., Cooper, C.D. and Dirks, K.T. (2004) Removing the shadow of suspicion: The effects of apology versus denial for repairing competence versus integrity-based trust violations. *Journal of Applied Psychology*, 89, 104–18.

Klostermaier, K.K. (1994) *A Survey of Hindusim*. Albany, NY: State University of New York Press.

Knee, C.R. (1998) Implicit theories of relationships: Assessment and prediction of romantic relationship initiation, coping, and longevity. *Journal of Personality and Social Psychology*, 74, 360–70.

Kochanska, G. (1997) Multiple pathways to conscience for children with different temperaments: From toddlerhood to age 5. *Developmental Psychology*, 33, 228–40.

Kochanska, G. and Aksan, N. (2006) Children's conscience and self-regulation. *Journal of Personality*, 74, 1587–617.

Koenig, H. (2009) Research on religion, spirituality and mental health: A review. *Canadian Journal of Psychiatry*, 54, 283–91.

Koenig, H., Pargament, K.I. and Nielsen, J.B.A. (1998) Religious coping and health status in medically ill hospitalized older adults. *Journal of Nervous & Mental Disease*, 186, 513–21.

Kohlberg, L. (1973) The claim to moral adequacy of a highest stage of moral judgment. *Journal of Philosophy*, 70, 630–46.

Kowalski, R.M. (ed.) (1997) *Aversive Interpersonal Behaviors*. New York: Plenum Press.

Kowalski, R.M., Walker, S., Wilkinson, R., Queen, A. and Sharpe, B. (2003) Lying, cheating, complaining, and other aversive interpersonal behaviors: A narrative examination of the darker side of relationships. *Journal of Social and Personal Relationships*, 20, 471–90.

Kucharski, L.T., Toomey, J.P. and Fila, K. (2007) Detection of malingering of psychiatric disorder with the Personality Assessment Inventory: An investigation of criminal defendants. *Journal of Personality Assessment*, 88, 25–32.

Lagaree, T.A., Turner, J. and Lollis, S. (2007) Forgiveness and therapy: A critical review of conceptualizations, practices and values found in the literature. *Journal of Marital and Family Therapy*, 33, 192–213.

Laible, D.J. and Thompson, R.A. (2000) Mother–child discourse, attachment security, shared positive affect, and early conscience development. *Child Development*, 71, 1424–40.

Lampton, C., Oliver, G. J., Worthington, E.L. and Berry, J.W. (2005) Helping Christian college students become more forgiving: An intervention study to promote forgiveness as part of a program to shape Christian character. *Journal of Psychology and Theology*, 33, 278–90.

LaPierre, L.L. (1994) A model for describing spirituality. *Journal of Religion and Health*, 33, 153–61.

Lawoyin, T.O. and Larsen, U. (2002) Male sexual behaviour during wife's pregnancy and postpartum abstinence period in Oyo State, Nigeria. *Journal of Biosocial Science*, 34, 51–63.

Lazar, A. (2006) Fear of personal death as a predictor of motivation for religious behavior. *Review of Religious Research*, 48, 179–89.

Lazar, A., Kravetz, S. and Frederich-Kedem, P. (2002) The multidimensionality of motivation for Jewish religious behavior: Content, structure and relationship to religious identity. *Journal for the Scientific Study of Religion*, 41, 509–19.

Lazare, A. (1995) Go ahead, say you're sorry. *Psychology Today*, 28, 40–2.

Leary, M., Springer, C., Negel, L., Ansell, E. and Evans, K. (1998) The causes, phenomenology, and consequences of hurt feelings. *Journal of Personality and Social Psychology*, 74, 1225–37.

Lester, D., Aldridge, M., Aspenberg, C., Boyle, K., Radsniak, P. and Waldron, C. (2001) What is the afterlife like? Undergraduate beliefs about the afterlife. *OMEGA – Journal of Death and Dying*, 44, 113–26.

Levenson, R.W. and Ruef, A.M. (1997) Physiological aspects of emotional knowledge and rapport. In W. Ickes, *Empathic Accuracy* (Chapter 2). New York: Guilford Press.

Levine, T., McCornack, S. and Avery, B.P. (1992) Sex differences in emotional reactions to discovered deception. *Communication Quarterly*, 40, 289–96.

Lewis, H.B. (1971) *Shame and Guilt in Neurosis*. New York: International University Press.

Lewis, M. (1992) *Shame: The Exposed Self*. New York: The Free Press.

Lewis, M. and Ramsay, D. (2002) Cortisol response to embarrassment and shame. *Child Development*, 73, 1034–45.

Lindsay-Hartz, J., De Rivera, J. and Mascolo, M.F. (1995) "Differentiating guilt and shame and their effects on motivation". In J.P. Tangney and K.W. Fischer (eds) *Self-Conscious Emotions*. New York: Guilford Press, pp. 274–300.

Lippke, R.L. (2008) Response to Tudor: Remorse-based sentence reductions in theory and practice. *Criminal Law and Philosophy*, 2, 259–68.

Lucas, R. (2005) Time does not heal all wounds: A longitudinal study of reaction and adaptation to divorce. *Psychological Science*, 16, 945–50.

Lutz, A., Brefczynski-Lewis, J., Johnstone, T. and Davidson, R.J. (2008) Regulation of the neural circuitry of emotion by compassion meditation: Effects of meditative expertise. *Public Library of Science*, 3, 1–10.

Maccoby, E.E. (1999) The uniqueness of the parent–child relationship. In W. A. Collins and B. Laursen (eds) *Minnesota Symposium on Child Psychology: Vol. 30. Relationship as Developmental Contexts*. Mahwah, NJ: Erlbaum, 157–75.

Maccoby, E.E. and Jacklin, C.N. (1980) Sex differences in aggression: A rejoinder and reprise. *Child Development*, 51, 964–80.

MacDonald, D.A. (2000) Spirituality: Description, measurement, and relation to the Five Factor Model of personality. *Journal of Personality*, 68, 153–97.

MacLaren, V.V., Best, L.A. and Bigney, E.E (2010) Aggression–hostility predicts direction of defensive responses to human threat scenarios. *Personality and Individual Differences*, 49, 142–7.

Mahoney, A., Pargament, K.I., Tarakeshwar, N. and Swank, A.B. (2001) Religion in the home in the 1980s and 1990s: A meta-analytic review and conceptual analysis and links between religion, marriage and parenting. *Journal of Family Psychology*, 15, 559–96.

Maltby, J. (2005) Protecting the sacred and expressions of rituality: Examining the relationship between extrinsic dimensions of religiosity and unhealthy guilt. *Psychology and Psychotherapy: Theory, Research and Practice*, 78, 77–93.

Maltby, J. and Day, L. (2003) Religious orientation, religious coping and appraisals of stress. *Personality and Individual Differences*, 34, 1209–24.

Maltby, J., Macaskill, A. and Day, L. (2001) Failure to forgive self and others: A replication and extension of the relationship between forgiveness, personality, social desirability and general health. *Personality and Individual Differences*, 30, 881–5.

Marchena, E. and Waite, L.J. (2001) Marriage and childbearing attitudes in late adolescence: Gender, race and ethnic differences. Paper presented at the meeting of the Population Association of America, Los Angeles, CA: March 2000.

Martel, J. (2010) Remorse and the production of truth. *Punishment and Society*, 12, 414–37.

Martin, R. and Watson, D. (1997) Style of anger expression and its relation to daily experience. *Personality and Social Psychology Bulletin*, 23, 285–94.

Marty, M.E. (1998) The ethos of Christian forgiveness. In E.L. Worthington, Jr (ed.) *Dimensions of Forgiveness*. Philadelphia, PA: Templeton Foundation Press, pp. 9–28.

Maselko, J., Kubzansky, L., Kawachi, I., Staudenmeyer, J. and Berkman, L. (2006) Religious service attendance and decline in pulmonary function in a high-functioning elderly cohort. *Annals of Behavioral Medicine*, 32, 245–53.

Maslow, A.H. (1970) *Religion, Values and Peak Experiences*. New York: Viking.

Maslow, A.H. (1971) *The Farther Reaches of Human Nature*. New York: Penguin.

Mastekaasa, A. (1995) Age variations in the suicide rates and self-reported subjective well-being of married and never married persons. *Journal of Community and Applied Social Psychology*, 5, 21–39.

Mauger, P.A., Perry, J.E., Freeman, T., Grover, D.C., McBridge, A.G. and McKinney, K.E. (1992) The measurement of forgiveness: Preliminary research. *Journal of Psychology and Christianity*, 11, 170–80.

Mayer, J. D., Caruso, D. and Salovey, P. (1999) Emotional intelligence meets traditional standards for an intelligence. *Intelligence*, 27, 267–98.

McCallister, B.J. (1995) Cognitive theory and religious experience. In R.W. Hood, Jr, (ed.) *Handbook of Religious Experience*. Birmingham, AL: Religious Education Press, pp. 312–52.

McCullough, M.E. and Worthington, E.L., Jr (1999) Religion and the forgiving personality. *Journal of Personality*, 67, 1141–64.

McCullough, M.E., Worthington, E.L., Jr and Rachal, K.C. (1997) Interpersonal forgiving in close relationships. *Journal of Personality and Social Psychology*, 73, 321–36.

McCullough, M.E., Bono, G. and Root, L.M. (2007) Rumination, emotion, and forgiveness: Three longitudinal studies. *Journal of Personality and Social Psychology*, 92, 490–505.

McCullough, M.E., Bellah, C.G., Kilpatrick, S.D. and Johnson, J.L. (2001) Vengefulness: Relationships with forgiveness, rumination, well-being, and the Big Five. *Personality and Social Psychology Bulletin*, 27, 601–10.

McCullough, M.E., Worthington, E.L., Jr, Maxie, J. and Rachal, K.C. (1997) Gender in the context of supportive and challenging religious counseling interventions. *Journal of Counseling Psychology*, 44, 80–8.

McCullough, M.E., Kilpatrick, S., Emmons, R.A. and Larson, D. (2001) Is gratitude a moral affect? *Psychological Bulletin*, 127, 249–66.

McCullough, M.E., Rachal, K., Sandage, S.J., Worthington, E.L., Jr, Brown, S.W. and Hight, T.L. (1998) Interpersonal forgiving in close relationships: II. Theoretical elaboration and measurement. *Journal of Personality and Social Psychology*, 75, 1586–603.

McNaughton, N. and Corr, P. J. (2004) A two-dimensional neuropsychology of defense: Fear/anxiety and defensive distance. *Neuroscience and Biobehavioral Reviews*, 28, 285–305.

Meek, K.R., Albright, J.S. and McMinn, M.R. (1995) Religious orientation, guilt, confession, and forgiveness. *Journal of Psychology and Theology*, 23, 190–97.

Menesini, E. and Camodeca, M. (2008) Shame and guilt as behaviour regulators: Relationships with bullying, victimization and prosocial behaviour. *British Journal of Developmental Psychology*, 26, 183–96.

Messias, E., Saini, A., Sinato, P. and Welch, S. (2010) Bearing grudges and physical health: Relationship to smoking, cardiovascular health and ulcers. *Social Psychiatry and Psychiatric Epiemiology*, 45, 183–87.

Miller, J.B. and Stiver, I. (1994) Movement in therapy: Honoring the "strategies of disconnection." *Work in Progress*, No. 65. Wellesley, MA: Stone Center Working Paper Series.

Miller, J.G., Bersoff, D.M. and Harwood, R.L. (1990) Perceptions of social responsibilities in India and in the United States: Moral imperatives or personal decisions? *Journal of Personality and Social Psychology*, 58, 33–47.

Miller, R.S. and Tangney, J.P. (1994) Differentiating embarrassment and shame. *Journal of Social and Clinical Psychology*, 13, 273–87.

Mills, J.F. and Kroner, D.G. (2003) Antisocial constructs in predicting institutional violence among violent offenders and child molesters. *International Journal of Offender Therapy and Comparative Criminology*, 47, 324–34.

Mills, J.F. and Kroner, D.G. (2005) An investigation into the relationship between socially desirable responding and offender self-report. *Psychological Services*, 2, 70–80.

Mills, J.F. and Kroner, D.G. (2006) Impression management and self-report among violent offenders. *Journal of Interpersonal Violence*, 21, 178–92.

Mills, J.F., Loza, W. and Kroner, D.G. (2003) Predictive validity despite social desirability: Evidence for the robustness of self-report among offenders. *Criminal Behaviour and Mental Health*, 13, 144–54.

Millspaugh, D. (2005) Assessment and response to spiritual pain: Part 1. *Journal of Palliative Medicine*, 8, 919–23.

Montgomery, C. (2002) Role of dynamic group therapy in psychiatry. *Advances in Psychiatric Treatment*, 8, 34–41.

Moreland, J.P. (1987) *Scaling the Secular City: A Defense of Christianity*. Grand Rapids, MI: Baker Books.

Motiuk, M., Motiuk, L. and Bonta, J. (1992) A comparison between self-report and interview-based inventories in offender classification. *Criminal Justice and Behavior*, 19, 143–59.

Murphy, J.G. (2007) Remorse, apology and mercy, *Ohio State Journal of Criminal Law*, 4, 423–53.

Murray, S.L., Holmes, J.G. and Griffin, D.W. (2000) Self-esteem and the quest for felt security: How perceived regard regulates attachment processes. *Journal of Personality and Social Psychology*, 78, 478–98.

Murray, S.L., Rose, P., Bellavia, G.M., Holmes, J.G. and Kusche, A.G. (2002) When rejection stings: How self-esteem constrains relationship-enhancement. *Journal of Personality and Social Psychology*, 83, 556–73.

Myers, D.G. (2000) The funds, friends, and faith of happy people. *American Psychologist*, 55, 56–67.

Nagel, T. (2002) *Concealment and Exposure: and Other Essays*. Oxford: Oxford University Press.

Neff, K.D. (2003) Self-compassion: An alternative conceptualization of a healthy attitude toward oneself. *Self and Identity*, 2, 85–102.

Neimeyer, R.A., Wittkowski, J. and Moser, R.P. (2004) Psychological research on death attitudes: An overview and evaluation. *Death Studies*, 28, 309–40.

Nelson, J.M. (2009) *Psychology, Religion and Spirituality*. New York: Springer Science.

Nielsen, A.L. (1988) Substance abuse, shame, and professional boundaries. *Alcoholism Treatment Quarterly*, 4, 109–37.

Nun Ioanna (1996) When the conscience falls silent and shame dies out. *Orthodox America*. Available online at: www.roca.org/OA/142/142d.htm, accessed 10 October 2010.

Nygaard, R.L. (1994) 'Vengeance is mine', says the Lord. *America*, 171, 6–9.

Öhman, A. (2000) Fear and anxiety: Evolutionary, cognitive, and clinical perspectives. In M. Lewis and J. M. Haviland-Jones (eds) *Handbook of Emotions*. New York: Guilford Press, pp. 573–93.

Olthof, T., Schouten, A., Kuiper, H., Stegge, H. and Jennekens-Schinkel, A. (2000) Shame and guilt in children: Differential situational antecedents and experiential correlates. *British Journal of Developmental Psychology*, 18, 51–64.

Oman, D., Shapiro, L.S., Thorensen, C. E. Plante, T.G. & Flinders, T. (2008), Meditation lowers stress and supports forgiveness among college students: A randomized controlled trial. *Journal of American College Health*, 56, 569–78.

Öner-Özkan, B. (2007) Future Time Orientation and religion. *Social Behavior and Personality*, 35, 51–62.

Paleari, F.G., Regalia, C. and Fincham, F. (2005) Marital quality, forgiveness, empathy, and rumination: A longitudinal analysis. *Personality and Social Psychology Bulletin*, 31, 368–78.

Paloutzian, R.F. (2009) The bullet and its meaning. In A. Kalayjian and R.F. Paloutzian (eds) *Forgiveness and Reconciliation: Psychological Pathways to Conflict Transformation and Peace Building*. New York: Springer, pp. 71–80.

Paloutzian, R.F. and Smith, B.S. (1995) The utility of the religion-as-schema model. *International Journal for the Psychology of Religion*, 5, 17–22.

Papyrakis, E. and Selvaretnam, G. (2011) The greying church: The impact of life expectancy on religiosity. *International Journal of Social Economics*, 38, 438–52.

Pargament, K.I. (1997) *The Psychology of Religion and Coping*. New York: Guilford Press.

Pargament, K.I. (2002) The bitter and the sweet: An evaluation of the costs and benefits of religiousness. *Psychological Inquiry*, 13, 168–81.

Pargament, K. I., Kennell, J., Hathaway, W., Grevengoed, N., Newman, J. and Jones, W. (1988) Religion and the problem-solving process: Three styles of coping. *Journal for the Scientific Study of Religion*, 27, 90–104.

Pargament, K.I., Koenig, K.I., Tarakeshwar, N. and Hahn, J. (2004) Religious coping methods as predictors of psychological, physical and spiritual outcomes among medically ill elderly patients: A two-year longitudinal study. *Journal of Health Psychology*, 9, 713–30.

Pargament, K.I. and Rye, M.S. (1998) Forgiveness as a method of religious coping. In E.L. Worthington, Jr (ed.) *Dimensions of Forgiveness*. Philadelphia, PA: Templeton Foundation Press, pp. 59–78.

Pattison, S. (2000) *Shame: Theory, Therapy, Theology*. New York: Cambridge University Press.

Patton, J. (2000) Forgiveness in pastoral care and counseling. In M.E. McCullough, K.I. Pargament and C.E. Thoresen (eds) *Forgiveness: Theory, Research and Practice*. New York: Guilford Press, pp. 41–64.

Paulhus, D.L. (1984) Two-component models of socially desirable responding. *Journal of Personality and Social Psychology*, 46, 593–609.

Paulhus, D.L. (1998) *Paulhus Deception Scales (PDS): The Balanced Inventory of Desirable Responding–7*. Toronto, Ontario: Multi-Health Systems.

Pavot, W., Diener, E. and Fujita, F. (1990) Extraversion and happiness. *Personality and Individual Differences*, 11, 1299–1306.

Pearce, L.D. and Axinn, W.G. (1998) The impact of family religious life on the quality of mother–child relations. *American Sociological Review*, 63, 810–28.

Pennebaker, J.W., Hughes, C.F. and O'Heeron, R.C. (1987) The psychophysiology of confession: Linking inhibitory and psychosomatic processes. *Journal of Personality and Social Psychology*, 52, 781–93.

Petrucci, C.J. (2002) Apology in the criminal justice setting: Evidence for including apology as an additional component in the legal system. *Behavioral Sciences and the Law*, 20, 337–62.

Pham, M.T., Cohen, J.B., Pracejus, J.W. and Hughes, G.D. (2001) Affect monitoring and the primacy of feelings in judgment. *Journal of Consumer Research*, 28, 167–88.

Piaget, J. (1932) *The Moral Judgment of the Child*. London: Kegan Paul, Trench, Trubner & Co.

Piedmont, R.L. (1999) Does spirituality represent the sixth factor of personality? Spiritual transcendence and the five-factor model. *Journal of Personality*, 67, 985–1013.

Plante, T.G. and Boccaccini, M.T. (1997) The Santa Clara Strength of Religious Faith questionnaire. *Pastoral Psychology*, 45, 375–87.

Plante, T.G., Vallaeys, C.L., Sherman, A.C. and Wallston, K.C. (2002) The development of a brief version of the Santa Clara Strength of Religious Faith Questionnaire. *Pastoral Psychology*, 50, 359–68.

Posner, M.I. and Rothbart, M.K. (2000). Developing mechanisms of self-regulation. *Development and Psychopathology*, 12, 427–41.

Powers, C., Nam, R.K., Rowatt, W.C. and Hill, P.C. (2007) Associations between humility, spiritual transcendence, and forgiveness. In R.L. Piedmont (ed.) *Research in the Social Scientific Study of Religion*, Vol. 18. Leiden: Brill.

Price, M.J. (2006) Litigating salvation: Race, religion and innocence in the Karla Faye Tucker and Gary Graham cases. *Southern California Review of Law & Social Justice*, 15, 267–98.

Proeve, M.J., Smith, D.I. and Niblo, D.M. (1999) Mitigation without definition: Remorse in the Criminal Justice System. *Australian and New Zealand Journal of Criminology*, 32, 16–26.

Propst, L.R. (1996) Cognitive-behavioral therapy and the religious person. In E.P. Shafranske (ed.) *Religion and the Clinical Practice of Psychology*. Washington, DC: American Psychological Association, 391–407.

Propst, L.R., Ostrom, R., Watkins, P., Dean, T. and Mashburn, D. (1992) Comparative efficiency of religious and non-religious cognitive-behavioral therapy for the treatment of clinical depression in religious individuals. *Journal of Clinical and Consulting Psychology*, 60, 94–103.

Rackley, J.V. (1993) The relationship of marital satisfaction, forgiveness, and religiosity. Unpublished doctoral dissertation, Blacksburg, VA: Virginia Polytechnic Institute and State University.

Raghunathan, R. and Pham, M.T. (1999) All negative moods are not equal: Motivational influences of anxiety and sadness on decision making. *Organizational Behavior and Human Decision Processes*, 79, 56–77.

Randall, P.E. (1997) *Adult Bullying*. London: Routledge.

Randall, P.E. (2002) *Adult Bullying: The assessment of victims and perpetrators*. London: Routledge.

Raskin, R. and Hall, C. (1981) The Narcissistic Personality Inventory: Alternate form reliability and further evidence of construct validity. *Journal of Personality Assessment*, 45, 159–62.

Rector, N.A., Bagby, R.M., Segal, Z.V., Joffe, R.T. and Levitt, R. (2000) Self-criticism and dependency in depressed patients treated with cognitive therapy or pharmacotherapy. *Cognitive Therapy and Research*, 24, 571–84.

Regnerus, M.D. (2000) Shaping schooling success: Religious socialization and educational outcomes in metropolitan public schools. *Journal for the Scientific Study of Religion*, 39, 363–70.

Richards, P.S. (1991) Religious devoutness in college students: Relations with emotional adjustment and psychological separation from parents. *Journal of Counseling Psychology*, 2, 189–96.

Robbins, B.D. and Parlavecchio, H. (2006) The unwanted exposure of the self: A phenomenological study of embarrassment. *The Humanistic Psychologist*, 34, 4, 321–45.

Roberts, R.C. (1995) Forgivingness. *American Philosophical Quarterly*, 32, 289–306.

Roberts, R.D., Zeider, M., Matthews, G. (2001) Does emotional intelligence meet traditional standards for an intelligence? Some new data and conclusions. *Emotion*, 1, 196–231.

Rogers, C. (1959) A theory of therapy, personality and interpersonal relationships as developed in the client-centered framework. In S. Koch (ed.) *Psychology: A Study of a Science. Vol 3: Formulations of the person and the social context*. New York: McGraw Hill.

Rogers, M.B., Loewenthal, K.M., Lewis, C.A., Amlot, R., Cinnirella, M. and Ansari, H. (2007) The role of religious fundamentalism in terrorist violence: A social psychological analysis. *International Review of Psychiatry*, 19, 253–62.

Rogers, R. (2008) An introduction to response styles. In R. Rogers (ed.) *Clinical Assessment of Malingering and Deception* (Chapter 1). New York: Guilford University Press.

Roth-Hanania, R., Busch-Rossnagel, N. and Higgins-Alessandro, A. (2000) Development of self and empathy in early infancy: Implications for atypical development. *Infants and Young Children*, 13, 1–14.

Rozin, P., Lowery, L., Imada, S. and Haidt, J. (1999) The CAD triad hypothesis: A mapping between three moral emotions (contempt, anger, disgust) and three moral codes (community, autonomy, divinity). *Journal of Personality and Social Psychology*, 76, 574–86.

Rusbult, C. E., Kumashiro, M., Stocker, S.L., Kirchner, J.L., Finkel, E.J. and Coolsen, M.J. (2005) Self processes in interdependent relationships: Partner affirmation and the Michelangelo phenomenon. *Interaction Studies*, 6, 375–91.

Rusbult, C.E., Verette, J., Whitney, G.A, Slovik, L.F. and and Lipkus, I. (1991) Accommodation processes in close relationships: Theory and preliminary empirical evidence. *Journal of Personality and Social Psychology*, 60, 53–78.

Russell, B. (1953) *Religion and Science*. London: Oxford University Press.

Rye, M.S., Loiacono, D.M., Folck, C.D., Olszewski, B.T., Heim, T.A. and Madia, B.P. (2001b) Evaluation of the psychometric properties of two forgiveness scales. *Current Psychology*, 20, 260–7.

Rye, M.S., Pargament, K.I., Ali, M.A., Beck, G.L., Dorff, E.N., Hallisey, C., Narayanan, V. and Williams, J.G. (2001a) Religious perspectives on forgiveness. In M.E. McCullough, K.I. Pargament and C.E. Thoresen (eds) *Forgiveness: Theory, Research, and Practice*. New York: Guilford Press, pp. 17–40.

Sackeim, H. A. and Gur, R. C. (1979) Self-deception, other-deception, and self-reported psychopathology. *Journal of Consulting and Clinical Psychology*, 47, 213–15.

Salsman, J. M., Brown, T.L., Brechting, E.H. and Carlson, C.R. (2005) The link between religion and spirituality and psychological adjustment: The mediating role of optimism and social support. *Personality and Social Psychology Bulletin*, 31, 522–35.

Santage, S.J. and Worthington, E.L. (2010) Comparison of two group interventions to promote forgiveness: Empathy as a mediator of change. *Journal of Mental Health Counseling*, 32, 35–57.

Santelli, A. G., Struthers, C. and Eaton, J. (2009) Fit to forgive: Exploring the interaction between regulatory focus, repentance, and forgiveness. *Journal of Personality and Social Psychology*, 96, 381–94.

Saroglou, V. (2002) Religion and the five factors of personality: A meta-analytic review. *Personality and Individual Differences*, 32, 15–25.

Saroglou, V., Pichon, I., Trompette, L., Verschueren, M. and Dernelle, R. (2005) Prosocial behavior and religion: New evidence based on projective measures and peer ratings. *Journal for the Scientific Study of Religion*, 44, 323–348.

Satterly, L. (2001) Guilt, shame and religious and spiritual pain. *Holistic Nursing Practice*, 15, 30–9.

Saucier, G. and Skrzypinska, K. (2006) Spiritual but not religious? Evidence for two independent dispositions. *Journal of Personality*, 74, 1257–92.

Schlehofer, M.M., Omoto, A.M. and Adelman, J.R. (2008) How do "Religion" and "Spirituality" differ? Lay definitions among older adults. *Journal for the Scientific Study of Religion*, 47, 411–25.

Schlenker, B. and Darby, B. (1981) The use of apologies in social predicaments. *Social Psychology Quarterly*, 44, 271–78.

Schmitt, M., Gollwitzer, M., Forster, N. and Montada, L. (2004) Effects of objective and subjective account components on forgiving. *The Journal of Social Psychology*, 144, 465–85.

Segal, Z.V., Williams, J.M.G. and Teasdale, J.D. (2002) *Mindfulness-based cognitive therapy for depression: A new approach to preventing relapse*. New York: Guilford Press.

Selenta, C. and Lord, R.G. (2005) Development of the levels of self-concept scale: Measuring the individual, relational, and collective levels. Unpublished master's thesis.

Shackelford, T. and Buss, D. (1997) Cues to infidelity. *Personality and Social Psychology Bulletin*, 1034–45.

Shackelford, T.D., Buss, D.M. and Bennett, K. (2002) Forgiveness or breakup: Sex differences in responses to a partner's infidelity. *Cognition and Emotion*, 16, 299–307.

Shapiro, S.L., Carlson, L.E., Astin, J.A. and Freedman, B. (2006) Mechanisms of mindfulness. *Journal of Clinical Psychology*, 62, 373–86.

Sharma, A. (2010) Social-psychological correlates of happiness in adolescents. *European Journal of Social Sciences*, 12, 651–62.

Shaw, J.C., Wild, E. and Colquitt, J.A. (2003). To justify or excuse? A meta-analytic review of the effects of explanations. *Journal of Applied Psychology*, 88, 444–58.

Shweder, R.A., Much, N.C., Mahapatra, M. and Park, L. (1997) The "big three" of morality (autonomy, community, divinity), and the "big three" explanations of suffering. In P. Rozin and A. Brandt (eds) *Morality and Health*. New York: Routledge.

Siegel, D.J. (2007) Mindfulness training and neural integration: Differentiation of distinct streams of awareness and the cultivation of well-being. *Social Cognitive and Affective Neuroscience*, 2, 259–63.

Silber, M.D. and Bhatt, A. (2007) *Radicalization in the West: The Homegrown Threat*. NYPD Intelligence Division: New York Police Department.

Silberman, I. (2003) Spiritual role modeling: The teaching of meaning systems. *The International Journal for the Psychology of Religion*, 13 (3), 175–95.

Simon, S.B. and Simon, S. (1990) *Forgiveness: How to Make Peace with Your Past and Get on with Your Life*. New York: Warner Books.

Simons, M.A. (2004) Born again on death row: Retribution, remorse, and religion. *Catholic Lawyer*, 43, 311–38.

Skinner, B.F. (1957) *Verbal Behavior*. New York: Appleton-Century-Crofts.

Slingerland, E. (2008) Who's afraid of reductionism? The study of religion in the age of cognitive science. *Journal of the American Academy of Religion*, 76, 375–411.

Smart, N. (1998) *The World's Religions*. Cambridge: Cambridge University Press.

Smedes, L.B. (1993) *Shame and Grace: Healing the Shame We Don't Deserve*. New York: HarperCollins.

Smillie, L.D., Pickering, A.D. and Jackson, C.J. (2006) The new reinforcement sensitivity theory: Implications for personality measurement. *Personality and Social Psychology Review*, 4, 320–35.

Smith, P.K. and Trope, Y. (2006) You focus on the forest when you're in charge of the trees: Power priming and abstract information processing. *Journal of Personality and Social Psychology*, 90, 578–96.

Smith, T.B., McCullough, M.E., Poll, J. (2003) Religiousness and depression: Evidence for a main effect and the moderating influence of stressful life events. *Psychological Bulletin*, 129, 614–36.

Smith, R.H., Webster, J.M., Parrott, G. and Eyre, H.L. (2002) The role of public exposure in moral and nonmoral shame and guilt. *Journal of Personality and Social Psychology*, 83, 138–59.

Smith, P.K., Jostmann, N.B., Galinsky, A.D. and van Dijk, W.W. (2008) Lacking power impairs executive functions. *Psychological Science*, 19, 441–7.

Sommers, J.A., Schell, T.L. and Vodanovich, S.J. (2002) Developing a measure of individual differences in organizational revenge. *Journal of Business and Psychology*, 17, 207–22.

Sorenson, A.M., Grindstaff, C.F. and Turner, R.J. (1995) Religious involvement among unmarried adolescent mothers: A source of emotional support? *Sociology of Religion*, 56, 71–81.

Sroufe, L.A. (2005) Attachment and development: A prospective, longitudinal study from birth to adulthood. *Attachment & Human Development*, 7, 349–67.

Stark, R. (2001) Gods, rituals, and the moral order. *Journal for the Scientific Study of Religion*, 40, 619–36.

Stouten, J., De Cremer, D. and Van Dijk, E. (2009) When being disadvantaged grows into vengeance: The effects of asymmetry of interest and social rejection in social dilemmas. *European Journal of Social Psychology*, 39, 526–39.

Strawbridge, W.J., Cohen, R.D., Shema, S.J. and Kaplan, G.A. (1997) Frequent attendance at religious services and mortality over 28 years. *American Journal of Public Health*, 87, 957–61.

Struthers, C. W., Eaton, J., Santelli, A.G., Uchiyma, M. and Shirvani, N. (2008) The effects of attributions of intent and apology on forgiveness: When saying sorry may not help the story. *Journal of Experimental Social Psychology*, 44, 983–92.

Stuckless, N. and Goranson, R. (1992) The vengeance scale: Development of a measure of attitudes toward revenge. *Journal of Social Behavior & Personality*, 7, 25–42.

Stuewig, J., Tangney, J.P, Heigel, C., Harty, L. and McCloskey (2010) Shaming, blaming, and maiming: Functional links among the moral emotions, externalization of blame, and aggression. *Journal of Research in Personality*, 44, 91–102.

Subkoviak, M.J., Enright, R.D., Wu, C., Gassin, E.A., Freedman, S., Olson, L.M. and Sarinopoulos, I. (1995) Measuring interpersonal forgiveness in late adolescence and middle adulthood. *Journal of Adolescence*, 18, 641–55.

Suh, E., Diener, E. and Fujita, F. (1996) Events and subjective well-being: Only recent events matter. *Journal of Personality and Social Psychology*, 70, 1091–102.

Sundby, S. (1998) The capital jury and absolution: The intersection of trial strategy, emorse, and death penalty. *Cornell Law Review*, 83, 1557–98.

Sussman, S., Nezami, E. and Mishra, S. (1997) On operationalizing spiritual experience for health research and practice. *Alternative Therapies in Clinical Practice*, 4, 120–5.

Tangney, J.P. (1990) Assessing individual differences in proneness to shame and guilt: Development of the Self-Conscious Affect and Attribution Inventory. *Journal of Personality and Social Psychology*, 59, 102–11.

Tangney, J.P. (1995) Shame and guilt in interpersonal relationships. In J.P. Tangney and K.W. Fischer (eds) *Self-conscious Emotions: Shame, Guilt, Embarrassment, and Pride*. New York: Guilford Press, pp. 114–39.

Tangney, J.P. and Dearing, R.L. (2002) *Shame and Guilt*. New York: Guilford Press.

Tangney, J.P and Salovey, P. (2010) Emotions of the imperiled ego. In J.E. Maddux and J.P. Tangney (eds) *Social Psychological Foundations of Clinical Psychology*. New York: Guilford Press.

Tangney, J.P., Miller, R.S., Flicker, L. and Barlow, D. (1996) Are shame, guilt, and embarrassment distinct emotions? *Journal of Personality and Social Psychology*, 70, 1256–69.

Tangney, J.P., Stuewig, J. and Mashek, D.J. (2007) Moral emotions and moral behavior. *Annual Review of Psychology*, 58, 345–72.

Tatman, A.W., Swogger, M.T., Love, K. and Cook, M.D. (2009) Psychometric properties of the Marlowe-Crowne Social Desirability Scale with adult male sexual offenders. *Sexual Abuse*, 21, 21–34.

Taylor, G. (1985) *Pride, Shame and Guilt: Emotions of Self-assessment*. Oxford: Clarendon Press.

Temoshok, L.R. and Chandra, P.S. (2000) The meaning of forgiveness in a specific situational and cultural context: Persons living with HIV/AIDS in India. In M.E

McCullough, K.I. Pargament and C.E. Thoresen (eds) *Forgiveness: Theory, Research and Practice*. New York: Guilford Press, pp. 41–64.

Thomaes, S., Stegge, H. and Olthof, T. (2010) Does shame bring out the worst in narcissists? On moral emotions and immoral behaviours. In W. Koops, T.J. Brugman, T.J. Ferguson and A.F. Sanders (eds) *The Development and Structure of Conscience*. Hove: Psychology Press, pp. 221–3.

Thompson, L.V., Snyder, L.H., Michael, S.T., Rasmussen, H.N., Billings, L.S., Heinze, L., Neufeld, J.E., Shorey, H.S., Roberts, J.C. & Roberts, D.A. (2005) Dispositional forgiveness of self, others, and situations. *Journal of Personality*, 73, 313–59.

Thorson, A. and Powell, F.C. (1988) Elements of death anxiety and meanings of death. *Journal of Clinical Psychology*, 44, 691–701.

Thurston, N.S. (2000) Psychotherapy with evangelical and fundamentalist Protestants. In P.S. Richards and A.E. Bergin (eds) *Handbook of Psychotherapy and Religious Diversity*. Washington, DC: American Psychological Association, pp. 131–53.

Tieger, T. (1980) On the biological basis of sex differences in aggression. *Child Development*, 51, 943–63.

Tomkins, S.S. (1963) *Affect/Imagery/Consciousness: The Negative Affects*, Vol. 2. New York: Springer.

Tracy, J.L. and Robins, R.W. (2004a) Show your pride: Evidence for a discrete emotion expression. *Psychological Science*, 15, 194–7.

Tracy, J.L. and Robins, R.W. (2004b) Putting the self into self-conscious emotions: A theoretical model. *Psychological Inquiry*, 15, 103–25.

Tracy, J.L. and Robins, R.W. (2006) Appraisal antecedents of shame, guilt, and pride: Support for a theoretical model. *Personality and Social Psychology Bulletin*, 32, 1339–51.

Tracy, J.L. and Robins, R.W. (2007) Emerging insights into the nature and function of pride. *Current Directions in Psychological Science*, 16, 147–50.

Tracy, J.L., Cheng, J.T., Robins, R.W. and Trzesniewski, K.H. (2009) Authentic and hubristic pride: The affective core of self-esteem and narcissism. *Self and Identity*, 8, 196–213.

Treynor, W., Gonzalez, R. and Nolen-Hoeksema, S. (2003) Rumination reconsidered: A psychometric analysis. *Cognitive Therapy and Research*, 27, 247–59.

Tsang, J. (2002) Moral rationalization and the integration of situational factors and psychological processes in immoral behavior. *Review of General Psychology*, 6, 25–50.

Tsang, J., McCullough, M.E. and Fincham, F.D. (2006) The longitudinal association between forgiveness and relationship closeness. *Journal of Social and Clinical Psychology*, 25, 448–72.

Tsang, J., McCullough, M.E. and Hoyt, W.T. (2005) Psychometric and rationalization accounts of the religion-forgiveness discrepancy. *Journal of Social Issues*, 61, 785–805.

Tsoudis, O. and Smith-Lovin, L. (1998) How bad was it? The effects of victim and perpetrator emotion on responses to criminal court vignettes. *Social Forces*, 77, 695–722.

Tudor, S. (2008) Why should remorse be a mitigating factor in sentencing? *Criminal Law and Philosophy*, 2, 241–257.

Twenge, J.M. and Campbell, W.K. (2003). "Isn't it fun to get the respect we're going to deserve?" Narcissism, social rejection, and aggression. *Personality and Social Psychology Bulletin*, 29, 261–72.

Uden, M.H.F. van, Pieper, J.Z.T. and Alma, H.A. (2004) Bridge over troubled water: Further results regarding the Receptivity Coping Scale. *Journal of Empirical Theology*, 17, 101–14.

Vallacher, R.R., Nowak, A. and Zochowski, M. (2005) Dynamics of social coordination. *Interaction Studies*, 6, 35–52.

Van Lange, P.A.M., Rusbult, C.E., Drigotas, S.M., Arriaga, X.B., Witcher, B.S. and Cox, C.L. (1997) Willingness to sacrifice in close relationships. *Journal of Personality and Social Psychology*, 72, 1373–95.

Vaughan, F., Wittine, B. and Walsh, R. (1996) Transpersonal psychology and the religious person. In E.D. Shafranske (ed.) *Religion and the Clinical Practice of Psychology*. Washington, DC: American Psychological Association, pp. 483–510.

Vitz, P.C. (1994) *Psychology as Religion: The Cult of Self-Worship*, 2nd edn. Grand Rapids, MI: Eerdmans Publishing.

Volling, B.L., Mahoney, A.J. and Rauer, A. (2009) Sanctification of parenting, moral socialization, and young children's conscience development. *Psychology of Religion and Spirituality*, 1, 53–68.

Wachholtz, A.B., Pearce, M.J. and Koenig, H. (2007). Exploring the relationship between spirituality, coping, and pain. *Journal of Behavioral Medicine*, 30, 311–18.

Wade, N.G. (2010) Introduction to the special issue on forgiveness in therapy. *Journal of Mental Health Counseling*, 32, 1–4.

Wade, N.G. and Meyer, J.E. (2009) Comparison of brief group interventions to promote forgiveness: A pilot outcome study. *International Journal of Group Psychotherapy*, 59, 199–220.

Wade, N.G. and Worthington, E.L. (2005) In search of a common core: A content analysis or interventions to promote forgiveness. *Psychotherapy: Theory, Research, Practice, Training*, 42, 160–77.

Wade, N.G., Worthington, E.L., Jr and Haake, S. (2009) Comparison of explicit forgiveness interventions with an alternative treatment: A randomized clinical trial. *Journal of Counseling and Development*, 87, 143–51.

Wade, N.G., Worthington, E.L., Jr and Vogel, D.L. (2007) Effectiveness of religiously tailored interventions in Christian therapy. *Psychotherapy Research*, 17, 91–105.

Wagner, J.A. (1995) Studies of individualism–collectivism: Effects on cooperation in groups. *Academy of Management Journal*, 38, 152–72.

Waite, L.J. and Lehrer, E.L. (2003) The benefits from marriage and religion in the United States: A comparative analysis. *Population and Development Review*, 29, 255–75.

Walker, L.W. and Pitts, R.C. (1998) Naturalistic conceptions of moral maturity. *Developmental Psychology*, 34, 403–19.

Walrond-Skinner, S. (1998) The function and role of forgiveness in working with couples and families: Clearing the ground. *Journal of Family Therapy*, 20: 3–19.

Walsh, J.A., Tomlinson-Keasey, C. and Klieger, D.M. (1974) Acquisition of the social desirability response. *Genetic Psychology Monographs*, 89, 241–72.

Watkins, E. (2008) Constructive and unconstructive repetitive thought. *Psychological Bulletin*, 134, 163–206.

Watson, P.J., Grisham, S.O., Trotter, M.V. and Biderman, M.D. (1984) Narcissism and empathy: Validity evidence for the narcissistic personality inventory. *Journal of Personality Assessment*, 45, 159–62.

Watts, C. and Zimmerman, C. (2002) Violence against women: Global scope and magnitude. *The Lancet*, 359, 1232–7.

Weiner, B., Graham, S., Peter, O. and Zmuldlnas, M. (1991) Public confession and forgiveness. *Journal of Personality*, 59, 281–312.

Weisman, R. (2009) Being and doing: The judicial use of remorse to construct character and community. *Social and Legal Studies*, 18, 47–69.

Wenzel, M. and Ozimoto, T.G. (2010) How acts of forgiveness restore a sense of justice: Addressing status/power and value concerns raised by transgressions. *European Journal of Social Psychology*, 40, 401–17.

Whisman, M.A. and Wagers, T.P. (2005) Assessing relationship betrayals. *Journal of Clinical Psychology*, 61, 1383–91.

Wiederman, M.W. (1997) Extramarital sex: Prevalence and correlates in a national survey. *Journal of Sex Research*, 34, 167–74.

Wiersbe, W.W. (2007) *Be Reverent: Bowing Before Our Awesome God*, 1st edn. Colorado Springs, CO: David C. Cook.

Williams, B. (1993) *Shame and Necessity*, Berkeley, CA: University of California Press.

Wink, P. and Scott, J. (2005) Does religiousness buffer against the fears of death and dying in late adulthood? Findings from a longitudinal study. *The Journals of Gerontology*, 60, 207–14.

Wink, P., Ciciolla, L., Dillon, M. and Tracy, A. (2007) Religiousness, spiritual seeking, and personality: Findings from a longitudinal study. *Journal of Personality*, 75, 1051–70.

Witty, M.T. (2005) The realness of cybercheating. *Social Science Computer Review*, 23, 57–67.

Witvliet, C.V.O., Ludwig, T.E. and Vander Laan, K.L. (2001) Granting forgiveness or harboring grudges: Implications for emotion, physiology, and health. *Psychological Science*, 12, 117–23.

Witvliet, C.V.O., Phipps, K.A., Feldman, M.E. and Beckham, J.C. (2004) Posttraumatic mental and physical health correlates of forgiveness and religious coping in military veterans. *Journal of Traumatic Stress*, 17, 269–73.

Wolfinger, N.H. (1995) Passing moments: Some social dynamics of pedestrian interaction. *Journal of Contemporary Ethnography*, 323–40.

Wood, L.A. and MacMartin, C. (2007) Constructing Remorse: Judges' Sentencing Decisions in Child Sexual Assault Cases. *Journal of Language and Social Psychology*, 26, 343–62.

Worthington, E.L., Jnr (1998) An empathy-humility-commitment model of forgiveness applied within family dyads. *Journal of Family Therapy*, 20, 59–76.

Worthington, E.L., Jr (2001) *Five Steps to Forgiveness: The Art and Science of Forgiving*. New York: Crown House.

Worthington, E. and Wade, N. (1999) The psychology of unforgiveness and forgiveness and implications for clinical practice. *Journal of Social and Clinical Psychology*, 18, 358–418.

Worthington, E.L., Jr and Drinkard, D.T. (2000) Promoting reconciliation through psychoeducational and therapeutic interventions. *Journal of Marital and Family Therapy*, 26, 93–101.

Worthington, E.L., Jr and Scherer, M. (2004) Forgiveness is an emotion-focused coping strategy that can reduce health risks and promote health resilience: Theory, review, and hypotheses. *Psychology and Health*, 19, 385–405.

Worthington, E.L., Jr and Aten, J.D. (2009) Psychotherapy with religious and spiritual clients: An introduction. *Journal of Clinical Psychology in Session*, 65, 123–30.

Worthington, E.L., Jr, Wade, N.G., Hight, T.L., Ripley, J.S., McCullough, M.E., Berry, J.W., Schmitt, M.M., Berry, J.T., Bursley, K.H. and O'Connor, L. (2003) The Religious Commitment Inventory-10: Development, refinement, and validation of a brief scale for research and counseling. *Journal of Counseling Psychology*, 50, 84–96.

Worthington, E.L., Hunter, J.L., Sharp, C.B., Hook, J.N., Van Tongeren, D.R., Davis, D.E., Miller, A.J., Gingrich, F.C., Sandage, S.J., Elson, L., Bubod, L. and Monteforte-Milton, M. (2010) A psychoeducational intervention to promote forgiveness in Christians in the Philippines. *Journal of Mental Health Counseling*, 32, 75–93.

Yang, M., Yang, C. and Chiou, W. (2010) When guilt leads to other orientation and shame leads to egocentric self-focus: Effects of differential priming of negative affects on perspective taking. *Social Behavior and Personality*, 38, 605–614.

Younger, J.W., Piferi, R.L., Jobe, R.L. and Lawler, K.A. (2004) Dimensions of forgiveness: The views of laypersons. *Journal of Social and Personal Relationships*, 21, 837–55.

Ysseldyk, R., Matheson, K. and Anisman, H. (2007) Rumination: Bridging a gap between forgivingness, vengefulness, and psychological health. *Personality and Individual Differences*, 42, 1573–84.

Yuki, G. and Falbea, C.M. (1991) Importance of different power sources in downward and lateral relations. *Journal of Applied Psychology*, 76, 416–23.

Zechmeister, J.S. and Romero, C. (2002) Victim and offender accounts of interpersonal conflict: Autobiographical narratives of forgiveness and unforgiveness. *Journal of Personality and Social Psychology*, 82, 675–86.

Zinnbauer, B.J. and Pargament, K.I. (1998) Spiritual conversion: A study of religious change among college students. *Journal for the Scientific Study of Religion*, 37, 161–80.

Zinnbauer, B.J., Pargament, K.I. and Scott, A.B. (1999) The emerging meanings of religiousness and spirituality. *Journal of Personality*, 67, 889–919.

Zondag, H.J. and van Uden, M.H.F. (2010) I just believe in me: Narcissism and religious coping. *Archive for the Psychology of Religion*, 32, 69–85.

Zuckerman, D.M., Kasl, S.V. and Ostfeld, A.M. (1984) Psychosocial predictors of mortality among the elderly poor. *American Journal of Epidemiology*, 119, 410–23.

Index

Please note that page numbers relating to Notes will have the letter 'n' following the page number.

Abramoff, J. 105
abuse x, xii, 236n
actions, forgiveness 163–4
Adam and Eve 78, 217
adultery 30
affect, religion and spirituality 136–8
After Death Belief Scale 220
afterlife, belief in 213–15; conceptualisation within major world religions 213, 216–18; fear of punishment 218, 220, 221, 222; patterns of belief 220–1; strength of belief 218–19
age factors: and afterlife 219; in vengeance 53–5
aggression ix, x, xii, 54, 59
agnosticism 19, 116, 142, 221
agreeableness 55, 57
Ahadi, B. 175
Aksan, N. 16, 18
Alferi, S.M. 144
Ali, Hadrat 50
Allah 50, 166, 217, 241n
Allen, E.S. 40
Allport, G. 42–3, 139, 141, 151
altruism 11, 24
Amarasekara, K. 107, 110
amygdala 63
Andrews, B. 99–100
anger 4, 59, 167, 235; righteous 8–9
animalistic behaviour 9
anxiety 145–7
apology 231–2; components 178–80, 195; definitions xiv; and forgiveness

176–82, 186–7; and guilt 87; individual responses to components 180–2; and remorse 96–7, 108; and vengeance 70–1
Aponte, H. 132, 189
Aquinas, T. xiii
Aquino, K. 52
Ardelt, M. 214
Ashmun, J. 61
Aten, J.D. 154, 155
atheism 19, 116, 142, 220, 221
atonement xiv, 74
attachment style 30–1
authentic pride 8
authoritarianism 20, 27, 229, 233
autism 15
automatic maladaptive thinking patterns 207–8
Autonomy, Ethics of 6
Avici hell 218
avoidance behaviour 218
Ayoub, M. 166
Azar, F. 74–5

Baetz, M. 143
Bagaric, M. 107, 110
Bailey, K. 220
Bainbridge, W.S. 140
balanced inventory of desirable responding (BIDR) 119
baptism 164
Barbee, A. 37
Barber, L. 70
Baron, R.A. 54

Barrett, J.L. 135, 136
Barro, R.J. 148
Barta, W. 236n
Barth, K. 116
BAS (Behavioural Activation System) 62, 63, 64
Baucom, D.H. 73
Baumeister, R.F. 65–7
Becker, D. 35
Behavioural Activation System (BAS) 62, 63, 64
Behavioural Inhibition System (BIS) 62, 63, 64
behavioural standards, external (compliance with) 23
being mode, in mindfulness 206–7
beliefs 130–1; in afterlife *see* afterlife, belief in; cognitive behavioural approach 142–3; forgiveness 162–3; and remorse xvii; and therapy 210; *see also* religion; religion and spirituality (RS)
Bellah, C.G. 57
belonging 29
benefaction 10
benevolence, and therapy 192–4, 209
Bennett, K. 236n
Bennigson, C. 176
Ben-Ze'ev, A. 2
Berger, P.L. 130
Bering, J. 213, 216, 222
Berkowitz, M.W. 22, 23–4, 26
Berscheid, E. 41
betrayal: anatomy 33–47; behaviour and significance 35–40; case study 31–2, 33; consequences of 42–7; definitions 33–5; evidence of 40–2; in interpersonal relationships ix, xi, xviii, 28–47, 226, 229–30; and remorse 46–7; and wrongdoing xi–xiii; *see also* infidelity
Betzig, L. 40
Big Five factor personality model 55, 57, 62, 63, 138
Big Three ethics of morality 6–7, 8, 9
Bilgrave, D.P. 201
BIS (Behavioural Inhibition System) 62, 63, 64
Blocher, W. 72–3
Bloom, A. 188

'body glosses' 109, 239n
Bohn, H. 48
Bolt, M. 168
Bonaventure, Saint xiii
Boschen, T.L. 80, 81
Branden, N. 43
Brault, R. 82–3
British Psychological Society, Code of Ethics 238n
Brown, R.P. 59
Buddha, Siddartha Gautama 101
Buddhism 129, 145, 189, 233, 239n; and afterlife 213, 218; and compassion 102; and conscience 20; and forgiveness 167; and mindfulness 101, 206
bullying ix, x, 93, 236n
Burris, C.T. 220
Buss, D.M. 40, 41, 236n
Butzen, N.D. 57, 58
Byron, G.G. 1

callous-unemotional traits 15, 27
Camodeca, M. 93
Campana, K.L. 175
capital punishment 109
Carlsmith, R.M. 52
carrot-and-stick approach to wrongdoing 212–18
Casey, K.L. 79
Chakrabarti, A. 48, 51, 76
Chambers, R. 208
Chandra, P.S. 167
Chang, C. 177, 181
cheating xii–xiii, 236n
Chen, S. 184–5
Cherlin, A.J. 149
Chesterton, G.K. 235
Chiaramello, S. 96
Child Abuse Potential (CAP) inventory 121, 123
childrearing: and conscience 20, 21–2; and religion 148–9
children: abuse of x, xii; emotional intelligence 203; shame and guilt 93; spontaneous religion 135
Choi, N. 228
Christensen, H. 57, 58, 237n
Christianity 128; and afterlife 213, 217–18; and CBT 157; and conscience

20; Ethics of Divinity 7; and
    forgiveness 74, 160, 164–5, 166;
    fundamentalism 136; Protestantism
    201; Roman Catholicism 165, 201;
    and shame 79–80, 83–4
cognition: and emotion 11;
    religion/spirituality 135–6
cognitive behavioural therapy (CBT) 73,
    101, 102, 157, 192
cognitive developmental theories 12, 15
cognitive reframing 73
Cognitive-Experiential Self-Theory
    (CEST) 162
Cohen, S. 151
collectivist actions 177
collusive forgiveness 194
commerce 10
commitment, relationship 184–5
Community, Ethics of 7
community support 82
compassion 82, 102; and therapy 99–103
compassionate mind training (CMT) 101,
    103
compensation 179, 181; monetary 81–2
conduct disorder 15
confession 87, 109, 152, 233
conscience xi, xviii, 1–27, 229–30, 232;
    absence of 15, 27; in children 16,
    21–6; components 26; definitions xiv,
    1, 26; development of 11–19, 135;
    moral development 22–3, 23; moral
    emotions 3–11; nurturing growth of
    21–6; and religion 19–21; and remorse
    xiii–xvi; stage model (Kohlberg)
    12–14; temperament and socialisation,
    interplay of 14–19, 22
conscientia xiii
conservatism, religious 150
contempt 9–10
contrition 109, 111, 209; defined xiv
conventional morality 13
conversion, religious 114–16, 124, 137
coping styles, religious 60, 142, 146, 155,
    238n
Cora-McKinley, A.L. 54
Corr, P.J. 62, 63
creation 128
criminal offending, and remorse xix–xx,
    105–25; assessment of expressions of
    remorse in criminal proceedings

110–13; context of offender remorse
    108–9; good actors 111, 113–14;
    psychometric assessment and socially
    desirable responding 120–4; self-
    interest, sentence reduction 111, 114;
    validity of remorse in criminal
    proceedings 107
Cross, S.E. 177, 178

Darwin, C. 43
Day, J.M. 20
Day of Judgement 50, 218
Dearing, R.L. 145–6, 149, 213–14
death: and afterlife 212, 213, 218–19,
    220, 221; in Christianity 217; in
    Hinduism 218; religion as preparation
    for 213; unforgiveness 227; see also
    afterlife, belief in
death anxiety 211, 219, 220, 223, 231;
    belief in afterlife 213–15;
    intrapersonal, interpersonal and
    transpersonal components 215; self-
    annihilation factor 220, 221
death jurors 108, 109
death penalty 53, 109
decentering 207
deception 35, 37
decisional forgiveness 160, 185
deferring coping style 60, 142
deities 213
Delaney, H.D. 156–7
Deluty, R.H. 201
demandingness 25
democratic family decision-making/living
    25–6
denial 81
depression xi, 67, 70, 141, 143–5
despair 115
DeSteno, D. 10
development, religion/spirituality 135
developmental plasticity 17
DeYoung, N.J. 59
Dezutter, J. 153
dharma (righteousness) 166
DiBlasio, F.A. 191, 192
Dickerson, S.S. 86
Dietz, S. 28
discomfort, tolerance of 207
discursive psychology 110, 239n
disgust 4, 9–10

dispositional forgiveness, and religiousness 168–9
dispositional vengefulness 55, 67–8
divine retribution, fear of xvii
divinity, conception of 132–3
Divinity, Ethics of 7, 9
Dixon, R.D. 219
doing mode, in mindfulness 208
Dollahite, D.C. 29, 200
Donohue, M. ix–x
dopamine 62
Dorff, E.M. 240n
Drigotas, S.M. 236n
Drinkard, D.T. 68–9
Duba, J.D. 199, 201
Dunne, M.P. 56
Dupree, W.J. 73
Dürer, A. 78
dying 221–5

Eastern Orthodox church 130
economic benefits of religion/spirituality 148
educational benefits of religion/spirituality 148
Edwards, L.M. 168
effortful control 17
eightfold path 206
Eisenberg, N. 4, 5, 8, 11
elevation 10–11
Eliot, G. (Mary Ann Evans) 159
Elkind, D. 135
Ellis, A. 74
Ellis, M.L. 15
Ellison, C.G. 49–50, 149–50
embarrassment 4
Emerson, R.W. 126
Emmons, R.A. 10
emotion disposition 4
emotional forgiveness 160
emotional infidelity 42, 237n
emotional intelligence 202–3
emotional substitution 90, 91
emotions/emotionality 163, 232; basic and higher-order emotions 2, 3; and cognition 11; moral emotions see moral emotions
empathy: and autism 15–16; defined 23; moral emotional process of 11; other-directed 11

empathy and forgiveness xx–xxi, 194–6, 209; gender factors 198, 209; grief 203–5; relationship quality 197–9; therapy within social contexts of 202–3
Empathy Forgiveness Seminar 74
Engel, B. 97
enlightenment 206, 218
Enright, R.D. 168, 193
Enright Forgiveness Inventory (EFI) 169, 170
Epstein, S. 161, 162
equivalency law 49, 50, 51
essentiality 190–2, 209
Eve after the Fall (sculpture by Rodin) 78
existential punishment 212
Exline, J.J. 219
experience 133, 138
extended family 238n
externalisation process 100
extrinsic religiousness 139, 141–2, 143, 146, 214; versus intrinsic religiousness 151, 231
Eysenck, H.J. 56
Eysenck Personality Inventory 62
Eysenck Personality Questionnaire (EPQ-R) 56, 57, 58
Eysenck Personality Scales (EPS) 120

Fall of Man, The (Dührer) 78
Fear–Flight System (FFS) 63
Fear–Flight–Freeze System (FFFS) 62, 63, 64
fearfulness 17–18
Fehr, R. 178, 180, 181–2
Feldman, S.S. 30
feminism 14
Ferch, S.R. 191, 193
Ferguson, T.J. 5, 79
Feshbach, N.D. 11, 16
fight–flight reaction 62
Fincham, F.D. 160, 197, 228
Finkel, E.J. 33, 46
Fitnes, J. 35
Five Factor personality model 55, 56
Flannelly, K.J. 143
Florian, V. 214, 220
Fluehr-Lobban, C. 82
Flynt, L. 126

forgiveness x, 159–87, 231; actions
    163–4; and apologies 176–82, 186–7;
    beliefs 162–3; and Buddhism 167; case
    study 189–94; and Christianity 74,
    160, 164–5, 166; decisional 160, 185;
    dispositional 168–9; emotional 160;
    emotions 163; and empathy *see*
    empathy and forgiveness; forgiving
    God 49; and Hinduism 166–7;
    interpersonal 160; interventions 72–3;
    in Islam 50, 166; and Judaism 165;
    and religion 161–7; whether a
    religion-forgiveness discrepancy
    167–75; self-cognitive variables 198;
    in therapy 191; transgression-specific
    168, 169–75; and vengeance 53
Frantz, C.M. 176
Freedman, E.M. 53
Freeman, R.B. 148
Freud, S. 12
Frick, P.J. 15
Friedman, H.H. 96
friendships, close 29
Fuller, R. 137, 138
fundamentalism 19–20, 80, 81, 115, 136,
    150, 158, 186; Islamic 171
Furnham, A. 117
Future Time Orientation 213

Gandhi, M. 1
Gaylin, W. 5
Gelfand, M.J. 177, 178, 180, 181–2
gender factors: empathy and forgiveness
    198, 209; in vengeance 53–5
Al Ghazali 82
Ghorbani, N. 220
Gilbert, P. 43, 101, 102
Gilligan, C. 14
Giner-Sorolla, R. 7
Glass, S.P. 35–6
God: comparative view 128; finding of,
    amongst prisoners xix–xx, 114–16;
    goodness of 19; vengeful 49
godliness 9
Goldstein, A. 240n
Gonzales, M.H. 45
Goodman, M.A. 200
goodness, of God 19
Goranson, R. 54, 59
Gordon, K.C. 193

Gorsuch, R.L. 168–9
grace 10
gratitude 10
Great Chain of Being, The 10
grief 203–5
group-norms 177
grudge bearing 64–8
Grych, J.H. 22, 23–4, 26
Guerra, V.M. 7
guilt xix, 4, 232; case study 89; and
    conscience 12; defined xiv, 86; and
    dying 221–5; genuine 87, 90; nature
    of 86–7; and religious orientation
    150–4; and remorse xv, 150–4; shame
    compared 5–7, 87–95
Guinote, A. 184

Hadith 166
Hadrat Ali 50
Haidt, J. 3, 8, 9, 10, 11
Hall, C. 62
Hall, J.H. 228
Halling, S. 228–9
Hamady, S. 82, 239n
Hamama-Raz, Y. 220
Hammurabi, Code of 49
Hansson, R. 40, 226
Hao, J.Y. 168–9
happiness 29, 30
harm, causing xi, 73, 226
Harris, C. 36
Hartling, L.M. 38
Hathaway, W. 207
Heartland Forgiveness Scale 168
heaven 212, 217, 218, 219
hell xvii, 211, 212, 217, 219
Hennessy, D.A. 54
Hess, M.B. 78–9
Higgins, R. 167
Hill, E.W. 192, 194, 202, 203, 205
Hill, P.C. 135
Hinduism 129; and afterlife 218; Ethics of
    Divinity 7; and forgiveness 166–7; and
    shame 85
Hoffman, M.L. 24, 237n
Hook, A. 99–100
Hope, D. 159, 160, 191
Horning, S.M. 142
hospice care 214
hostility triad 8

hubristic pride 8
Human Development Study Group 193
humanism 130
humiliation 39
Hunsberger, B. 136, 150
hygiene, maintenance of 9

illness 148
immanence 128, 129, 131
impression management (IM) 109,
    117–25
impulsivity 63
Index of Religiousness 57
Indian religions 129
individual salvation 81
induction 24, 237n
infidelity xiii, 28, 229; clues of 40–2;
    emotional 42, 237n; harm caused by
    73; sexual 35, 36, 42, 226, 227, 237n;
    see also betrayal
Infidelity-Specific Treatment Model 73
Ingersoll, R.E. 131, 132, 133
Ingersoll-Dayton, B. 227, 228
in-groups 162
insight-oriented therapy (IOCT) 73
integration 133
integrity 2–3, 117–24
intentionality 192, 209
internal behaviours 101–2
Interpersonal Behaviour Survey (IBS)
    120–1, 122
interpersonal forgiveness 160
interpersonal relationships: betrayal in ix,
    xi, xviii, 28–47, 226, 229–30; power
    in 183–4; religion and vengeance xix,
    48–77; 'trials' 37
Interruption Theory 41
intimate relationships see interpersonal
    relationships
intrinsic religiousness 139, 141–2, 148,
    153, 214; and depression 144–5;
    versus extrinsic religiousness 151,
    231
inwit xv, xvi
Islam 128; and afterlife 217; and
    conscience 20, 21; equivalency law 51;
    and forgiveness 50, 166; ill-treatment
    of women 241n; Qur'an 21, 50, 64,
    76, 79, 83, 166, 217; and shame 82–3
Izard, C.E. 8

Jacklin, C.N. 22, 54
Jackson, L.M. 150
James, A. 142–3
Jang, S.A. 31
jealousy 36
Jennings, D.J. 66
Jeremiah (Prophet) 83
Jesus Christ 30, 49, 74, 84, 164, 165,
    212, 218, 237n
John (New Testament) 165, 238n
John March Ministries 61–2
Johnson, J.L. 57, 58, 64
Johnson, R.E. 177, 181
Jorm, A.F. 57, 58, 237n
Judaism: and afterlife 216–17; and
    conscience 20; equivalency law 49, 50;
    and forgiveness 165, 166; Levirate
    marriage in 81–2, 238n; and revenge
    64; and shame 81–2; and therapy 201;
    and vengeance 49
Judgement Day 50, 218
Jun, J. 228
Jung, C. 213
justice, or vengeance 51–3
Justitia (Roman goddess of justice)
    237n

Kabat-Zinn, J. 206
karma (Buddhist concept) 167
Karremans, J.C. 53, 185
Katchadourian, H. 92, 235
Kaufman, G. 78
Kavka, G.S. 236n
Keltner, D. 183
Kendrick, D.T. 54
Keng, S. 208
Kim, P.H. 108
Kingdom of God 164
Kinlaw, B.J.R. 219
Kochanska, G. 2, 14, 15, 16, 17, 18,
    22
Koenig, C. 214
Koenig, H. 126, 141, 144, 146
Kohlberg, L. 12–14, 15, 23–4, 240n
Kolko, D.J. 236n
Kowalski, R.M. 37, 38
Kravertz, S. 214, 220
Kroner, D.G. 118–20
Kuran see Qur'an
Kyd, T. 48

Lagaree, T.A. 190
Laible, D.J. 15
Lambert, N.M. 29
Lampton, C. 161
LaPierre, L.L. 133–4
Larsen, U. 40
Lawoyin, T.O. 40
Lazar, A. 215
Lazare, A. 97
Leary, M. 44
Lester, D. 219
Levels of Self-Concept Scale (LCS) 182
Levine, T. 38
Levirate marriage, in Judaism 81–2,
    238n
Leviticus, Book of 9, 165
Lewis, H.B. 85
Lewis, M. 86, 90
Likert scale 57, 58, 74
Lindsay-Hartz, J. 90, 91
Lippke, R.L. 107, 114
longevity and mortality 147–8
Lord's Prayer 164
Lucas, R. 70
Luke (New Testament) 84, 164, 212,
    237n
Lutz, A. 102

Maccoby, E.E. 22, 54
MacLaren, V.V. 63
MacMartin, C. 110, 111
Maimonides 216
maladaptive thinking patterns 207–8
malingering 124
Maltby, J. 152
Mammen, O.K. 236n
Mansfield, K. 106
Mark (New Testament) 164, 165
Marlowe-Crowne Social Desirability Scale
    (MCSDS) 119, 170
marriage 29, 30, 40, 160, 199, 232;
    Levirate, in Judaism 81–2, 238n
Martel, J. 109
Marxism 130
Maselko, J. 148
Maslow, A. 132, 133, 138
Mastekaasa, A. 30
Matthew (New Testament) 30
Mauger Forgiveness Scale 57
McCallister, B.J. 136

McCullough, M.E. 10, 55–6, 58, 64, 163,
    168, 169, 170, 199
McGuire, M.T. 43
McLeary, R.M. 148
McNaughton, N. 63
meaning 132
meditation 140, 145
Meek, K.R. 151, 152
Menesini, E. 93
mental health xx; religion and spirituality
    141–7; and unforgiveness 227;
    vengeful rumination and grudge
    bearing, effects 67–8
mesolimbic dopamine system 63
metalanguage 92, 239n
Meyer, J.E. 72
Michel, D. xvi
Middleburgh, C. 240n
Miller, A. 28
Miller, J.B. 38, 85
Miller, R.S. 4
Mills, J.F. 118–20, 123–4
Millspaugh, D. 225, 241n
Mind, Theory of 11
mindfulness: and Buddhism 101, 206;
    defined 206; and therapy 205–8
mindfulness-based cognitive therapy
    (MBCT) 206, 207
Mishneh Torah 240n
modelling 25
Molière (Jean-Baptiste Poquelin) 116
moral depravity 10
moral development 13, 22–3
moral emotions: contempt and disgust
    9–10; elevation 10–11; embarrassment
    4; empathy 11; gratitude 10; and
    moral behaviour 1–2; other-focused 8;
    pride 7–8; righteous anger 8–9; self-
    conscious 3–4, 7; shame and guilt 5–7;
    see also guilt; shame
moral maturity 2
moral rationalisation/reasoning 23–4, 173
morality: Big Three ethics of 6–7, 8, 9;
    intellectual and upper-class
    conceptions of 14; morality-identity
    distinction 93; religion as bastion of
    19; stages 13
Moreland, J.P. 19
Moses, Law of 30
mother–child dyads 15

Muhammad, Prophet 166
Mullett, E. 74–5
multifaith communities 139–40
Murphy, J.G xv–xvi, 115, 116, 236n
Murray, S.L. 36–7
mutually responsive orientation (MRO)
    18, 19, 22
mystery 133

Nagel, T. 43
narcissism: covert/overt 60, 61; non-
    pathological 238n; as predictor of
    vengefulness 58–62; and psychoticism
    62
Narcissistic Personality Disorder 59
Narcissistic Personality Inventory 62
natural ladder (*scala naturae*) 10
needs 161–2
Neff, K.D. 102
neglect of children xii
Nelson, J.M. 147, 148, 213, 234
neuroticism 55
New South Wales Law Reform
    Commission 110
New Testament 49, 83–4, 164
Nicene Creed 218
norms, within relationships 33–5
Nun Ioanna 83, 98–9
nurturance 24
Nussbaum, M. xix
Nygaard, R. 53

obedience 20
observer-based schedules 138
OCEAN (openness, conscientiousness,
    extraversion, agreeableness and
    neuroticism) 55
Okimoto, T.G. 52–3
Old Testament xix, 49, 164
Olthof, T. 93
Oman, D. 208
Organisational Revenge Scale 54
organised religion 140
original sin 164
Osiris, Judgement of xv
other-deception 118
other-oriented induction 237n

pain 221–2, 225
Paleari, F.G. 197, 198, 199

Paloutzian, R.F. 172
parent–child attachment 18–19
Parent–Child Relationship Inventory
    (PCRI) 121, 123
parenting styles 24, 148–9, 229
Pargament, K. 60, 137, 142, 146, 155
Parker, K. F. 115
Parlavecchio, H. 4
pastoral counselling 234
Pattison, S. 79–80, 98–9, 100
Patton, J. 234–5
Paul (Apostle) 1, 84, 240n
Paulhus deception scales (PDS) 119
peak experiences 133, 138
PEN (psychoticism, extraversion and
    neuroticism) 55, 56
Penance 165
penitence xiv
personality: Eysenck's model 62; and
    friendship 29; religion and spirituality
    138–9, 158; theory 12; and vengeance
    55–8, 76
Personality Assessment Inventory (PAI)
    120, 122
Personality Inventory for Children (PIC)
    121
Petrucci, C.J. 97
Peyton, W. 114–15
physical abuse xii
physical health, religion/spirituality
    147–8
Piaget, J. 12, 15, 135
Piedmont, R.L. 196
Pilkonis, P.A. 236n
Pitts, R.C. 2
Plante, T.G. 168
plasticity, developmental 17
play 133
Plutchik, R. 137
positive thinking 70
Posner, M.I. 17
post-conventional morality 13
post-traumatic stress disorder (PTSD)
    68
Powell, F.C. 219
power, in interpersonal relationships
    182–5
prayer 82, 140
pre-conventional morality 13
pride, moral 7–8

prisoners, finding of God xix–xx, 114–16
Proeve, M.J. 107, 111
Propst, L.R. 157
Protestantism 165, 201, 219
psychoanalytic theory 12, 15
psychodynamic therapy 100
psychology: discursive 110, 239n; and
    religion 234; and shame 85–6
psychometric assessment 117, 145; case
    study 121–3; and socially desirable
    responding 120–4; and transgression-
    specific forgiveness 170–1
psychopathology 15, 27
psychotherapy, spiritual base 132
psychoticism 62, 76; and vengeance 56–8
psychoticism, extraversion and
    neuroticism (PEN) 55, 56
punishment: in afterlife, fear of 218, 220,
    221, 222; existential 212; role of 51–2;
    see also afterlife, belief in

Qisas (retaliation) 239n
Qur'an 21, 50, 64, 76, 79, 83, 166, 217,
    239n, 240n, 241n

racism 9
Rackley, J.V. 169
Ramsey, D. 86
Randall, P.E. 54, 236n
Raskin, R. 62
rational emotive behaviour therapy
    (REBT) 74
rationalisation, transgression-specific
    forgiveness, and religiousness 171–5
REACH intervention (Worthington) 72,
    75, 238n
rebirth 218
receptive coping style 60
recidivism 107
recompense 50
reconciliation 69, 197
Rector, N.A. 102
Reformation 165
regret xiv, 106
regulation of behaviour 14–15
rehabilitation 111
Reinforcement Sensitivity Theory (RST)
    62–4
rejection 36
relationship commitment 184–5

relationship quality: dissatisfaction 41–2;
    empathy and forgiveness 197–9
relationship to divine 133
religion xix, xx, 127–31; as bastion of
    morality 19; and conscience 19–21;
    coping styles 60, 142, 146, 155, 238n;
    definitions 128, 236n; extrinsic and
    intrinsic religiousness 139, 141–2,
    143, 144–5, 146, 148, 151, 153, 214,
    231; and forgiveness 161–7;
    fundamentalism 19–20, 80, 81, 115,
    136, 150; organised 140; and
    psychology 234; religious conversion
    and remorse 114–16, 124; remorse and
    repentance xvii; and shame see religion
    and shame; and spirituality see religion
    and spirituality (RS); spontaneous 135;
    vengeance, religious teaching (mixed
    messages) 49–51; see also God; specific
    religions
religion and shame: Christianity 83–4;
    Islam 82–3; Judaism 81–2
religion and spirituality (RS) 126–58; and
    affect 136–8; afterlife, belief in see
    afterlife, belief in; children and
    parenting 148–9; and cognition
    135–6; connections between 126,
    134–40, 158, 231; contraindications
    149–50; and development 135;
    educational and economic benefit 148;
    guilt, remorse and religious orientation
    150–4; immanence 128, 129, 131;
    intervention 154–7; mysticism 233;
    and personality 138–9, 158; protective
    factors 140–7; and social benefits
    139–40; therapy and religious people
    199–202; transcendence 128, 129,
    131, 132, 134, 139, 141, 231; well-
    being 147–50; see also beliefs
religion-forgiveness discrepancy 167–75
religiosity 56–7
Religious Commitment Inventory (RCI)
    58
religious conversion 114–16, 124, 137
religious pain 222
remorse x–xi; acknowledgement 112; and
    apology 96–7, 108; assessment of
    expressions of in criminal proceedings
    110–13; and betrayal 46–7; and
    conscience xiii–xvi; context of offender

108–9; and criminal offending xix–xx, 105–25; definitions xiv; feigned 103, 107, 230–1; genuine xvii, 45, 103, 109, 111, 112, 230, 231–2; and guilt xv, 150–4; integrity/impression management 109, 117–24; propensity to 140–1; religious conversion 114–16, 124; religious orientation 150–4; and reparation 95–9; and repentance xvii; suffering 112; transformation 113; validity in criminal proceedings 107; and wrongdoing xiii, xv
reparation, and remorse 95–9
repentance xv, 115; definitions xiv
restorative justice 52–3, 237n
resurrection 221
revenge 83, 171
revenge tragedies 48
righteous anger 8–9
Robbins, B.D. 4
Robins, R.W. 6, 8, 85–6
Rodin, A. 78
Rogers, M.B. 150
Rogers, R. 124
Roman Catholicism 165, 201
romantic relationships 28, 29, 41; see also interpersonal relationships
Romero, C. 185
Rothbart, M.K. 17
Rozin, P. 8, 9
rule violation, acknowledgement 181
rumination 226, 228; and mindfulness 207, 208; negative 70; vengeful 64–8
Rusbult, C.E. 33, 46
Rye, M.S. 170

Salsman, J.M. 138–9
salvation 167
Sandage, S.J. 73–4
Santa Clara Strength of Religious Faith Questionnaire 168
Santelli, A.G. 45
Saroglou, V. 56
Satterly, L. 221, 223, 224, 225
Saucier, G. 134
Saunders, C. 221
Scherer, M. 160
Schlehofer, M.M. 138
Scott, J. 145–6

Segal, Z.V. 206–7
self versus behaviour distinction, shame and guilt 94–5
self-actualisation 132
self-annihilation factor, death anxiety 220, 221
self-consciousness 3–4, 7
self-construals 177, 178, 187
self-control 22
self-criticism 103
self-deception 117, 118
self-directed coping 60, 142
Self-Enhancement Seminar 74
self-esteem 23, 36–7, 42, 60
self-forgiveness 174–5, 239n
self-gratification 13, 18, 21
self-regulation 14
self-report inventories, psychometric 121, 125
septo-hippocampal structures 63
sexual assault 110
sexual boredom 42
sexual infidelity 35, 36, 42, 226, 227, 237n
Shackelford, T.D. 40, 41, 236n
shame xix, 78–104; appeasement value 43; avoidance of 43; and Christianity 79–80, 83–4; defined xiv, 79; and expressions of guilt 90; guilt compared 5–7, 87–95; and Islam 82–3; and Judaism 81–2; nature of 79–86; and psychology 85–6; remorse and reparation 95–9; and South-Asian peoples 84–5
shame-proneness 99–100
Shapiro, S.L. 206
Shaw, J.C. 177
Sheets, V. 54
Shoemaker, A. 168
Shweder, R.A. 6, 7
Sikhism 51
Silberman, I. 162
Simons, M.A. 116, 117
sin 164, 165, 241n; weight of xvi–xviii, 211–35
Skrzypinska, K. 134
Slingerland, E. 136
Smart, N. 129, 130
Smedes, L.B. 80, 88
Smith, B.S. 172

Smith, P.K. 183, 185
Smith, R.H. 92–3
Smith, T.B. 141, 142, 144
Smith-Lovin, L. 43
social benefits, religion and spirituality
    139–40
social classism 9
social learning theory 12
social orientation 22
social-domain theory 15
socialisation 5, 14–19, 22
socially desirable responding (SDR) 117,
    119, 120–4
Sommers, J.A. 54
Sorenson, A.M. 144
sorrow 230
soul, weight of ix–xxii, xxi, 211–35
South-Asian peoples, and shame 84–5
spiritual pain 224–5
Spiritualism 131
spirituality 131–4; defined 132; and
    disgust 9–10; religion–spirituality
    connections 126, 134–40, 158, 231; see
    also religion and spirituality
Sroufe, L.A. 18
St Michael xv
stage model (Kohlberg) 12–14, 23–4
Stark, R. 19
Stegge, H. 5, 79
Stiver, I. 38
Stoddart, S. (Pastor) 211, 212, 222, 241n
Structured Inventory of Malingered
    Symptomatology (SIMS) 123
Struthers, C.W. 176
Stuckless, N. 54, 59
Subkoviak, M.J. 169, 170
Suh, E. 69
Sundby, S. 108–9
Sussman, S. 134
synderesis xiii

Talmud 81, 239n
Tan, E. 207
Tangney, J.P. 4, 5–6, 7, 8, 85, 87–9, 94,
    100, 153
Tatman, A.W. 119
Taylor, G. 88
Temoshok, L.R. 167
temperament 14–19, 22
terminal illness 147–8

Terror Management Theory (TMT) 212
terrorism 150, 162
theism 19
Theory of Mind 11
therapeutic factors for groups (Yalom) 72
therapy xx–xxi, 188–210; benevolence
    192–4, 209; and compassion 99–103;
    essentiality 190–2, 209; forgiveness
    and empathy 191, 202–3;
    intentionality 192, 209; and Judaism
    201; and mindfulness 205–8; non-
    disclosure in 99–100; religious beliefs
    210; and religious people 199–202;
    and vengeance 71–6
Thomaes, S. 5
Thompson, L.V. 69
Thompson, R.A. 15
Thorsen, A. 219
thoughts, being ashamed of 3
Three Factor personality model 56, 57
Thurston, N.S. 154
Toews, J. 143
Torah 81, 216, 240n
tort law (compensatory damages) 49
total pain 221–2, 225
Tracy, J.L. 6, 8, 85–6
trait anger 237n
transcendence 128, 129, 131, 132, 134,
    139, 141, 231
Transgression-Related Interpersonal
    Motivations Inventory (TRIM)
    174
transgression-specific forgiveness, and
    religiousness 168, 169–75;
    psychometric issues 170–1;
    rationalisation 171–5
Treynor, W. 67
trust, betrayal of xi–xii, 28
truthfulness 37, 119
Tsang, J. 164, 168, 169, 170, 171, 172,
    173–4, 193
Tsoudis, O. 43

unforgiveness 160
unforgiving self 226–9

valence 237n
Van Lange, P.A. 53
van Uden, M.H.F. 60–1
Vaughan, F. 134

vengeance xix, 230; age and gender as predictors of 53–5; defined xiv; and forgiveness 53; or justice 51–3; personality factors as predictors of 55–8, 76; and psychoticism 56–8; Reinforcement Sensitivity Theory 62–4; religious teaching about (mixed messages) 49–51; and therapy 71–6; turning away from 68–71
Vengeance Scale 54, 59
vengefulness: dispositional 55, 67–8; narcissism as a predictor of 58–62; vengeful God 49; vengeful rumination, grudge bearing and health 64–8
venial sins 241n
Vitz, P.C. 241n
Volling, B.L. 149

Wachholtz, A.B. 143
Wade, N.G. 71, 72, 72–3, 155
Wagers, T.P. 226–7
Wagner, J.A. 177
Walker, L.W. 2
Walrond-Skinner, S. 194
Walsh, J.A. 117
Watts, C. 39
Watts, R.E. 199, 201
Weisman, R. 109, 111, 112, 113
well-being: physical health 147–8; religion and spirituality 147–50
Wells, A. 142–3
Wenzel, M. 52–3
Whisman, M.A. 226–7

Wiederman, M.W. 40
Wiersbe, W. 105
Wiesenthal, D.L. 54
Williams, B. 78, 88, 92
Wilson, M. 61–2
Wink, P. 138, 145–6
Witvliet, C.V.O. 68
women, ill treatment in Islam 241n
wonder 138
Wood, L.A. 110, 111
Word of God 84
Wordsworth, W. 239n
workplace bullying x
world religions 128; and afterlife 216–18
World to Come 216
Worthington, E.L., Jr. 68–9, 71, 72, 73–4, 154, 155, 160, 168, 169, 170, 194
Wright, T.L. 35–6
wrongdoing: and betrayal xi–xiii; in Buddhism 167; carrot-and-stick approach 212–18; in children 16; and remorse xiii, xv

Yalom, I. 72
Yama (God of death) 218
Yang, M. 94
Ysseldyk, R. 67

Zechmeister, J.S. 185
Zimmerman, C. 39
Zinnbauer, B.J. 131, 137
Zondag, H.J. 60–1